Mary Hickson

Ireland in the seventeenth century

The Irish massacres of 1641-2

Mary Hickson

Ireland in the seventeenth century
The Irish massacres of 1641-2

ISBN/EAN: 9783744741057

Printed in Europe, USA, Canada, Australia, Japan

Cover: Foto ©ninafisch / pixelio.de

More available books at **www.hansebooks.com**

IRELAND IN THE SEVENTEENTH CENTURY

OR

THE IRISH MASSACRES OF 1641-2.

CONTENTS

OF

THE SECOND VOLUME.

	PAGE
DEPOSITIONS—*continued*	
MASSACRE OF PROTESTANT COLONISTS AT SHRULE—*continued*	1
ENGLISH CATTLE TRIED IN COURT, AND ALLOWED BENEFIT OF CLERGY	5–7
MASSACRE OF PROTESTANT COLONISTS AT ARDGLASS	12
,, AT AGHALON	20
THE MURDER OF THE REV. MR. MONTGOMERY	28
DEPOSITION OF DEAN BARTLEY'S SERVANT	36
MASSACRE OF PROTESTANT COLONISTS AT SILVER MINES	37
,, AT CASHEL	40
MURDERS OF CHILDREN IN CARLOW	51
MASSACRE OF PROTESTANT COLONISTS NEAR KILKENNY, AND AT ROSS	53–61
DESECRATION OF PROTESTANTS' GRAVES IN KING'S COUNTY	69
MASSACRES OF PROTESTANT COLONISTS IN KING'S COUNTY	70
MANGLING OF THE CORPSES OF PROTESTANTS IN KILKENNY	75–78
DEPOSITION OF BARNABY DUNNE, ESQ., OF BRITTAS	80
DESECRATION OF PROTESTANTS' GRAVES IN KILDARE	84
MURDER OF MR. AND MRS. NICHOLSON AT MOUNTRATH	90
MASSACRE OF MORE THAN A HUNDRED PROTESTANT COLONISTS IN THE CHURCH AT LOUGHGALL	91
MASSACRE OF PROTESTANT COLONISTS AT RATHKEALE	93–95
DEPOSITION OF DAME BARBARA BROWN, ANCESTRESS OF THE EARL OF KENMARE	96
MASSACRE OF PROTESTANT COLONISTS IN CLARE	99

CONTENTS OF THE SECOND VOLUME.

DEPOSITIONS—*continued*   PAGE

DEPOSITION OF LADY HARRIS, WIDOW OF SIR THOMAS HARRIS, AND MOTHER OF SIR EDWARD DENNY OF TRALEE CASTLE	102
MASSACRE OF PROTESTANT COLONISTS AT KILLARNEY	105
SIEGE OF TRALEE CASTLE	107–121
MASSACRE OF PROTESTANT COLONISTS NEAR NEWMARKET	122
,, NEAR MACROOM	137
,, AT COOLE	139
,, AT CAPPOQUIN	141
THE CASE OF HENRY O'NEIL OF GLASDROMIN	144
RECORDS OF THE HIGH COURT OF JUSTICE	171
TRIAL OF SIR PHELIM O'NEIL	181
TRIAL OF LORD MUSKERRY	192
CASE OF COLONEL MACSWEENY	205
TRIAL OF VICAR GENERAL EDMUND O'REILLY	219
LIST OF EXAMINATIONS TAKEN AGAINST CAPTAIN SANTHY OR SANKEY FOR MURDER OF AN IRISHMAN	230
LETTER OF CAPT. STOPFORD ON BEHALF OF LIEUT.-GEN. O'FARREL	231
LIST OF PERSONS TRIED IN HIGH COURT AND VERDICTS	232
ORDER OF CROMWELL RESPECTING THE WIDOW AND ORPHANS OF TIRLOGH O'BYRNE	236
ORDER OF FLEETWOOD, CORBET AND JONES ON THE PETITION OF DANIEL O'HAGAN	237
LETTERS OF CROMWELL ON BEHALF OF JAMES BARRY AND TIBBOT ROCHE	238
LETTER CONCERNING LORD MUSKERRY AND COL. CALLAGHAN	239
CATHOLIC ACCOUNTS OF THE MASSACRES AT SILVER MINES, FETHARD, CASHEL, AND SHRULE	240
APPENDIX	
EXAMINATION OF DERMOT OGE	257
PETITION OF WEXFORD IRISH AGAINST PLANTATIONS	263
THE COMMISSIONERS' REPORT ON THE WEXFORD PLANTATIONS	266
PROJECT FOR THE PLANTATION OF LONGFORD	276
ARGUMENTS OF THE LONGFORD IRISH AGAINST PLANTATIONS	281
ARTICLES AND CONDITIONS OF THE LONGFORD PLANTATION	283

CONTENTS OF THE SECOND VOLUME.

APPENDIX—continued

	PAGE
Memorial of Grievances of the Longford Irish	293
The King's Irish Wards	300
Letter of the Lords Justices on the Plantations of Ely O'Carrol, Leitrim, and the MacCoghlan's Country	303
Selections from Documents Concerning Phelim O'Byrne	306
The Established Church in Ulster	324
Discourse Concerning the Settlement of the Natives in Ulster	327
Letter of Lords Justices on the Irish Parliament and Army, 12th of May, 1641	332
Letter of Sir W. Parsons on Poyning's Act, 12th July, 1641	334
Irish Privy Council to Vane, 30th June, 1641	336
Parsons to Vane on Parliament and Graces, 8th August, 1641	339
Relation of the Plotting of the Rebellion by Lord Maguire	341
Relation of the Same by a Franciscan Friar	355
Sir W. Cole to the Lords Justices, 11th Oct., 1641	359
The Lords Justices to the Lord Lieutenant, 25th Oct., 1641	361
Examination of Owen O'Connolly	367
Examination of Hugh MacMahon	368
Declaration of Dean Kerr	370
Brodie's Note on the Royal Commission to Sir Phelim O'Neil	373
Outbreak of the Rebellion in the County Cork from a Contemporary Anonymous MS.	379
Outbreak of the Rebellion in Kerry from the MS. Autobiography of the Rev. Devereux Spratt	384

ADDENDA:

Examination of Rev. George Creichtoun	388
Extracts from Cromwellian Council Books	397
Examination of Nicholas Simpson, M.P.	398
Letter of Dr. Ingram, F.T.C.D., on the O'Byrne Depositions in the College Library	405
Note on Depositions and Fascimiles	407

FACSIMILE

To face page 141.

THE IRISH MASSACRES OF 1641.

DEPOSITIONS
(*continued*).

CXVIII.

The Examination of JAMES LYNCH *concerning the murders committed at Shrule, taken Nov.* 23*rd,* 1652.

Saith, that on Friday night the convoy that was with the English lay with them at one Bourke's of Kinlough's, within a mile of Shrule, and the next day towards evening came to Shrule the Lord of Mayo and his son, then Sir Theobald Bourke, now Lord of Mayo, being with them; the said Lord of Mayo then demanded the castle of Shrule from this examt.'s brother, Pierse Lynch, who answered that one of the Lord Clanricarde's houses being already surprised, he would let none into the castle without the said Lord Clanricarde's orders, upon which answer the said Lord of Mayo, with the English and their convoy, went to one Robert Lambert's house in the town of Shrule (*illegible*) the castle side of the bridge, and there lay that night, and the next morning a brother of this examt.'s, William Lynch, being a friar, went forth of the castle in his habit, but this examt. nor any of those in the castle durst (not) stir forth, in regard that they had denied the said Lord of Mayo entrance. And being at dinner, a sentinel upon the top of the castle called to them and told them of the murder. This examt. further saith, that Mr. Beucannon's son was killed in the arms of his, this examt.'s, brother William, but he knoweth not the murderers. After the murder was committed this examt. observed the old Lord of Mayo with one Henry Brinkhurst (*sic*) and two horsemen more whom he knows not riding towards the church, where they halted, and within a quarter of an hour after he saw the young Lord of Mayo ride from the other side of the bridge and follow his father; but where the said young Lord was or what he did in the murder this deponent

2   THE IRISH MASSACRES OF 1641.

knoweth not. He likewise saw one Edmund Bourke of Cloughans with a sword drawn, in whose company was one Kedagh Feinne and his son, with two of the Clooneanodas (sic), one of whom told him, this examt., the next morning, when he desired their assistance in burying the corpses, that it was enough (trouble) for him to kill them, and not to bury them. He likewise saw one Richard Burke (*illegible*) Hugh O' (*illegible*) living near Tobberkedagh, and one of his sons, and he saw in the morning Major Browne, and Andrew Browne his brother, but whether they went out of town before or after the murder this examt. knoweth not. He likewise observed Ulick Bourke and William Bourke his brother to be there, James Mac Eneas MacDonnell (*torn*) now at Castle Hacket, Hugh O'Duynane, who, as this examt. heard, showed gold rings belonging to the English (*torn*).

Note.

The rest of this examination is so torn or faded as to be quite indecipherable; but he was again examined on the 14th of April, 1653, and further said that 'Richard MacTibbot (Burke) of the barony of Kilmaine was the person who murdered Mr. Gilbert, when he was flying from Shrule to Cong, under the protection of Friar William Lynch, his (the examt.'s) brother.' The friar made the following deposition on the 23rd of April, 1653, from which it would appear that Mr. Gilbert was not killed before he reached Cong. This discrepancy in the evidence of two Catholic witnesses, brothers, shows the extreme difficulty the Cromwellian Commissioners had to contend with in their efforts to ascertain the truth, and how indefatigable and impartial those efforts were.

CXIX.

WILLIAM LYNCH FITZPETER, of Galway, Franciscan friar, aged forty years, being duly sworn on the Holy Evangelists, and examined, deposeth that he, the said deponent, came into Shrewle to see his father, then residing in the castle at Shrewle, the night before the murder was committed, and that on the day the said murder was committed, the said deponent, being a Franciscan friar, came out of the said castle, when the murder was acting on the bridge of Shrewle aforesaid, to shelter some of the British, and that one Bouchannon's (sic) son was twice or thrice, at least, forcibly taken out of this deponent's arms. And this deponent further saith, that the murderers, whom this deponent, being a stranger, knew not, threatened to kill this deponent if he let not the son of the said Buchannon go, and that the son of the said Buchannon was forcibly taken out of this deponent's arms, and murdered. And further saith, that Mr. Gilbert, his wife and children were sent by the said deponent unto the house of Mr. Robert Lambert of Shrowle, and were there sheltered until midnight (after the said murder was committed) under beds. At which time this deponent, with his two foster brothers, Edmund MacGilloroman, yet living in Shrowl, and William MacGilloroman, deceased, came with horses of Peter Lynch's, this deponent's father, and convoyed the said Mr. Gilbert, with his wife and two children, unto Fryar's Island, on the lands of Moyne, where they stayed twenty-four hours, expecting the conveniency of this deponent to carry them towards Cong ; the said wife and children of Mr. Gilbert the said deponent left in the said island, until a better conveniency might be assured for their safe conveyance thence. And on Wednesday after the murder, he, this deponent, went with the said Mr. Gilbert out of the island towards Cong, and about a quarter of a mile from the island there appeared out of an ambush Donogh O'Kennie and Richard McTibbot, who, as this deponent hath been informed, had waited for this deponent's coming along with the said Mr. Gilbert all that morning. And the said Donogh McKennie and Richard McTibbot, after saluting this deponent, came up with a firelock, which was in the hand of the said Donogh, unto whom this deponent cried, that they should not draw any blood from the said Mr. Gilbert, the said Donogh being a follower of this deponent's father, whereupon the said Donogh and Richard came up with the said firelock, unto whom this deponent again said to abstain from meddling with the said Mr. Gilbert, and this deponent endeavoured as much as in him lay to preserve the person of the said Mr. Gilbert from the said Donogh and Richard, yet, notwithstanding the said deponent's entreaties and endeavours to defend the said Mr. Gilbert, the said Donogh came with his firelock to shoot him through ; whereupon this deponent took hold of the said firelock, so as the shot was thereby diverted from the body of the said Mr. Gilbert, and only pierced his skin, and grazed his arm, who immediately fell, and then the said Donogh and Richard stripped the said Mr. Gilbert of his clothes, and what he had about him, leaving him so stript with this deponent, who took his foster-brother's mantle, and put the same about him, and carried him, the said Mr. Gilbert, along unto Mr. Andrew Lynch's, at Ballymacgibbon, which Andrew relieved the said Mr. Gilbert with clothes, and then the said Andrew and this examinant conveyed the said Mr. Gilbert safe to Cong. And further saith not.

Taken before me,
ROBT. ORMSBY.

WILLIAM LYNCH FITZPETER.

CXX.

THOMAS JOHNSON, Vicar of Tullagh and Killycomen, in the county of Mayo, sworn and examined, saith, that on or about the 10th of November, 1641, after the present insurrection and rebellion was begun, divers rebels of the baronies of Costello and Gallen in the county of Mayo, whose names he knoweth not, in forcible and rebellious manner came and broke into this deponent's house, at Ballynow, in the same county, and then and there rebelliously and by force and arms, seized on, took, and carried away this deponent's household goods, books, and all things they pleased, which they found, and so departed away. And the next morning those, or some other rebels, not known to him, forcibly also at the same place took and carried away all his cows and young cattle, two horses, and his sheep, all worth fifty pounds, and above. And then or soon after, one Malachi, the titulary Archbishop of Tuam, seized on this deponent's church living, and took upon him to give and confer it on one Eiver O'Conaghan, a popish priest, who thereupon entered thereunto, and received the profits thereof ever since, worth 80*l.* per annum, a year's profit being now lost. And this deponent himself, having fled for safety of his life to Castlebar, being Sir Henry Bingham's castle in the same county, and staying there until about Candlemas in that year, 1641, the said Henry Bingham at that time, upon certain terms, and articles, betwixt him and Miles, Lord of Mayo, delivered the castle aforesaid to him, the said Lord of Mayo, to keep for him during the rebellion, there being at that time and for a month before a siege maintained against that castle by the arch-rebel, Edmund Bourke of Braskagh (*sic*), in the barony of Owles, gent., at which time of the delivery of the said castle, he the said Miles, Lord of Mayo, undertook to convey the said Sir Henry Bingham, and all the English and Scottish in the castle, with their clothes, unto the fort of Galway. And, thereupon, they coming the first day to Ballinacarragh, in the same county, a town belonging to the Lord of Mayo, this deponent there fell sick and was forced to turn back again, and in his return to Castlebar he was set on and surprised by one Murrow O'Hargan (*sic*) a rebel, who was a ploughman to Patrick Harte, gent., who stripped this deponent of all his clothes, and in that state he came to Castlebar, aforesaid. But fearing to stay there, this deponent fled to the house of Walter Bourke of Tyrloghe, Esq., who gave him not only clothes, but kept and defended him against the rebels, although the Popish priests and friars laboured to have him put to death. And as to the said Sir Henry Bingham, he went to the town of Neale, where he stayed for some time. But as for the rest of the English and Scottish that went along with the said Lord of Mayo, which were about fourscore or upwards, whereof the Lord Bishop of Killalla was one, and eight Protestant ministers besides, the said Lord of Mayo and his company brought them all along to the bridge of Shrule, where a great number of the rebels of the county of Mayo and the county of Galway met them, and then and there assaulted and set upon them (they being all without weapons, and not suffered to take away any from Castlebar aforesaid), and slaughtered and murdered the most part of those English and Scots, and amongst the rest six of those ministers, the Bishop being shrewdly wounded, and but two of the ministers escaping. And the said Lord of Mayo's company flying to the rebels, and he and his son Sir Theobald Bourke also flying away, left those they conveyed to the usage and mercy of the rebels; the ministers' names then slain being Dean Farges (*sic*) of Killala, Mr. Corbett, Mr. Bingham, Mr. Barnard, Mr. Rowledge (*sic*) and the Bishop of Killala's chaplain, whose name he, this examt., cannot express.

And further saith, that the rebels in the barony of Costello and Gallon, in the said county of Mayo, in mere hatred and derision of the English and their very cattle, and in contempt and derision of the English law, did ordinarily and commonly prefer, or seem to prefer, bills of indictment, and brought the English breed of cattle to be tried by juries, and having in their fashion arraigned these cattle, their scornful judges, then sitting amongst them, would say (of the cattle in the dock), '*They look as if they could speak English! give them the book and see if they can read*,' pronouncing the words '*Legit aut non*' to the jury. And then, because these English cattle stood mute and did not read, the Irish judges would pronounce sentence of death against them, and so they were committed and put to slaughtering.

And this deponent further saith, that in the time he stayed with, and was protected by, the said Walter Bourke, the young priests and friars demanded of Stephen Lynch, prior of Strade, in this deponent's own hearing, if it was not lawful to kill this deponent, because he would not turn to mass, which prior answered that it was as lawful to kill them as to kill a sheep or a dog. And divers of the Irish rebellious soldiers then told this deponent to his face, that were it not for fear of offending the said Walter Bourgh, they would make no more conscience or care of killing him than they would do of a pig or a sheep. And the said Walter Bourgh (sic) being threatened to have his house burned over his head, and to be pillaged of his goods, if he kept this deponent any longer, he gave him a pass under his hand to take to the Earl of Clanricarde at Loughrea, which brought him thither accordingly in safety, where, as otherwise without God's miraculous delivery, he could not, as he is verily persuaded, have escaped murdering. And this deponent ever after that time lived by the noble and free charity of that good Earl, until of late that his Lordship sent him and divers other Protestants away with a convoy. And this deponent further saith, that one of those rebellious murderers aforesaid, named Kedagh Roe MacJames Clandonnell, boasted at his return from Shrule that he had killed with his own hands four of the Protestants, namely, Mr. Barnard, commissary; Mr. Corbett, minister; Edward Jones, and Mr. Smith, a merchant. And in triumph of that his villany, the said Kedagh brought their blood upon his hands, arms, and weapons to Ballinacarragh aforesaid, sixteen miles distant from Shrule, and being advised to wash his hands, arms, and weapons of that blood, he answered, with an oath, that he would not wash off the English blood until he came to Ahcedrinay (sic) to Rory Oge's house. And this deponent saw the said Kedagh afterwards wear a suit of clothes he knew to be Mr. Barnard's, the same which he wore when he parted from this deponent at Ballincarragh aforesaid.

And further this examt. saith, that after the massacre at Shrule, he, this deponent, having a daughter blind of both eyes, who went to seek relief up and down the parish of Turlogh, where he had been vicar, with a little boy that led her, also this deponent's child, these two poor children of his being met on the highway by one Manus MacJames, brother to the before-mentioned Kedagh, that bloody rebel, knowing them to be this deponent's children, took the boy and tied him to a tree and there left him, and the poor girl, weeping and in great fear, almost starved with cold, when and where he is persuaded they had both perished, had not one Donnell O'Duggan by accident come that way, who, knowing the children, loosed the boy from the tree and sent them both away.

And this deponent also saith, that while he was at Turlogh

aforesaid, in Mr. Walter Bourgh's house, divers friars of the order of St. Dominick in their white habits, knowing this deponent to have been vicar of that parish, and that he would not turn to mass, persuaded one Tirlogh Duffe, footman to the said Walter Bourgh, to set up two cars to hang this deponent on, but he refused, and certifying to his said master the same, the master sharply reproved those friars. And he gave warning to all his tenants to relieve this deponent and suffer none to hurt him, which they accordingly performed, and so by God's great mercy and providence his life was saved, and he was sent with the pass to the noble Earl of Clanricarde, as aforesaid. And this deponent further saith, that he heard divers of the soldiers at Mr. Walter Bourke's house earnestly protest and say that they heard that Sir Charles Coote had given them some overthrow, and that they were preparing to go against Castle Coote; that the titulary Archbishop of Tuam, Malachi Keely (*sic*), had assured them all that they need not fear, for that the English should not have power to fight against them, but should be delivered into their hands, so as they (the Irish) might cut their (the English) throats, or kill them at their pleasure. And that they should have the Holy Ghost to say mass unto them thrice before they went into battle.

Jurat. 14*th Jan.* 1643,   THOMAS JOHNSON,
HEN. JONES.   *Vicar of Turlogh and Killycomen.*
HEN. BRERETON.

Note.

Mrs. Fargy, or Varges (the name is as usual spelt in various ways in the deposition), widow of the Dean of Killala, sworn before the Commissioners on the 19th of October, 1642, confirmed much of the contents of the foregoing depositions. She says that, beside the Bishop and the Dean and six other clergymen, there were about fifty-five Protestants, amongst them her father, ' John Beucannon, Esq.,' and that all the men in this party, except the Bishop and two of the clergymen, were murdered at Shrewle bridge. Several women were also murdered, two of them being *enceinte*; all the rest were stripped naked, and the examt. ' knew not what became of them.' She further swore that she often heard the rebels say that they meant to ' *root out all the English and Scottish because they had gotten all from them (the Irish) by their courts and assizes.*' Walter Bourke, who sheltered Mr. Johnson, was also examined on oath before Sir Robert Meredith, when he swore as follows :—

"This examt. saith, that such was the hatred of the English by the Irish, in the county of Mayo, that they could not endure to see a beast of English breed live amongst them, and not only destroyed those cattle, but with all derision and scoffing carriage used to bring a book before the cow or sheep of English breed, that they had taken from the English, and ask it whether it could read, and in case they were disposed at that time to spare the cow or sheep, one of them answered it could read, and bade that its appearances (recognisances) should be entered; but if they (the Irish) were otherwise disposed, they killed it. In conclusion, he saith they left not a beast living that they took from an English Protestant."

This treatment of the unfortunate English cows was a double satirical punishment of their owners and 'their courts and assizes.' So late as 1688, three rebels and cattle-stealers were allowed at a Wicklow assizes to plead the old exemption of punishment, under 'the benefit of clergy;' but two of them being returned by the ordinary '*non legit*' were hung; the third, and most guilty, it was said, escaped. Corbet, the minister murdered at Shrule, was the author of some severe pamphlets against the Covenanters and the Jesuits, whom he charged with being in a confederacy against the king and the Church of England. He was said to have been assisted in those writings by Maxwell, Bishop of Killala, also a high churchman. Baillie says that Maxwell 'received a warning from heaven, as distinct and loud as any used to be given on earth, to reclaim him from his errors, for with his eyes he did see that miserable man John Corbet, who took upon him the shame of penning a rabble of contumelious lies against his mother church, hewed in pieces in the very arms of his poor wife; the prelate himself, in the meantime, was stricken down and left with many wounds as dead, by the hand of the Irish, with whom he had been too familiar' (*Vindication of the Church of Scotland*, p. 2). Corbet had been a Presbyterian minister in Scotland, but adopting Episcopalianism Wentworth gave him a valuable living in the diocese of Killala, displacing Adair, the low church bishop of that see, and putting Maxwell in his place. The latter was a learned and able prelate, but a violent persecutor of the Presbyterians. He died in Dublin in 1646, 'quite worn out and spent,' says Ware, 'with the miseries of the times.' An immense number of depositions were taken respecting the massacres in Sligo and Mayo. Andrew Adair, of Magowney, in the latter county, Esq., swore that he believed above six hundred Protestants had been murdered in Mayo and Sligo by the rebels, and that he observed one John Reynolds, who had murdered Mr. Trafford, minister at Longford Castle (v. *Deposition of Mrs. Trafford*, p. 349, vol. i.), to tremble most fearfully when he heard that minister's name mentioned. Thomas Hewitt, of Belcarron in Mayo, swore that the Irish had often told him that they had drowned between two and three hundred Protestants in the river of Moyne, within ten miles of Strade, taking them out in boats on the river and throwing them into it. Whether this was all vain and wicked boasting, or a true relation of crimes they had actually committed, it is hard to say. The mixture of superstitious devotion and bloodthirstiness in the rebels is curiously shown in the deposition of another witness, the widow of Michael Darby, gentleman, of the Crenght in Roscommon, who swore that her husband, 'having died of fatigue and cold while he served against the Irish, she and her father-in-law, Mr. Corshead, a minister, went into the castle of Elphin, then held by Bishop Tilson, which was besieged by the rebels.' She goes on to say that when the besiegers 'saw that they could not prevail, but that many of their party were slain, then they would say and confess that God fought for the besieged. Howbeit, such was their foolish superstition, that those besiegers would blame one another for breaking the stone font in St. Mary's church at Elphin, where, they said, St. Patrick had left the print of his knee, and for other abusing of that church, being our Lady's church, and they said therefore God was against them.' A tolerably well-known passage in the writings of Erasmus, in which he describes a 'religious' of his acquaintance planning an atrocious murder, and after praying for its success, 'purely and piously,' assassinating his victim, occurs to one when reading these and other similar annals of Irish crime.

CXXI.

ROBERT NESBITT, being of the age of twenty years, or thereabouts, being duly sworn upon the Holy Evangelist and examined, saith, that he lived with his father, Robert Nesbitt, in Ardnaglass, within the barony of Tiroragh (*sic*) and county of Sligo, at the beginning of the rebellion, and that the said Robert, with his wife and five small children, were constrained to continue in the same place for a year and a half, or thereabouts, after the said rebellion began, until about the month of May, in the year 1643, at which time this deponent saith there came a company of Ulster men to the said town of Ardnaglass, commanded by one Captain MacSweyne, who (during the time of their abode this deponent saith) they were hired (*sic*) by the MacSweynes of Ardnaglas to murder his father, his mother, and their children; whereupon, on a Saturday at night, these murderers came to this deponent's father's house and quartered there all night, and did dress a beef for their supper, which Roger MacSwyne of Ardnaglas had given them as a part of their hire; and on the Sunday morning the aforesaid murderers bound this deponent's father, Robert Nesbitt the elder, and in the meantime this deponent's mother went to the said Roger MacSwyne's house, and told him that they had bound her husband and intended to murder them all, and prayed him for God's sake to save them; whereunto the said Roger replied that what was to be done was by his command, for he had given orders to them, and commanded her to depart, adding withal that, if they (his men) did not kill the thieves, as he named them, that he would do it himself; notwithstanding which answer this deponent's mother came back to the house where her husband was bound, and immediately they tied the said deponent's mother, Emmeline Nesbitt, with ropes of hair, and drew them all, to wit, the father, mother, and five children, to the place where they intended to act the murder, and before they came to the place this deponent, with his two sisters, Helen and Mary, shrunk back out of the way, and hid themselves. The rest were led on to the slaughter, when they murdered the father, and also the mother by . . . . she being then great with child, and threw a young child, newly weaned, into the river. Whereupon, the eldest son, whose name was John, fled away (being then sixteen years or thereabouts) until he met with one Owen O'Dowd, now living in Ardnaglas, unto whom he addressed himself, and told him that the Ulster men had killed his father and mother, and prayed him to save his life, unto whom the said Owen replied that he would, and yet he brought him back to the murderers, and delivered him unto their hands, who killed him. And this deponent, being further examined, saith, that Roger MacSwyne, Edmund McSwyne, Alexander McSwyne, Roger McSwyne FitzAlexander, Hugh McSwyne, and divers others, were all of them contrivers and assistants of the murderers in the fact; and, further, he, this deponent, saith that they, the said McSwynes, were always jealous that the said persons should escape into the English quarters, and discover their actions, which was the cause they murdered them after so long a time. And further this deponent saith not, but that one George Evans, now living near Donegal, can testify to what this deponent hath saith.

ROBERT NESBITT +

Being present, 16th June, 1658,
CHARLES GORE.

CXXII.

ROBERT LYDFORD, of the abbey of Boyle (*illegible*) in Major King's house, being duly sworn and examined, saith, that at the breaking out of the rebellion in 1641, he lived at Shrone, in the county of Sligo, and soon after Candlemas in that year Sir Robert Hannay, with his lady, children, and many of the British nation who had lost their substance by the rebels, little surviving but their lives, were, by a convoy of the county Mayo, from whence they came, brought towards Ardnaglas, but the said convoy being surprised by the means of Roger Oge MacSweyne of Ardnaglas, and his brother Brian MacSweyne, the most of those distressed people fell into the enemies' hands, and were murdered; but this examt. more particularly saw one Connor MacNamee pulling a pretty youth of those prisoners, who, being brought within twenty yards of the place where this examt. was then hiding himself, near the church of Skreine, and took him (the youth) by the hair of the head with one hand, and with the other hand cut his, the said youth's, throat, by stabbing him through the same several times with an Irish skean, and then seeing a poor churl accidentally pass by, caused him to drag the said corpse to an open grave in the said churchyard, and there to bury it. And when he, this deponent, had so done, he saw the said Connor follow an old British man, who carried a young child in his arms, and driving the old man before him out of this examt.'s sight, to murder him, as this examt. verily believes, but what was done with the old man this examt. knoweth not. He, this deponent, further saith, that there were three of the number of those British at the same time hanged by the inhabitants of the country thereabouts, which one Owen MacEdmunds, living there, perceiving, and that the said Connor, with other wicked persons, were saying that they would pass from Ardnaglas to the Skreine, where this deponent lived, there to kill all British inhabitants, did hastily run to this deponent to advertise him what he (Owen) hath heard spoken, and to put this deponent upon his guard against the said rebels' approach thither, which he did the best he might by hiding himself up and down the country. This examt. further saith, that one Thomas Coote and his wife, and one Thomas Carurie (*sic*), and two Englishmen were soon after that time murdered at (*illegible*) by Hugh O'Connor, son of Tiegue O'Connor of Sligo, Esquire, deceased, and his brother, Cathal O'Connor, and that Tiegue O'Connor of Sligo, Esquire, and the said Hugh and Cathal O'Connor, brethren, went together into the barony of Tireragh, with many idle persons calling themselves soldiers, following them, a little while after the murder at Sligo was committed; and the first night they all lay at Ardnaglas, and from thence went forward into the barony, and within four or five days returned back and lay at (*illegible*) aforesaid, when and where the said murder was committed, but whether the said Tiegue O'Connor of Sligo, the eldest brother of the three, was there at the instant doing of the same, this examt. cannot tell. This examt. further saith, that Robert Nesbitt and his wife, a British couple, and inhabitants of Ardnaglass, were soon after that time stabbed and murdered, but by whom this examt. doth not know, the said woman being great with child, and this examt. heard that when she was killed . . . as was commonly reported in the country, and further saith not.

ROBERT LYDFORD.

Taken before me,
ROBT. PARKE.

CXXIII.

The Examination of EDITHA GARDINER *of Portumna, aged about twenty-five years, wife to Richard Gardiner, one of my Lord President's troop, December* 18*th,* 1652.

Being examined upon oath, saith, that in the beginning of the war, her husband, Richard Gardiner, with his two brothers, Matthew and Archibald Gardiner, and Mr. Walker, and Mr. Shauld, ministers, with others, were besieged in the steeple of Roserke Abbey, in the barony of Tyrawly, for three quarters of a year, by the Barretts, and others of the enemy in that country; being so long besieged they sent to Mr. Edmund Burke of Rappagh, to deliver the place to him, if he would give them a safe convoy for this examt., her mother, Mr. Walker, and his man, to Abbey Boyle in the county of Roscommon, it being an English garrison, her husband and some others that were in the steeple being to remain there with Mr. Burke's people; whereupon Edmund Burke of Rappagh came and received the place, and sent his brother Richard Burke, a friar, and six soldiers to convey them, two of whom left them at Ardnaree, and the friar, and the other four went on with them to Ballyjordan, where they broke their fast. And when they were going from them after breakfast, the said Friar Richard Burke bid them go the shortest way unto Lough Cuiltoge, over a bog, and he would meet them, and sent four soldiers of Edmund Bourke along with them, and about half an hour after they were gone out of the town where they broke their fast, about seven or eight of the town's people followed them, and fell upon Mr. Walker and his man, and killed them; and being demanded whether the four soldiers who were to convey them did offer to prevent the killing of them, she saith they did not, and she further saith, that, before the town's people came to them, the said guard fell upon this examt. and her mother, and stript them to the skin, saying, they (the guard) had as well do it as others, and when this examt.'s mother saw the people coming, she had some small linen and a gold ring, which she gave to the soldiers, and asked them to take her and this examt. aside and save their lives. Being examined whether she knew any of her convoy, she saith that she knew none but Richard Burke, the Friar, and one Gilduffe, and being asked whether the said Edmund Burke did punish any of the soldiers, she saith she doth not know, and saith that the soldiers told Mr. Burke and her husband that they (Mr. Walker and his man) were killed. And after Mr. Walker and his man were killed, this examt. and her mother went to Bally-cottle, to this examt.'s father-in-law, where they remained, and afterwards her mother was murdered, going between Ballimote and the Boyle, but by whom she doth not know, and this examt. went to Roserke, and stayed there with her husband, till the Lord President came into the country, with a party for their relief. And this examt. being demanded if she knew anything of the murder that was committed between the Moyne and Killaly, saith that she heard that one James Dexter did instigate the people to murder them, in regard that some of the British had gone away in his boat.

Taken before me the day
and year above written,
  CHA. COOTE.

Note.

Editha Gardiner's husband swore to the same effect, stating how the rebels had burned the town and forced the English to retreat into the church tower, or steeple (tower), and that he had heard, that when James Dexter's boat was stolen by three Scotchmen who escaped in it to Ulster, he (Dexter), and some Irishmen, gathered all the rest of the Scotchmen of that neighbourhood, and drowned them in the sea and the river at Moyne.

CXXIV.

Julian Johnson, the relict of John Johnson, clerk, preacher of God's word, parson of Athenry, Donmore, in the county of Galway, sworn and examined, saith, that since the present rebellion began in this kingdom, a little before Christmas, 1641, her husband, then alive, and she, were robbed and despoiled of their means, goods, and chattels, to their loss of 1,655*l.* sterling, by, and by the means of, the Lord Clanmorris, and his soldiers, who at first in a fawning and seemly fair manner, as a man seeming to partake with the Rt. Hon. Earl of Clanricarde, came into her house, and by his promises of loyalty to his Majesty, and love to her husband, was kindly entertained by them, but when he, by information, had discovered and searched out where all their goods were, he then discovered his former dissimulation and treachery, and deprived them of all their said goods to the value aforesaid. But before that time, viz. about the beginning of November, 1641, her said husband and she were forcibly robbed at Corrindely, in the county Leitrim, and thereabouts, of goods worth 760*l.* by the treacherous rebel Owen McQuillen, then bailiff and receiver of rents, and others whose names she cannot express. And afterwards her said husband and she, forsaking both those counties for safety, retired to the island called the Inch in the King's County, to the house of Capt. Robert Smith, and stayed there about five weeks, and then her said husband and her eldest son, and one Mr. Baxter, a minister, and the said Captain Smith, and twenty more Protestants of their company, being all slain in a skirmish by the sept of the O'Molloys, and their soldiers, she, this deponent, was robbed at the same Captain's house of goods and chattels worth 241*l.* more. And then and there the said Captain Smith's wife was also robbed of all her goods, and she and this deponent, after several days' restraint with those rebels, were constrained to eat and drink with those that murdered their husbands. And saith, that Paul O'Molloy, a friar, was the principal man in that slaughter and robbery, who quickly after that skirmish, in a triumphant rejoicing way, said, '*It was brave sport*' to see the young men, meaning some of the young Englishmen, then slain, defending themselves, '*their eyes burning in their heads.*' And saith also, that the rebels robbed her of her clothes, and that that friar, though often entreated, would give her none of her clothes again, because, as he said, and as was indeed true, because she was a minister's wife.

DEPOSITIONS.   15

And then all the Protestants were turned out of the island, stripped of all they had, and denied any of their meat and provision, which the rebels had surprised, almost surfeited themselves on, and had then thrown on a dunghill. And saith that, although this deponent and the said Captain Smith's wife escaped away, and lived, yet the rest, being in all about one hundred and forty, being turned out without their clothes, died of hunger or starving. And this deponent, after her removal from the island, being brought to one John McFarrell's house, she heard some one of the cruel rebel soldiers then and there boast and brag of the brave sport he and others had, in setting on fire the straw with which a stripped Englishwoman had tied about her, and how bravely he said, 'the fire made the English jade wince.' And this deponent afterwards endured many miseries coming to Dublin, where she now is in great want and misery, her former sufferings being too many to be related, and she charged with nine small children, who for a year have been maintained by the Rt. Hon. the Earl of Clanricard, Captain Chidley Coote, and Captain Parsons, out of their mere worthy bounty and charity.

JULIAN JOHNSON.

Jurat. 8th Feb. 1648,
HENRY JONES.
HEN. BRERETON.

CXXV.

RALPH LAMBART, late of the town of Galway, gent., sworn and examined, deposeth that he was robbed and despoiled of leases, goods, and chattels, worth 401*l.*, and upwards, at the beginning of this rebellion. And further saith, that himself and his family, with many other pillaged Protestants, repaired for refuge to Loughrea and Portumna. And saith that one Hugh Langridge, a house-carpenter, being a servant of the late and present Earl of Clanricarde for twenty-eight years, and a dweller in Loughrea, about July, 1642, had occasion to go to the woods to cut timber about five miles from home, taking with him his son of the age of fifteen years, and lodging in an empty house one night in a scattered small village, there came five men and broke in upon them both asleep, the chief of these men being one Rowland Bourke, formerly a soldier in the said Earl's foot company, but who, through some misdemeanours, was cashiered; they first bound the said Hugh with his son, and then led them forth in their shirts, a quarter of a mile, and then bound them to two trees about twenty yards asunder, and then began to cut, hew, and stab them, as long as they perceived any life in them, the said Rowland with his sword, and another with the said Hugh's own axe, and the rest with darts and skeans; the father received seventeen wounds, and the son nine, and as soon as the malefactors had ended their said mischief, they forthwith returned back to the said house, to pillage further the said Hugh's tools and victuals, and in a while the said Hugh, being a strong-hearted old man, began to revive, and asked his son if he were living, who answered that he was so wounded that he could not tell whether he would recover or not, for his head was almost cut open, but his throat had escaped. The father replied he feared he never could recover, for that he had received a stroke under his ribs with his own axe, and that his bowels were coming through it, but he desired his son if he (the father) should die, to commend him to his wife and other children, and to report of his usage, and so, commending himself and his family to Almighty God by an earnest prayer, he began to sing a psalm, and by that time the cruel rebels returning from the house, the said Rowland Bourke said, '*Are you singing? then I'll sing with you!*' and struck him on his head with his sword, so as his brains did appear, as this deponent hath seen, within three days after, when the corpse was brought into the town, but the youth was cured at the Earl's charge, who did keep him some time. Also this deponent saith, that about July, 1642, there was a poor old minister named Mr. Korbett, living in the time of peace within four miles of Loughrea, but in the troubles he remained at Loughrea, for relief and safety as the rest did, yet in expectation of kindness from his former parishioners, he went towards his parish, and by the way had his head cut off by two young cowboys, one of whom was apprehended by Captain Thomas Leicester, who should have him hanged for that murder, but that one of Captain Burke's soldiers then being on the mainguard, let him out of the stocks, and this deponent heard that prisoner say, when he was demanded why he murdered so harmless a person, that he thought it a good service to God, seeing that Mr. Korbett was an Englishman, and especially because he was a minister. Moreover, this deponent saith that he had a son at nurse with one that dwelt at Clancannon, upon the Bourke's land, so that this deponent could not send for him, it being January, 1641, and the child was beaten by one of Hubert Buie Bourke's soldiers, so that it died in three days after. This deponent further saith that, about February, 1642, there was a cruel murder committed at the abbey of Boyle, by Charles McDermott, one of the great McDermott's sons, and his men, who one night came into the said town of Boyle, and there murdered many persons, amongst them this deponent's sister and her child, and her husband, William Stewart, were there slain, as this deponent hath been credibly informed by both English and Irish. . . . And further saith, that he heard it credibly reported, that about December, 1641, one Con O'Rourke of the county of Leitrim, then a new made colonel, did produce a supposed commission from his Majesty, under the broad seal, wherein full power was given to the Irish to banish all the English, and despoil them of all their goods, but this deponent hath been credibly informed by some of the Irish, that the said broad seal was the seal of a patent for lands that the said colonel had gotten at Mohill, when he took it from Mr. Henry Crofton, and that he, the said Con, or his son, did forge the said commission to the said seal.

RALPH LAMBERT.

Jurat. 9th July, 1615,
Coram HEN. JONES.
HEN. BRERETON.

CXXVI.

COLONEL FRANCIS TAAFE, being duly sworn and examined, deposeth and saith, that he knew Charles O'Connor and Hugh O'Connor, the brothers of O'Connor Sligo, and he heard of a horrid murder committed in Sligo upon Mr. Stewart, William Walsh, and divers others, wherein the said Charles and Hugh were principal actors. He further saith, that Major-General Lucas Taafe and this examt. did, with five hundred men, apprehend the said persons and brought them prisoners to Ballinafad in order to try them for the said murder, where they were kept prisoners for a long time (but the certain time he doth not remember), during which time he believed the said Major-General Taafe sent to such as had the chief authority in this province, desiring that the said parties might be brought to a trial, and at length, finding it very inconvenient to continue there any longer in that place, the said Major-General caused them to be conveyed to Castle Coote, to the intent they might be there brought to justice, as he believes, where Lieut.-Gen. Bourke there was with an army, who then commanded in chief both in the army besieging that place, and in the whole province where the said Charles and Hugh were left prisoners, and were within a week set at liberty, but by what means or by what order he knoweth not. He further saith, that about a twelvemonth ago he saw the said Hugh O'Connor come into the Lord Clanricard's army near Ballyshannon, and discover himself to his lordship and desired that he might be questioned for the aforesaid murder, who promised and engaged that so soon as he got into Ballyshannon he would have the said Hugh hanged, which was prevented by the sudden approach of the English army, and the said Hugh is now in actual rebellion, not daring to come in because of the murders, as this examt. is informed.

FRANCIS TAAFE.

Taken before us 13th of May, 1653,
CHARLES COOTE.
WALTER CARWARDINE.

Note.

The deponent Colonel Francis Taafe was the fourth son of the first Viscount Taafe by his wife, the daughter of Lord Dillon, and having gone abroad after the Cromwellian Settlement, and married an Italian lady, he died at Naples leaving a son Charles. The elder brother of Colonel Taafe, Major-General Lucas Taafe, married, first, Elizabeth Stephenson of Dunmoylan, county Limerick, by whom he had a daughter; and secondly, Annabella, daughter of Captain Thomas Spring (*v.* Deposition CLXXXVI.) of Kerry, by whom he had a son, Christopher, who married and left issue a son, Abel Taafe of Tipperary, living in the early part of the last century.

CXXVII.

MARGARET KELLY, of Dundalk, in the county of Louth, widow, aged forty years or thereabouts, taken the 24th of June, 1654, being duly sworn and examined, deposeth and saith, that on or about the 23rd of October, 1641, this examt., then living at Carrickmacross, in the county of Monaghan, did there and then see Patrick MacEdmund MacMahon, Patrick MacToole MacMahon, where they now live she heard not, Toole MacEward now in the county of Down, Patrick MacCollo Roe MacMahon, Hugh Rander (*sic*) O'Collan, and Patrick O'Lerdy (*sic*), all three prisoners, now in Dundalk gaol, and several other rebels whose names this examt. remembereth not. She saith that the said rebels did then and there seize on the several English inhabitants and Protestants of the town of Carrickmacross, and amongst them seized on John Jackson, George Gedden, and Thomas Alsdersly, and committed and kept them prisoners in the said town, until the 1st of January, 1641, and then the said rebels having erected a gallows near to the Castle of Carrickmacross, this deponent did see the said Patrick MacCollo Roe MacMahon, Hugh Rander O'Collon, Patrick Lerdy, Patrick MacEdmund MacMahon, Patrick MacToole MacMahon, and Toole MacEward, and several other rebels aforesaid, carrying the said John Jackson, George Gedden, and Thomas Aldersly, to the said gallows, and the said rebels being come to the gallows she did then see them ready to hang the said Jackson, Gedden, and Aldersly, and this examt. having gone a little way into the said town, and returning immediately, did as she was passing by see the said Jackson, Gedden, and Aldersly hanging dead upon the said gallows, and the said Patrick MacCollo Roe MacMahon, Hugh Rander O'Collon, Patrick O'Lerdy, Patrick MacEward MacMahon, Patrick MacToole MacMahon, and the said Toole MacEward standing at the said gallows among the other rebels, aiding and assisting at the hanging of the said Jackson, Gedden, and Aldersley. This examt. further saith, that about a month or six weeks after the 1st of January aforesaid this examt. did see the said Hugh Rander O'Collon and Toole MacEward present, and assisting other rebels at Carrickmacross aforesaid at the hanging of Mr. Russell and his wife, whose Christian names deponent remembereth not, and further saith not.

MARGARET KELLY.

Taken and deposed before me the day and year aforesaid,
    THOMAS DONGAN.

CXXVIII.

ANNE MOORE, of Portfreany, in the county Down, aged fifty years or thereabouts, duly sworn and examined, saith, that at the beginning of the rebellion she and her husband, Edward Moore, lived in the parish of Ballydowney, and they removed from their own house (when all the goods they had therein were taken away by the Irish party) to the house of Philip Kelly, being a neighbour of their own, where they tarried one night, and the next morning this examt.'s husband went into one John Porter's hard by to hear what news there was, and at his coming into the said Porter's house he was seized upon by Callo McKnogher and others, whose names she remembers not, to about the number of six persons, when he, her said husband, was taken a little way and killed by them. And the cause of this examt.'s knowledge is that she chanced to look out of the said Philip Kelly's house towards John Porter's, when she saw the said Callo and the others carrying her husband by the said Porter's house; upon which she hasted after them as fast as she could, but before she could come unto them her said husband was killed and the Irish had left him full of wounds. And she further saith, that the saw the corpse of one Hugh Wild, who was murdered at the same time, by the same party. And she saw his entrails coming forth of his body; and she did hear among the Irish, while she was their prisoner, that one Pat Oge O'Hoolihan was amongst them that committed these murders. And further saith not.

ANN + MOORE.

Jurat. 13 *May*, 1653,
 EDWARD CONWAY.
 GEO. RAWDON.   *Note.*

John Porter, sworn, confirmed the above in all particulars, adding that Art O'Huolihan, a priest, was amongst the party that committed these murders.

CXXIX.

EDWARD WILSON, of Lattmarkmurphy, in the parish of Augh (*illegible*), in the barony of Dungannon, county of Tyrone, gent., being duly sworn and examined, deposeth and saith, that in the beginning of the present rebellion, and by means thereof, to wit on the 23rd of October last, he was robbed or otherwise despoiled of his goods and chattels worth 870*l.*, by, or by the means of, Shane Oge MacCanna (*sic*) of the barony of Truagh, county of Monaghan, gent., Toole MacCanna and his brother Cuconnaght MacCanna, Patrick MacCanna and his brother, and several of the septs of the Mac-Cannas. And this deponent saith, that there was murdered at Aghalon aforesaid, by the rebels, men, women, and children, to the number of one hundred persons or thereabouts, some whereof they killed with swords, others they hanged, others they shot to death, others they hung up by the arms, and with their swords did hack them, to see how many blows they could endure before they died, and others they knocked on the head with hatchets. And further this deponent saith, that he heard it credibly reported by men of credit that the rebels of that county publicly said that the king of England should no longer be their king, saying further,

' Hang him, the rogue! he has been too long our king already!'
and they said the king of Spain should be their king, and they
drank his health in the house of a Scotchman they had murdered. And further saith, that he hath also heard it credibly
reported that at other times the rebels said Sir Phelim O'Neil
should be their king.

EDWARD WILSON.

Jurat. 16*th October*, 1742,
    Coram JOHN WATSON.
        WM. ALDRICH.

CXXX.

The said EDWARD WILSON, of Lattmarkmurphy, in the parish of
Aghalon, in the barony of Dungannon, being duly sworn and examined, on behalf of Robert Rowan, a little child, son to James
Rowan, late of Magharnabaly, in the county of Armagh, gent., murdered by the rebels, deposeth and saith, that the said James Rowan
before the rebellion began was worth and had in estates, lands,
leases, ready money in his house, and money owing him by men
now in actual rebellion, and in other goods and chattels to the
value of 2,000*l.* and above; and having such an estate as aforesaid,
was, since the rebellion began and by means thereof, expelled from,
deprived, robbed, or otherwise despoiled of all his means and estate
aforesaid, and after half a year's imprisonment was himself murdered
in prison. And his wife and four small children, going towards
Clannaboys for safety of their lives, were all most cruelly murdered
by the rebels on the highway, to wit, the mother was knocked on the
head, being great with child, and two of her children were hanged
over their mother's shoulder before they murdered her, and the other
two children were knocked on the head and so killed; and at the
same time and place four of her servants were also murdered by the
rebels. And saith, that the rebels that robbed the said James Rowan
aforesaid were the inhabitants of the Newry. But the names of
those rebels that committed the aforesaid murders, nor their places
of present abode, this deponent knoweth not. And that the estate
of the said James Rowan aforesaid, by the death of his wife and her
other children, of right belongeth to the said Robert Rowan.

                                            his
Jurat. 12*th October*, 1642,   EDWARD + WILSON.
    WM. ALDRICH.   mark
    JOHN WATSON.

22 THE IRISH MASSACRES OF 1641.

Note.

John Henderson, gent., sworn on the 2nd of May, 1653, before Colonel George Rawdon, deposed that he and about forty other Protestants were imprisoned at Armagh in the spring of 1641, by order of Tirlogh Roe O'Neil, that he looked out one morning of a window in the back of the gaol, and saw 'James Rowan, an inhabitant of Newry, brought thither by one Walter Bodley, Hugh Modder MacCadden (*sic*), and Neil O'Mallan, with others whose names he knoweth not, and there murdered by them.' Henderson further swore that Mr. Griffin, curate of Armagh, William Cammoge, and others to the number of about twenty, were all taken away from Armagh to Munolly, about twenty-four miles distant, and all murdered except Cammoge, who escaped and told him the fate of the rest, and that thirty-six persons were drowned or murdered by the rebels at the Tollwater.

CXXXI.

The examination of HUMPHREY STEWART, taken before me, this 3rd day of May, 1653, being aged forty years or thereabouts, who being duly examined and sworn, saith, that the next day after the town of Lisnogarvey was burnt by Sir Phelim O'Neil, and his army returning home scattered, this examt. coming down to the Tollwater the same day saw Joseph Hanley, his wife, and their children, cast into the Tollwater, with one Henry Taylor, son of William Taylor, and there drowned by Donnell O'Neill McCann, David McVeagh, Edmund Roo MacElevay, and Neil O'Doven, whereupon this examt. was glad to fly back into the woods for shelter and there hid himself. And as for the drowning at Portadown, he, this examt., saith, that he and one James Jackson being at plow for Mr. Jones, about Lammas last, there came to them when they were ploughing one Toole Oge McToole *dubh* MacCann, and they falling into discourse about the great murders committed at Portadonne, this examt. charged the said Toole with being one of them that committed them, to which the said Toole answered, that he did nothing but what he had command for; for that Toole McRory had the command of many men and him amongst the rest, and that he commanded them not to suffer any of the British nation to pass over the bridge, without money and some of their clothes, and this examt. saith, he heard there were drowned by the said men about seven score men, women, and children, among whom were William Taylor, with four or five children, Alexander Rose, with six or seven children, John Jackson and his wife, Edward Eaton, James Rumbold, and very many more of this examt.'s neighbours, but this examt. knoweth not the names of those that were at the said drowning, but heard from many it was done by the command of the said Toole McRory McCann, and further saith not.

  Geo. Rawdon.   Humphrey Stewart +

CXXXII.

  John Hickman, late of Tinakeertagh, in the parish of Armagh, county of Cavan, yeoman, sworn and examined, saith, that in the beginning of the present rebellion, viz. about the 24th of October, 1641, he, this deponent, was deprived, robbed, or otherwise despoiled of his lands of inheritance, worth 48*l.* yearly, and is like to lose the future profits thereof, until a peace be established, and of goods and chattels worth 116*l.* more. And also this deponent's house was taken up by the rebels, Hugh O'Reily, gent., of Drumnaloe, and Hugh McDonough Malmore O'Reilly of Ardlough, in the same county, Owen O'Gowen of Cordnashure, who forcibly took from this deponent his horse and stripped his father-in-law and his wife of their clothes. And further saith, that when this deponent and his wife and children intended to come away from the rebels, one Donnell O'Leary, his brother-in-law, who is an Irishman and yet a Protestant, being not allowed to come away with them, took this deponent into his own house, and there kept him for about one year together, during which time the rebels sent them word and threatened them all with death, if they would not go to mass. And the rebels forcibly took from his said brother-in-law, Donnell O'Leary, the possession rents and profits of his land, and some of his goods, and promised to restore all unto him if he would forsake the Protestant religion and go to mass. And further saith, that whilst he was so kept at his said brother-in-law's house, he and his brother-in-law drew out of the river of Lough Erne the corpses of six persons that the rebels had formerly drowned, which corpses they buried. And this deponent observed that although those corpses had lain long in the water, yet they were not torn, nor eaten by the fish, nor devoured, but their skins were whole. And further saith, that since those persons and other Protestants were drowned in that river, which is called Lough Erne river, this deponent hath heard divers of the rebels complain that they could not get bream, pike, or other fish in that river, since the English were drowned there, as formerly they had done, and they used to say that they (the Irish) thought all the fish and the English had gone away together.

JOHN + HICKMAN.

Jurat. 16*th Feb.* 1642,
RANDAL ADAMS.
WILL. ALDRICH.

CXXXIII.

RANDALL ADAMS, clerk, duly sworn, saith, that about the 1st of November, 1641, being in company with some of the chief gentlemen of Westmeath, near the place of his and their residence, he heard some of the said gentlemen profess and say to some friars then in their company, that they, the friars and their fellows, were the cause of this great and mischievous rebellion, and showed to their face what little, and indeed no cause they had to have begun so many foul abominable actions; as first, generally they enjoyed the highest benefits the kingdom could afford, and that none even of the best and greatest, all things considered, could be so fully made partakers of them, the benefits aforesaid, than they were, and for further convincing them of their damnable villainy, they instanced, in very many particulars at first, the great freedom they had in religion without control, and that they, the friars, had generally the best horses, clothes, meats, drinks, and all provisions, delightful or useful, as none others had, or could hope to have, the like on such cheap and easy terms, for they had all without care or cost of their own, and many other privileges, beyond any of their own function either regular or secular, through the Christian world; and therefore those gentlemen most bitterly cursed them, the friars, to their teeth, saying they hoped God would bring that vengeance home to them which they, by their wicked plots, laboured so wickedly to bring on others. The gentlemen before named that spoke these very same words were Sir Phelim Tuite, Knt. and Baronet, Edward Tuite, Esq., justice of the peace, and Andrew Tuite, Esq., justice of the peace.

RANDALL ADAMS.

Jurat, August 22*nd*, 1642,
JOHN WATSON.
WM. ALDRICH.
HEN. BRERETON.

CXXXIV.

The Examination of CHRISTOPHER HAMPTON, *taken before me, by direction of the Right Honourable the Lords Justices and Council, this* 11*th of December*, 1641.

The said Hampton, being sworn by the clerk of the Council, saith, that he and divers others coming ashore on the 5th of the present at the Skerries, within ten miles of this city, one called Father Malone, with many accompanying of him, laid hands upon this examt. and the rest, and stripped them of all they had, and likewise entered into the ship, and rifled and took away what was there, which being done, the said Malone sent this examt. and the other passengers by a warrant under his hand, from constable to constable, to Roger Moore, colonel in the army. According to the warrant of the said Malone, this examt. being brought before Mr. Roger Moore, he after some time let this examt. and the rest go free and at large. This examt. further saith, that at the same place and time there was present at the Church of Duleek, in consultation, sundry of the Lords of the Pale, namely the Lord of Gormanstown, the Lord Netterville, the Lord of Slane, the Lord Louth, the Lord of Iveagh, the rest were unknown to this examt.

ROBERT MEREDITH.

Note.

Was this Father Malone the provincial of the Jesuits before mentioned (*v. ante*, p. 386) or a parish priest in Wicklow? This outrage was committed on the day that Sir Charles Coote was sent from Dublin into Wicklow, and six days later another English bark was plundered in the same neighbourhood, as appears by the next deposition.

CXXXV.

The Examination of DAVID POWELL, *taken before me, Sir John Temple, Knt., December* 14*th*, 1641.

David Powell, one of the inhabitants of Clontarf, saith, that a bark belonging to Philip Norrice, of Liverpool, ran aground near Clontarf on the 11th of December, that some dwellers of (*sic*) Raheny, to the number of fourteen, came and pillaged the said bark, and took away all the best commodities that were then in her, and that when one Evers and a miller came to help to save the goods, they fell upon them and wounded the miller to death, and caused Evers, for fear of losing his life, to turn Papist. On the 14th of December the inhabitants of Clontarf, chiefly fishermen, came and took away out of the said bark such coals and salt and ropes as were left in the said barque and carried them to their houses. And saith further, that FitzSimmons of Rahenny, gent., was amongst those at Rahenny that pillaged the bark all night. And saith further, that there came some of the rebels on the 12th of December to Clontarf, and that they came to the house of this examt., finding no other English in the town, and rifled all he had, and said they would set fire to his house if he would not leave it, and that they would not leave an Englishman dwelling upon the land, and they said they would go from thence to Howth.

J. TEMPLE.

(*Unsigned.*)

Note.

The above deposition appears to be a copy of a lost original.

CXXXVI.

JOSEPH SMITHSON, minister and preacher of God's Word in the parish of Clonskerme (*sic*), in the county of Dublin, and barony of Rathdown, being duly sworn and examined, deposeth, that in December last, upon (*illegible*) day at night, he was robbed in household goods to the value of 40*l.*; in hay, 50*l.*; in (*illegible*) 3*l.*; in bills and bonds, 10*l.*; in the loss of his glebe lands and garden, 5*l.*; in divers hens, geese, ducks, pigs, and turkeys, 18*s.*; offerings and other duties, 5*l.* And that his wife was that night taken prisoner in her own house at Dean's Grange, county Dublin, by the servant of Richard Rochfort of the same parish, in the county of Dublin, gent., viz. Phelim Malone and John Carrick of (*illegible*), and others whose names are James Goodman of Ballinley, Alexander Rochfort and Patrick Sherman of the Kill, all of the parish and county aforesaid, and being so taken in her own house, her apron pulled off and herself dragged out by the hair of her head, she was then pinioned and set upon her own horse, her clothes plucked from her, and they drove her horse through bogs to one Mr. William Wolverston, of Stillorgan, in the said county, Esquire, who gave command to the rebels to hang her but not upon his land. Afterwards she was carried, still on horseback, a matter of twenty miles after the same manner. And this deponent further saith, that the said Mr.

Wolverston told him, this deponent, that he would pay no more tithes but to the mass priest. And this deponent is like to be deprived of the same tithes which since the rebellion began Mr. Wolverston hath detained from him. And saith also, that Mr. Richard Rochfort, a wilful Papist, kept from this deponent as many tithe furs as came to 5l., and said to this deponent that he kept them in hopes to see the Protestants buried in them. And this deponent is like to be deprived of those tithes also due from the said Rochfort since the rebellion, he peremptory denying to pay them. And further the said Rochfort did say to one Thomas Frisby, that if he would get him Mr. Smithson and his wife he would shoot them to pieces with his pistol. And further this deponent saith, that he credibly heard that the robbers that took away his wife were of the council of (*illegible*) the said William Woolverston aforesaid, and of one Patrick Coleman, Nicholas Farrell, Daniel McQuin, Nicholas Rochfort, and William Taylor, of Stillorgan, being all Papists and rebels, as he considereth. And this examt. is credibly informed that the said rebels have most barbarously and cruelly hanged his said wife till she died, and a servant woman of hers also. And this examt., for fear of the cruelty of the said Wolverston, Rochford, and the rebels before mentioned, was enforced to fly from his benefice, with his two sons, whither they dare not return, but are deprived of the benefit thereof, being worth yearly 40l., and above, and being as aforesaid robbed of his other goods, hath no means whereby to maintain himself and his children, but they are all exposed to great want and misery.

JOSEPH SMITHSON.

Jurat. coram nobis, 18*th Jan.* 1641,
WM. HITCHCOCK.
WM. ALDRICH.

Note.

In former times Wicklow was well stocked not only with the red-deer which Strafford loved to hunt (*v.* Introduction, *note* p. 71), but with otters and other small wild animals, the furs of which were valuable. In a letter to Strafford, Laud thanks him for a gift of a cloak lined with Irish furs, in which it appears from the above deposition portions of the Established Church tithes were sometimes paid.

CXXXVII.

DENNEY, the relict of JAMES MONTGOMERY, clerk, parson of Donnamayne, in the county Monaghan, being duly sworn and examined, deposeth and saith, that since the beginning of this present rebellion and by means thereof, her said husband, and she, this deponent, were expelled from, deprived, robbed, or otherwise despoiled of their goods and chattels to the value of 708*l*. And further saith, that the rebels that so robbed and despoiled them were Colonel MacMahon MacBrian, and Patrick MacLaughlin, Colonel MacQuin, Colonel MacArt Ardle MacMahon, and Ewer MacCallan. And she further saith, that on May day last, when the rebels were beaten at Ardee by the English army, they all came to Carrickmacross, and then they killed her, this deponent's, husband, and said they would not leave a minister alive in Ireland, because, as they said, the English army killed all their priests at Ardee. And the chief captains and colonels in the Carrick said they did God good service in killing the ministers. And this deponent saith also, that at Christmas last the rebels most cruelly murdered, at three several times, nineteen Englishmen, and since Christmas killed and drowned, at or near the Carrick, of men, women, and children, to the number of eighty-nine persons. And saith, that the persons that did these murders and cruelties were Colonel MacBrian MacMahon, a chief rebel in Carrickmacross, Ewer MacLoughlin, a rebel bishop who was the chief director and causer of these murders, and Patrick MacLoughlin, a colonel also among the rebels. And this deponent further saith, that such was the cruelty of those that murdered her husband, that after they had hanged him up they cut his head from his body and stabbed him with skeans. And that one Friar John, who was one of the principal murderers, took hold of her husband's leg while he was hanging, saying, '*Go tell the devil I sent thee to him for a token.*' And the same rebels did commonly say that the Protestants were to be all crushed. And this deponent saw one who termed himself to be the priest of Carrickmacross sprinkle water on and christen anew one Francis Williams, of Carrickmacross, and his wife, who were formerly Protestants, but turned to mass, he further saying they could not be Christians until they were so christened. And the rebels before her husband's death prest him much to turn to mass, but he told them he would die in his own religion.

DENNEY MONTGOMERY +

Jurat. 17*th November*, 1642,
    JOHN WATSON.   RANDAL ADAMS.
    WM. ALDRICH.   ED. PIGOTT.
    HEN. BRERETON.

DEPOSITIONS.   29

CXXXVIII.

JOHN JOICE, Vice-Constable of the Black Castle, of Wicklow, sworn and examined, saith, that since the beginning of this present rebellion, and by means thereof, he was deprived of his goods and chattels hereafter expressed, viz. upon and from his farms of Greenane and Ballinowle, in the county of Wicklow, and within Wicklow aforesaid, of beasts and cattle worth 100*l*., horses worth 80*l*., sheep worth 26*l*., new tanhouse and bark worth 100*l*., in his haggard of corn and hay 100*l*., hogs, rents, owing by tenants that are now in rebellion, 15*l*., by those rebels following, Luke Toole of Castle Kevin, Tiegue Ogo Birne of Ballinvallagh, Esquire, an ancient traitor in the time of Queen Elizabeth, Brian Birne of Killnamonagh, gent., Walter Birne of Neuragh, gent., John McBrian Birne of Ballinater, gent., Luke Birne of Killwanagh, gent., James Birne of Tinwillin, gent., William (*illegible*) of Ballireagh, Brian McDonogh of Behanagh, Donogh Commian of Kilnemanagh, gent., Thomas Archbold of Wicklow, gent., Alexander McDonell of the same, gent., John Coghlan of Wicklow, gent., all of the county of Wicklow, Patrick Bane O'Cullen, James McOwen Doyle, Owen Doyle, a butcher, Edmund O'Cleary, Art McShane, Gerrot McShane, Shane O'Cleary, Michael Passmore, Brian McArt, Edward McBrian, Tirlogh Birne, Nicholas Doyle, Turlogh Doyle, Harry Barnewall, Richard Barnewall, Patrick McDermot, James Corley, Nicholas McBroder, Henry White and John his son, Tadey Newman, Richard Hore, Shane McEdward, Thomas White, James White, William McIlderry, Edward Connell, Shane McMurrogh, Edward and Peter White, Fitz Andrew; Richard Kinn, Edward Duffe, William McDermot, John McDermot, Tiegue O'Cullen, Hugh O'Ronon, Richard O'Ronon, Laughlin O'Ronon, Patrick and Nicholas O'Ronon, Walter White, Richard Cottner, Gillernow Cottner, John Toole, William Kearny, James McRichard, Henry Bronocke, James McDermot, Donnell Roe Slater, Nicholas McMurtagh, George Sherlock, Laughlin McTirlagh of the town of Wicklow. And further saith, that Oliver Masterson in the county of Wexford, gent., James Fullam of the city of Dublin, shoemaker, Tiege McDonnell Enos, Tirlagh MacGerald, who are now in actual rebellion, were and are indebted to this deponent in several sums amounting to 88*l*. 4*s*., and by means of their being in rebellion he hath lost the same.

And this deponent further saith, that Thomas Mullinex, gent., now resting by commission in the castle of Wicklow, told this deponent, and so have others whom this deponent gives credit unto likewise informed him, that Philip Birne of Barnasoile, in the county of Wicklow, gent., son-in-law to Mr. Edward Leech of the Grange near Wicklow, was, about seven weeks since, by or by the means of the said Mr. Mullinex, apprehended in Dublin for partaking with the rebels, and especially for writing a letter to him and this deponent for delivering up the castle of Wicklow unto the rebels. And that the said Philip Birne was brought before Sir Charles Coote, and there examined and committed, and threatened to be hanged, but how he was enlarged this deponent knoweth not. Howbeit, by some means he hath gotten fresh liberty, and at or about the 6th or 7th of April last this deponent received another letter from him, which followeth in these words, viz.—

MR. JOHN JOICE.—So it is, though (as) you partly know, I intend to assault the Castle of Wicklow, before I depart, I do not desire to take the lives of any Christian, so I desire you and the rest to prepare yourselves to serve God, so I rest

Yours as you deserve it,
PHILIP BIRNE.

Which letter this deponent received about the 7th of April aforesaid, 1642, which letter was thus endorsed, ' To John Joice and the rest in the castle of Wicklow.' And afterwards this deponent received a letter from the said Luke Birne, colonel of the rebels, thus directed, viz. ' To my loving and respected friend Mr. John Joice, and the rest of the gentlemen in the castle of Wicklow, these.'

COURTEOUS GENTLEMEN.—It is not unknown to men of your litteration (sic) and experience, that it is no perfect point of Christianity that men should, in scorn of other Christians, rather untimely perish between hope and despair than yield to many well-disposed men of note, as many other gentlemen of your country have done and some to myself, for which they received the benefit of faithful promises faithfully performed to their content in the present, and ever shall, by God's grace subsisting, which gentlemen like (illegible) and quarter of goods and lives shall you receive, with all sufficient security of performance, if it shall please God Almighty to mollify your hearts, no longer to stand in your own light, and to listen with attentive ears to your own good and safe desires, wished by your true and affectionate friend to do you service; in expectation of your answer I rest.

LUKE BIRNE.

April 26th, 1642.

Since which time this deponent received another letter, delivered unto him about the last of April, 1642, from the said Walter Birne, thus directed, ' To Mr. John Joice and the rest of his company.'

DEPOSITIONS.

Mr. John Joice.—Being not otherwise employed, I am bold to write to you and the rest of my neighbours here with you; we were not wont to be so long in one town, but we drank and made merry together. For my part I am here since the day that Thomas Marcer was killed, who I protest should not be killed if I were present; in the meantime, I gave way to others to send letters to you, which I know to be no great purpose. But if you were in that mind or in that want whereby that you would leave that place, which I know to be no pleasant place for you, my word should be as (*illegible*) as any man's in the country. I will not threaten you, nor tell you of anything that is like to befall you, for I know you would not believe it, but I will tell you some news, that you may believe if you please. The English army took the castle of Carrigmaine on Sunday last, was sinnoige (*sic*) and killed fourteen men, that were warders there, and many women and children. But there was killed of the English Sir (*illegible*) the colonel, his lieutenant, five captains, and 200 soldiers. So I rest yours as you are mine,

WALTER BIRNE.

8th April, 1642.

Notwithstanding which letters, and the often assaults and attempts of the rebels aforesaid, whereby some of the people of the castle perished, the castle was not taken, but the enemy from time to time repulsed by his Majesty's small number of soldiers there. And this deponent further saith, that the rebels in the town of Wicklow have burned, pulled down, and destroyed 23 of this deponent's houses or tenements in Wicklow, upon one of which this deponent spent 160*l.* in buildings, by which burning and spoiling this deponent hath lost to the value of 500*l.* And this deponent hath afterwards been despoiled by the rebels of corn in the ground worth 40*l.*, and there is now due unto him by one Dudley Birne of Ballinmacshannon, who is now in rebellion carrying arms against his Majesty and his loyal subjects, and therefore this deponent maketh accompt that he shall lose by the same 10*l.* sterling. And this deponent is also expelled from, deprived and forcibly dispossessed by the rebels of his lands of inheritance lying in the Ranelagh worth 40*l.* per annum, whereof one year's profit is already lost, and this deponent is like to be deprived of their future profits until a peace be established. So as his present losses by means of the rebellion come to 1,102*l.* 4*s.* and his future loss to 40*l.* per annum as aforesaid.

JOHN JOYCE (*sic*).

Jurat. 10*th August*, 1642,
JOHN WATSON.
WM. ALDRICH.
HEN. BRERETON.

Note.

John Joyce held the Black Castle of Wicklow, the ruins of which I believe still remain, for three years after he made this deposition, until the rebels, despairing of being able to take it by force or persuasion, obtained admittance by treachery and set it on fire, when the brave warder perished in the flames. From Byrne's letter it is evident that Joyce had lived on good terms with his neighbours in times of peace, but when they went into rebellion he was their stoutest opponent, until the Black Castle became his funeral pyre. (See the trial of his murderers hereafter given.)

CXXXIX.

EDWARD DEANE, late of Oghran, in the county of Wicklow, tanner, sworn, saith, that on or about the first day of November last he was by the rebels robbed and despoiled of his goods to the value following: of corn worth 10*l.* and above, of beasts, garrons, and sheep worth 100*l.*, household goods worth above 20*l.*, leather and bark worth 250*l.*, wearing apparel worth 10*l.*, in all 380*l.* And this deponent and his wife and seven children were expulsed from their house and his farm at Oghran aforesaid, whereof he had a lease from Captain Bryford for 48 years in being under the rent of 3*l.* per annum, his interest therein being worth 100*l.* And for another lease of 29 years in being of a farm in Tennekilly in the same county, whereof his interest was worth 20*l.* at least. And that the parties that so robbed him were Luke Toole of (*illegible*), within the county Wicklow colonel of 500 rebels, Luke Byrne of Killarlonon, in the same county, gent., captain of 100 rebels, John MacBrian, the son of Brian MacPhelim, gent., Turlogh MacHugh Duffe, lately resident with Mr. Job Ward of Knockreagh and steward of his court, another captain of 100 rebel soldiers, and about 500 others in their company and under their command. And that divers of those rebels said they were the queen's soldiers, and fought for her, and they made a proclamation that all the English men and women that did not depart the country should be hanged, drawn, and quartered in 24 hours, and that the houses of the Irish that kept any English children should be burned. And afterwards the same rebels, or some of them, did murder and hang one Edmund Snape, and Thomas Hanpath, smith, and others, being Englishmen. And further saith that the rebels about the same time did prey and despoil the said Captain Byford, Nicholas Bretnay, Thomas Holman, Clemence Stephens, widow, David Stanhope, Peter Deane, Thomas Walton, James Shuttleworth, and Stephen Sandes, all this deponent's neighbours, and English people, and their wives and families, of their goods and clothes. And the rebels burnt two Protestant bibles, and said it was hell fire that burnt, and burnt all this deponent's rescripts, bonds, and leases.

EDWARD DEANE.

Jurat. 7*th Jan.* 1641, *cora nobis,*
   ROGER PUTTOCK.
   JOHN WATSON.

CXL.

DAVID ROCH, of Dublin, labourer, duly sworn upon the Holy Evangelists, deposeth and saith, that at the beginning of the rebellion in Ireland he lived with Robert Kennedy, Esq., of Ballygarney, as plowman. And saith, that he did then know John Leeson, shepherd to the Earl of Meath, and Nathaniel Snape, sometime servant to Mr. Silvester Kennedy, son to the said Robert Kennedy, and that they were both English Protestants. He further deposeth, that at the beginning of the rebellion aforesaid Colonel Luke Toole, of Castle Kevin, in the said county, having the chief command of the rebels there, entered into possession of the house at Ballygarney, belonging to the said Robert Kennedy, Esquire. This deponent further saith, that whilst the said Luke Toole was in the said house he (this deponent) saw the said Nathaniel Snape and John Leeson brought into the said house, as prisoners to the said Luke, by some under his command, but their names he knoweth not. And about a half an hour after he saw the said Nathaniel Snape and John Leeson brought out of the said house, and carried to two thorn-trees, near to the said house, and there hanged until they were dead, and, as some of the soldiers under the said Luke Toole told this examt., the same was done by directions of the said Luke. This deponent further saith, that the said Snape and Leeson were, as he believeth, hung because they were English Protestants, and he saith that after they were dead he did help to bury them. And further he cannot depose.

·DAVID + ROCHE.

11*th Jan.* 1652,
   JAMES DONNELAN.   DUDLEY LOFTUS.
   THOS. DONGAN.   THOMAS HOOKE.

The said David Rorke is bound in 10l. to give evidence against Luke Toole for the aforesaid murder in the High Court of Justice at Dublin, the first day of the sitting of that court, and not to depart hence without license, &c.

CXLI.

LUKE TOOLE, of Castlekevin, in the county of Wicklow, aged seventy-five years or thereabouts, examined before us, saith, that at the beginning of the rebellion he was summoned by Hugh McPhelim Byrne, Lieutenant-General of the running army for the Irish, to be at Ballygarny, to join with others of the Irish army there, to give opposition to Sir Charles Coote, who about that time with a party of the English army marched into the county Wicklow. He saith, that he being come to Ballygarney, found Phelim McRedmond Byrne, who commanded in chief over this examt., and the rest of the party at Ballygarney. He further saith, that he coming in and entering into the said town of Ballygarney, there was a man hanging upon a bush near the house of Ballygarney, at which his horse started, and upon inquiry he, this deponent, was told by some of the soldiers there that the man was a shepherd, but to whom he, this deponent, cannot now remember, nor doth he know the man's name, nor whether he were English and Protestant. He saith that he did not give any order for the hanging of the said shepherd, or any other person at Ballygarney, neither doth he know of any other that gave an order for the hanging of any one there, nor doth he know of any other man that was hanged there. He saith he doth not know of any Englishman or Protestant being brought into the said house at Ballygarny, before him, this deponent, or any other person, he, this deponent, and the rest of his party having gone away early the next morning, after his coming there as aforesaid, to meet the said Sir Charles Coote. He further saith that he neither saw or know John Leeson or Nathaniel Snape.

LU. TOOLE.

27th Jan. 1652,
 JAMES DONNELLAN.   THOS. HOOKE.
 ISAAC DOBSON.   DUDLEY LOFTUS.
 THOS. DONGAN.

CXLII.

ELIZABETH LEESON, late of Delgany, in the county of Wicklow, widow, sworn, deposeth and saith, that since the beginning of the present rebellion, viz. about a month before Christmas last, her late husband, John Lisson (sic), late of Delgany aforesaid, was hanged at Ballygarney, in the county of Wicklow, by Morgan McEdmund and Brian of the Killory in the said county, and Brian Fynn of the Doune in the said county, yeoman, as this examt. was informed, and as they both confessed afterwards to this examt. herself. And further saith, that ever since her said husband's death she lived with John Walshe of Killenargy, with whom her said husband formerly lived, and that about three weeks before Easter the said Morgan McEdmund and Brian Fynn, with two others, whose names she knoweth not, came to the said John Walsh's house, he and his wife being absent, and from thence violently took her to Ballygarney, in the said county, to one Captain Toole, a commander of the rebels, and to George Hacket, then marshal there, who threatened to hang this examt., except she could procure security to be true to the Irish army, and thereupon sent her to Arklow gaol, where she had been committed in a most miserable manner, but that one of their commanders there, whose name she knoweth not, took pity on her and let her go abroad, by means whereof she escaped, and coming to Dublin was several times on the way threatened to be hanged by the rebels, and at Bolton Hill, in the said county, upon Monday in Easter week, several rebels, whose names she knoweth not, took her and put a rope about her neck and tied her up to a gallows, until she was almost hanged, but afterwards took her down and said she should not be hanged but shot to death, which the said rebels would have done, but that their chief commander sent her away, after he had sworn her not to go near the English army. And she further saith, that before her said husband was hanged as aforesaid, they were robbed of cows, horses, household goods, provisions and clothes, besides clothes which she had to leave at Mr. Walsh's house, when she was taken away from thence, to the value in all of 56*l*., all which were taken from her by the said Morgan McEdmund, Brian MacFinn, and Philip O'Reilly, near about the Killory aforesaid, and others whose names she knoweth not.

ELIZABETH LISSON (sic).

Jurat. 21st *April,* 1642,
 WILLIAM HITCHCOCK.
 WILLIAM ALDRICH.

CXLIII.

GEORGE TWELLY, sworn and examined, saith, that at the beginning of the rebellion, and about a quarter of a year before, he served Dean Bartley, of Truaghtown, in the county of Monaghan, and that on the rising of the rebellion one Neil MacCannan possessed himself of the Dean's house, and took him prisoner, together with about fifty or three score English and Scots, men, women, and children, all of the said Dean's family and tenants, and about a month after, he, the said Neil MacCannan, conveyed the said Dean to Enniskillen, and promised to protect the servants and the rest of the said family and tenants with him at Truaghtown, which he accordingly did for the space of three-quarters of a year, about which time Sir Phelim O'Neil and many more rebels in his company came to Truaghtown, to make merry, as this examt. then surmised, who perceiving so many English and Scots there, he, the said Sir Phelim, uttered words to this effect in English : ' *Cozen* (sic) *Neil MacCannan, I wonder you keep so many English and Scots about your house.*' ' *Why,*' said MacCannan, ' *they be poor servants of the Dean's and I keep them under myself, you need not fear what they can do, poor things, they had rather have a bit of meat than to do any mischief against you or I.*' Sir Phelim replied, ' *I desire that you make away with them, for they may do mischief hereafter, if their army should be near us, and any escape from you.*' Then said MacCannan, ' *I have kept them, Sir Phelim, so long, that I am loath to see them suffer death now.*' Sir Phelim hastily made answer again, ' *Plague on them !* ' or some such reviling words, ' *set out all your guards, and let me see a fire made for them before I go hence !* ' ' *No !* ' said MacCannan, ' *I will not,*' and thereupon some difference about it seemed to arise betwixt them, and Sir Phelim told MacCannan that he might be assisting at his own death in keeping these servants alive, and MacCannan then said, that notwithstanding that, he would protect them, and did so accordingly. That this discourse, or the substance of it, this examt. was earwitness of himself, being one of the servants of the said Dean, when he was a prisoner under the aforesaid MacCannan. And further saith not.

GEORGE TWELLY.

Taken before us (illegible), 1652,
R. TIGHE.
R. RYEVES.

CXLIV.

ANNE SHERRING, late wife of John Sherring, of the territory of Ormond, at the Silver Works, in the county of Tipperary, aged about twenty-five years, sworn and examined, deposeth and saith, that about Candlemas was two years ago, the said John Sherring, her then husband, going from his farm which he held from Mr. John Kennedy, Esq., near to the Silver Mines, one Hugh Kennedy, one of the brothers of the said John, a cruel rebel, with a great number of Irish rebel soldiers, then and there forcibly assaulted and set upon her said husband, and upon one John Brooke, William Loughlin, and eighteen more English Protestant men, and about ten women and four children in their company, and then and there first stripped them of their clothes, and then with stones, pole-axes, skeans, swords, pikes, darts, and other weapons most barbarously murdered and massacred them all; in the time of which massacre a most loud and fearful noise and storm of thunder and lightning, wind, hailstones, and rain began, the time being on a Sabbath day, about an hour before night, the former part of that day being all very fair. But that thunder, lightning, and tempest happening suddenly soon after the massacre began, much affrighted and terrified this deponent and many others, insomuch that those very murderers themselves confessed it to be a sign of God's anger, and a threatening of them for their cruelty, yet it restrained them not, but they persisted in their bloody acts till they had murdered her husband and the rest of these Protestants, and had hacked, hewed, slashed, stabbed, and so massacred them that they were all cut to pieces, her husband for his part having thirty grievous wounds then and there given him, some near or through his heart, some mortal wounds in his head, some in his belly, and in either arm four wounds, and the rest in his back, legs, thighs, and neck. And that murder done, those barbarous rebels tied withes about the necks of those murdered and drew them out of the refining mill, where they slew them and threw them all or most of them into a deep hole, formerly made, one upon another, so that none of those men, women, and children escaped death; howbeit, one Thomas Laddell, a Scotchman, and Thomas Wallop, who then and there received many grievous wounds and had been left on the ground for dead, crawled up, after the rebels were gone away, and with much difficulty escaped with their lives. And further saith, that such was God's judgment, upon the said Hugh Kennedy, for that bloody act, that he fell into a most desperate madness and distraction, and could not rest day nor night, yet coveting to do more mischief on the English, but being prevented and denied to do it, he about a week after drowned himself in the next river to the Silver Works. But his barbarous and wicked soldiers went on in their wickedness, and afterwards bragged how they had killed a minister and his wife and four children near the city of Limerick. And this deponent is too well assured that those and other Irish rebels in that part of the country executed and committed a great number of bloody murders, robberies, and outrages, against the persons and goods of the Protestants, so as very few escaped with their lives, and none at all saved their goods. And further saith, that all the Popish gentry in the country thereabouts, especially all those of the septs and names of the O'Brians, the Coghlans, and the Kennedys, were all actors in the present rebellion against his Majesty, and either acted or assisted in murders, robberies, cruelties, and rebellions aforesaid. And she further saith, that by means of the said rebellion her said husband and she were in Ormond aforesaid, about Candlemas 1641, robbed and stripped of goods to the value of 160*l.* at the least. And that the said John Kennedy, being their landlord, was the man that so deprived them thereof, and the other rebels stripped her.

ANNA + SHERRING.

Jurat. coram nobis, 10*th Feb.* 1648,
  HEN. JONES.
  HEN. BRERETON.

Note.

Several depositions were taken about the murders at the Silver Mines. Amongst others William Timms, gentleman, sworn before Jones, Brereton, and Aldrich, on the 26th of May, 1645, deposed, that he was made prisoner by the Irish and that he and his wife and children were robbed and stripped. He confirmed Mrs. Sherring's statement as to the murders and the mangling of the unburied corpses, and he goes on to relate how either through inability or disinclination to punish the murderers, they as usual escaped serious punishment.

'After the cessation proclaimed in October, 1643, this deponent coming from Cork to Sir George Hamilton's house, where he had sent his wife and children before him, he stayed there and at the Silver Mines until about the 14th of January, 1644, when there came directions from the Supreme Council at Kilkenny unto the said John Kennedy of Dounally, to apprehend and bring into prison the persons of all those that committed the said murders at the Silver Mines. Whereupon the said John Kennedy apprehended and carried to prison all the known murderers saving his brother Hugh, who had before that time drowned himself, and one Hugh O'Coghy, who was servant to himself, the said John Kennedy, which said Coghy, whether to prevent some confession and discovery of his said master's wicked acts, or to preserve him, the said Coghy, to act more mischief, this deponent cannot tell, he, the said John Kennedy, did not or would not apprehend, but rather sent or suffered him to go away, and stay until the danger was passed over, amongst a wicked company of priests and friars. And when the other persons so apprehended and imprisoned for that foul massacre aforesaid had been imprisoned for some time, and slightly questioned for the fact, then they were either suffered to escape, or set at liberty and so came home again. And then the said Coghy returned home unto his said master's house, where he was entertained and harboured as formerly, served and attended his master, and for anything this deponent knoweth to the contrary he doth so still, without being punished for his wicked acts.'

Another witness, John Powell, sworn and examined on the 15th of July, 1645, confirmed the truth of Mrs. Sherring's and Mr. Timms' depositions, adding that when John Clark was murdered at the Silver Mines, his wife flung herself on her knees before Hugh Kennedy crying out, '*I have but a shilling left, but I will give it to you to save my child!*' on which he took the child by the legs, 'dashed out its brains against the stones, and then his followers ripped up the woman, who was great with child, and murdered her with the rest.' (*MS. Depositions, Tipperary, T.C.D.* p. 407.) See the royalists' and Catholics' account of the massacres at Cashel and Silver Mines and the fate of the murderers hereafter given.

CXLV.

GILBERT JOHNSTON, late of the town of Cashel, parish of Cashel, within the county of Tipperary, husbandman, duly sworn and examined, deposeth and saith, that about the 1st of January last, 1641 (O. S.), this deponent was robbed and forcibly despoiled of his goods, &c., to the value of 82*l.*, part consisting of debts due to him by Papists now in actual rebellion, as Philip O'Dwyer of (*illegible*), and James Butler of Ballynahinch, in the county aforesaid. And further saith, that about the same time this deponent and divers other English and Protestants betook themselves for their safeguard into the city of Cashel, yet the mayor of the city, James Sall, and the corporation of the same admitted the undernamed persons with forces and arms to enter the same, namely Philip O'Dwyer aforesaid, Charles O'Dwyer, James Butler of Ballynahinch aforesaid, they being accompanied by five hundred or six hundred men, and having entered the said city, in a most rebellious and inhuman manner they stripped the most part of three hundred persons there, men, women, and children, English Protestants. This deponent further saith, that at that time he and to the number of forty more, young and old, in one company, being all stripped as aforesaid, by the direction of the said parties were in one flock stark naked driven to one of the gates of the city, and then and there in a most barbarous manner, before they could get out of the gate the said parties and their followers and servants murdered John Linsay, clerk, Thomas Charleton of Cashel, sadler, Mr. Carr, a schoolmaster of Cashel, and this deponent was dangerously wounded in his head, arms, and thighs, and was left for dead amongst the corpses under the gate, where he lay from four o'clock in the forenoon until four in the afternoon, during which time, it being then frosty weather, this deponent's body, after he came to himself, was frozen to the ground with his own blood, and the blood of those that were killed close by him, so that he had much to do to loose himself from the ground. After this while, and during the time that the murders and stripping were committed, the said Philip O'Dwyer (*torn*) stood in a window at the said mayor's house, perceiving what was done. And after this deponent recovered himself, in the way going to (*illegible*) was apprehended by some of the said party's company, as he believeth, and commanded to stand to a post, where they shot several shots at him, to wrest a confession out of him where his money was, being before robbed and stripped of all that he had. Yet God miraculously rescued him from them.

About the 3rd of January, aforesaid, this deponent, his wife, and children went to Golden Castle, in the same county, to save their lives, where two hundred persons, young and old, English and Protestants, got themselves in for fear of the rebels, and were afterwards closely besieged by Pierce Butler of Bansha, and divers others of the gentlemen of that county, till towards Easter following, the besieged having no relief for a long while, but a little oatmeal and water, divers of them died, and at length the provisions being spent, the survivors ventured to steal away by night, and coming in the way towards the English quarters, in a place hard by Closhguire, in the said county, were assaulted by the rebels, who then and there cruelly murdered some of them, some others they hanged; this was in or about Easter last, the names of those that were so murdered this deponent partly knoweth, namely James Hook of Golden, aforesaid, tanner, George Crafford and Jane his wife, who was great with child, which child they took up and tossed upon a pike, Anthony Patten of Ballygriffin, miller, and his wife, James Guthrie of Ballygriffin, yeoman, and the names of the rest he knoweth not, or doth not remember. He also saith, that the said parties being come away from Golden Castle, the wife of George Miller being then left sick, as soon as the rebels entered, they dragged her out of bed by the legs down stairs, till they knocked out her brains.

GILBERT + JOHNSTON.

Jurat. coram nobis, 20*th Feb.* 1642,
PHIL. BISSE.
THOS. BETTESWORTH.

CXLVI.

ELLISH MEAGHER, *alias* JEANES, sworn and examined, 23rd of August, 1642, saith, that she is aged thirty-three years, and is the wife of Thomas Jeanes, of Captain Perry's troop in the Lieut.-General Cromwell's regiment, and that she was formerly married to Peter Palfrey of Cashel, and that she did nurse a child to Robert Brown of Cashel, in the year 1641. That at the latter end of December, viz. the 31st of the month, 1641, Philip O'Dwyer of (*illegible*) entered the town of Cashel, with a number of the Irish in arms and plundered all the English and Protestants of the said town, and the next day, the 1st of January, they fell a killing of them, and murdered John Beane, innkeeper, with his brewer and tapster, whose name she remembereth not, Mr. Ralph Carr, schoolmaster, about eighty years old, Thomas Charleton, commonly called Thomas Sadler, Richard Lane and his two daughters, John Linsey, Mr. Bannister, minister, a man who was a tyler and his wife great with child, John (*blank*), a glazier's son, about eleven years of age, Peter Murdoch and his child about seven years old, John Anderson, an old woman about eighty years of age, and six more, whose names this examt. remembereth not, but she saw them lie dead. That she herself received eleven wounds, and many other women and children were then and there wounded. That of the murderers of the English, Richard O'Molony, of Captain Patrick Boyton's company, William Conway, John O'Herrick (*sic*), Thomas O'Gorman, Richard and William Fleming, James Minoge and others, were afterwards killed or are since dead, whose names she remembereth not, they being of the town of Cashel, as for others who also acted in those murders and cruelties, she remembereth them not by name, being strangers unto her and she knoweth not who wounded her. That between thirty and forty women and children were then stripped quite naked, and kept in guard together under the upper gate, about three or four hours, and after the gate was opened, they were sent out in frost and snow, naked, and betook themselves to Moyldrom, two miles from Cashel, where they were entertained by James Sall, until about ten days or a fortnight after they were sent for to be returned to Cashel, by Colonel Philip Dwyer aforesaid, then governor of the town, by whom they were committed to prison, where the poor creatures were again stripped of the clothes they had gotten at Moyldrum, and the plasters that were laid on their wounds were plucked off lest they should be cured. And that while these women and children aforesaid were at Moyldrum, all the English Protestants were cast into a dungeon at Cashel, being in water up to their knees, and that they were sent away afterwards by a convoy to Clonmell, which convoy was commanded by the said Captain Patrick Boyton, and Pierse Boyton, his lieutenant, that three of the said Protestants were by the said convoy killed, by John O'Herick aforesaid, who killed then and there the aforesaid glazier's son. That some men followed the convoy, especially to kill Edward Bourke, one of the said Protestants, whom they wounded, but he was rescued by Richard Conway of Cashel, who went with the convoy. That she, this examt., did see the said O'Herick afterwards in the company of the said Boytons, and that neither of them did hinder the said persons of their company from killing the English in the way aforesaid. This examt. further saith, that one named George (*blank*), an Englishman, was murdered on the way between Ardmaile and Cashel, but by whom she knoweth not.

ELLISH + MEAGHER.

Deposed before us,
the day and year above written,
HEN. JONES.
CHAR. BLOUNT.

CXLVII.

The Examination of NICHOLAS SALL, *of Cashel, taken the 24th of July,* 1652.

This examt. sworn and examined, saith, he is aged forty-five years or thereabouts, and further saith, that he is an inhabitant of the town of Cashel, and was there resident on the 31st of December, 1641, when Colonel Philip O'Dwyer and his party did enter the said city with about 2,000 men, and that so soon as they entered they began to plunder the English and Protestants, bringing in all their plunder to Mr. Beane's house, which was appointed as a storehouse for the said goods. And further saith, that the next morning early they murdered divers English Protestants to the number of fifteen or sixteen; he further saith, he did not see those persons as they were being murdered, but heard that they were murdered by one James Roche of Ballygriffin, the sons of John MacMaghunagh of Crossall, and Edmond MacDonagh and William MacShane. And further saith, that Philip MacThomas O'Dwyer of Moorestown cast a dart at one Mr. Bannister, smiting him in the leg as he was running away to save his life, by which means he came to a stand, and then they murdered him, as this deponent was credibly informed, and that William MacPhilip of Ardmaile killed Thomas Sadleir, as he was credibly informed, and further saith not.

NICHOLAS SALL.

Jurat. coram nobis,
HEN. JONES.
JOHN BOOKER.

CXLVIII.

EDMUND SPILLANE, of Cashel, aged about twenty years, deposeth, that he was present when one Conogher MacShane Glas and his son murdered Mr. Francis Bannister, and took some of his money away.

 JOHN BOOKER.
 NATH. WILLMER.
 JOHN HACKET,
  Mayor of Cashel.
 28*th Aug.* 1652.

CXLIX.

WILLIAM POWER, of Cashell, sworn and examined, saith, that he was at Cashel when Philip Dwyer and his forces came thither, and that he saw one Thomas Charleton murdered by William MacPhilip O'Dwyer of Ardmoile, and that he also saw one William Beane, innkeeper, murdered by James Roche of Griffinstown, and that when he was standing in the street Thomas Brown, cooper, was murdered by the said Roche, and that he was present when John Dwyer of Knockgorman thrust with a naked sword at Mr. Beane, the innkeeper's ostler, wherewith he wounded him, and further saith not.

CL.

JOAN MEAGHER, of Cashel, aforesaid, aged about thirty-five years, being sworn on the Holy Evangelists, deposeth and saith, that she saw Mr. Bannister and John Linsey murdered by some of the party that came into Cashel, but their names she knoweth not.

CLI.

ELLEN HANRAHAN, aged sixty years, deposeth, that she did see one William McPhilip of Ardmoile murder Thomas Sadlier, and that she did see four or five of the soldiers of the O'Dwyers murdering John Linsey.

CLII.

CATHERINE HOGAN, aged fifty years, deposeth, that she saw Mr. Beano and his tapster murdered by some of the soldiers that came into the town, whose names she knoweth not, but was informed by divers of the neighbours that Philip MacShane of Killnamanagh and his sons were the murderers.

CLIII.

DANIEL BOURKE, of Cashel, deposeth that he was present when Thomas Sadlier and Ralph Carr were murdered, and that Connor FitzJohn Regan of Poulvaly and William MacPhilip of Ardmoile were the chief actors in those murders. And further saith not.

Note.

The foregoing depositions of Spillane, Power, Meagher, Ellen Hanrahan, Catherine Hogan, and Daniel Bourke appear to be copies of originals taken before Booker, Willmer, and Hacket, the Mayor of Cashel, for the High Court of Justice in 1652-3. They are all unsigned by deponents.

CLIV.

JOHN HACKET, Mayor of Cashel, duly sworn and examined, the 24th day of August, 1652, deposeth and saith, that he was an inhabitant of Cashel, and there present when the rebels entered the city aforesaid, being on New Year's Eve, 1641, and that the chief commander of the Irish party was one Philip O'Dwyer, a colonel, and with him there entered into the aforesaid town, Tiegue Ogo O'Meagher, Donogh O'Dwyer, brother to the said Philip ; Thomas Purcell, brother to the baron of Loghmoe, Philip Magrath of Cluain, in the Ormond ; Philip McThomas O'Dwyer, Philip MacTiegue Ryan of Kippensally, Thomas Roe Regan of Clonulty, Hugh McShane Regan of Clonulty, James Roche of Ballygriffen, the three sons of Daniel MacMahounagh O'Dwyer of Crossall, James Bourke of Soarte, and many others, whom this deponent knoweth not, all of whom began the same day to strip and plunder the English of that city, and cast them into prison, and the next day, being

New Year's Day, in the morning at the daybreak, they began to wound and murder the said English, killing outright sixteen of them, men and one woman, viz. Ralph Carr, William Beane, John Linsey, Richard Lane, Thomas Charleton, Thomas Browne Cooper, William Manifold, *alias* Captain Kerog, and his wife, William Bean's ostler, whose name this deponent remembereth not, and further saith, that James Roche of Ballygriffen, and the three sons of Daniel MacMahounagh O'Dwyer of Crossall, Thomas Roe Ryan, Hugh MacShane Ryan, aforesaid, Brian Carney of Tiefknockan, were the chief actors in the murder of the Protestants aforesaid, and further saith, that Edmund McRoss O'Dwyer of Knockgorman, Owny MacCollum and Thomas McWilliam Dwyer of the same, were then keepers of the magazine, and John Dwyer of Gurtonaske, Philip Magrath of (*illegible*) in Ormond, Tiegue Oge O'Meagher, Donogh O'Dwyer, Thomas Purcell, Philip MacThomas Dwyer, Philip MacTiegue Ryan, and James Bourke aforesaid, were some of the chief murderers, and further saith, that James Roche aforesaid bragged that he had revenged the death of his wife, by killing two of the English with his own hands, and Philip MacShane being slain by some of Captain Peisley's troop, the son of the said Philip made his brags that he had revenged the death of his father, for that he had killed twice as many of the English in Cashel, and that he had killed Thomas Charleton, for that he, the said Charleton, was one of the troop under the command of Captain Peisley, and that he heard it was he (Charleton) had killed his father. And further saith not.

JOHN HACKET,
Deposed before us, the day and   Mayor of Cashel.
year first above written,
HEN. JONES.
JO. BOOKER.

CLV.

DONATUS O'CONNOR, late of Ardtramon, in the county of Wexford, clerk, duly sworn and examined, deposeth and saith, that since the beginning of the present rebellion, viz. a week or thereabouts about All Hallowtide, 1641, this deponent was by the rebels at Ardtramon and Castlebridge in the same county deprived, robbed, and otherwise despoiled of his means, goods, and chattels, to his present loss of 120*l.*, and of the rents and profits of the church livings worth 200*l*. yearly, but who they were that so despoiled him he cannot tell, since at that time he had fled for safety of his life to the town of Wexford, where he stayed two days, until his wife, children, and family came to him, and afterwards he and they stayed there until about the 1st of March, subsisting principally on the means they had from friends in the country thereabouts, and then by, or by the means of, Nicholas French, and other priests and friars there, he, this deponent, because he was a Protestant minister, was put in prison in a most dark, odious, loathsome dungeon, exceedingly fraught with the ordure of former prisoners imprisoned there, which dungeon indeed hath killed him indeed, as he knoweth, but that God gave him strength and power to survive and overcome that heavy calamity, and yet there the deponent endured restraint until about the 1st of July following, at which time the great God, his sure deliverer, gave him a way to go from thence by the warrant of the Lord Mountgarrett, and the Lord Gormanston, and others of the rebellious council at Killkenny to appear before the said council, in which town he stayed for three months longer, viz. July, August, and September, and part of the present month of October, when the rebellious party often endeavoured to seduce or draw him from the Protestant religion to mass and the Popish religion. But he, this deponent, by the help of God continued constant in his true religion as a Protestant, and endured his misery, restraint, and want, which was very much, with the fitting patience of a true Christian. And within that time he was greatly taxed with malice and plotting against them, the said rebels, especially by one Mr. Hore of Killsallaghan, in the county of Dublin, Esq. (one of their grand council), for writing a letter in his, this deponent's, own blood to his father in England, which letter the rebels intercepted, pen and ink being denied him, and for other acts against them. And whilst this deponent was in restraint in Kilkenny, he observed by general report that seven heads of Protestants, whereof one was that of Mr. Bingham, a minister near Ballinakill, in the Queen's County, were cut off, and brought by the rebels to Kilkenny, where a gentlewoman of the rebels, in her malice, drew out a skean and stabbed the said Mr. Bingham's head through the cheeks. And further saith, that whilst this deponent was at Kilkenny, the great councillor men that sat there, with, for, or amongst the rebels were, first the Lord Mountgarrett, the Lord Gormanston, the Lord Netterville, Sir Edward Butler, Sir Richard Butler, Pierce Butler of Monihore, in the county of Wexford, Esq., the said Philip Hore, Richard Bealing, son-in-law to the said Lord Mountgarrett, David Rowth (*sic*), titulary Bishop of Ossory, the titulary bishop of Downpatrick, and divers other titulary bishops and abbots whose names he knoweth not, and divers Jesuits and friars, and amongst the rest one that called himself Sir Nicholas Shea, who lately, as was generally there reported, came from Rome, and brought with him a great deal of ammunition to Wexford, and that called himself the parson of Callan by jurisdiction from Rome. And another, a Franciscan friar, by name, as he styled himself, Sir Richard Synnot, was a rebellious councillor there. And one Nicholas French, a seminary priest, who, being at Wexford, when this deponent was a prisoner there, said, upon controversy concerning the jurisdiction of the Church of Ireland, that if Charles, meaning the King's Majesty, were there himself, he would not give him an inch of right over the Church. For that he, meaning the King's Majesty, hath no power over it, or words to that effect. And saith, that the said French and Synnot, being at Wexford in the beginning of the rebellion, when the state of Dublin had sent gunpowder or other provision there, to be transported to Duncannon, they undertook to convey it with their assistants, but they, being the chief guides, they carried it to the rebels there, being about two or three barrels of powder, with shot and match. And further saith, that the rebels from time to time divulged that the cause of their insurrection was, that ten thousand at least of the Protestants in England and Ireland had put their hands to a note to hang all the Papists at their own doors, unless they came to church within a short time afterwards, and so would excuse their rebellion and bloody acts committed. And therefore, they alleged, it was time for them to prevent the danger the Puritans intended to do them. And saith, that this deponent was told by an Irish captain, who came lately out of France, that the Romish priests sent from Dublin by the State as banished men, not long after their arrival beyond sea, falsely and publicly divulged, or caused to be divulged, over France and Spain, that the English had committed divers outrages and cruelties in Ireland upon the Romish Catholics, namely, ripping up women great with child, throwing children into the fire, and other supposed barbarous cruelties, which this deponent is assured the rebel Irish in this kingdom were guilty of, and manually exercised against the Protestants. And further saith, that the rebels frequently protested that the Lords Justices and Council here, and all that took their parts, or the part of the

Parliament of England, were notorious rebels. And saith, that the rebels have often, in this deponent's hearing, commonly observed that they would not if they might be pardoned, and every one called home to his own living, submit, unless that all the church lands and livings of Ireland were restored to the Romish Church, and that they might enjoy their religion freely, and that the Protestant religion might be rooted out of the kingdom, and the Church of Rome restored to its ancient jurisdiction, powers, and privileges, within this kingdom of Ireland. And the rebels also publicly and frequently villified the Protestant religion, and all Protestants, and said that the priests formerly banished should return to Ireland. And this deponent hath been credibly and secretly told, that he hath been put to death by the rebels, if they had had a competent number of their bishops together, who would have degraded him first, but because they had not he escaped with his life, as they told him, he having been formerly been a Romish priest, but the light of truth gave him power to become a Protestant. And this deponent did still observe, that the Romish priests and friars did frequently in their sermons and in other ways persuade the rest of the Romish faction to extirpate and root out all the Protestants in the kingdom. And saith, it was generally reported amongst the rebels of Kilkenny that the Pope of Rome had engaged himself to give 50,000*l*. per annum for the maintaining of the wars in Ireland, against the Protestants, so long as the said war should continue, and that the rebels expended 60,000*l*. more for their colleges and religious houses to that end. And this deponent continued a prisoner at Kilkenny, until within the present month. But then the great God in whom he trusted offered him a way of escape.

DONATUS O'CONNOR.

Jurat. 28*th October*, 1642,
WILL. ALDRICH.
HEN. BRERETON.

CLVI.

ROBERT WADDING, of Killstoune, in the county of Carlow, gent., duly sworn and examined, deposeth and saith, that he was robbed and despoiled of his sheep, cows, goods, and chattells by the Bagenals of Dunleckny, the Byrnes, and Nolans, to the value of 2,385*l*. 9*s*. 2*d*. And this deponent further saith, that coming to Leighlin to make inquiries for his sheep aforesaid, thinking the rebels to have departed that town, at the house of one John Carron, this deponent was beset by ten or twelve of the rebels, armed with guns, pikes, and skeans drawn, some they held at the deponent's throat, some at his breast and back, and took his money from his pocket, likewise his cloak and hat, and were unbuttoning his doublet, insomuch that he verily thinks they would have stript him naked, but that Owen Garkagh O'Birne in the interim came in and rescued this deponent out of their hands, and procured this deponent his hat and cloak again, whereat they were grieved, but durst not oppose him, he being powerful amongst them, but they swore they would inform against him that he was a protector of Protestants. However, they would not let this deponent go until the said Owen O'Birne made a solemn promise unto them he would not depart with this deponent until he, the said Owen, had delivered him unto the priest to be reconciled, as they termed it; who accordingly brought this deponent to the house of Mr. Reynolds, where the priest of that parish, one Butler, was so busied in giving absolution to the poor English Protestant inhabitants thereabouts that this deponent had to wait his leisure, and while he was so attending it, this deponent heard him, the priest, before absolution given, tender to them an oath to this effect, viz. that they should continue true and faithful subjects to the king of England, and should honour and obey him in all matters temporal, and that they should acknowledge the Holy Church of Rome to be the true Church, and the Pope of Rome to be supreme head of the Church of Ireland, and should honour and obey him in all causes spiritual whatsoever. In conclusion, the priest's leisure serving, he came to this deponent, and told him by way of advice that his only course was to go to mass, and to hold with them, and by so doing this deponent should get restitution of all his goods that he had lost, and should live among them and come to great preferment, if not, there would be no living in this country for the deponent, for no Protestants must abide therein. Whereupon this deponent seemed to take time to consider of the matter, and desired a pass to Carlow, where he might have further conference with Sir Matthew Roth concerning the same, which being obtained, this deponent missed of going to Father Matthew Roth, and betook himself to the Castle of Carlow, where the English kept in hold, until he had the opportunity of coming to this city.

ROBERT WADDING.

Jurat. 17*th March*, 1641,
  ROGER PUTTOCK.
  JOHN STERNE.

CLVII.

ANNE HILL, wife of Arthur Hill of Hacketstown aforesaid in the county of Carlow, sworn and examined, deposeth, that about the 7th day of November last she lost from Hacketstown aforesaid three cows worth six pounds, robbed from her by the hand of Pierce Grace of Bordkillmore, in the county of Wicklow, as she is credibly informed, who is now in rebellion, and who, accompanied by one Maurice Bane, *alias* Birne, and others, this deponent divers times since the beginning of the rebellion saw in Hacketstown, rifling the houses of Protestants, among others robbing the house of John Watson, Archdeacon of Leighlin. And this deponent further saith, that she lost from the lands of Killerlonagh, in the county Wicklow, a mare worth 3*l*. ster., but by which of the said rebels she knoweth not. And further saith, that the said Maurice Bano, *alias* Birne, of (*illegible*) in the said county of Wicklow, with certain other rebels of the said county under the command of Luke Birne, robbed and despoiled her of household goods to the value of 80*l*., and of 20*s*. in money, and drove her with her four small children from her house and grounds which she held in Hacketstown aforesaid, worth 30*l*., and took away from her hay worth 30*s*. and of household provisions worth 7*l*. 10*s*. And she further saith, that as she was coming to Dublin, through the lands of Bordkillmore, in the said county of Wicklow, she was assaulted by Mortogh Ewy (*sic*) of Hacketstown aforesaid, and one William of Killolonagh, in the parish of Kiltegan, county of Wicklow, accompanied with about nine or ten more, who pulled off her back a young child of about a year and a quarter old, and threw it on the ground and trod on it so that it died, and stripped herself and her four small children naked, threatening to kill her and drown them. And through the cold contracted by such usage her other three children are since dead.

ANNE HILL +

Jurat. April 17th, 1641,
JOHN WATSON.
WM. ALDRICH.

CLVIII.

DAME ANN BUTLER, wife unto Sir Thomas Butler, of Rathhelin, in the county of Carlow, knight, and baronet, duly sworn and examined, deposeth and saith, that about St. Patrick's Day last and since she was robbed and deprived of her lands, rents, goods and chattels, to the value following, by means of this rebellion, in sheep, cows, oxen, young cattle and old, in breeding mares, saddle mares, horses and other cattle, to the present loss of 1,542*l*. at least. In corn in the haggard, the house, and the ground, which by means of this rebellion she utterly despaireth to have any profit by, to the loss of 1,412*l*. In household goods, provision, and furniture necessary for a house 832*l*. 5*s*. 4*d*. In plate 200*l*. at least, in rents due from those that are rebels and from others that are undone by the rebellion 750*l*., and more. Money lent to Mr. John Thompson, who by means of this rebellion is utterly disenabled to pay 100*l*. Houses burnt, wasted, and depopulated 70*l*., so as this deponent's losses by this rebellion amount to the sum of 4,906*l*. 5*s*. 4*d*. And this deponent further deposeth, that the parties that so robbed and despoiled her were Sir Morgan Kavenagh of Clonmullin, in the county of Carlow ; and Walter Bagenal of Dunleckny, Walter Butler of Polestown, living in the county Kilkenny, Thomas Daniels of Killeghan, the son of Oliver Costae, a captain of the rebels, Ambrose Plunkett of (*illegible*), James Allen of Linkerstoune, Turlogh Brian of (*illegible*), all these being freeholders, living in the county of Carlow ; Tybot and Walter Butler of Tully, sons to James Butler of Tully, in the county Carlow, who besieged this deponent's house, with about six or seven hundred men, and in the dead of night burnt the outer gate of her house, and at length with great violence did approach and undermine the said house, so as this deponent, her husband, and family were constrained to desire quarter, and had only their lives promised. And after the rebels had in this violent way entered, she and her husband, not being able in any way to resist, the rebels set strict guard over them, and brought them from their said dwelling unto the castle of Leighlinbridge, where they kept herself, her husband, and children for two weeks, and from thence conveyed them under a strict guard to the town of Kilkenny. And there they were brought before the Lord of Mountgarret, when Walter Bagenal and James Butler, brother to the Lord Mountgarret, did use all means possible to move the said Lord to put them all to death, alleging that they were rank Puritan Protestants, and desperately provoking in these words, saying, ' *there is but one way, we or they*,' meaning Papist or Protestant must perish, to which malicious provocation the said Lord Mountgarret would not hearken. And this deponent further deposeth, that Walter Bagnall, with his rebellious company, apprehended Richard Lake, an English Protestant, and his servant, with his wife and four children, and one Richard Taylor of Leighlinbridge, his wife and children, Samuel Halter of the same, his wife and children, an Englishwoman called Jones, and her daughter, and as she was credibly informed by Dorothy Reinolds, who had several times been witness of these lamentable particulars, that they violently compelled another Englishwoman, who was newly delivered of two children in one birth in her great pain and sickness, to rise from her bed and took the infant that was alive, and dashed out its brains against the stones and afterwards threw him into the river Barrow. And this deponent one day having a piece of salmon for dinner, Mr. Brian Cavenagh's wife being with her, she refused to eat any part of the salmon, and being asked the reason, she said she could never again eat any fish that came out of the Barrow, because she had seen twenty-three Protestants and other carcases taken up out of it. And this deponent saith, that Sir Edward Butler did credibly inform her, that James Butler of Tenahinch had hanged and put to death all the English that were at Goran, and thereabouts, Jane Jones, servant to this deponent, going to their execution, and as she conceived they were about the number of thirty-five, and she was told by Elizabeth Humes that they were all executed. And further saith, that being in restraint and having intelligence that some of her own cattle were brought thither by Walter Bagenal, she petitioned, being in great extremity, the Lord Mountgarett to procure her some of her own cattle for her relief, whereupon he recommended her unto the mayor and corporation of Kilkenny, who concluded that because she and her family were Protestants and would not turn to mass, they should have no relief.

Ann Butler.

Jurat. 7th Sept. 1642,
  Fran. Pigott.
  John Watson.

CLIX.

Sir Edward Butler, Knt., aged sixty-six or thereabouts, being duly sworn and examined, saith, that about the 1st of May, 1642, there came a company of James Butler of (*illegible*) and his servants with others, armed, into the town of Graigue in the county of Kilkenny, to search, as this examt. was informed, for his tenants, then inhabiting the town, being English men and women, and there they seized upon the bodies of John Stone, his wife and son, Walter

Shirly, with others whose names he remembereth not, who they carried out of the town and hanged, some of them upon the lands of (*illegible*) near Graigue; the rest were carried further by Gibbon Forestal, Garrett Forestal, Donogh O' (*illegible*) now in Connaught, whither he went with his master James Butler, and others whose names he remembereth not. And this examt. is confident that James Butler was then at home in his house, but he doth not certainly know whether Colonel Bagenal's wife was there or not, but saith that she doth frequent the place and continue there sometimes two months or thereabouts. He further saith, that soon afterwards he heard that Morris Kelly with others brought divers English prisoners from Gowran to Graigue, amongst whom was Henry White, tenant to this examt., at which time there was there Edmund Butler, Sir Walter Butler, Captain Shortall, and Captain John Butler, this examt.'s son, and this examt. hearing that these prisoners were so carried away, he sent his servant Andrew Barlow to use his utmost endeavour to save Henry White, by reason he was his, examt.'s, tenant, who prevailed with Colonel Edmund Butler, then commanding in chief, that he got off the said White, and the rest, as he heard, were conveyed to Ross, and near to that place put to death, as he was informed; and that the said Kelly did convey them to Graigue, and thence to the gates of Ross, and that he, this examt., sent his said servant and another to mediate to save their lives. Being demanded what he knoweth of the death of Richard Lake, he saith he heard he was hanged, and further saith not.

EDWARD BUTLER, Knt.
Taken on the 18th August, 1652, before us,
  HEN. JONES.
  HEN. STAMER.

CLX.

SARAH FRANCIS, *alias* BOULGER, aged thirty-six years or thereabouts, duly sworn and examined, saith, that she lived at the Graigue at the beginning of the rebellion, and continued there five or six years after. That she is the daughter of Barnaby Boulger of the Graigue, and was formerly married to Walter Shirley of the Graigue, who by his trade was a carver and joiner. That he, her said husband Walter Shirley, did work with James Butler of Tennahinch near the Graigue, and made up a gate for his house at Tennahinch. That there then lived at the Graigue of English, John Stone, Robert Pyne, William Stone, one John, servant to the said John Stone,

Zachary Pyne, a child of about a year and a half old, Joseph Valentine married to the examt.'s sister Katharine, and Walter Shirley her husband, as before mentioned, Margaret Stone, wife of John Stone, Margaret their daughter, then wife to Thomas White of Goran, Barbara Pyne, wife of the said Robert Pyne, and others whom she, this examt., remembereth not. That Walter Bagenal, Esq., now called Colonel Bagenal, was at Tennahinch about the beginning of May, 1642, where was also his wife, and Colonel Edmund Butler was there also. And this examt.'s husband did make some pistol and carbine stocks for Colonel Bagenal and others, he being promised thereupon a protection to live quietly in the country. And the said Shirley, this examt.'s husband, having finished his work and brought it home, obtained from the said Bagenal fifteen shillings for it, and a protection under the said Bagenal's hand for his quiet living in the place. But before her said husband could recross the bridge of Graigue on his way to his house, he was followed by one from Tennahinch to deliver back the pass he had received, which he refusing to do he was brought back to Tennahinch house, where it was taken from him, but by whom this examt. remembereth not. The same day James Butler of Tennahinch and the said Colonel Edmund Butler went from that place on horseback; this deponent did see them going, but did not know that Colonel Bagenal was with them. The same night about midnight Dermot O'Donoghue and Connor More, servants of James Butler aforesaid, knocked at this examt.'s house, and she opening the door, they entered and took away her husband, and the examt. going forth found all the rest of the English taken out of their houses and carried over the bridge of the Graigue by James Butler's followers. That this examt., fearing some mischief to her husband, went to Ballyogan to her landlord Sir Edward Butler, living about a mile from the Graigue, to desire his assistance for preserving her husband. That returning with a paper signed by the said Sir Edward Butler, those persons in whose hands her husband was, seeing her coming with the paper, hanged her husband forthwith, and cut him down when he was so hanged before she, though making all haste, could come to him; that a little way from thence they did also hang Joseph Valentine aforesaid, this examt.'s brother in-law, his wife, this examt.'s sister, being then present, who came along with this examt. from Ballyogan aforesaid, and overtook her husband before he was hanged. Being demanded who of the Irish were present at these executions and driving away of the English, she said that she saw Garret Codd, Gibbon Forestall, and about ten more that she knoweth not the names of. She further saith, that John, the aforesaid servant of John Stone, was also hanged on the same tree that her husband was hanged on and at the same time, and that John Stone and the rest of the English were carried towards Ross, and by the way murdered. She further saith, that the same day towards evening, William Stone, son of John Stone, working at the river on a ship for Sir Charles Coote, was brought to the Graigue and hanged on the same tree that her husband was hanged on. And that one . . . Bennett of Ross came riding thither post to save William Stone if he could, but could not prevail by reason of Mrs. Ellen Butler, who then lived in the house of James Butler of Tennahinch aforesaid, and opposed his saving said Stone. That this examt. did that day see the said Bennett on horseback bareheaded, and that she was told by others that he had neither cloak, band, or hat on, through riding in haste to save the said William Stone. She further saith, that she hath heard that Gerard Codd, Gibbon Forestal, and a servant of Henry Bagenal's were present at the execution of the said Stone.

SARAH FRANCIS +

Deposed before us, 16*th October*, 1652,
 THOMAS HERBERT.
 HEN. JONES.
 THOMAS WILSON.

Note.

 James Butler of Tennahinch, mentioned in the foregoing depositions, was the younger brother of Lord Mountgarrett, who was the father of three sons, viz. Edmund Roe, his heir; Edward of Urlingford, whose examination is hereafter given, executed in 1653, like Bagenal, for his share in the murders at Kilkenny in 1641-3; Richard, also a captain in the Irish army in those years. Carte's abstract of the missing portion of the *Plunket MSS.* which Mr. Prendergast copied for Colonel Plunket Dunne (*v. ante*, p. 107, *note*) gives the following account of Bagenal's conduct, but it is shown to be wholly untrustworthy on the vital point of his guilt by the documents here printed for the first time :—

 "When Colonel Bagenal," says Carte's MS., "was by the Supreme Council made governor of the county Carlow, Mr. James Butler of Tennahinch, brother to the Lord Mountgarrett, was competitor with him for the place, and missing his aim,

DEPOSITIONS.

advised him to write a warrant to put William Stone to death. Bagenal, just then turned of thirty (Butler about sixty), ordered it. Butler advised the wife of the man who had Bagenal's order to keep it carefully for preventing future danger. Bagenal when a hostage ten years after was arraigned for this and other murders in Lady Butler's deposition, who was summoned to give witness against him, though the whole story was but hearsay from one Dorothy Reinolds, wife to a native of the country, enemy to Bagenal, on account of his estate. Nor does she charge Bagenal with the murder of the thirty-five, and in her evidence she deposed nothing of consequence against him at his trial, so that he had been acquitted, if they had not arraigned the wife of the man, as egging Bagenal thereto, who by his order executed Stone. She (this woman) heroically sent for a friend of Bagenal's and told him, ' Sir, your friend Colonel Bagenal will be tried for the death of Stone, and I am imprisoned for it, all they aim at from me is, to get the warrant my husband had for his (Stone's) execution, thereby to charge Bagenal. Here, take the warrant, carry it to Colonel Bagenal, my life is not worthy to be saved where he is in danger, if he thinks it will injure him let him burn it, I'll leave myself to God, if it will do him no hurt, bring it to me again.' Bagenal after perusing it returned it. It was thus:

' Whereas proof is made before me that William Stone, a late convert, hath lately and often resorted to the garrison of Duncannon with intelligence as a spy. These are therefore to require you to apprehend the said William Stone and him so apprehended to hang till he be dead,'

or words to this purpose. Bagnal though a hostage was tried and put to death at Kilkenny, though he apprehended no guilt either on evidence of the warrant or rather his own confession, and yet so ill an opinion of their sentence (sic) that they sent in vain to Leighlin Bridge for intelligence of Sir John Temple's thirty-five murdered persons. As to Sir John Temple's charges against Bagenal of designs against Lady Butler, &c., they needed only to have left them to the rabble and it had been done." (*Carte Papers*, Bodleian Library, pp. 418 *et seq.*)

The original pages of the *Plunket MSS.* of which the above professes to be an abstract have long been lost or destroyed, so that we have no means of testing its accuracy. But whether the abstract be true or false the account it gives of Bagenal's conduct and the charges on which he was condemned and executed is, as I have said, shown by Lady Butler's deposition to be wholly untrustworthy. Plunket probably, and Carte certainly, were too blinded by party prejudice to acknowledge, what they must both have well known, that no prisoner in the High Court of Justice was ever found guilty of murder and executed for it, when he could bring reasonable proof that the death of the person laid to his charge occurred in open war, or that such person, man or woman, was adjudged by the rules of such war a spy, and had been seized and sentenced to death while acting in that capacity. A prisoner in the High Court, like Lord Muskerry, as will be seen hereafter, was tried separately for each murder of which he was accused. When he could prove that one of those, say, four or five murders charged against him was really a case of sentence of death against a spy, he was pronounced not guilty of that charge and then the rest were heard in turn, and if they were proved to have been murders of persons who had never acted as spies, but lived peaceably and were unarmed, the prisoner was pronounced guilty of murder and executed accordingly, although he had been cleared of the guilt of the spy's death. Carte's theory, which he would have us to take for truth, that the finding of the warrant with the woman whose husband had hung William Stone would have secured the condemnation of Bagenal, and saved her and her husband, and that she acted ' heroically ' in sending it to him, is untenable. The production of such a warrant as Carte gives would have almost certainly procured a verdict of 'not guilty' for Bagenal, the woman, and her husband, inasmuch as it distinctly states that Stone was regularly employed as a spy against the Irish army. The warrant which is in the books of depositions in Trinity College differs somewhat from Carte's copy and is as follows :—

"Whereas proofs have been made before me that Mr. William Stone (*illegible*) is a spy and hath of late resorted to Duncannon, and that he would be a guide to the enemy to distress the country and the inhabitants thereof, this order is given to apprehend the body of the said William Stone, and having so apprehended him to hang him, for which this shall be your warrant. Dated at Tennahinch, May 2nd, 1642.

" WALTER BAGENAL."

It was often difficult to ascertain whether the person killed had been really acting as a spy between the hostile armies. Prisoners brought before the High Court endeavoured sometimes to prove by perjury that their victims were spies (knowing the result would be a verdict of 'not guilty') when in fact they were nothing of the kind, but inoffensive men and women, endeavouring to live in peace, or to escape to Dublin or England. Some of the rebels, as we have seen (*v.* Depositions IV.: XXII.), put a very wide interpretation on the word spy and murdered or wished to murder those poor fugitives, lest they should 'carry news to England' or the English army. The judges in 1652-4 had no easy task to ascertain the truth in such cases, but the prisoners were allowed to make the best defence they could, and call witnesses on their behalf. If William Stone had never been hung, it is probable that Bagenal would have been condemned on the evidence of Lady Butler, who swore positively that he had urged Lord Mountgarret to murder her and her husband. She may have been too willing to listen to rumours, and may have been deceived by Dorothy Reynolds and Jane Jones, but she was an eye-witness and an ear-witness of what she relates about Bagenal and James Butler, and no impartial person will reject her testimony. Taken in connection with the depositions of Mrs. Shirley, Morris Kelly, and others, the evidence was quite enough to condemn Bagenal. Carte's observations on her deposition are alike incomprehensible and absurd. The following letter from Lady Butler to her brother-in-law, Brian Cavenagh, son of Sir Morgan Cavenagh, is amongst the MSS. in Trinity College. Lady Butler and Mrs. Brian Cavenagh were the daughters of Sir Thomas Colclough of Tintern. The spelling of this letter, bad as it is, is quite as good as that of many ladies of rank in both islands between 1600 and 1780 :—

"*To my loveing brother, Bryan Cavenagh, Esq.*

"Dear Brother,—I am hartily greaved for the troble yow are in, and do condoale with yow, as being one that hath felt it. And now I was told by Bryan MacWilliam who came from the county Carlow, that they will preasently apprend yow and committ yow to the Black Castle of Loughlin. Yow do not know what may befall yow in it and I do think it is the saffer way for yow to come hither, where my Lord of Mountgarret is, who I hope will use yow no wors than he hath used us; but he hath been earnestly prosed to take away my life by your unkle James and Bagenal, but I thank God he refused it. So God grant yow may find the same favor at his hands but yow must instantly heaste away. Thus beseeching the Almighty God to direct yow to the beste and to grant yow favor amongst them first,

"Your trewly loveing sister,
"ANN BUTLER."

Brian Cavenagh's mother was the sister of Lord Mountgarret and of James Butler of Tennahinch. From her marriage with Sir Morgan Cavenagh (chief of the Slught Dermot) descends the present Art MacMurrogh Cavenagh of Borris House, Carlow, formerly M.P. for Wexford.

CLXI.

ELIZABETH ENNIS, *alias* HARRIS, aged fifty years or thereabouts, sworn and examined, saith, that she knew Edward Butler of Urlingford, second son to the late Lord Mountgarret, two years before the rebellion began, and about a week after Easter, in the year 1642, this deponent with several others, to the number of eighteen men, women, and children, were carried from Freshford to Ballyraggett, by a company of foot soldiers, whom this deponent doth verily believe were commanded by Captain Edward Butler aforesaid, who was then in Ballyraggett, commander in chief of the castle and company, and upon the application of Mr. Clerk and Mr. Byfield, both of Parkscrone, English Papists, prevailed with the said Captain Edward Butler to spare the life of this deponent, and one Anno Deals, and this deponent's husband, who was horse-rider to the said Edward Butler's father ; and this deponent was told by Mr. Clarke and Mr. Byfield aforesaid that the said Edward Butler told them that if he hanged his father's horse-rider, his father would hang him ; whereupon the said horse-rider was saved, with his wife and children, and being demanded by whose order the five English Protestants who were then in prison in Ballyraggett with her, this examt., were put to death, she saith, that the said Clarke and Byfield told her that it was by Captain Edward Butler's order, and she further saith, that she knoweth that the said Captain Edward Butler durst not come into his father's, the late Lord Mountgarret's sight, for his hanging of the said five persons.

ELIZABETH + ENNIS.

Sworn before us, the 5th Feb. 1652,
RICHD. STEPHENS.
(*illegible*) EVANS.

This examt. being further asked whether the aforesaid five persons were hanged, were thrown into a pit, and buried before they were dead, she saith that she often heard from several persons of credit that said they saw it, that they saw the persons that were so hanged, as they lay in the pit, throw back the earth with their hands upon the enemy, the persons that suffered thus being two men, two women, and a boy.

CLXII.

ANNE BRADFORD, aged about thirty years or thereabouts, duly sworn and examined, saith, that she was born in Gowran, in the county of Kilkenny, but descended from English parents, and that she living in Gowran, with her parents, at the beginning of the rebellion, that Walter Butler of Polestoune and Pierce Butler, son to Sir Edward Butler, came to Gowran, and the places there adjacent, and seized upon and took all the English inhabitants they could find, and gathering them together put them into prison in Gowran, where they continued a fortnight or thereabouts, and afterwards took them and pretended to send them with a convoy to Ross, and bound them two and three together, and that Morris Kelly of Gowran aforesaid, being ensign to Captain Pierce Butler, commanded the said convoy, who conveyed them within a musket shot of Ross, and there left them, who were in number about thirty or forty, young and old, as she thinks, viz. Thomas White, this examt.'s brother, her husband's father, mother, and sister, James Bromfield, and his wife and three children, Arthur Scott and his wife, one Thurston and divers others, whose names she remembereth not. And saith, that after the convoy had left there, the said Kelly went into Ross and presently after there came out of the town of Ross seven or eight persons, with swords and batts in their hands, and did drive them all below Ross for a mile to a woodside, and there they murdered all these English, except this examt.'s husband's sister, and her four children, but who these murderers were or their names she knoweth not.

ANNE + BRADFORD.

August   , 1652, examined before us,
 HEN. JONES.
 JO. STAMER.

CLXIII.

The Examination of MORRIS KELLY, *of Gowran, taken before us this* (blank) *day of August,* 1652.

This examt. saith, that at the time of plundering, when the rebellion first broke out, and he came out of (*illegible*) and was in Gowran, and when Captain Pierce Butler raised his foot company he was made ensign of it against his will, as he now allegeth, and saith that about eight or nine weeks after he was made ensign, the rendezvous being at Tennahinch, near the Graigue, he repaired thither and then divers English people, viz. Erasmus Bradfield, James Blomfield, Arthur Scott, with divers others, men, women, and children, to the number of 134 persons as he remembereth, being then prisoners, brought from Gowran to Graigue, were delivered to this examt. by Colonel Edmund Butler, Major Robert Shortall, Captain Pierce Butler, and Sir Walter Butler, and James Butler of Tennahinch, who were all present together, and saith that Colonel Edmund Butler, then commanding in chief, commanded this examt. and gave him orders to receive the said English into his charge, and to convey them to Ross, which he did, and delivered the said order to Captain James Duffe, who there had the command of a company of foot, according to the directions thereof, which said Duffe was by the said orders commanded to convey them to Duncannon; but what the said Duffe did therein this examt. knoweth not, but said that at the first he refused to receive the said orders, but afterwards he took them; and this examt. saith he left the English prisoners at the gate of Ross, and at his return in three days he heard that they were murdered, but by whom he knoweth not. And further saith, that he received the said prisoners bound, yet notwithstanding when he was marched out of the commander's sight he unbound them.

The examt. being demanded why he did strike Alexander Bradford and threaten that neither he nor any of his generation should be living within a month, he denied that he struck the said Bradford, or used any such threatening language. He further saith, that after he heard that the English who were committed to his charge, whom he safely conveyed to Ross, and left there, were murdered, he laid down his arms and never bore arms after.

Examined before us, MORRISH KELLY.
HEN. JONES. JOHN STAMER.

CLXIV.

The Examination of EDMUND SCOTT, *of Balliraggett, gent., aged forty years or thereabouts, sworn and examined saith,*

That in the beginning of the rebellion he lived under Edmund Butler, Esq., who was elder brother of Edward Butler of Urlingford, Esq., and living in the town of Ballyraggett; in the year 1641 (*sic*) there was brought six or seven English Protestants, from Freshford to Ballyraggett, by the said Edward Butler and his company, and this deponent saith that there was a little boy amongst the prisoners about sixteen years of age, that was going to be hanged, and the mother of the said child, whose name this deponent knoweth not, earnestly besought this deponent to beg for her son's life, whereupon this deponent went presently to his own house, where the said Edward Butler then was, and desired him that he would be pleased to give the said boy's life to this examt., and that he would keep him to be his servant, whereupon the said Edward Butler said that he should have the boy, and sent a token to the Marshal by this examt., that was then executing the prisoners, but before this deponent could return to the place of execution the boy was hanged, and this examt., being asked what commander was then in the town of Ballyraggett, at that time, saith he knew or heard of no other but the said Edward Butler. And further saith not.

EDMUND SCOTT.

Taken before us, 31st Jan. 1652,
RICH. STEPHENS.
ARTHUR BELL.

CLXV.

The Examination of EDWARD BUTLER, *of Urlingford, Esquire, in the county of Kilkenny, taken before Colonel Thomas Herbert and Robert Doily, Esquire, members of the High Court of Justice sitting at Dublin,*

Who saith, that he hath lived at Urlingford in the county Kilkenny for twenty years past or thereabouts, and that he is the second son of the late Lord Mountgarrett, and that his eldest brother is called Edmund. And being demanded if he was in that party of 600 or 700 horse and foot, which his brother commanded, and fought with, against four score Englishmen in the year 1642, a little before Michaelmas near to Ballinakill, in the county Kilkenny, at which time that Irish party killed amongst others Lieutenant Gilbert, Ensign Alfrey, Mr. Thomas Bingham, a minister, Robert Graves, Richard Bentley, and others whose heads as a trophy of that victory were sent to be set up at Kilkenny, a piper playing before them; he, the examt., saith he was not in that fight, but at his own house at Urlingford, about ten miles from Ballinakill, but heard of the Englishmen that were then killed, and that his cousin Walter Butler was also killed there, and he, this examt., was at the burial of the said Walter Butler the next day, his brother Edmund was also at that burial. Being further demanded if he had not the command of a foot company that year, or the year after, he said that he had such command that year, and that so soon as that fight aforesaid was ended, he laid down his command, and was not in arms since, but continued at his aforesaid dwelling-house at Urlingford, and hath not since meddled with any military employment.

Being demanded if he was governor of Ballyraggett in the year 1642, and if any of his foot soldiers were quartered there, he saith he never was governor there, nor did any of his foot live in that place to his knowledge, but he confessed that he was in the town of Ballyraggett about Easter after the rebellion broke out, and in one Edmund Scott's house there. Being demanded if he saw any English people brought prisoners into Ballyraggett at the time he was there in Scott's house, he saith he did not that night hear anything of them, but that next morning, being the next day of his coming thither, he was told by Mrs. Scott, wife to Edmund Scott, that there were some prisoners then going to execution, and she earnestly desired this examt. to save their lives if he could, and that thereupon he went in person to the place where the marshal's man was hanging them, and he did see three hanged, an old man, an old woman, and a boy, and that he saved all the rest who otherwise had been hanged, all having ropes about their necks, that he was so troubled at it, that he called the marshal's (Cantwell's) men rogues, and demanding of them by whose order they hanged these prisoners, they could not show any order in writing for the fact, but alleged it was by the provost marshal Cantwell's order. Being demanded if there were not five hanged at that time, he said he saw but three, nor did he hear of any more being executed of that company.

DEPOSITIONS.

Being questioned if upon Mrs. Scott's begging the boy's life, he did not give the said Scott a token by which the marshal should deliver the boy to Mr. Scott, he said he is assured Mr. Scott never did ask such a ring of him, nor did he, the examt., give him any token to have the boy delivered to him or any other. Being demanded if Mrs. Scott did desire him to save one Anne Trout, *alias* Deals, who was going to execution and was one of those brought from Freshford to Ballyraggett, he said that Mrs. Scott did not name any one to him in particular, but in general words coming hastily into his chamber betimes in the morning, she told him that some English people were going to be hanged, and desired him to use the best means he could to save them, and he thereupon presently went to the place of execution, with his sword in his hand, and did save all that were not put to death, as he hath already declared. Being also demanded if Mrs. Scott did not entreat him to save the life of a poor Scotch woman who was then to be hanged with the others, and if he did not send his man with her to the guard near the gallows, he, this examt., saith, that he did save that poor Scotch woman, whose name is Kincade, wife to a corporal in the Earl of Ormond's regiment, and to that end went thither in person, denying that he sent his man thither, but remembereth that Mrs. Scott, and he thinks her husband, also went with him to the said place of execution. Being demanded if Mrs. Scott went upon her knees to beg from him the lives of those poor English people, he saith not, nor any other person did so, as he remembereth. Being demanded if he knew Mr. Bifield and Mr. Clerk, he said he did know them, and that they lived at Parkscrone, half a mile from Ballyraggett. Being questioned further if those two gentlemen did not intercede to him for the saving Elizabeth Ennis, *alias* Harris, and her husband, who was ambler or rider to his father, and were likewise then to be executed, he, this examt., saith, that he well remembers they were led to execution with the English before mentioned, and that he then saved their lives also. But remembereth not that they spoke with him before Mrs. Scott and he went together to the place of execution, but well remembers that he saw them and the said Bifield and Clarke in town that day.

Being questioned if at his apprehension by Sergeant Williams and Jeremy Weaver he did not desire them to shoot him, being sure that he should be hanged if he came to Kilkenny, he said that their usage was so violent and uncivil towards him, taking from him his money, jewels, and cloaths, that he confessed in his passion he desired them to shoot him, rather than to use him so, but denied that he was afraid of going to Kilkenny, or that there was any word spoken of it at that time. Being lastly demanded why, having solemnly engaged himself to the Countess of Ormond to see the poor stripped English safely conveyed from Kilkenny to Waterford, at the first outbreak of the rebellion, he forsook them at Knocktopher, and thereby exposed them to the rage of the bloodthirsty Irish, he, this examt., saith, that he did promise the Countess to secure those English (*illegible*) Waterford, and accordingly went with them to Knocktopher and two miles further, and being that cold and snowy day surprised with a quartan ague, he was so ill that he was thence carried in a horse litter to Urlingford, and for a month after was forced to keep his bed, and that if those English received any bad usage afterwards, he could not help it, but denies that those English were plundered that night or had any loss of life or goods while he had charge of them. And further saith not.

EDWARD BUTLER.

Taken before us,
26 *Feb.* 1652,
THOS. HERBERT.
R. DOILY.   *Note.*

The following are also in the Kilkenny volume of depositions.

For ye Lord Pressident of ye high Court of Justice in Dublin, These,

MY LORD—I have sent your Lordship the enclosed examinashuns aganst Mr. Edward Butler, second son to the late Lord Mountgarrett, and I shall only give your Lordshipp my knowledge conserning him. When I had reseived orders from the hands of the parliment to aprehend all such perssons in these ptes, that had bin guilty of sheding the English inoscent blood in the first year of the rebellion, I sent a pty in the night.to cease the sd Butler, but he was not at home, and he, hearcing that there was a cesuir of blood guilty persons, he fledd into the boggs and fastnesses out of ye parlement's quarters for his safty, and thaire continewed, untill he was going in a disguise habitt to Spain with some Irish offisers, and was providencialy taken between Thomastown and Waterford, by some soldiers that knew him of Captain Frank's troop. I shall not ad but remayne My Lord,

your Lordshipp's humble servant
D. AXTELL.

DEPOSITIONS.

(*Enclosure* 1.)

The Examination of JEREMIAH WEAVER, *of Captain John Frank's troop, against Edward Butler, of Urlingford, Esq., taken before us on oath* 31*st Jan.* 1652.

This deponent saith, that when the said Edward Butler was apprehended by him, he made resistance and laid hands on Captain Heygate's sergeant's carbine, and called to some Irish officers there to assist him, saying, ' Will you leave me so ? ' This deponent asked him for arms, he denied to have any but a knife, but being searched by me I found a *maddeogue* or skean with the haft in his hand and the blade in the sheath. The said Edward promised me 100*l.* to run away with him for Spain, and promised to make me a captain there, and he then desired to be shot by me and the others that apprehended him, for he knew that he should be hanged if he were brought to Kilkenny, and further saith he feared nothing but false information.

JER. WEAVER.

Taken before us,
RICH. STEPHENS.
JOHN HEYDON.

(*Enclosure* 2.)

The Examination of Sergeant ROBERT WILLIAMS, *against Edward Butler, son of the Lord Mountgarret.*

That the said Edward Butler when he was apprehended laid hands on my carbine. I asked him if his name was Butler, he said it was not, he asked me why I laid hands on him, he being under protection and having his protection in his pocket. Then the said Edward Butler desired those Irish officers that were present to assist him, saying, ' Will you leave me thus ? ' I asked him for arms. He said he had not any but a knife, but being searched by one Joshua Weaver, of Captain Frank's troop, a *maddeogue* (Irish dagger) was found about Mr. Butler, the haft thereof in his hand and the blade in a sheath. The said Edward Butler desired me and the rest to shoot him, for he said he knew if he were brought to Kilkenny he should be hanged, and further he saith he feared nothing but false information.

ROBERT + WILLIAMS.

Taken before us,
on oath, 31*st Jan.* 1652,
RICHARD STEPHENS.
WM. HEYDON.

CLXVI.

MAGDALEN REDMAINE, late of Dowry in the King's County, widow, the relict of Thomas Redmaine, who was one of the soldiers that were slain with Captain Smith by the rebels, sworn and examined, deposeth and saith, that since the beginning of the present rebellion, viz. on or about the 26th of December, 1641, when her husband was slain, she, this deponent, was deprived, robbed, and despoiled of her goods and chattels, consisting of tanned leather, bark, green leather, corn, cattle, worth 114*l*. 10*s*. 4*d*., by the rebels Costiny Molloy, gent., Art Molloy, Shane O'Farrell, and their accomplices and soldiers whose names she cannot express. And further saith, that this deponent and divers other Protestants, and amongst them (*illegible*) widows, after they were all robbed, were also stripped naked, and then they covering themselves in a house with straw, the rebels then and there lighted the straw with fire and threw it amongst them on purpose to burn them, when they had been all burnt or smothered, but that some of the rebels, more pitiful than the rest, commanded these crueller rebels to forbear, so as they did, yet the rebels kept them (the English) naked in a wild wood from Tuesday till Saturday, in frost and snow, the snow unmelted long lay upon some of them, so as three children died in their arms. And when this deponent and the rest endeavoured to have gone away for refuge to the Birr, the rebels turned them back, saying they should go to Dublin, and when they attempted to go towards Dublin, they (the rebels) hindered them again and said they should go to the Birr, and so tossed and haled them to and fro, yet at length such of these poor stripped people as died not in the hands of the rebels escaped to the Birr, where they were harboured and relieved by one William Parsons, Esq., and yet there died at the Birr, of those poor stripped persons, about forty of men, women, and children. And this deponent and those other stripped people that survived lived miserably at the Birr aforesaid until they and the rest had quarter to come from thence to Dublin.

MAGDALEN REDMAINE +

Jurat. 8*th March*, 1642,
JOHN WATSON.
WM. ALDRICH.

Note.

It has been said by not a few writers on 1641, that no massacres or even murders of unarmed persons were committed in Leinster, but such writers must change their opinion after reading the above and many other depositions in the Leinster volumes. Isabel, the widow of Christopher Porter, one of the poor women so mercilessly treated, as Mrs. Redmaine relates, sworn and examined before the same commissioners, confirmed all she had related of the cruelty of the Leinster Irish.

CLXVII.

NICHOLAS WALSH, of Harristown, in the King's County, clerk, duly sworn, deposeth, that on the 6th of December, 1641, he was robbed and despoiled of his goods and means worth 888*l.*, by the hands and means of Henry MacOwen Dempsy, Colonels Donogh, Nicholas and John Dempsy, Brian MacGlashny Dempsy, and others their kindred and followers. And this deponent further saith, that on the 16th of the said month of December he was robbed of and lost in the castle of Castle Dermot, county Kildare, ready money, plate, rings, jewels, and household goods worth 200*l.* by Pierce FitzGerald of Ballysonan, now a colonel among the rebels, Luke FitzGerald of Molamoy, Ensign Gerald FitzGerald of Castleroe, and their servants. Further he saith, that the graves in the churchyard and church of Harristown were digged up, and the corpses of Protestants that were there interred for seven years at least before that time were taken up and their bones and bodies thrown into ditches, and other base places, by the directions of the Vicar-General James McShane Dempsey. And a poor Englishman called Toby Emmet being by the rebels drawn to go to the mass, was on the same day of his reconciliation returning homeward hanged, the rebels themselves saying that they hanged the English after their reconciling to the Roman Church, that they may pray for their souls.

NICHOLAS WALSH.

Jurat. 6*th Jan.* 1642,
JOHN STERNE.
WM. ALDRICH.

CLXVIII.

RICHARD TAYLOR, late of the Birr, *alias* Parsonstown, in the King's County, shoemaker, sworn and examined, deposeth and saith, that about All Hallowtide, 1641, the rebellion began about Birr and the country thereabouts, and then this deponent being bound prentice unto and living with one William Remington, an English Protestant, stayed with his said master working at his trade. And saith, that soon after Hollandtide aforesaid, or thereabouts, the murders and cruelties after-mentioned were committed by the rebels, viz.: One Mary Nelson, a Scottish Protestant, was at Craghan, in the county of Tipperary, very near the Birr, assaulted by two rebels, viz. by one William Oge and William Buie of Craghan aforesaid, and as she was stoutly defending herself, one Donogh McThomas of the Birr aforesaid, a bloody butcher coming towards her, she conceiving him to be her friend, cried out to him and said, ' *For God's sake help me !* ' whereunto he answered ' *I will help you I warrant you,*' and thereupon coming behind her, he with a beef-axe first knocked her down, and then with the axe cut her in the head and hand, and then with the others gave her thirty wounds, so as then and there she was barbarously murdered. And at the same time and place there were six more Protestant women, viz. Ellen Palmer, and one Mary Taylor, and four others murdered by the three rebels before named, and others to the number of a hundred or thereabouts, which seven murdered Protestants were all stripped stark naked and left lying on the ground weltering in their blood in the open air for a day and a night, and then Mr. Parsons, governor of the Birr, made such means that they were sent for and carried there and buried in this deponent's presence. And about the same time was murdered at the Birr one Thomas (*illegible*), servant to Mr. Heyward, an English Protestant, each of the said so murdered having several wounds. And further saith, that about a quarter of a year after these murders were committed, viz. about Candlemas, 1641, one Edward Garner of the Birr, a tailor, and his wife, being taken from the Birr aforesaid with a convoy towards Dublin, were on the way, at a place called the Island in the King's County about three miles from Birr, murdered by one Turlogh Carroll, now of the Birr aforesaid, and his companions, as they were travelling at night a little beyond the convoy, which said Carroll and his wife did then and there strip naked the said Garnet and his wife, saving that they left her a pair of stockings on her legs, and there they were left lying. And about a week after a Popish priest, called Father Cahir Farrell, coming by with his boy, and being displeased that the woman had her stockings left upon her, said to the boy that he would give him sixpence to pull off 'that English sow's stockings,' which the boy oftsoon performing, found 5l. in her stockings, which they then carried away, but left the dead bodies there still until the crows and ravenous creatures devoured them.

About Easter, 1642, one Edward Erwin, late of the Birr, being sent from Birr towards Banagher to fetch salt, was met by the way at Dolnagh in the MacCoghlan's country, in the King's County, by some of the Coghlans and their confederates, the soldiers of John MacCoghlan, chief of the country, since knighted as is reported, who carried him thence to Ormond, hard by Tinnelogh, in the county of Tipperary, where they first half hanged him, and then letting him recover breath, buried him alive in a hole with rubbish and stones, yet so that about a month after the dogs drew the body out of the ground and devoured the flesh.

And this deponent further saith, that quickly after the time the town and castle of Birr was upon a siege taken from the English by the Irish rebels, viz. about February, 1642, there was left in and about the town to the mercy of the rebels about seventeen of the children of the English, whose parents were either formerly slain by the rebels or dead, as namely, three children of one Samuel Smith of the Birr, named Euseby, Anne, and Margaret, who, being almost starved with hunger and cold, and denied to come into their father's house by one Robert Tew that had gotten possession thereof, those three poor children for shelter from the cold crept into an oven in the back yard of their father's house, whither that inhuman rebel, Robert Tew aforesaid, brought some straw and putting it into the oven with the children set it on fire, so as then he burnt all three in the oven to death. About the same time a young Irish rogue called Adam, son of the said Robert Tew, with a cudgel knocked on the head and killed another of those fatherless children, that was the daughter of one Patrick Taylor, a Protestant, and that done tied a withe about her legs and drew her up and down, making that good sport and recreation.

In or about the month of February aforesaid, 1642, two other of those fatherless children, by name Grace Middleton and Anne Middleton, children of John Middleton (who with his wife was formerly hanged to death at Castletown by John O'Carroll of Clontisk,

Esq., and his soldiers), were at Birr aforesaid knocked on the head and murdered when they came to beg relief by certain stranger rebels that were said to have come thither out of the Pale, whose names this deponent cannot express. Howbeit they are or very lately were dwelling at the town of Birr aforesaid. And the residue of all those fatherless children, save only one, are also murdered or starved to death at or about Birr. All which this deponent knoweth to be true, for that from the very time of the beginning of the rebellion until about the 15th of March, 1644, he was restrained and kept at Birr aforesaid, by and amongst the rebels, to make shoes and boots for them, and then by God's providence he escaped from them one morning when they were at mass. And this deponent saw most of the murdered bodies aforesaid, and might have seen more of them if he durst have gone to them, and at length God delivered him out of their hands, who doubtless else would have murdered him also, wanting not malice to do so.

RICHARD TAYLOR +

Jurat. 21st October, 1645,
HEN. JONES.
WM. ALDRICH.

CLXIX.

MARTHA MOSLEY, the relict of Samuel Mosley, late vicar of Carlow, now deceased, sworn and examined, saith, that about th beginning of November, 1641, when the rebellion was begun at Carlow, her said husband was then alive. And that then he and she, this deponent, were forcibly expelled, deprived of and from the possession of his benefices, or church means, and of their goods and chattels to the value in all of 1,000*l.*, and above, by Thomas Davells of the Queen's County, Esq., Mr. Wall of Loughlan, in the county of Carlow, Esq., and Robert Harpole of the Queen's County, Esq., and their soldiers and partakers, whose names she knoweth not. And that this deponent's husband and she, and their four children, and her mother fled from their habitation into the Castle of Carlow, where they remained for about one year, and there endured much grief and calamity, insomuch indeed, that she thinketh it was the death of her said husband, and also of her mother. And she further saith, that during the time that she and the rest were in the said castle, viz. betwixt St. Stephen's Day, 1641, and the week before Easter, the said castle was besieged by the said Thomas Davells, Wall, Harpole, and their soldiers, and by Walter Bagenal of

Dunleckny, Esq., and Robert Evers of Cloghnory in the county of Carlow, gent., and their soldiers and accomplices, whose names she cannot tell. And saith, that one night, whilst that siege lasted, there was slain and hurt near to the castle and church, to the number of twenty-five, men, women, and children, English Protestants, who were most barbarously mangled, hewed, and slashed by the rebels. And one woman who had her hand cut off this deponent, by God's assistance, cured, as she did divers others whilst she was there. And amongst the rest she so cured, there was a poor stripped woman, that the night aforesaid was most miserably wounded, and had several great cuts through her skull, and one in her face, who was left for dead, and lay there for twenty-four hours, and at length, by God's great help, recovered her senses, and so much strength that she crawled and came into the castle, being a most miserable object of pity, and although such as saw her despaired of her recovery, yet God, working through such means as this deponent used to her, she afterwards very well recovered.

About Whitsuntide, 1642, one Hugh Everard and Edward Howe, two Protestants, were, within a musket-shot of the castle, both murdered, mangled, and cut to pieces most barbarously by the said Mr. Harpole and his soldiers. The wife of one Jonathan Lyn and her daughter were also surprised by the rebels, as they were gathering corn, and were from that place carried to Stapletown wood, where and when those two poor women were hanged upon a tree by the hair of the head all night. And the next morning they were cut down by the rebels, and being found to have life in them, the cruel villains then and there killed them outright. About the latter end of August, 1642, one Bennet Bower went out of the castle to get in corn, and there went with him one Alice Chevening and her little son, and another woman, that had been formerly his servant, all which four about a quarter of a mile from the castle were met by the soldiers of the said Harpole, who then and there took the said Bower prisoner, murdered the little boy and his mother, and the said other woman, the poor child's head being pitifully mangled and his belly so opened that his bowels fell out, and one of the women's throat being almost cut through, and the other pitifully mangled.

MARTHA MOSLEY.

Jurat. 29th October, 1643,
  HEN. JONES.
  HEN. BRERETON.

Note.

Charles Jowell, gent., of Dourigally, in the King's County, swore before Jones and Brereton that of twenty-two families, his near neighbours, in all about one hundred and twenty persons, he believed only his sister and two others survived. The rest were stripped, and in one way or another were murdered by the rebels. He was himself sheltered by one Nicholas White and Brian Molloy, but was beaten and wounded because he refused to go to mass. While he was at White's house, one Ellinor Bycroft and her two children were murdered in that neighbourhood, their bodies being thrown into a hole in a ditch before they were quite dead, and the earth cast over them while they were 'groaning miserably.' He also swore that the rebels read aloud in his presence the commission which they said they had received from the King, and showed a broad seal attached to it. It would almost appear that there was more than one of those mysterious real or forged documents in circulation in 1641. If so they were probably all forgeries.

CLXX.

JAMES BENN, late of the city of Kilkenny, shoemaker, sworn and examined, deposeth and saith, that since the beginning of the present rebellion, that is to say, about the 26th of December, 1641, he, this deponent, at Kilkenny aforesaid, was deprived, robbed, or otherwise despoiled of leather, household stuff, and other things worth 30*l*. by one Mr. Codd, a commander of rebels, who that day came into the said city, and one Bourke and other accomplices and soldiers of or with the said Mr. Codd, whose names this deponent cannot remember; which said rebels then and there forcibly robbed and pillaged all the Protestants in that part of the city, or suburbs, called the Irish town, of their goods. The gates of the city being at that time shut, and some others, especially Roe Purcell, merchant, then sheriff of the said city, and son-in-law to Patrick Murphy, now mayor of the same city, and his servants, and others as well Papist inhabitants of the same city, and other devilish rebels of the country that they had called to partake with them, robbed and dispossessed the rest of the Protestants in the city.

And further saith, that one of the rebellious cruel soldiers, about

Easter, 1642, did in Kilkenny aforesaid, in this deponent's own sight, most barbarously and wickedly with a sharp skean rip open the belly of a poor English young woman, that fled thither from Castlecomer, for safety, so that her entrails tumbled out, and she received them in her arms, and at the same time stabbed and wounded the mother and brother of the said young woman, and had killed them outright, as this deponent is verily persuaded, but that he sent one Richard Lawlor, a shoemaker, to rescue them, who carried the two, the mother and son, to one Thomas Archer, then mayor of the city, to whom complaint being made of these outrages, he so far sleighted it, that he turned them scornfully away, so that the villainous rebels of the city, viz. some men, but mostly women and boys there, threw stones on them and dirt in the streets, and pursued and beat them out of the town. But as to the poor young woman, she crawled away with her bowels on her arms, out of the town, and died that night under a hedge. And further saith, that on the Sunday, in the morning next after that this deponent was robbed of his goods, he went to the church of St. Canice to pray, where he saw one Mr. Smith, a Protestant minister, late of Ballynckill, and one Mr. Lemon, a Scottish Protestant, late a schoolmaster in Kilkenny, which Mr. Smith was then and there stark naked, and the said Lemon had only a pair of breeches on, both having been stript in the church, and standing trembling near the altar; when this deponent not being able to relieve them, left them in that poor state. And the same morning the deponent met coming out of the church one Mr. Jones, late minister at Stroncarty, who was stript of almost all his clothes, and had a great wound in his shoulder, given him by the rebels.

And further saith, that whilst this deponent remained at Kilkenny, which was from the beginning of the rebellion until about the 26th day of June, 1643, then he, this deponent, observed and saw in the houses and shops of Andrew Murphy, James Archdeacon, Pierse Archer, Robert Tobin, and divers other merchants in the said city, the Protestant bibles and prayer-books torn in pieces, and used as waste paper to wrap up soap, starch, candles, and such wares as they sold. And further saith, that although after they were robbed this deponent and some of the English were suffered to stay at Kilkenny, yet the rebels gave them nothing, but they lived by their hard labour. And when they had gotten anything, it was taken from them, by cesses, presses, and soldiers. And this deponent and the rest of the Protestants were often threatened to be

hanged, so as they stood in fear of their lives till they got away.
And further, this deponent hath been credibly told by some of the
Romish and rebellious citizens there, that the titulary Bishop of
Cashel and Turlogh Oge O'Neil, brother to the devilish rebel Sir
Phelim O'Neil, and the Popish citizens of Kilkenny aforesaid,
petitioned and earnestly moved the council at Kilkenny, that all
the English Protestants there should be put to death, whereunto
one Richard Lawless, an alderman of the city, in excuse of them
answered and said, that the English were all robbed before, and he
saw no cause that they should lose their lives. And at divers other
times, when it was pressed that the English should be put to death,
the Lord Mountgarrett, and his son, Mr. Edmund Butler, and Mr.
Philip Purcell, by their strength, means, and occasions prevented it,
they being, as the deponent believeth, commanded by God Almighty
so to do. And further saith, that the said Sir Phelim O'Neil, about
a month or six weeks since, came to Kilkenny (out of the north),
where this deponent left him and his lady, and the other grand
rebellious councillors.

And further saith, that about a month since, one Captain
Chambers being taken prisoner by the rebels, and promised fair
quarter, was brought to Kilkenny, when and where the base rebel,
Captain Robert Harpole of Shrule, having begged leave to have him,
caused his, the said Harpole's own men to hang the said Captain
Chambers upon a gate, and before he was dead they cut off his head
and let his body fall to the ground, and cruelly and indecently
mangled it. And the stripped body was carried away into a ditch,
with the head, and there buried, as this deponent was credibly informed by one Brian MacShane, his apprentice, whom he, this examt., sent purposely to see how they used the said Captain Chambers,
not daring to go himself.

JAMES BENN.

Jurat. 3rd July, 1643,
  WM. ALDRICH.
  HEN. PIGOTT.

Note.

As I have already said, the fewness, comparatively speaking, of
massacres in the province of Leinster was made up for by out-
bursts of ferocious bigotry in the destruction of churches, the digging
up of Protestants from the graves in which they had rested for
months or years, and the casting of their bones into ditches and roads.
Nothing can whitewash some of the Roman Catholic clergy from

the guilt of these outrages. The order of the ' moderate ' Bishop of Ferns respecting the burial of Francis Talbot, given at page 155, vol. i., and the testimony of innumerable witnesses at Kilkenny, Wexford, Carlow, and other Leinster counties, show that the people acted only in accordance with the mandates of their priests, when they profaned the graves of the Protestants. And we have equally good evidence to show that up to the eve of the rebellion those same priests were, even in that intolerant age, treated with courtesy and even kindness by the Protestants of those counties. A somewhat rare edition of Lord Castlehaven's ' Memoirs of the Irish Wars of 1641,' published in 1815, contains Lord Anglesey's letter of observations and reflections thereupon, written in 1680. Of the terms on which the Roman Catholics and Protestants lived in 1640-1 Lord Anglesey says, ' there never was more unity, friendship, and good agreement, amongst all sorts and degrees, excepting in the standing root of mischief, the difference in religion, than at this time, or more mutual confidence. . . . I remember very well the summer before the rebellion, the titular Bishop of Ferns coming on his visitation into the county of Wexford, where I then dwelt, at the request of the Popish priest, I lent most of my silver plate to entertain the said Bishop with, and had it honestly restored.' How this courtesy and tolerance, which, needless to say, would never have been exhibited to a heretic bishop by a Spaniard or Italian in their native countries, in 1640, was repaid by the Bishop of Ferns and his brethren we know. John Mayer, sworn on the 29th of May, before Henry Jones and Henry Brereton, deposed that the rebels of Kilkenny had brought into the town the heads of ' Mr. Alfrey, son of the Lord Lieutenant's comptroller, Lieutenant Gilbert, Mr. Bingham a clergyman, and four others,' which heads they knocked against the stones, cut, slashed, and mangled, and scorched the face of Mr. Bingham. They then placed his head on a pole, and laid a leaf of a book before it, ' *scornfully saying he might preach now if he would, for his mouth was open enough!* ' The same witness adds, that the rebels robbed the Protestant churches, broke the pulpits, and made gunpowder in some of them, ' swearing they would turn the bodies of the Protestants out of their graves that had been buried a year before.' Long before Cromwell's soldiers came over to desecrate, as is popularly supposed, the churches, they were desecrated, plundered, and their bibles and service books kicked into the kennel and trampled on by the orthodox Catholics.

CLXXI.

ANN, wife of MERVIN MAUDSLEY, late of the city of Kilkenny, gentleman, duly sworn and examined, deposeth and saith, that since the beginning of the present rebellion, viz. about the 1st day of (*illegible*) past, her said husband and she were, at Kilkenny aforesaid, deprived, robbed, and despoiled of their means, goods, and chattels, consisting of household goods, linen, apparel, beer in the cellar and other things, to the value of 69*l*. 15*s*. ster. And saith, she knoweth not the names of the rebels that so robbed them, but was credibly informed and believes that they were the rebellious soldiers serving under the command of Philip Purcell of Ballifoyle in the county of Kilkenny, Esq., son-in-law to the Lord Mountgarrett and captain of a company of rebels. And about the same time some of the rebels in Kilkenny aforesaid struck and beat a poor Englishwoman, until she was forced into a ditch, where she died, those barbarous rebels having first ript open and let her child's guts about her heels and most cruelly murdered her, being about sixteen years of age. And further saith, that Joan Smith, this deponent's mother, who dwelt in the house of her, this deponent, was also by the rebels robbed and despoiled of her goods worth 60*l*. And further saith, that one (*blank*) Cantwell, provost marshal for the rebels, at or near Kilkenny, and his company hanged seven Englishmen that they found on the way from Ballin (*torn*), whereof one was a tailor, named Richard Philips, and they also hanged an Irishman, because he was in company with these Englishmen. All which eight persons were hanged in the town of Kilkenny, on a house of newly-framed timber. And also the rebels called on the Lord Mountgarrett to have all the English there hanged, he answered, that he would pistol any who made such a request again, for that the English who were left would gladly enough go away and leave the country, if they knew how; which this deponent knew they would, for the rebellious Irish would still abuse and oppress those English whom they had not slain or banished, and would commonly call them English dogs.

ANN MAUDSLEY.

Jurat. March 28th, 1643,
HEN. BRERETON.
WM. ALDRICH.

CLXXII.

RALPH BULKELY, of the town of Carlow, parish clerk, sworn and examined, saith, that since the beginning of the present rebellion, that is to say, in the months of November and December, 1641, and since, he was robbed and forcibly despoiled of goods and chattels to the value of 231*l*. by the Irish Papists and rebels, viz. Robert (*illegible*) of Clownagh in the same county, gent., a captain of rebels since slain in rebellion, Robert Harpole of Shrewle in the same county, another captain of rebels, Thomas Davells, Esq., of the Queen's County, Edmund Wall of Loughane, and Edward Wall of Ballynakill in the county of Carlow, Esq., another commander of rebels, Walter Bagenal of Dunleckny, another of their commanders, who at the first, upon his promise of loyalty and to do his Majesty service, procured to himself arms from the stores in Dublin and then most perfidiously and treacherously turned rebel and used those arms against his Majesty and his loyal Protestant subjects, Murtogh Oge (*blank*) of Castletown, Esq., James Butler of Tully, Esq., Garret (*illegible*) of Brisholstown (*sic*), Esq., and generally all the other gentry and commonalty of Irish Papists, within the county of Carlow. . . . And this deponent and many of the English for the safety of their lives fled to the Castle of Carlow, to the number of 600 men, women, and children, many being very poor and having nothing to eat when they came thither. And further saith, that such was the providence and mercy of God to them in the said castle, to save them from the rebels, that a great flood fell into the river of Carlow aforesaid, about the beginning of December, 1641, and continued until after Candlemas following, in such a height, that he never saw the like there, where he hath dwelt eighteen years. Insomuch that none could approach the castle but upon a narrow causeway, which they might with difficulty defend. Howbeit the rebels before named and divers others of the country on St. John's Day of Christmas, 1641, while the flood was high, came into the town of Carlow, and took it, and the Irish of the town joined and resorted with them, and set and kept several corps de garde, and hemmed in all those in the castle, so that they could not stir out, so much as to fetch a pail of water, but they were slain. And afterwards, viz. a little after Candlemas, the flood still continuing, those rebels secretly in the night time with cotts, and on horseback approached unto, and summoned the castle, and laid siege thereunto, and also to the church, and with pickaxes and sledges broke down the church wall, but were repulsed, and many of them slain, but those of the English that were found out of the castle, these rebels most barbarously murdered, some of them being children, that were slain hanging at the breasts of their poor mothers, and some very old people that could scarcely go. And the said rebels, to their great loss of men, continued the siege until the morning following, but were much annoyed and hindered by the water, insomuch that when they were quite repulsed, and forced to leave the siege, many of them were put to deep wading and swimming, and some in the cotts slain, wherein that flood and the narrowness of the pavement, afforded to the besieged Protestants not a little relief and advantage. By which repulse these rebels were, as he conceiveth, so deterred, that afterwards they did not attempt to besiege the castle or the church, but yet lying in the town, kept the Protestants in the castle until his Majesty's army did, about Easter following, march thither, and then all that were there besieged went away with the army.

RALPH BULKELY.

Jurat. 8th Jan. 1643,
HEN. JONES.
HEN. BRERETON.

CLXXIII.

BARNABY DUNNE, of Brittas, in the Queen's County, Esquire, being duly sworn and examined, deposeth, that about the end of November, 1641, and since, he was robbed and deprived of his goods, rents, chattels, and other profits as followeth, by and through the commotions and rebellions begun in that and other parts of the kingdom of Ireland, viz. of corn, sheep, cows, oxen, garrans, and plow harness, which he left as a stock in his lands of Ballyvadock, Rahmoro, and part of the lands of Stradbally, held by Robert Robinson, Thomas McCarroll, and Walter Fullam, his farmers, worth 400*l.*, which stock was taken for the most part, as he credibly heard, by Henry Dempsey, Con Dempsey, Murtagh Dempsey, Failly Dempsey, Rossa and Nicholas Dempsey, William Cosby, otherwise called William Kelly, and others their adherents. In cows, mares, sheep, horses, colts, swine taken and stolen from him in Irregan, worth 400*l.*, by and through the means of Daniel *duna*, Arthur and Rory *duna*, John McWilliam Conraghy, and others, their adherents and confederates. In corn and malt at Brittas, and corn in ground, and household furniture and stuff which he is not permitted to possess or move from thence for not joining with these rebels, and because he is a Protestant, worth 300*l*., of his rents due and payable at Michaelmas, and Easter 400*l*., and the same for two years to come, 800*l*., which he doth not expect to receive by reason of the rebellion and the banishment of his English tenants that he had in Iregan, to the number of twenty and upwards, part of whom he was driven to keep and relieve at his house of Brittas, until at length they came with much difficulty to the fort at Maryborough after Easter last, and partly by reason of the wasting, burning, and destroying of his houses, mills, and other improvements that were thereon by this unnatural rebellion. Also the rent of the impropriate rectory of Iregan for harvest, 1642, worth 100*l*., and is like to lose the future profits thereof (until a peace be established) through the intrigues of Ross Geoghegan, titulary Bishop of Kildare, who doth claim the same, and inhibited the inhabitants of the country by himself and Tiegue Delahunty, priest, to pay this examt. the said rent and the rents and profits of the impropriate rectory of Kilruish and Collier's land, in the said diocese, worth 34*l*. per an., and is likely to lose the future profits thereof, also of arrears of rents and tithes before the last year, and debts due by persons who are likely to grow desperate, and not be recovered through this rebellion, 400*l*., also 100*l*. due on a mortgage or rentcharge on part of the lands of John Carroll of Clonlish in the King's County, Esquire, and the said rentcharge for Michaelmas, 1642, 15*l*., also a mortgage on the lands of Rory Oge of Banellileg, Daniel *duna* of Tinnahinch and John *duna* of Coulloghlane, in Iregan, in the Queen's County aforesaid, 100*l*., of which they intend to deprive him, this examt., being now not amenable to his Majesty's laws, nor he, according to their new ways and laws, capable to partake thereof or recover the same. All which amounteth to the full sum of 2,134*l*. sterling.

This examt. further saith, that about Christmas, 1641, one Tiegue MacRory Dunne, who sometime lived with him, spake to Sybil, wife to this deponent, as she told him this deponent, and as the said Tiegue afterwards confessed, that there was no safety for her life or this deponent's in Iregan, unless they went to mass. Whereupon this deponent discharged the said Tiegue out of his house, and bade him or any of them that were Papists to burn and kill him this deponent, and his wife, and their children, if they, the

Papists, could or durst, for that he, this deponent, and his family, would not join in the rebellion, nor change their religion.

He further saith, that one Robert Story, an Englishman that then lived at Mr. Richard Redish's house, affirmed unto him that about that time one Tiegue Delahunty, a mass priest, that lived in Iregan, desired him, the said Robert, to carry a message from him to the said Sybil, which was that if she did not go to mass she must leave Iregan, and go to her father, Sir Robert Pigott.

He also deposeth, that Daniel Dunne of Tomgraney, gent., and Arthur Dunne of Ballynahonne, gent., told him that it was certain that there was some powerful personage in the Irish army in the north that used to sit under a tent cloth or canopy, and that none but prime men or commanders were admitted to his or her presence, some saying it was the young prince, others the queen or the queen mother. And said, that those that begun this commotion gave it out for certain that they had the king's commission to do what they did, and that they were to extirpate or banish all the English and Protestants that would not become Roman Catholics.

He also saith, that Phelim Dunne of Lackamore, and Elinor FitzGerald, wife to Brian McDonnell, told him that the titulary bishop and the priests said they could not consecrate the churches wherein to celebrate the mass, until the corpses of the Protestants should be removed thereout.

He further saith, that in January last, or February, the fore-named Ross Geoghegan, titulary bishop, came with others to this deponent's house at Brittas where he then was, being sickly, saying that this deponent was one of his charge, and that he was bound to labour to reduce him to be of the Roman Catholic religion, whereupon divers arguments about religion, the king's prerogative and supremacy, past between them, which this deponent put down in writing, and upon the said Geoghegan's earnestness, this deponent alleged that he was the king's sworn officer, as being a justice of the peace and twice a high sheriff, and had sworn the oath of supremacy which he held to be lawful, and he in conscience tried to observe the same ; to whom the said titulary bishop replied that it was an unlawful oath, pretending it might safely be dispensed with, further urging that God would not permit any to have power above his vicar on earth, meaning the Pope. Whereupon this deponent alleged a passage that fell out concerning the King of Hungary being in league with the Turk, who, by the persuasion of a legate from the Pope, violated his oath in breaking that league and joined in battle with the emperor against the Turk. And the Turk having a copy of the league and oath taken betwixt them called upon Christ Jesus to avenge Himself upon the perfidious Christian that brake the oath taken in His name, upon which it was observed as remarkable that the Turk gained the victory against the Christian army.

And further this deponent saith, that about the end of that month of February, one Brendan Conn, a friar, as he heard him to be, came to this deponent, labouring to persuade him from being a Protestant, and to join and subscribe to a writing that he, the friar, had drawn up, the contents whereof, as this deponent remembereth, was to bind himself to join with the undertakers of that commotion in their confederation for banishing the English that would not conform to the Roman Catholic religion, and doing such further acts as the undertakers or rebels would appoint, which this deponent refused to yield unto. During which time some forbearance was shown to this deponent in permitting him and some of his English tenants to remain there, hoping from time to time they would be as they (the rebels) were. And divers messages and threatenings were brought to this deponent from Florence FitzPatrick, Arthur Molloy, and some of the Dempsies, and divers others that if he did not put away his English tenants and servants and become as one of them, they would pull him out by the heels and take all he had. And this deponent, seeing the dangerousness of the time, and perceiving the rebel's evil intentions and cruel dealings with others, and proclamations for robbing all Protestants, and to kill them if they would not leave these parts, though the said rebels pretended to be authorised by the king to do as they did ; which this deponent believeth not, for that his Majesty would surely stand by his Protestant subjects, and as soon as he, this examt., got a little cured of his sickness, he being altogether unable to suppress or resist them, being one against many thousands, fled unto the house of his father-in-law, Sir Robert Pigott, at Disart, in the month of March last. And saith, that some of his servants in the night time, as they told this deponent, brought unto him to Disart aforesaid, two beeves, twenty-six muttons, some plate, and a little linen, for which he heard Daniel Dunne and his rebellious adherents threatened to hang the said servants, and in a rage wounded one of them. So that they durst not any more come with any relief to this deponent.

BARNABY DUNNE.

Jurat. 22nd Nov. 1642,
 Cora WM. ALDRICH.   RANDAL ADAMS.
  JOHN WATSON.   HEN. BRERETON.

CLXXIV.

THOMAS HUETSON (sic), of the town and county of Kildare, an English Protestant, sworn and examined, saith, about a month or three weeks since one John Courtney of Kildare aforesaid, weaver, and Martin Courtney, his son, Walter White of the same town, labourer, Buonaventure Berry of the same town, the reputed son of William Berry of the same town a Popish priest, and Thomas Berry of Kildare aforesaid, near kinsman of the said William Berry, and divers other rebels of the Irish, did in the cathedral church of Kildare aforesaid dig up the graves of Dominick Huetson, this deponent's brother, who had been buried about twenty months, and of Christian Huetson, this deponent's grandmother, who had been buried about one week, and took their corpses out of the same graves in the church, and laid them both in a garden, outside the walls of the churchyard, which was done by the council and procurement of Ross McGeoghegan, titulary Bishop of Kildare, and James Dempsy, the Popish vicar general, William Berry, priest, Dominick Dempsy, guardian to the friars, who live in Kildare aforesaid, James Flanagan of the same, a friar, Brian O'Cormady of the same, friar, and other friars, whose names he now remembereth not. And further saith, that the same William O'Berry (sic) brought this deponent before the said titulary bishop, and informed him that this deponent was looking in the church window when the corpses of the said brother and grandmother were being taken up, and that he writt down the names of those parties that so took them up, and desired to know what must be done with this deponent, to which the said Bishop Geoghegan answered that if he found the report to be true, and that this deponent would do anything against their Catholic cause, he would imprison and hang him. And further deposeth, that some of the parties above named, with divers others of the town of Kildare, said that they could not sanctify or hallow the said church of Kildare until the heretics' bodies were removed out of it.

THOMAS HEWETSON.

Jurat. 15*th Feb.* 1641,
ROGER PUTTOCK.
WM. ALDRICH.

Note.

Ralph Walmesly, farmer, of Ballynegulshy near Birr, sworn and examined, deposed to the murder of his mother and his infant child by an Irishman who was sent to convey them to Birr by Lady Herbert. He also deposed as to several other murders of which he had heard and to the seditious speeches, drunkenness and profligacy of a friar. But he spoke in high terms of the kindness shown to him by Captain Turlogh Molloy and John McFarrell, gent., of Ballycally in the Queen's County, saying that ' he (this deponent) is confident that the said Molloy and McFarrell were much grieved at the ill-treating of the English, which appeared not only by the said Molloy's and MacFarrell's loving words, but by the real courtesies they did the English at divers times.'

CLXXV.

The joint Examinations of EDWARD SALTINGHALL, *late of the Grange, in the parish and county of Armagh, gent., and* GEORGE LITTLEFIELD *of the said county.*

These deponents, being duly sworn and examined, say, that Manus O'Cahan of the Grange, in the county of Armagh aforesaid, colonel of the rebels, Brian O'Kelly of Charlemont, captain of the rebels, Patrick O'Mallan late of Munroy (*sic*) in the county of Tyrone, another captain of the rebels, caused to be gathered together and put into the church of Loghgall, in the said county of Armagh, three score and ten persons, all English Protestants, and there kept them two days and two nights, and afterwards sent them with one hundred soldiers to (*blank*). And the rebels did in (*illegible*) aforesaid likewise suddenly gather all the English there together and drove them to the bridge of Portadowne, and threw them all over the bridge into the water, they being in all 154 Protestants who were then and there most miserably drowned. And afterwards the three rebels last above named gave to the rest of the English a pass to go into England that they who were left behind should not be afraid.

And further saith, that the said Manus O'Cahan and Brian O'Kelly, and Shane O'Neil, and Art Oge O'Neil, gent., did take William Blundell of Grange, yeoman, in the said county of Armagh, and put a rope about his neck and threw him into the Blackwater near Charlemont, and did draw him up and down in the water to make him confess his money, who thereupon gave them 21*l.*, yet within three weeks after he and his wife and his three children were drowned by the rebels, and one more of his children being left behind in Grenan, was afterwards taken by Patrick O'Donnelly of Knockaconey, in the county of Armagh, gent., out of the same house, who caused it also to be drowned. And further saith, that Samuel Law of Grenan in the parish of Armagh, yeoman, was forcibly taken out of his house at Grenan aforesaid, by the rebels Neil Oge O'Neil and Donogh O'Hagan, and Phelimy O'Mallon, all of Grenan aforesaid, and brought to a wood and there they put a withe about his neck, and therewith drew him up and down by the neck until he was glad to promise to give them ten shillings. And further saith, that Art MacHugh Boy O'Neil and Neil Modder O'Neil, both captains of the rebels, caused divers of the inhabitants of Armagh to be put to death, namely, James Chappell, Esq., Thomas Whitacre, gent., Thomas Glover, gent., Mr. Starkey and his two daughters, William Wollard, yeoman, Thomas Collier, hatter, Christian Symonds, shoemaker. And there were also divers other persons by the rebels put to death, as namely, William Marriott and his son, and Robert Spring, all of Loughgall, gentlemen, who were hanged upon the butcher's stalls before their own doors, and their houses set on fire and burnt. And the rebels also murdered William Galvin and his brother's wife and children, Thomas Sadlier, John Keighley and Peter Keighley, Samuel Birch, Thomas Foster and James Berrall, Robert Berrall, Patrick Erwin, Joshua Griffin, James Rodes and John Bartlett, all of Armagh. And further saith, that one Loughlin MacArtee (*sic*) of Horkly, in the county of Armagh, boldly affirmed that he had killed one Thomas Woodward of Horkly with a blow of his stave, and that he made a woman help to hang her husband.

And saith, that the rebels Patrick MacPhelimy of Ballymoilmurry in the county of Armagh did forcibly and cruelly throw one John Hale of Ballimacroome into a river, when he swimming over to the other side, the said Patrick ran on a piece of wood that lay over the river, and with an axe knocked out the said Hale's brains. And also saith, that Neil O'Hologan, William O'Hologan, and Patrick Ballagh O'Donnelly, all of Torgardan, in the parish of Kilmore, and county of Armagh, yeomen, did maliciously kill and murder Richard Roe of Kilmanin, in the county of Armagh, yeoman, because he had justly caused some of their friends to be hanged. And that Phelimy Mac (*illegible*) and Redmond Roe O'Crelly, both of Ballaghkernon, in the county of Armagh, yeomen, did take their master, Henry Pilkington, gent., out of Loughgall aforesaid, professing much kindness unto him, because he was their master, and said they would keep him (*illegible*). But as soon as they had got him within less than a quarter of a mile of his own house, they, thinking that he had money hidden thereabouts, took his own garters and tied them about his neck to make him confess the money. But because he would not confess to any they hanged or strangled him on the highway, and stripped him of all his clothes and put his head into a ditch and there left him. And further saith, that the said Manus O'Cahan and Brian O'Kelly received at one time from one William Fullerton, parson of Loughgall, 35*l.* upon promise to send a convoy with him and one Richard Gladwich to Lisnegarvy, and gave the said William Fullerton a pass to go.there safe and sound. But when the convoy of rebels had carried or brought them about two miles on their way, they cut off their heads. And the rebels James O'Donnelly and Hugh MacManus, both of Dromoly, in the county of Armagh, gent., did take and imprison John Richardson, gent., and Christopher Blake Francis Hill, butcher, and Ambrose Castleman, baker, all of Loughgall, in the said county of Armagh, until they were forced to give them all the money they had, and then promising to get them a convoy to the Newry, at length, when they had got their money, hanged the poor men. And further saith, that one George Lawlis, a rebel, of Loughgall, yeoman, resolving to kill John Corrider, told him he would do so, but bid him first say his prayers, whereupon the said Corrider kneeling down to pray, the said Lawlis instantly cut off his head as he was upon his knees. And one Patrick O'Donnelly of Knockerony, in the county of Armagh, gent., being cured of a wound which he had in his arm by William Wollard of Armagh, chirurgeon, about a week after most barbarously and ungratefully killed the said Wollard. And the rebels Hugh O'Farrel of Mountjoy, in the county of Armagh, gent., did most barbarously murder one Alexander Corrider and Richard Humfrey and his wife, after they had given him all their money and wealth. And further saith, that Hugh O'Quin and Art O'Lockane (*sic*), both of Annaghe, in the county of Armagh, rebels, most cruelly murdered Williams of Drumakroffe, in the county of Armagh, yeoman, when he was naked and his wife and children were looking on, and also that John Proctor of the Balmeton, in the parish of Armagh, was killed by the said Hugh because he could give him no money. But before they killed the said Williams they kept him in the court of guard till he was scarce able to go, and then they let him out, cut off his head and held it up to his wife and children.

And after the rebels were gone away, his sorrowful and poor wife burying him in the garden, one Patrick O'Daly, a rebel, took up his corpse and threw it into a ditch.

And further saith, that Patrick O'Kelly, Hugh O'Kelly, Patrick MacEarny, Shane MacCoddam, Ann ny Coddam, all of Clonedan, in the county of Armagh, caused twenty-three of the poor English who were made servants to Brian O'Kelly to be drowned because two Englishmen that were in (*illegible*) company at the siege of Drogheda fled into the city from the rebels. And these deponents heard divers of the rebels often say, that if Owen MacArt should not ere long come out of Spain, they would make Sir Phelim their king.

            EDWARD SALTINHALL,
Jurat. 1st *June*, 1642,   GEORGE LITTLEFIELD.
WM. ALDRICH.
WM. HITCHCOCK.

Note.

I have given the foregoing as a specimen of one of those very unreliable depositions which the Royal Commissioners sometimes received. One-fifth of it may be reliable, the rest is evidently mere hearsay. (*v.* Introduction, pp. 135, 145.)

CLXXVI.

RICHARD HUDSON, of (*illegible*) Street, Dublin, carrier, aged forty-five years or thereabouts, duly sworn and examined, saith, that on the 24th of October, 1641, at the beginning of the rebellion, he was living at Kildargin in the territory of Idough, in the county of Kilkenny, within two miles of Castle Comer, and saith that about a month before Christmas, 1641, a company of the rebels, to the number of fifty or thereabouts, fell upon this examt.'s house, and robbed and stripped this examt., and that Edmund Brenan, late of Ardee, deceased, was commander of these rebels. And further saith, that the country being full of rebels, this examt. ran for safety of his life into Castle Comer, in the said county, and there continued, and saith, that after his coming to the said castle of Castle Comer, the said Edmund Brenan, who was captain, one Thomas Butler, brother to one Richard Butler, who lived in Castle Comer, was made captain of the rebels in garrison in the said town of Castle Comer, and that during his being in such command, a youth called Richard Barnard being sent out of the castle, on some occasion into the town, one Lisagh Brenan took the said Barnard, and carried him and hanged him upon his father's tenter hooks, till he was dead, his father being a clothier by his trade, the said youth being so hanged on the tenter hooks within view of the said castle. And further saith, that an Englishwoman, the wife of a collier, being sent with a letter from some of the Irish to Captain Farrer, who was in the same castle, was by some of the Irish soldiers shot before the gate of the castle and died there of the shot. And further saith, that about the second week of Lent then following, quarter being offered to those that were in the said castle, he, this examt., and many of the English left the said Captain Thomas Butler, and some of his soldiers followed them and by force took from thence one Richard Philips, and one John Showell, whom the said Thomas Butler carried to Kilkenny and there hanged them until they were dead. And further saith not.

 GERARD LOWTHER.   RICHARD + HUDSON.
 EDWARD BOLTON.
 THOS. DUNGAN.

CLXXVII.

LUCY SWIFT, of Ballyraggett, duly sworn and examined, deposeth and saith, that she lived in Idough in the beginning of the rebellion, and being demanded what she knew of the murders committed in Idough, she said that one Lewis Davis, a Welshman, was murdered by one James McWilliam O'Brenan, now in prison, and James McDonnell, living in Idough, and that one William Stretton was murdered by Melaghlin McTiegue, and that Barnaby Dempsy hanged this examt.'s godmother Lucy Coale in his own town, where she then lived.

Taken before us, 14*th Sept.* 1652,
 WILLIAM HEYDON.
 (*illegible.*)

CLXXVIII.

ELIZABETH LAWLESS, being examined upon oath, what she knoweth of the murder of Richard Barnard, son of Alexander Barnard, deposeth that about Shrove Tuesday, in the year 1641, she, this deponent, being in the town of Castlecomer, did see Lewis Brenan strike at the said Richard Barnard (being then young, about nine or ten years of age) with his sword drawn, and gave him first a deep wound upon his head, and presently after on his face, and this examt. thereupon saw the said Richard fall to the ground, and the said Lewis Brenan, not being therewith satisfied, in pursuance of his bloody and murderous disposition, took off a hempen cord from a greyhound's neck, and put it about the said Richard's neck, and dragged him to his father's tenter hooks, and there the said Lewis hanged him, the said Richard, and being demanded what she knew or conceived to be the reason of this murderous and bloody action, she saith she knoweth no reason, unless it was because he, the boy, was of English parents, and further saith, that the said boy came out of the said castle of Castle Comer, not an hour, or thereabouts, before he was murdered, and saith that the said Lewis Brenan did exceedingly vaunt, after he had perpetrated that bloody murder.

ELIZABETH LAWLESS +

Taken before us,
JOHN STAMER.
(illegible.)

Note.

William Collis of Kildare, saddler, sworn before Brereton and Jones in 1649, deposed that Walter White of Kildare, a commander of the rebels, said in his (Collis's) hearing, that he thought ' *the worse of himself the day he saw any of the breed of English walk along the streets of Kildare*,' one of many proofs showing that the rebels of English descent, but Irish by birth, were more inveterate haters of the English rule than were the rebels of old Irish descent and name. English writers of the seventeenth century noticed that it needed only one generation to make the colonists of Ireland more rebellious than the Irish themselves. John Glasse of Mountrath swore on the 8th of April, 1642, that Mr. and Mrs. Nicholson were offered their lives if they would go to mass, but that they refused to do so, ' the wife showing even more resolution than her husband,' and ' when they pressed her,' says the deponent, ' to burn her bible, she said she would die on the point of the sword first, which they both made good on the Sabbath day, the morning after Twelfth Day last, when they were cruelly butchered and murdered before mass time by the followers of Florence FitzPatrick.' The wife of FitzPatrick, according to several witnesses, was a most cruel persecutor of the Protestants. Oliver Davoren of Rathmore, in Kildare, sworn before Sterne and Aldrich, in January, 1641, deposed that he was robbed of goods worth 281*l*. by one Lynch of Rathmore, but that ' he saw no murders although he heard that they were committed.' He further swore that the said Lynch said in his (deponent's) presence that ' it was no sin to rob and spoil heretics, and that Catholics were not bound to spare them as neighbours.'

CLXXIX.

The Examination of ALICE GREGG, *the widow of Richard Gregg, late of Loughgall, in the county of Armagh.*

(Harleian MSS., Brit. Mus. III. 5,999.)

This examt., duly sworn, deposeth that one Dogherty, a colonel of the rebels, with others his soldiers and partakers, stripped at one time three hundred Protestants about Loughgall of their clothes, and then drove them like sheep into the church of Loughgall, and there the said Dogherty publicly said to his bloody and rebellious crew that all these, meaning the Protestants so imprisoned, should be put to death, both men, women, and children, and then and there caused the door of the church to be shut and locked, and left them naked, save that some few covered themselves with straw, where in that state they remained for four days after, having but very poor allowance of victuals, and indeed scarce enough to keep their bodies and souls together, and then by the command of the said Dogherty, his merciless soldiers, with their skeans, set upon this deponent, her husband, and children, and in the same church gave her eight wounds in her head, and divided and cut her son John Gregg whilst he was yet alive into quarters, and threw them in his father's face; then they stabbed her husband, and gave him seventeen or eighteen wounds, and so murdered him, and cut him in quarters in this deponent's sight. And then and there in the same church the said rebels stabbed and quartered or otherwise cut in pieces at least one hundred more Protestants, especially those that were able to bear arms, and continued in their bloody massacre and murder, which, as this deponent is verily persuaded, had fallen upon all the rest, but that one Captain O'Reilly forbade them to kill any more; so that these bloody and barbarous villains, merely out of awe, desisted, and about a day after this deponent so wounded, and many others all severely wounded, were turned out of the church, and were suffered to go up and down the country naked, to taste of the cold and sorrowful charity of the usurping, merciless, and pitiless Irish. And this deponent is confident and partly knoweth, that the rebels put to death, by drowning in the flood, famine, hanging, and extreme tortures, almost all the Protestants in the county thereabouts. Insomuch that one in a hundred hardly escaped with life, as this deponent is verily persuaded. And further saith, that many of the poor Protestants that fled the bloody hands of the rebel soldiers were afterwards most brutally murdered by the very Irish cripples, and those women of base condition that kept them company, which cripples and idle women did much vaunt the glory of such their cruelties, wherein they had no little assistance from their children, that, as far as their powers extended, assisted and exceeded them in their merciless and bloody acts.

Jurat. 21*st July*, 1643,
 Coram JOHN WATSON.
  WM. ALDRICH.

CLXXX.

(Harleian MSS., Brit. Mus. III. 5,999.)

THOMAS PERKINS, clerk, late curate of Lynally, in the King's County, duly sworn, deposeth, that one Mr. Gearnye, who had been in the said parish forty years, and was then near a hundred years old, was killed by the Dempsies in his own house, and buried in a ditch by the common road, and they murdered also one John Ap Hugh, and his wife, being sick in bed.

Note.

The above are accurate copies of the originals in the books in Dublin, omitting details of the deponent's pecuniary losses. (*v.* Introduction, p. 129.)

CLXXXI.

WALTER DISSECOMBE (*sic*), a British Protestant of Mountrath, in the Queen's County, sworn and examined, saith, that since the beginning of the rebellion, viz. about the 11th of January, 1641 (O. S.), he was robbed of goods worth 10*l.* by Captain Edmund Butler and Tiegue (*illegible*). This deponent further saith, that he knoweth Mr. John Nicholson and his wife were murdered upon the Sabbath day morning, about seven of the clock, by the servants of Florence FitzPatrick, to whom they (Mr. and Mrs. Nicholson) betook themselves for protection, and this deponent hearing where and how they were murdered, and finding the report true by finding the said parties murdered in a wood near Mountrath in such a cruel and barbarous manner as is hardly to be expressed, and this deponent, desiring to do the neighbourly and Christian office to bury them in the best manner he was then able, he was pursued to all extremity of his life because he tried to bury them, and the rebels came to his house with their swords drawn to dispatch him, asking in Irish 'where that English churl was that buried Nicolson and his wife,' and they sought him all day in the neighbouring houses, thrusting their swords into the hay to see if they could find him, but it pleased God to offer an unexpected occasion to draw him from his own house at the instant they thought him there, and his life was saved by betaking himself to Maryborough. He heard that they inquired whether the dogs and crows had as yet devoured Nicolson and his wife, and it was answered they had not, for they were buried by Disskcome, whereupon they (the Irish Catholics) professed he should 'need to-morrow someone to bury himself.'

WALTER DISSKCOME +

Jurat. 11*th April*, 1642,
RANDALL ADAMS.
ROGER PUTTOCK.

CLXXXII.

ANNE SOUTHWELL, late of Ballenekilly, county of Limerick, widow, relict of Captain John Southwell, lately slain by the rebels, duly sworn and examined before us, deposeth and saith, that about Christmas last, and divers times since the beginning of the present rebellion, she was robbed and forcibly despoiled of her goods and chattels worth 1,472*l*. 10*s*. She further saith, that she was robbed of all her goods, quick and dead, by the hands and means of William Cullum of Lismoly, county Limerick, gent., and his eldest son; James FitzGerald of Kilkenane in said county, gent., Edmund Pursell of Ballincullane, gent., and their soldiers to the number of 800. She also saith, that her said husband was, on Easter Tuesday last, shot and killed by an ambush of rebels at Grange bridge in the said county as he was on his way to relieve Newcastle. She saith that one Maurice Herbert of Rathkeale, in the said county, Esquire, about Candlemas last did hang three Englishmen of Rathkeale, but their names she knoweth not. She also saith, that Mrs. Anne Woodhall, wife to Mr. Woodhall, gent., with her daughter Anne, and Josias Walker, gent. and his wife; Anne Gerald, wife to Maurice Fitz-Gerald, Mr. Jennings, a minister, Mr. Escott and his wife, late of the Castle of Mahonagh, with divers others, unknown, to the number of forty, were stripped naked by Thomas McGibbon of Mahonagh, gent., and his followers, who hanged eight of those so stript parties unknown. This act was done about Christmas last. She also saith, that she saw two letters under the hands of Richard Stevenson of Dunmoylan, and Maurice Herbert of Rathkeale, Esq., aforesaid, therein persuading this deponent's husband, to whom they directed the said letters, to change his religion and join with them, and that suddenly too, for otherwise it would not serve his turn, 'notwithstanding all our.puritan helps that we were likely to have out of England and Scotland.' She lastly saith, that Mr. Thomas Philips of Ballyea, in said county, formerly a reputed Protestant, since this rebellion is turned Papist.

ANNE SOUTHWELL.

Jurat. coram nobis,
29th Sept. 1642,
PHIL. BISSE.
RO. SOUTHWELL.

Note.

This deponent was Anne, eldest daughter and co-heir of Sir John Dowdall of Kilfinny Castle, in the county Limerick, by his wife Elizabeth, daughter of Sir Thomas Southwell of Poylong in the county Cork, Captain John Southwell was the eldest son of Edmund Southwell, Esq., of Castle Mattress, in the county Limerick, by Catherine, daughter and heir of Garret Herbert of Rathkeale, in the same county. Thus Captain Southwell and the Herberts of Rathkeale (the descendants of an Elizabethan or early Tudor colonist) were relatives, which accounts for their warning him to change his religion. Captain Southwell died *s. p.*, his widow Ann married William Piggott, Esq., of Kilfinny, by whom she had a son and heir, John Piggott, and two daughters, Martha married to Lieutenant-Colonel Stamer of Clare, and Elizabeth married Thomas FitzGerald of Woodhouse. The Rathkeale Herberts lost almost everything in 1649, and the family is now extinct in the male line. The last notice I have been able to find of them is in the will of Morgan O'Connell of Kilfinny in 1747 (my great-great-grandfather), which mentions his 'nephew Garret Herbert of Rathkeale.' For Lady Dowdall's curious account of her spirited defence of Kilfinny Castle against the Irish in 1642, see the appendix to Belling's *History of the Irish Catholic Confederation,* edited by Mr. Gilbert as before mentioned. One of her five daughters and co-heiresses marrying Sir Hardress Waller, that regicide's life was spared after the Restoration in consideration of the Dowdall's loyalty.

CLXXXIII.

THOMAS SOUTHWELL, of Cloughkeltred, in the county of Limerick, gent., duly sworn and examined, deposeth and saith, that he was robbed and despoiled by the rebels of goods and chattels worth 1,854*l.* He further saith, that Thomas Whitby of Rathkeale, husbandman, James Bowerman of the same, husbandman, Edward Parsons of the same, labourer, John Gale, tailor, John Sworder, labourer, Maurice Branagh, an Irish Protestant, Tiegue McConogher, of the same, an Irish Papist, yeoman, but true to him (this deponent), Edward Harding of the same, were taken away about Lady Day last and half hanged by Maurice Herbert of Rathkeale, and Garret Herbert, his son, a captain of rebels, who threw three of the said English into the river Deele; also he saith, that a poor English maid of Rathkeale was thrown off the bridge into the said river, by the said Herbert's soldiers, and she swimming to the shore was beaten off by them, and brained with stones. Not long after one Stubbs, near Rathkeale, a fellmonger, was murdered, as is conceived, by the said Herbert's directions; also he saith, that about the beginning of September last one Robert Rice of Rathkeale, gent., was murdered in his bed, after quarter given to the Castle of Callow where he was, also Thomas Russell and Thomas Eggshill of the same, husbandmen, were murdered at Rathkeale by Stephenson's followers immediately after the report came that Oliver Stephenson was killed in battle.

THOS. SOUTHWELL.

Jurat. coram nobis,
14*th* October, 1642,
 PHIL. BISSE.
 TRISTRAM WHITCOMBE.
 RO. SOUTHWELL.

Note.

Thomas Southwell was the younger brother of the husband of the former deponent and the fifth son of Edward Southwell by Catherine Herbert of Rathkeale. For his services in 1641 he was appointed Commissioner for the precinct of Limerick in 1653, and in the following year was High Sheriff for the counties of Limerick, Kerry, and Clare. After the Restoration he was created a baronet, and from him descends the present Lord Southwell.

CLXXXIV.

DAME BARBARA BROWNE, late of the town and parish of the Hospital, in the barony of Small, in the county of Limerick, duly sworn and examined on behalf of Sir John Browne, Knt., her husband, deposeth and saith, that on the 1st day of January, 1641 (O. S.), and since, by the means of the present rebellion in Ireland, her said husband lost, or was robbed of goods and chattels, &c., worth 3,800*l*. She also saith, that the said lands and house of Hospital, oxen, cows, and steer were taken away by Murtogh O'Brian of Duharra, of Upper Ormond, in the county of Tipperary, gent., and John O'Kennedy, of the same, on the 1st of January aforesaid, and the horses and mares were taken away about the same time by John Lacy of Karrigkelle (*sic*), near the said Hospital, gent., Maurice Hurly of Knocklong, eldest son of Thomas Hurley of Knocklong, Esq., and the household stuff was taken away by Maurice Baggot of Baggotstown, in the same county, gent., about the 21st of March last past, and Dermot O'Brian of Coonagh, gent., and his followers; another part of the household stuff left at the castle of Lough Gur, near Any, was taken away by the Lord of Castleconnel, Captain Pierce Walsh of the Abbey of Owny, Esq., in the said county, and their followers. The rest that was kept at the Castle of Limerick was taken when the said castle was taken by the besiegers with General Purcell, &c. The corn in the haggard was taken away by Morris Baggot and Dermot O'Brien aforesaid, on the 1st of March, 1641, the corn in the ground, as she is informed, was reaped and taken away by means of the said Lord Castleconnell, the houses were demolished by rebels whose names she knoweth not.

She also saith, that the Castle of Castletown, where she fled for refuge, was besieged upon the 26th of March, 1642, by Luke Purcell of Croagh, Lieut.-General; Captain John FitzGerald, second brother to Thomas FitzGerald of the Glyn, Esquire, Lieut.-Col. Garret Purcell of Curragh, and divers others to the number of two or three hundred rebels, who lay close to the castle, so that the besieged could not stir out; during which time she often heard the besiegers say that they had the King's authority for what they did. During the siege one Thomas Hill, shoemaker, of Castletown, was killed by a shot from the besiegers, and at length for want of water the place was yielded up, about the 13th of May following; having been besieged five weeks and odd days, the quarter was for their lives and wearing clothes, and a few other commodities. After the quarter was given and taken, this deponent was conveyed to Cork by a sufficient convoy, the said Patrick Purcell conducting her with wonderful civility all the way, and as they were going along the said Purcell, in a serious manner, told this deponent that he had been twice excommunicated before he would take up arms, and that he would rather suffer for his religion than take up arms as he did, if he thought that there was not the king's authority for it. She also saith, that being brought near Macroom, the Lord Castleconnell, her nephew, mightily tempted her to mass, promising her thereupon a restitution of what she had lost, which she denying, he wished her to leave her children with him, that they might be bred up Catholics under him, promising her withal that none but Papists should possess a foot of land again in Ireland. And further she cannot depose.

BARBARA BROWNE.

Jurat. coram nobis, 4th Feb. 1642,
PERCY SMITH.
PHIL. BISSE.

Note.

This deponent was the daughter of John Boyle, Bishop of Cork, and the wife of Sir John Browne, Knt., son of Sir Thomas Browne, who had a grant in 1604 of the preceptory or Hospital of Awney, in the county of Limerick (a foundation of the Knights of St. John), with the lands around it. The wife of Sir Thomas Browne was maternally descended from an old Anglo-Irish family, named Brown, settled in Limerick and Kerry before the twelfth century (and not related in blood to her husband, who was an Englishman), who were Masters or Warders of Awney before 1560. The sister of Sir John Browne was the mother of Lord Castleconnell, whom Dame Barbara Browne therefore calls her ' nephew.' Her only daughter Elizabeth, heiress by survival of her brother to Hospital, married Captain Thomas Browne of Molahiff, county Kerry, and had by him a daughter, who married her cousin Nicholas, second Lord Kenmare, ancestor of the present Earl of Kenmare. Castletown, the seat of Sir Hardress Waller, Lady Dowdall's son-in-law, was a rich booty for the rebels if the immensely long bill for damages in the form of a deposition, furnished by its owner in 1644-9, be not exaggerated. The inventory of lands, houses, corn, hay, cows, horses, household furniture, &c., in this deposition of Sir Hardress Waller's covers five or six pages of the Limerick book, and over each one of them the pen has been drawn.

It would have been too unmerciful to inflict the reading of this tedious inventory on the king and parliament. But to modern readers it has some interest as giving us an idea of the fine and useful articles in an Irish gentleman's country house in 1641, and their separate money values, compared with the value of similar articles at the present day. The following are a few of the items:—

	£
Hangings and tapestry for drawing-room	100.
Eiderdown and feather beds and flock do., with bolsters, pillows, blankets, rugs, and caddows	80.
Canapies (*sic*) and vallances	15.
One dozen of Turkey work cushions	3.
Do. of chairs	26.
Half a dozen very rich cushions	6.
Half a dozen cushions of satin richly embroidered	8.
Six green broad cloth stools richly embroidered, with a large carpet, and cupboard cloth richly embroidered	16.
Three large cloth carpets, and one dozen of chair covers, same cloth, three cupboard cloths of same consisting of sixteen yards of broad cloth	5.
One large couch with bed and bolsters of rich taffeta	5.
Two very rich Turkey carpets	10.
Four copper vessels for brewing, washing, &c.	26.
Four iron pots valued at	2.
A great iron jack, being a thing hard to be got in this kingdom	3.
In white earthenware of all sort, basin, ewers, and candlesticks	10.
One great chest of books	60.
One pair of great bossed andirons of brass and two pair bound with brass	10.
Three pairs of plain iron andirons, half a dozen spits, and four great dripping-pans	3.

It is strange to find an 'iron jack' costing more than half as much as a 'Turkey carpet.' The 'caddows' in the first item must have been counterpanes, the word was used for such articles in Ireland until the middle of the last century. The 'Turkey work' must have been a kind of 'crewel work,' the former name being the most appropriate to describe the useless expenditure of woman's time, lounging on one embroidered cushion to embroider another. Every pound in the above probably represented ten of our present money.

CLXXXV.

BEATRICE, the wife of CHRISTOPHER HOPDITCH, late of Esuddogh (*sic*) in the county of Clare, sworn and examined, saith, that since the beginning of the present rebellion, that is to say about Christmas, 1641, this deponent and her said husband were robbed and dispossessed, at Esuddogh and Kilfenora, of horses, cattle, corn, provision, and other things, their goods and chattels, worth 150*l.*, by the rebels, John Anderson now of Esuddogh, yeoman, Dermot O'Brian of Dromore Castle in the county of Clare, Esquire, nephew to the Earl of Thomond, Moyle MacBrody of the parish of Inshicrony in the said county, gent., Cahil O'Roghan of the same, gent., Garrald O'Flannigan of Kilfenora, gent., and their soldiers and servants, whose names this deponent cannot express. And further saith, that her husband and she being for safety of their lives fled to the castle of Inshicrony, they were there robbed and deprived of their household stuff, provisions, and the rest of their goods and chattels, worth fifty pounds, on the 21st of March, 1641, and then and there her husband was cruelly murdered by John O'Grady, James Oge O'Grady, Brian O'Grady, Loghlin Oge O'Grady, Gilladoffe O'Shaughnessy, William O'Shaughnessy, and Cahill O' (*illegible*), all of the parish of Inshicrony, gent., and by divers others of the neighbours thereabouts, whose names she cannot remember now. And further saith, that the rebels aforesaid, or some of them, also at that time and at Inshicrony aforesaid, cruelly murdered one Peter Newman, this deponent's brother-in-law, Richard Adams and his wife, whom they undertook to convey away, but murdered her on the way; Anthony Davies, Robert Hart, Robert Blenkinsopp, John Holland, Richard Blagrove, Thomas Watson, a servant of Mr. Heathcote of Inshicrony and William Abbot, all English Protestants, and proper able men, and they also murdered the wife of Thomas Watkins, and her two children, and another child of William (*blank*) the turner, and generally robbed and stripped of all their means all the Protestants in the country thereabouts, and carried arms with, for, and amongst the other rebels, and committed divers outrages and cruelties.

And at length this deponent for more safety fled to the castle of Ballially in the said county of Clare, and she and about a hundred more Protestants were there from about the 20th of June, 1642, last past, until about the 4th of September following, besieged by the rebels aforesaid, and by Connor O'Brien of Leminagh, and Christopher O'Brian, brother to the Lord of Inchiquin, Dermot O'Brian of Dromore, nephew to the Earl of Thomond, Connor O'Brian, eldest son to Sir Donnell O'Brian, Knight, Loghlin McLoughlin near to Kilfenora, and a great number of rebel soldiers, whose names she cannot express. But she often observed seven several colours displayed and flying amongst them; which said rebels having brought with them from Limerick a brass piece of ordnance, did therewith make several shots against the castle of Ballially, and prepared and brought near the same castle baskets of earth, and engines, called sows, and thereby, and by their shots against the said castle those within it durst not go out, and were driven to that extremity for want of victuals that they were glad to eat the flesh of horses, dogs, and to feed upon nettles and other weeds, so that divers sickened and died, and some that had five or six children in the beginning would have none left alive at the end of the week. And at length the assailant rebels, as it seemed, growing partly weary of all their attempts, came to a parley with those in the castle, and offered terms of fair quarter to be given upon surrender. And so much and so far that the said Christopher Brian, by his adulations and fair speeches, prevailed and persuaded with one Maurice Cuffe, who was one of the chief gentlemen in the castle, that he and the wife of Mr. Winter Bridgeman, and one Mr. Hill, Thomas Cuffe and John Cruise, that they went out to the said Christopher Brian and the rest of the rebels. But they were no sooner gone a little out of the castle but that the rebels laid violent hands on the said Morrice Cuffe, Mrs. Winter Bridgeman, and Mr. Hill and made them prisoners. But the other two, viz. the said Thomas Cuffe and John Crewse, suddenly overran them and fled back into the castle, and the other three were kept prisoners for ten days or thereabouts. Then the rebels erected a gallows in sight of the castle, whither they brought the prisoners, threatening to hang them if those in the castle would not surrender it. But that way prevailed not, and they took away the prisoners again and kept them in great misery for a good space. At length when the said Morrice Cuffe writ a letter to the castle, telling in what misery he and the other prisoners were, and what little hope there was of relief, those that then commanded in the castle, and others therein, pressed by extreme want of meat, and seeing no means of relief, took quarter to go away with their lives and half their goods, and so did depart away, and left the castle to the rebellious enemy.

And then this deponent being very sick and weak, getting to an

Irishman's house near there was there kept for some time. But being laboured to go to mass, she and her children privately escaped away, and at length, though she was very weak, got to the castle of Barnesmore in the night, and from thence got to Galway, and from thence by sea to Dublin. And further saith, that in the acting of cruelties the rebellious women were more fierce and cruel than the men. And amongst the rest one Sarah O'Brian, sister to the said Dermot O'Brian, undertook to convey out of the castle of Dromore the said Peter Newman and his wife, this deponent's sister, and their family, so as she might have their goods. But when she had gotten their goods, she suffered the barbarous rebells there first to cut off the said Peter Newman's arm, and afterwards extremely to torture him, and at length to shoot him to death, and after the said Sarah had stripped the said Peter's wife and children of their clothes turned them away, exposed to the dangers of those persons whom, as she told this deponent, she had hired to kill them. But they having notice of her bloody intentions did by God's assistance escape the danger by going another way.

BEATRICE + HOPDITCH.

Jurat. 24th May, 1643,
    JOHN STERNE.
    HEN. BRERETON.

Note.

Andrew Chaplin, a Protestant clergyman, one of the besieged in Ballially Castle, sworn and examined on the 12th of May, 1643, before Commissioners Bisse and J. Wallis, made a long deposition, in all things confirming Mrs. Hopditch's evidence. He says that—

"About the 6th of August, 1642, the said besiegers of the castle of Ballially, or some of them near the said castle murdered or caused to be murdered the undernamed persons, namely Adam Baker late of Ballymacagill, in the county of Clare, yeoman, Ambrose Webster, miller, of Inish in the said county, John Walker, yeoman, of Lisson in the said county, Thomas White, mason, late of Knockderry in the said county, John Twisden, yeoman, late of Ballyvanny in the said county, John Sutche, yeoman, late of Ballyally, John Burgess, yeoman, late of Inish aforesaid, Robert Harte, yeoman, of the same place (*illegible*), whereof being murdered, and then stripped, their corpses lay about the ground not far from the castle walls, and were not suffered by means of the said parties to be buried, until the dogs and crows did pick and eat up their carcasses."

CLXXXVI.

ELIZABETH HARRIS, relict of Sir Thomas Harris, Knt., late of Tralee in the county of Kerry, sworn and examined, deposeth and saith, that since the beginning of the present rebellion her said husband, Sir Thomas Harris, and she were by means of the rebellion despoiled and robbed of their plate, money, jewels, household stuff, beasts, money, cattle, horses, and other goods and chattels amounting to the sum of 2,000*l*. And that she by means of the present rebellion is deprived and expelled from the possession of rents and profits of lands assigned and appointed to her for life for her jointure amounting to 500*l*. per an., one year's profits being already lost, and the future profits she is likely to lose and be deprived of until a peace be established. And she further saith, that, as she is credibly informed and hath too great cause to believe, her said husband, Sir Thomas Harris, after he had defended the castle of Tralee for six months, or thereabouts, against the violent assaults and attempts of the rebels, he was driven and exposed to such wants, that he drank puddle and corrupted water, and by that means and other wants he died, and that after his death the remainder of the men that assisted him, wanting a governor and means, were forced to leave or surrender the said castle, being not able any longer to keep the same.

ELIZA. HARRIS.

Jurat. Jan. 4th, 1642,
JOHN WATSON.
WM. ALDRICH.

Note.

This deponent was Elizabeth, daughter of Sir Anthony Forrest, Knt., of Huntingdon, and wife of Arthur Denny, Esq., of Tralee Castle, eldest son of Sir Edward Denny, Knt., by his wife Margaret Edgecombe, daughter of Piers Edgecombe of Mount Edgecombe, and maid of honour to Queen Elizabeth. Sir Edward Denny, the cousin german of Raleigh and Sir Humphrey Gilbert, had obtained a grant of Desmond's chief castle and town of Tralee, with a fine estate around it, for his gallant services against the rebels in 1570-84. His eldest son, Arthur Denny, died in 1619, leaving a son and heir, Sir Edward Denny of Tralee Castle in 1641, and M.P. for the county, who had married in 1625 Ruth, daughter of Roper, Lord Baltinglas, and cousin maternally of Sir Philip Sidney. Sir Edward

DEPOSITIONS. 103

Denny had by this lady nine children (from his eldest son descends the present Sir Edward Denny, Bart.), the youngest, a daughter, was only a few weeks old when the rebellion began in Ulster. His mother, who made the above deposition, had married secondly Sir Thomas Harris, Knt., of the old family of his name at Cornworthy, Devonshire, and when Sir Edward Denny went to join the troops under Sir William St. Leger in Cork (having sent his wife and young children to England) he left his castle of Tralee to the care of his stepfather. Lord Kerry was appointed governor of Kerry by St. Leger, and at his request Sir Edward Denny, who had a garrison at Castlemaine, delivered the ward of that place to Captain Thomas Spring, by whom it was soon after surrendered to the Irish. Pierce Ferriter, owner of a good estate and the Ferriters or Blasquet Islands on the west coast of Kerry, was appointed captain of some troops collected in that neighbourhood, whom Lord Kerry supplied with arms, but in a few weeks Ferriter carried off both men and arms to the rebel side, and proceeded to besiege Tralee Castle. He was a man of considerable ability, and a long poem in Irish, written by him on the death of a son of the Knight of Kerry, who died in Spain *circa* 1640, has been translated by Crofton Croker and published in the Percy Society publications. Lord Kerry fled to Cork, and from thence to England, in February, 1641-2. His brothers joined the rebels. The depositions here given and a document in the appendix show the sufferings of the besieged at Tralee. Dr. Smith when writing his history of Kerry in 1750 had access to an interesting journal kept by Elkanah Knight, a steward of Sir Edward Denny's, who was in the castle during the siege. This MS. has of late years been lost or stolen, but from Smith's abstract of its contents we are able to test and supplement some of the following depositions.

CLXXXVII.

STEPHEN LOVE, late of the town and parish of Killarney, in the barony of Magunihy, within the county of Kerry, a British Protestant, duly sworn and examined before us by virtue of a commission bearing date 5th of March, 1641, concerning the robberies and spoils since this rebellion committed upon the British and Protestants in the province of Munster, deposeth and saith, that on or about the 15th of November, 1641, Edmund Hussey of Rath, in the said county, Esquire, steward and overseer to Sir Valentine Browne

Bart., now under age, came to Killarney aforesaid, and there warned the English inhabitants of the same to consult together and muster there under and according to the tenor of their respective leases, being bound by them severally to have so many men in readiness in times of open insurrection, which being then denied, amongst others, by this deponent, fearing he and the rest thereby to be betrayed of their firearms, and also because the Papists generally deceived great statesmen, this deponent then and there told the said Hussey that he and the rest (of the Protestants) had doubtless reason to mistrust them. The said Hussey then made answer, ' *This national distinction will breed a national quarrel,*' and pressing them further saith, ' *Nay, and it shall breed a quarrel.*' This deponent saith that since that time the said Hussey has gone into actual open rebellion and is one of the committee for the said county.

From the best information and intelligence this deponent could learn, the said Hussey was from time to time a messenger between the enemy and Sir Thomas Harris, and the rest of the English in the castle of Traloe, who were besieged from the 14th of February, 1641, until the Christmas following, during which time the English in the castle endured extreme misery, being at least five or six hundred souls when they went into the same, and there were three hundred of them perished through the extremity of the siege, some of them being driven to eat bran and tallow, and others raw hides; this was occasioned by the hands and means of Donnel MacCarthy of Ballinearrig (*sic*) in the same county, gent., then colonel in the said siege, Captain Florence MacFineen, commonly called *Sugan*, since killed in rebellion, Donogh MacFineen of Ardtully, Esquire, Pierse Ferriter of Ferriter's Island, in the said county, gentleman, then captain of a company, Tiegue MacDermot and Cormac Carty of Tiernagouse, in the said county, gentlemen, Captain Morris MacEligot of Ballymacelgott (*sic*), in the said county, gentleman, Walter Hussey of Castle Gregory, gentleman, Phelim MacFineen of Tullaghie, gent., Dermot O'Dingle of Ballinacourty, gent., Nicholas MacThomas of Ballykealy, gent., Garret MacPatrick, *alias* Pierse, near Ballinfroyne in the same county, gent., Garret MacJames FitzGerald of Ballymora, gent., John FitzGerald, commonly called John *Atlea* (*i.e.*, of the hills or sides of the hills) of Glandine, gent., Edmund FitzMaurice of Listohill (*i.e.*, Listowel), gent., James Knowde of Abbeydorna, Esquire, Francis Knowde, his brother, of the same, gent., Pierse FitzJames FitzPierse of Ardfert, gent., Donogh MacGillicuddy of Castlecorr, gent., Arthur O'Leary of Kilcours (*illegible*), Owen

O'Sullivan, *alias* O'Sullivan Mor of Dunkerron in the same county, Esquire, Donell O'Sullivan of Coolmagort, gent., Owen Donell MacCarty, *alias Moyle* of Dunguile, gent., Owen MacDermot O'Sullivan of Formoyle (in Iveragh), gent. Fineen MacDermot MacFineen of Kenmare, gent., now high sheriff of the same county of Kerry, Tiegue O'Donoghue, *alias* O'Donoghue of Glanflesk in the same county, gent., and Jeffrey, Daniel, and Tiegue O'Donoghue, his sons, of the same, gent., Cormack Reagh MacCarthy of Lyshingoune in the same, gent., and Donogh MacCormac, his brother, gent., Donell MacMoirtaghe, *alias* Moriartaghe, of Castle Drum, gent. Owen MacFerris of Ballymalis, in the same county, gent., and John and Donnell Ferris of the same, gentlemen, Thomas MacTirlogh of Noghoval, in the same county, gent. Tirlogh MacDermot O'Connor, son and heir of Dermot McTirlogh of Ballygowan, in the said county, gent., Thomas Plunkett of Gorthainvoga (*sic*) in the same, gent., John and Patrick Plunkett, his brothers, of the same, gentlemen, Richard McElgott of Ratanny, in the said county, gent. John Field, doctor of physick, a most pestilent and pernicious enemy to the English nation, and one of the Committee for the said county. Florence MacCarthy of Castle Logh (*illegible*), governor of the said county. James Browne, gent., of Ross, Morris FitzEdmund of Clonratt, gent., Edward Spring of Killaghie, gent., Thomas Spring of Stradbally, Esquire, Daniel Creagh of Castlemaine, gent., John Pierse of Killiny, gent., one of the attornies of his Majesty's Court of Common Pleas, and (*illegible*) of the said county's Council, Caroll O'Sugrue of Castle Curr, in the said county, gent. (*illegible*), Mortogh McEgan of Cam (*illegible*), in the said county, gent. The above named parties, either in their own proper persons or by their counsel and assistance, were at several times at the siege of Tralee, as also at the sieges of other castles in the said county, where the English betook themselves for safety.

This deponent further saith, that about Easter the above named Phelim MacFineen MacCarthy, being exasperated against the English for the death of Captain *Sugan*, who about that time was killed in open rebellion, hard by Cork, came to the castle of Ross in the same county Kerry, where divers English Protestants were living, and then and there drew and hauled out of the castle the undernamed persons, namely Thomas Whittell and Margery his wife, two old people past three score years of age, or thereabouts, Patrick Haysam, and Mary his wife, then great with child, John Heard and his wife, George Linegar, the widow Hawkins, aged three score and ten years, and to the number of nine others, who no sooner came a little distance from the castle, than they were all immediately stripped by the means of the said Phelim, and kept up close and naked in the market-place of Killarney, and afterwards being conveyed two miles from the town, they were in a most inhuman manner murdered, one of the women being buried alive.

About the latter end of November last, this deponent being then in the castle of Ballycarthy, where the said Florence came to take possession of the same from Robert Blennerhassett, Esquire, he then observed these particulars following; first, the said Florence then and there produced a list of all the names of the lords and commons assembled in their parliament at Kilkenny, and then in this deponent's presence did aver that Nicholas Plunket, Esq., and counsellor-at-law, was speaker of the said parliament; he likewise produced a rough draft of the several acts concluded in the said assembly, namely, that all manner of persons, of what degree, state, or condition soever, should take the oath of union and association in this general cause, as they termed it, otherwise to be dealt withal as enemies and accounted of the malignant party, and to maintain the Roman Catholic cause, to the uttermost of their skill and endeavour, and not to embrace any particular pardon until such time as a general pardon was granted for the whole kingdom, &c., &c. . . . During the siege of the castle of Traly aforesaid, William Bolton of Glanoroght, in the said county, carrier, Lawrence Tristram of Traly aforesaid, gaoler, John Abraham of Ballycarthy, husbandman, English Protestants, were hanged at Traly, by direction or appointment of the said persons or some of them, likewise John Carty of Cloghane in the said county, husbandman, being sent from Ballycarthy aforesaid by Captain John Hasset to Cork to Sir Edward Denny to give intelligence how the English and Protestants stood in the county, at his coming back was apprehended by the abovenamed rebels or some of them and then and there was hanged at Traly aforesaid. This deponent lastly saith, that John Pierse, above named, John Madden of Rattoo, in the said county, gentlemen, Christopher Holcome of the same (*illegible*), and his wife Ellen Holcome, and their daughter Anne, Richard Curtis, yeoman, of the same, Richard Linegar and his wife Mary, of the same, being formerly English Protestants, are since this rebellion turned Papists, and further deposeth not.

Jurat. coram nobis, 3rd Feb. 1642,
    PHIL. BISSE.
    THOS. BETTESWORTH.

DEPOSITIONS.   107

Note.

This appears to be a copy made by the Commissioners. It is signed by them, but not by Stephen Love. The omitted portion merely relates to the proceedings of the Confederation at Kilkenny, as told by Florence MacCarthy to Robert Blennerhassett, after the surrender of Ballycarthy. Sir Valentine Browne, second baronet, the son of Sir Valentine Browne, by Mary, sister of Donogh Lord Muskerry, was a child of three years old when the rebellion broke out.

CLXXXVIII.

MICHAEL VINES, late of the town and precinct of Tralee, in the county of Kerry, shoemaker, a British Protestant, duly sworn and examined before us by virtue of his Majesty's commission, deposeth and saith, that about the last of January, 1641 (O. S.), he lost, was robbed, or forcibly despoiled of his goods and chattels, worth 340*l.*, part consisting of debts due by Papists who are now out in open rebellion, as Walter Hussey of Castle Gregory, gent., Garret McJames of Ballymacthomas, gent., John MacJames of Ballymacequim, gent., John Huggan of Lixnaw, tailor, Patrick Purcell of Croagh, in the county Limerick, gent., John *a Clee* of Caragh, in the county of Kerry, gent., Conagher O'Dynan of Liselton, Dermot O'Dingle of Ballinacourty, gent., Thomas MacEdmund of Dunlow, gent., John MacVaine (*sic*) of Ballymacthomas, gent., Morrish FitzGerald of Gallerush (*sic*), gent., Pierce Ferriter of Ballyferriter, gent., Nicholas Trant of Ventry, gent., John Golden (*sic*) of Ventry, gent., Patrick Trant of Ventry, gent., all of the said county of Kerry, and divers others, and therefore this deponent cannot get any satisfaction. This deponent further saith, that he and his wife and seven children were forced to go into the castle of Tralee in the possession of Sir Edward Denny (*illegible*) there was the short castle of the freehold of Stephen Rice of Dingledecuish, gentleman, a Papist and out in rebellion where they were closely blocked up and besieged nearly three quarters of a year by Colonels Donogh Oge MacCarthy of (*illegible*) and Edmund FitzMaurice of Ardagh, Esq., Captain Pierse Ferriter of Ballyferriter, Esq., Capt. Dermot O'Dingle of Ballincourty, Esq., Capt. Walter Hussey of Castle Gregory, Esq., Capt. Donnell McMortogh of Castle Druim, Capt. Morrish McElgot of Ballymac Elgot, Esq., Capt. Garrott MacJames of Ballymacthomas, Esq., Capt. John FitzGerald of Caragh, *alias* John A Clee, Esq., Capt. MacFineen MacCarthy of Clonaragh, Esq., Capt. Florence MacFineen MacCarthy, *alias* Captain Sugan, Esq., Capt. James Browne of Killarney, Esq., Capt. Florence MacCarthy of Pallasmor, Esq., Capt. O'Sullivan Mor, Esq., Captain MacGillacuddy, Esq., who was formerly a Protestant, but is since turned Papist, near Bally (*illegible*), and Captain O'Donoghue of the Glins near Killarney (who, as it was credibly reported, undertook the undermining of the said castle), and divers others, to the number of about a thousand armed men, and this deponent saith, that during the time of the siege they were undermined at four quarters of the castle, and the warders within countermined against them again.

And further he saith, that they (the Irish) brought four sows which the warders of the said castle broke and burnt killing those within them, and again they (the Irish) brought a great piece, and shot fourteen shots at the castle, and beat down the battlements of the said castle, and this deponent likewise saith, that he heard Captain Pierce Ferriter and other rebels did say, that they had the King's Commission for what they did, and therewithal he sent a copy of the same unto the warders of the said castle, and said that we were the rebels and those (with him) the king's subjects, and further, he, this deponent, saith, that they were forced to eat raw salt hides, that did stink, and to drink water that was as black as ink, and as thick as if it were thickened with flour, and other water there was full of yellow clay, and he saith, that there died of want, or were killed by the enemy to the number of at least two hundred men, women, and children, and during the siege of the said castle there was killed outside it, as this deponent was credibly informed by some of the rebels themselves, the number of three hundred. And he also saith, that the castle was yielded upon quarter for their lives, and a suit of clothes a piece, and that (*illegible*) Bradfield of Tralee, yeoman, John McMorrish of (*illegible*), yeoman, John O'Lenane of Tralee, yeoman, John McMurrogh of Ballycarty, yeoman, who before this rebellion were Protestants, have since turned Papists, and go under the rebel's colours and do fight for the rebels against the English, and further he saith that two that were English Protestants before this war have since turned Papists, and convoyed powder to the rogues for using against the English castles, their names are these, John Hollis and George Hollis of the Island of Kerry, brothers, and yeomen.

He also saith, that one John Williams, *alias* John Roe, heretofore of the town of Tralee, servant to one Thomas Day of Tralee, and since one of the warders of the short castle of Tralee aforesaid, about midsummer last stole forth out of the ward, and ran to the enemy that besieged the said castle, and discovered to them the designs of the English of both castles concerning the prey of cattle near the castles which they had gotten for their relief, and had it not been for the aforesaid discovery by which their design was defeated and they of the castle for want of provision enforced to yield (*sic*) two months sooner, which John Williams from that time went and bare arms amongst the rebels. This deponent also saith, that he was credibly informed by many that John Blennerhassett of Ballycarty, *alias* Captain John Hassett, about Christmas Day, 1641, when the enemy was going from Castlemaine towards Tralee Castle, with a piece of ordnance for the battery of the said castle, the carriage of the piece then failing on the way, did send a carpenter to the carriage to mend the same for the enemy. This deponent also saith, that Robert Blennerhassett of Ballycarty aforesaid, father to the said John, said to this deponent, that the Irish never did him any hurt, his ground being ploughed and sown by the rebels his tenants, who robbed many of the English thereabouts, but as for him (Vines) and others of the English Protestants, he, Robert Blennerhassett, said that the ground was the worse that the English trod upon it. This examt. also observed that Robert Blennerhassett would suffer harmless the Irish to cut whatever wood they wanted for their use, and never contradict them, but that if any of the English went to the wood to cut but a stick of wood, then they would be presently threatened and beaten by his servants whom he had appointed and who were very rebels.

This day also came before us NICHOLAS ROBERTS, late of Ballymaceligot, within the county of Kerry, husbandman, who being duly sworn and examined, saith, that the deposition concerning the names of the besiegers of Tralee Castle are true. The deponents (Vines and Roberts) also say that about the last day of November, about the time that the castle of Ballycarthy was yielded to the rebels, they saw these persons sworn upon the bible and on their knees to the oath of association with the rebels, viz. Robert Blennerhassett aforesaid, John West of Kilcow, Esq., James Conway of Cloghane, gent., Henry Huddlestone of the Grange, in the parish of Ratass, gent., before Charles MacCarthy Mor of the Pallace, Esq., Donell

Oge MacCarthy near Killarney, Esq., Dermot O'Dingle, Esq.,
Commissioners of the association at Ballycarty Castle.

          MICHAEL VINES.
          NICHOLAS + ROBERTS.
Jurat. coram nobis, 18*th June*, 1643,
 PHILIP BISSE.
 THOMAS ELWELL.
       Note.

 There were two castles in the town of Tralee in 1641, the larger or 'great castle,' as it was called, being a 'restoration' of the old castle of the FitzHenrys and the FitzGeralds, Earls of Desmond, which had been destroyed in the wars of 1580-1602. Two short entries in the diary before quoted (*v.* Introduction, p. 52) kept by Sir Edward Denny, which records the general feeling about Stafford's advent in Ireland, are as follows:—

 "22d of December, 1627, I finished this great castell and came with my mother to live in it.

 "20th November, 1629. My wife and I began housekeeping in this castell."

 It stood nearly on the site of the present Denny Street, a rather handsome outlet of Tralee, backed by the present Sir E. Denny's demesne, and a fine range of mountains between Tralee and Killarney. The 'Short Castle' mentioned in the deposition as the freehold of Stephen Rice, a member of an old Anglo-Irish family settled in Kerry, as far back as the eleventh century, stood a little to the west of the larger fortress, on the east side of the present 'Square' of Tralee. It was forfeited with large estates in the west and north-west of Kerry in 1649, although the Rices do not appear to have had any share in the outrages committed by the rebels. But they were, as they have always been (until one of the junior branch, the ancestor of Lord Monteagle, conformed in the last century), Roman Catholics, and Stephen Rice had been M.P. for Kerry in the troubled Parliament of 1613. In 1634 his two sons were M.P.'s for Dingle, but five years after, in Wentworth's last Parliament, they were unseated, and Christopher Roper and Sir George Blundell, Englishmen, utter strangers to the borough, were elected in their stead. Robert Blennerhassett, who had been M.P. for Tralee, was also unseated in 1639, and Thomas Maule, with a Henry Osborne, were elected for the same place. Out of the eight members for Kerry and its boroughs in 1639, four were strangers to the county, probably officers in the army, and only one of the remaining four, Sir Valentine Browne, was a Roman Catholic. According to the diary of Elkanagh Knight before mentioned the English and Irish Protestants who had crowded into the 'Great Castell' of Tralee were hearing the church service read on Sunday, the 23rd of January, 1641-2, by the Rev. William Fell and the Rev. Nathaniel Harrison, when the sentinels on the battlements perceived the rebels approaching from the west. The siege continued from that day until the following July or August, when Sir Thomas Harris and many others having died of want and hardship, the unfortunate remnant of the garrison surrendered upon quarter, which appears to have been honourably observed by Ferriter. But before the surrender his soldiers had committed many cruel murders. Knight's diary mentions that on one occasion they took an Englishwoman, and stripping her, broke a hole in the ice on the river and set her standing in it, keeping her there until she was frozen to death or starved in the sight of those within the castle. While the siege went on a certain Henry Lawrence, called by Knight an 'English Roman Catholic,' who if he were not the subsequently well-known president of Cromwell's Council was assuredly a relative of his, kept moving in a rather mysterious fashion between the contending parties. On the strength of his nationality, he was admitted into the great castle, where some movements or words of his arousing the suspicions of the garrison, Sir Thomas Harris ordered him to be arrested and searched, when the following passport was found in his pocket:—

"I have employed this gentleman, Mr. Henry Lawrence, upon some special occasions for the furthering and advancing Catholicism, to go to Tralee, and from thence to Castle Drum, or the camp, wherefore I pray the Irish and English not to molest or hinder him in body or goods. Given under my hand, this 8th of February, 1641.
"PIERCE FERRITER."

He was dismissed from the castle, and appears to have returned to the rebel camp.

His signature and that of Hardress Waller appear to a deed securing the jointure lands of Elizabeth, Lady Harris, before mentioned, the mother of Sir Edward Denny, née Forrest. Her niece, Martha Lyn or Lynn, was the wife of John Blennerhassett, eldest son of Robert of Ballycarty, in 1641. Richard second Earl of Barrymore, whose sister married Sir Arthur Denny, married Martha, daughter of Henry Lawrence. The first husband of Cromwell's mother was a Lynn, and the families of Denny, Waller, Barry, Forrest, Lynn, and Lawrence in 1640-70 were certainly connected by marriage and ties of friendship. That President Henry Lawrence himself played a strangely double part in politics is matter of history, and his religious opinions seem to have been as insincere as his politics.

CLXXXIX.

ARTHUR BLENNERHASSETT, late of Ballycarty, in the county of Kerry, gent., deposeth and saith, that upon the 2nd of February, 1641, or thereabouts, the undernamed persons, gentlemen and freeholders of the said county, in a rebellious and hostile manner, came to besiege the town and castle of Tralee in the said county, namely Florence MacCarthy of Carrigprehane, Esq., since made governor of Kerry, Donnell MacCarthy of Castle Logh, colonel of rebel forces, Edmond FitzMaurice of Tubrid, Esq., Garret FitzGerald of Ballymacdaniel, gent., John FitzGerald of Caharragh, *alias* John *atlea*, gent., Donell Moriarty of Castledrum, gent., Florence MacCarthy of Glanaroght, gent., since killed in actual and open rebellion, Fineen McDermot MacCarty, of Creggane, gent., Owen O'Sullivan, *alias* O'Sullivan Mor, gent., Donogh MacGillacuddy, *alias* O'Sullivan of Castlecurr, gent., Tiegue Donoghue, *alias* O'Donoghue of Killaghie, gent., James Browne of Killarney, gent., Maurice MacElgot of Ballymac Elgot (*sic*), gent., Captain Roger O'Donoghue of Ross, gent., Nicholas MacThomas (a FitzMaurice) of Ballykealy, gent., Garret Pierse of Aghamore, gent., Pierse Ferriter of Ballysybil, gent., Tiegue MacCarthy of Tiernagouse, gent., Walter Hussey of Castle Gregory, gent. This deponent further saith, that the said parties, with their forces, consisting sometimes of three hundred armed men, at other times of five hundred, sometimes of a thousand, continued the siege of the said castle till the beginning of August following, during which siege the English Protestants in the castle, being in number five hundred persons, young and old, or thereabouts, endured much misery, the enemy having cut off all relief from them so that by the time the said castle was delivered up, divers of the besieged men, women, and children, English Protestants, were shot and murdered, namely Lawrence Tristram of Tralee aforesaid, merchant, Hugo Dashwood of the same, shoemaker, Henry Jones of the same, merchant, Edward Westcombe of the same, shoemaker, John Truby, late of Ballymacfine, husbandman, John Dickson of

Portally, shoemaker, Valentine James of Portally, John Gooding of Tralee, yeoman, Jeffrey Bayley, in or near Portally aforesaid, merchant, Lawrence Tristram the elder, gaoler, of Tralee, who was apprehended by the rebels and hanged in the market-place of the said town, Joseph Collier of Ballyvelly, yeoman, Edward Barrett of Tralee, yeoman, John Turner of the same, yeoman, Mary Batchelor of the same, widow, Elizabeth Vine of the same, widow, Andrew Rawleigh of the same, tailor, Robert Haysam of the same, smith, Edmund Commane of the same, yeoman, and divers innocent children, at least half a score, were shot and murdered in or about the said castle, during the siege, by the same parties and their confederates. This deponent's cause of knowledge is, that all the time the said castle was besieged this deponent lived in another castle hard by the same, and had daily credible information of the passages that past in the said siege, and was likewise an eye-witness of the delivering up of the said castle into the hands of the said parties, whereby he came to know that the premises are undoubtedly true.

About the 3rd of September last, the undernamed persons, officers, and commanders among the rebels gathered their forces together, consisting of six or seven thousand armed men, horse and foot, on purpose to assault and set upon the English garrisons in the county of Cork, and take them, namely the Lord Viscount of Muskerry, the Lord Roche, the Lord of Ikerrin, the Lord of Castleconnell, Theobald Purcell Baron of Loghmoe, Garret Barry, General of their forces in Munster, Patrick Purcell of Croagh, in the county of Limerick, Esq., Lieut.-General of the same forces, Maurice Fitz-Edmund of Castle Ishin, in the county of Cork, gentleman, Oliver Stephenson, since killed in open rebellion, late of Dunmoylan, in the county of Limerick, Esq., Cormac MacCallaghan Carty of Sugreena, in the county of Kerry, gent., Dominick Fanning, late mayor of the city of Limerick, Edmund FitzGerald of Clenlish, in the said county of Limerick, gent., Edmund MacSheehy of Ballyvellan, in the same county, gent., Thomas Oge of Ballykealy, in the county of Kerry, gent., and their said forces having met together with colours flying in a rebellious and hostile manner, entered upon the confines of the county of Cork, and would have advanced further to effect their enterprise if not then seasonably resisted by the English forces. This deponent's cause of knowledge herein that he was prisoner with the said party, and therefore present, whereby he observed the said parties, and such of them in arms commanding such companies of horse and foot whereby to maintain their hostilities and open rebellion.

JANE GUARD, the wife of (*illegible*) Guard, late of Tralee aforesaid, a British Protestant, was produced as witness only touching the siege of the castle of Tralee. She deposed and saith, that she saw the above-named parties, and each of them severally maintaining the said siege, and continuing it during the time above mentioned, and that the persons above named being English and Protestants were then and there shot and murdered by the said parties. Her cause of knowledge is that she being a dweller in the town of Tralee aforesaid, she knew the said gentlemen to be at several meetings in the same, and also that she being in the said castle during the siege she observed and saw the said parties shot and murdered in the said castle.

Jurat. coram nobis, 25*th* Feb. 1642,
PHIL. BISSE.
THOS. BETTESWORTH.

A. BLENNERHASSETT.
her
JANE + GUARD.
mark

Note.

Arthur Blennerhassett was the third son of Robert Blennerhassett mentioned in Vino's deposition, and the ancestor of the family of his name settled since the 17th century at Riddlestown, near Rathkeale, in the county Limerick, a place which in the 12th century was owned, as its name implies, by the De Ridels or De Rudels, an old English family, passed from them to the Rices, and by a Rice heiress marriage to the Windalls, whose heiress married the grandson of this deponent. Many of the so-called murders in this deposition were probably the result of gun or cannon shots fired at the castles in Tralee during the siege.

CXC.

WILLIAM DETHICK, late of Killvallehagh (*recte* Killballylahiff), in the parish of Killiny in the barony of Corcaguiny, within the county of Kerry, gent., a British Protestant, duly sworn and examined before us by virtue of his Majesty's commission, &c., deposeth and saith, that about the last of January, 1641, and since the beginning of this present rebellion, he lost, was robbed, and was forcibly despoiled of his goods and chattels to the value of 402*l*. 10*s*. Also he saith, that his (*illegible*) and goods were taken at the time aforesaid by Walter Hussey of Castle Gregory in the said barony, gent., Owen MacMoriarty of Castle Drum, gent., Owen MacDonnell

Oge of Keelgarrylander (*i.e.*, the wood of the garden of Launder or De Launder, an old English name hibernicised into Lander) in the said barony, gent., and their associates to the number of a hundred men in a hostile manner. He also saith, that his ammunition, viz. one of his guns, was taken away by Owen MacDonnell Oge aforesaid, and another of his guns was taken away by John MacMorrish Fitz-Gerald of Knockglass in the said barony, about the time aforesaid. He also saith, that his money was taken away by the captains and commanders at the siege of Tralee, whose names shall be set down in their due place, about the latter end of August last past. He also saith, that the persons above mentioned who took away his goods were they also who robbed most of the Protestants in that part of the barony aforesaid (commonly called by the name of the half barony of Lettrogh), about the time aforesaid, the said parties being accompanied by Edmund MacShane FitzNicholas FitzGerald of Tierbrin in the said barony, gent., John Craud (*sic*), *alias* John FitzGerald of Knockglass, gent., having also in the said action Captain Thomas MacPhilip FitzGerald of Doylus, in the same barony, gent., who is a freeholder; John MacDermot of Tralee aforesaid, yeoman, Tiegue MacShane O'Sullivan of Cappaclogh, yeoman, Nicholas FitzEdmund FitzGerald of the same, yeoman, together with his four sons, all that that he hath.

Also this deponent saith, that after the battle of Newton, in which the rebels had an overthrow, among which the MacCarthys of Kerry had a share, some of the county having the fortune to return home, found in the town of Killarney many old decrepit men and women and young children, Protestants, to the number of sixteen, who could not get into some castle for refuge thereabouts, and all those persons were taken by the MacCarthys and their followers in those parts, and being stripped, were first whipped up and down from one end of the town to the other, then they were taken altogether, and a great hole being made for the purpose, they were thrown into it, and so buried alive. This the deponent saw not with his own eyes, but he dares avouch it for truth, because he hath heard it most confidently related from the mouths of many Protestants who are of good credit, and from many of the rebels themselves, some whereof have boasted and gloried in that wicked act, others in their relation of it speaking with some remorse and pity. He also saith, that one John (*illegible*) of Lixnaw, in the barony of Clanmaurice aforesaid, yeoman, a Protestant, being permitted by one Thomas Stack of those parts, gentleman, to live peaceably and enjoy what he had, at length, about Christmas last, as he was digging potatoes in his garden, four or five of the rebels there came and most cruelly murdered him and threw him into a river. Two or three more were killed there that night, but unknown to deponent.

Also he saith, that upon the 26th of January, 1641, a part of the enemy's army, to the number of two hundred, marched through the town of Tralee, and encamped that night at Ballyvelly, where they met a party of five hundred more, and the next night they lay at Cloghane, and from thence went to Castlemayne, pillaging and stripping the country where the English were, and driving their preys before them as they went. Also he saith, that upon the 15th of February last was twelvemonths, *Ann. Dom.* 1641, the town of Tralee was taken and plundered, where there was a great deal of pillage; at that time one Lawrence Tristram, the jailor there, was hanged and laid naked for two days together before the castle. The same day the two castles of Tralee were straitly besieged, and the burning of their premises seen at the distance of a mile and half a mile, as at Ballyvelly, and (*illegible*), in the greater of the two castles was Sir Thomas Harris, Knt., who also died there about the Easter following, besides him there were as warders about four score fighting men, besides three or four hundred men, women, and children.

In the lesser castle at Tralee John Freeman was deputy constable for the Lord of Kerry, and besides him were about thirty fighting men, whereof this deponent was one; besides other men, women, and children in all to the number of about six score. The besiegers were to the number of two and twenty hundred, sometimes more, having about one hundred horse, the chief commanders were Donell Oge MacCarthy, colonel from near Killarney, Esq., Captain Nicholas MacThomas FitzGerald and Major (*torn*) of Ballykenly, Esquires, Captain Florence MacCarthy of near Killarney aforesaid, Esquire, who was governor of the county from the beginning of the rebellion, and so continued for the space of seven or eight months, until the castles were yielded up, and then the Lord Muskerry was made governor of the whole county; Captain Fineen MacCarthy of Ardtully in the barony of Glaneroght, gent., Captain O'Sullivan Mor of Dunkerron, Esquire, Captain MacKillakudagh (*sic*) of the barony of Magunihy (as he believeth), gent. These captains are all of the part of Kerry aforesaid which they call Desmond, Nicholas FitzThomas aforesaid excepted; besides other commanders of the other parts of Kerry, viz. Edmund Fitz-

Morris of Lixnaw, Esq., Captain Walter Hussey of Castle Gregory, in the barony of Corcaguiny, gent., Captain Pierce Ferriter, Captain Dermot O'Dingle of Ballinacourty, gent., Captain Donnell Mac-Moriarty of Castledrum, gent., Captain John FitzGerald of Glandine, *alias* John *atlea*, gent., Captain Garret MacPatrick FitzGerald of Aghamore, in the barony of Clanmaurice, gent., slain at Liscarrol, Captain Morris MacEligot of Ballymaceligot, gent., and John his brother, Captain Morris FitzEdmund Gerald of Clongoukhat (*sic*), in the barony of Corcaguiny, gent., with divers others whose names this deponent cannot now remember, who laid close siege unto these castles within thirty yards and sometimes within thirty feet of them, from about February 12th until the four or five and twentieth of the August following, the enemy watching most commonly during the siege about 300 every night. About the latter end of March, after the beginning of the said siege, the enemy brought three sows towards the west, whereof two were set close to the wall, which were first broken with great stones from the castle, and after fired, and two or three rebels were burnt in them. After this, upon the 27th of April ensuing, they brought four sows towards the castle, and a piece of ordnance, out of which they discharged thirteen shots, which broke down some of the battlements of the castle, but no hurt besides, of these sows two were brought near the castle wall, but were burnt and two rebels in them.

The 18th of May after, they began to undermine the small castle, they of the castle countermined, and beat them out of their works, having killed a great many of them. About a fortnight after, being the latter end of May, having assaulted them again, they of the castle killed at one shot two of the rebels, by name, Tirlogh McCarty of Tralee, and a Lieutenant Tirlogh MacShee that came out of the Low Countries lately.

After this there were daily acts of hostility past betwixt those of the castle and the enemy, until the castle was yielded up; during the said siege those of the castle from time to time killed no less than a hundred of the enemy, and that by the enemy's own confession, and those of the castle during all that time lost no more than five men upon service out of the small castle, and about eighteen or nineteen out of the great castle, that were lost by venturing out for relief. Besides these there died out of both castles through the sickness, called the scurvy, no less than about four score persons, men, women, and children, during the time of the siege. The deponent often heard the rebels and besiegers call those of the castles 'English dogs and rebels,' and (say) that they had kept them long enough in Ireland already, and that now they (the Irish) would spend their lives, but that they would leave not a man of them (the besieged) alive in this kingdom, and that it was the king's pleasure that they (the Irish) should do so by virtue of his commission, and often when those in the castle were at their devotions of preaching, praying, and singing, the rebels underneath would mock them in a most reproachful manner.

At length, the provisions of both castles being wasted, they (the besieged) being kept alive for a time with eating of cats and raw hides, they were enforced to yield it up upon quarter of their lives and wearing clothes, which castles afterwards the besieged burnt; also he saith, that Ellis Wheywall (*sic*) of near Stradbally, in the barony of Corcaguiny, miner, Richard Walker of Kilgobbin, in the said barony, yeoman, together with his brethren Richard and Arthur Walker of the same, yeomen, Thomas Goodenough of the same, yeoman, William Farryn of Ballyenough (*sic*), in the barony of Trughenackmy, yeoman, Richard Bigford of the Kerries, in the said barony, yeoman, John Pierce of Ballynallard (*sic*), in said barony, gentleman, formerly reputed to be Protestants, are since this rebellion turned Papists. He also saith, that after the delivering up of the said castles upon quarter, he, this deponent, repaired to John FitzGerald's castle of Ennismore, where he often heard some of the priests and friars that usually resorted thither say, that it is true the rebels had not the king's commission for what they did, but that, however, the king did connive and wink at it. And further he cannot depose.

WILLIAM DETHICK.

Jurat. coram nobis, 17*th May,* 1643,
PHIL. BISSE.
JAMES WALLIS.

Note.

This deponent was probably the son of Humphrey Dethick, one of the first twelve free burgesses of Tralee named in the charter granted 31st of March, 1611, Robert Blennerhassett being provost. Humphrey Dethick was also the latter's colleague in the representation of the borough in 1613. I have in the above deposition, as in the former ones, omitted the long inventory of lost goods, lands, &c., and their money value. Amongst them salt works carried on in Killballylahiff and tucking mills there are mentioned, showing how the son of the M.P. for Tralee did not disdain trade, and how the industrial resources of even the most remote districts in the west of Ireland were being utilised by the colonists until the land was once more reduced to a waste by an ill-advised rebellion. A curious proof of the dislike of the Irish to mercantile pursuits is furnished in the before-mentioned Irish poem by Pierce Ferriter, the rebel leader, translated for the Percy Society by Crofton Croker, Describing the wailing of the *banshee* or guardian spirit for Maurice FitzGerald, son of the Knight of Kerry, who died on the eve of the rebellion, Ferriter says :—

> The prosperous traders
> Were filled with affright,
> In Tralee they packed up
> And made ready for flight,
>
> For there a shrill voice
> At the door of each hall
> Was heard, as they fancied,
> Regretting *their* fall.
>
> They fled to concealment,
> Ah! fools thus to fly—
> For no trader a Banshee
> Would utter a cry!

Acting out what he wrote, Ferriter marched with his Hussey and Geraldine associates to Tralee, sweeping poor Mr. Dethick's salt pans and tucking mills into the sea and the rivers, and leaving the districts of Castle Gregory and Killballylahiff in a state of desolation and poverty, from which they have never thoroughly recovered to this day.

CXCI.

DANIEL SPRATT, late of the town and parish of Tralee, in the barony of Trughenacmy, county of Kerry, clothier, a British Protestant, duly sworn and examined before us by virtue of his Majesty's Commission, &c., deposeth and saith, that about the latter end of January, 1641, he lost, was robbed, and forcibly despoiled of his goods and chattels, and of debts which before this rebellion were esteemed good, but now become desperate (by reason that the debtors, as Daniel Chute of Tulligarron, Esq., in the said county, are impoverished Protestants), to the value of 157*l*. Also he saith, that about the time mentioned his goods were taken by Captain John

FitzGerald, *alias* John *aclee*, of the said barony, within the said county, gentleman, and divers others that were at the siege of Tralee Castle, whose names he knoweth not. And further he deposeth, that whilst he was one of the warders of the said castle, he saw Mr. Edmund Vorkley, the elder, of Tralee aforesaid, gentleman, come to the grate of the said castle and seemed to be importunate with the warders of the said castle to give it up to the enemy before they had been a month besieged, when, as there was no such necessity, they (the warders and people within) having then, to Mr. Vorkley's own knowledge, provision to hold out for a great while against the enemy, Mr. Vorkley being amongst the rebels from the beginning of the rebellion, and being pressed to come within the castle, where his wife was, but did not, but sent for his wife out of the castle, and left her at the castle of Ballycarty. This deponent also saith, that when the castle of Tralee was yielded up, and when all the rest had only quarter for life, and one suit of clothes apiece, that the said Mr. Vorkley had no less than about eleven horse-loads of clothes, that he brought from the castle of Tralee to the castle of Ballycarty, and further he deposeth that about a fortnight before Michaelmas last, 1642, he saw Captain John Crosbie of Ballingarry Island discourse freely with the rebels that came within a bow-shot of the island, and brought them forth drink, and drank freely with (*illegible*) Fitz-Maurice, McEligot of BallymacEligot, gent., Captain Walter Hussey of Castle Gregory, gent., and Dermot O'Dingle of Ballynacourty, gent.

DANIEL SPRATT.

Jurat. coram nobis, 15*th June*, 1643,
PHIL. BISSE.
HEN. RUGGE.

Note.

The eleven horse-loads of clothes, which naturally provoked the clothier, Mr. Daniel Spratt, to jealousy, was certainly an unreasonable proportion for one man to bear away with him from Tralee Castle, unless he were a rival clothier, which it does not appear Mr. Vauclier was. But it is very likely that he had strong sympathies, notwithstanding his Protestantism, with the rebels, for he was the brother-in-law of O'Sullivan Mor, their wives being the grand-daughters of Jenkin Conway of Killorglin before mentioned, and the nieces of the wife of Robert Blennerhassett of Ballycarty. During the earlier years of the rebellion Vauclier and the Blennerhassetts seem to have been endeavouring to conciliate the rebels, or to 'keep in' with both parties, but in the end they were glad to adhere to the side of the Parliament. The island of Ballingarry, a most picturesque spot, now an isthmus, on the beautiful north-west coast of Kerry, not far from the mouth of the Shannon, was fortified and gallantly held for several months by Colonel David Crosbie, who sheltered there many Protestants from the surrounding districts and from Tralee. A short sketch of the siege of Ballingarry in 1642-3, and of the beauties of the coast in that neighbourhood, which I drew up for the 'Leisure Hour,' after spending a summer day there two or three years ago, will be found in the number of that periodical for February, 1882. The locality is full of interest for the artist, the antiquary, and the lover of fine coast scenery. Captain John Crosbie mentioned in Mr. Spratt's deposition was the Catholic nephew of Colonel David Crosbie. Captain, afterwards Sir John, Crosbie, baronet, from the first adhered to the Irish and Catholic side, and could only have been at Ballycarty as an ambassador from the besiegers. MacEligot and MacGillacuddy, colonels in the Irish army, were also nephews of Colonel David Crosbie. When Ballingarry was at last taken by the Irish, through the treachery of the two warders appointed to guard the drawbridge connecting the precipitous shores of the island with the cliffs on the mainland, Colonel David Crosbie's life was saved only through the influence of his nephews, and his niece Katherine MacGillacuddy who was with him in the castle or fort. He managed, with their help, to escape to Cork, and returning to Kerry in 1649, was made governor of the county by Cromwell, which enabled him to save not a few of his friends and relatives from transplantation. The confused state of parties in Kerry, owing to the constant intermarriages amongst the Irish and the Elizabethan or earlier colonists, was far from advantageous to the English who had come to the county in the reigns of Charles I. and his father, and the depositions of these later colonists are full of complaints of the apparently friendly intercourse which from time to time existed between those who were opposed to one another in religion and politics. John Abraham, Josias White, and Nicholas Roberts made a joint deposition before Archdeacon Bysse and a magistrate or commissioner named Elwall, of which only a copy remains. It is nothing more than a repetition of the evidence given by Vines and Roberts, with the exception of the following passages:—

"The deponents further say that about New Year last, 1642, there went forth from the castle of Ballycarty nine men and one woman, who lost their lives going to the English castle called Newmarket, when they were taken by the rebels. The names of the said persons were these, John Ellis, near Stradbally, in the barony of Corcaguiny, gent., and his son, Thomas Ellis ; Thomas Goodwin of the Currens, barony of Trughenacmy, tailor, John Williams of Killontierna, in the said barony, husbandman, Andrew Morgan of the Currens aforesaid, butcher, and his son William : James MacGarret of Ballycarty aforesaid, husbandman ; John Prosser of Killarney, mason ; Robert Ingledew of Killarney aforesaid, butcher ; and Elizabeth Dashwood of Tralee, wife to John Dashwood, shoemaker, who, as was reported, was thrashed (*sic*) to death, but among these Robert Ingledew, tiring upon the mountains behind the rest of the company, was brought back by six of the rebels to the said castle of Ballycarty, who, being brought there, Mrs. Hannibal (*sic*) 'Hassett, wife of Captain Edward 'Hassett, being there, began to complain to her father-in-law, Robert Blennerhassett, of the cruelty of the enemy towards the rest, and beseeching him very earnestly to take some course to save the said Robert Ingledew, his answer was, ' *He is a cow-stealing rogue, and let them do with him even what they will*,' and upon that the rebels carried him about a mile from the place, and murdered him most cruelly. They also say, that the cause these persons fled out of the castle, before it was yielded up, was that they were daily threatened by the Irish ward there, so that they stood in danger of their lives, being accused of stealing cattle from the enemy for their relief, before the castle was yielded up. And although Mr. Robert 'Hassett told all the English of the castle that he had gotten quarter for them all for life and goods, and a convoy to be conveyed on to the next English garrison in the county of Cork, yet it afterwards appeared to the contrary, there was no such matter, for the said Robert 'Hassett confessed to one of those deponents, Nicholas Roberts, and to others, that the truth was he made no quarter at all, but referred him and all the English ward to Mr. Florence MacCarthy's own breast. They also say that without any consent or foreknowledge of any of the warders when the castle was to be yielded up, the said Robert Blennerhassett called unto him all the warders and caused them to be all disarmed of their arms (*sic*), which were their own proper goods, and so they were delivered up to the Irish ward, he himself being permitted to live within the castle among the Irish. They also say that about the time of the siege of Tralee they saw two or three of the Irish of Glaneroghe (*sic*) whose names they know not, rebels, permitted to come within the grate, in company of Captain John Blennerhassett, and there eat and drink in the little buttery, with their arms, skeans, and swords, where lived Robert 'Hassett; also they say that in Captain John 'Hassett's house, that was situated within the bawn of the said castle, they have often seen divers of the prime rebels of that country to come in and out, to eat and drink and be merry. Also Florence MacCarty, about the latter end of August last, came to Captain John 'Hassett's house, within the said bawn, and lay there one night, and so went away next morning, the said Florence being then a prime man at the siege of Tralee. The said John 'Hassett was often seen to parley with divers others of the rebels, and letters passed to and fro betwixt them. They also say, that the warders of Ballycarty Castle, with the rest, might and would often have relieved the castle of Tralee when they were besieged, and often propounded the design to do so to the said Captain John 'Hassett, but he never would consent that they should fall upon that design. They also say that John Abraham the elder, one of those deponents, and the aforesaid Josias White, with his wife and two children, and Richard Page's wife of Tralee, and Mary the wife of John Boyse of Tulligarron, in the parish of Ballymaceligot, husbandman, were all stripped by the rebels. They also say that John MacThomas FitzGerald, late of Tralee, tailor, and Anne his wife, Gibbon Supple of Tralee, tailor, James O'Connor of the Kerries, in the parish of Tralee, gentleman, Garret More of Tralee, gent., Richard Bigford of the Kerries aforesaid, husbandman, also the wife of the second son of Patrick MacEllistrum of Tralee, gent., John Pierce of Tralee (*illegible*), formerly reputed Protestants, since the rebellion turned Papists, also one Mr. Chafe (*sic*) of Lixnaw, gent., and his wife Frances, and one called MacWilliams of the same, gent., William Jones of the Currens, husbandman, Thomas Morgan of the same, husbandman, George Murrow of the Disert, husbandman, Walter Kirby of near Stradbally, husbandman, and his two sons Richard and William, Peter Brian, miller, of Tralee, and his wife, John MacAuliffe of the same, miller, also Anne and Elizabeth Reens, daughters to Mrs. Reens of Cornfield, near Potally (*sic*), widow, Katherine Conway of Killorglin near Castlemayne, widow, also Mr. Traws (*sic*) of Kill (*illegible*) near Currens, widow, Arthur White of Ballyfinnoge, husbandman, and farmer, reputed Protestants heretofore, but since not only (are) turned Papists, but live among the rebels, and do duty and service for them; lastly, these deponents say that Lawrence Tristram, when the rebels put a rope about his neck (*torn*) if he would go to mass, said he would not. And that (*illegible*) of Tralee, tailor, and John Hall of Glancrogh, husbandman, put into the gaol as ward, were taken out and hanged at the market cross of Tralee, on the (*illegible*) of February last was a twelvemonth, being before promised quarter for life by Captain Dermot O'Dingle and his company; a third person that was of the ward, who was called the black man of Glancrogh, being shot ran into the castle of Tralee, and there died; a fourth called (*torn*) Marwood being taken prisoner, after awhile made his escape to the castle of Ballycarty, and further they cannot depose.

" *Jurat. coram nobis*,
Phil. Bisse.
Thos. Elwell."

" Josias + White.
John + Abraham.
Nich. + Roberts."

Note.

The lady styled 'Mrs. Hannibal 'Hassett' in this deposition, by a mistake which betrays the cockney origin of the deponent, was the daughter of Mr. or Captain Vauclier, mentioned in Mr. Spratt's deposition, and her christian name must have been Annabel, a very common name in the Spring family (which was connected by marriage with the Conways, Blennerhassetts, Husseys, Browns, and FitzGeralds), although in a voluminous pedigree of the Blennerhassetts, written between 1690-1786, she is called 'Mary, daughter of Edward Vauclier, Esq.' The deponent, however, who know her husband and father personally, and who had resided in her house, could not have been mistaken as to her christian name except through his failure to discard the cockney H. The place now known as Ballycarty is a small townland to the east of Ballyseedy demesne, still the property of the Blennerhassetts. There is a small square tower on Ballycarty, which was probably a Geraldine fortress before 1584. At that time the present Ballyseedy was included in Ballycarty, as appears by the Elizabethan maps of the Denny estate in the Rolls House, and the castle or mansion mentioned in the depositions stood a little to the south-west of the present Ballyseedy House. Extensive ruins still remain thereabouts of a castle or mansion with a bawn or strong outward wall.

CXCII.

EDWARD VOAKLEY (*Vauclier*), late of Tralee, in the barony of Trughenacmy, county of Kerry, gent., being duly sworn and examined, &c., deposeth and saith, that about the 20th of January, 1641, he lost, was robbed, and forcibly despoiled of his goods and chattels to the several values following, viz. of cows, horses, mares, oxen, sheep, and sums to the value of 400*l*.; of household stuff to the value of 21*l*.; of ready money to the value of 120*l*.; of wearing apparel to the value of 50*l*.; of corn and hay in house and haggard to the value of 260*l*.; of debts to the value of 500*l*., which ere this rebellion were esteemed good debts, by reason that some of the debtors are become impoverished Protestants, as John Mason, John Barret, Arthur Rawleigh, and divers others whom this deponent doth not now remember, and the rest Papists and rebels, as Garret FitzGerald of Ballymacdaniel, gent., Fineen MacDermot Carthy of Glaneroght, gent., Thomas Malone of the parish of Clogherbrien, gent., Edmund More O'Shane of Ardglass, gent., Conogher Trassy of Ballinorogh, husbandman, Phelim MacFineen Carthy of Drommavally, gent., Christopher Hickson of Knockglass, gent., John Granal (*sic*) of the same, gent., all of the county Kerry aforesaid, and divers others whose names he cannot remember. Also he says, that by means of this rebellion he is dispossessed of the benefit of certain leases in the said county, as first, of the lease of New Manor near Tralee, where he had a term of eighty years to run and upwards, worth above the landlord's rent 70*l*. per annum, in which, together with his improvements and housing, now burnt to the ground, he is damnified to the value of 600*l*. Also a lease of certain lands in Ballymullen wherein he had a term of eleven years, if a certain woman so long lived, worth 10*l*. above the landlord's rent, wherein he conceives himself damnified in 50*l*.; also a lease of Gorthataumple, wherein he had a tenure of ninety-seven years, worth above the landlord's rent 7*l*. per annum, damnified herein 100*l*. Also certain leases of certain houses in the town of Tralee wherein he had a tenure of ninety-nine years to come, all of them being burnt all to three, the number burnt thirteen, he conceives himself damnified to the value of 600*l*., the whole of his losses in goods and chattels amounting to the value of 3,600*l*. Also he saith his goods were taken away by Garret FitzJames Gerald of Ballymacdaniel, and Walter Hussey of Castle Gregory, gent., and their followers. His household stuff and money were taken by the besiegers of Tralee Castle, whereof these were the chief: Donnel MacCartie of Castlelogh in said county, gent., Florence MacCartie, formerly living with his father, O'Donovan, in the county of Cork, gent., Garret MacPatrick of Aghamore, gent., Fineen Mac-Dermot Carthy of Glanerogh, gent., captain among the rebels, Donogh MacFineen Cartie of Ardtully, gent., Captain Tiegue Mac-Dermot MacCormac Cartie of near the Currens, gent., Captain Dermot O'Dingle O'Moriarty of Ballinacourty, Captain Donnel MacMoriarty of Castledrum, and Captain O'Sullivan Mor of Dunkerron, Esquire, Captain Fineen MacDaniel Carthy, *alias* Captain *Sugan*, near Glanerogh, gent., and divers others to the number of one thousand. He also saith, that Daniel MacMoriarty of Castledrum aforesaid, gent., hath possessed himself of this deponent's house in Tralee, and certain other tenements belonging to that house. Also he saith, that divers Protestants to the number of forty, as Arthur Barham of Clogherbrien, Robert Brooke of Carrignafeely, Robert Lenthal of Tralee, Thomas Arnold and John Cade of Tralee, Griffin Floyd of Killarney, William Wilson of the same, dyer, Donnell O'Connor of Killarney, maltster, Robert Warham of Tralee, John Godolphin of Tralee, shoemaker, Hugh Roe of Tralee, barber, Benjamin Weedon, hosier, Henry Knight, tailor, Richard Hore of New Manor, husbandman, were all treacherously killed by O'Sullivan More of Dunkerron and his followers to the number of five or six hundred, this deponent having the command of the said Protestants (there being two more that escaped) saved his life by leaping off a rock into the sea, being enforced to swim at least a mile, and so got away, having first received fourteen wounds with swords and skeans, and one shot in the right shoulder, and one deep wound in his back with a pike; this was done about midsummer last near Ballinskelligs in the said county. He also said that eleven men and one woman were murdered on the 15th of January last, coming out of the county of Kerry from the castle of Ballycarty, which was then lately yielded upon quarter, in which castle they were, they were murdered in the mountains near Newmarket by the rebels of Cork and MacAuliffe of Duhallow, in the county Cork, the names of those that were murdered were these: John Ellis of Ballyduff in said county and his son, Andrew Morgan of the Currens, butcher, Elizabeth Dashwood, wife of William Dashwood of Tralee, shoemaker, Hugh Williams of Ballymariscal, Thomas Goodwin of the Currens, John Norris, servant to the ward of Ballycarty, and divers others to the number of eleven. This deponent also saith, that being employed

DEPOSITIONS.   127

about midsummer last by Sir Edward Denny, his captain, from
Cork into the county Kerry, to give notice to the castle ward which
were in some distress, to prevent the yielding of the hold to the
enemy, upon his intelligence of the Lord Forbes, his coming
towards those parts to relieve them. He was by the way taken
prisoner about the *black walk* in the middle of the mountain called
Slieve Lougher by Tiegue MacAuliffe of Castle MacAuliffe, Dawn
MacAuliffe, Conogher Ceogh near Liscarroll, and Owen O'Callaghan
of near Newmarket, to the number of 500 men, who brought him to
the camp near Adare, where there were about 7,000 then prepared
to fight against the English, among whom were Garret Barry, their
General; Patrick Purcell, Lieutenant-General; Charles Hennessy,
Sergeant-major General; Garret Purcell, Lieutenant-Colonel; Lord
Roche, the Lord of Castle Connell, the Baron of Loghmoe, *alias*
Theobald Purcell; O'Sullivan Bear; O'Sullivan Mor; Dominick
Fanning, mayor of Limerick; Edmund FitzThomas Gerald, captain.
Deponent was detained twenty-three days, but was afterwards
exchanged for Captain James Brown, taken at Newtown a little
before. He also saith, that while in restraint he heard it generally
spoken among them that they, the rebels, fought for the king's prerogative, and that we were the rebels and traitors, and that they
were not preferred to any places of honour, and that they were not
made judges of assize, and had not the liberty of their religion. He
also saith, that the besiegers of Tralee burnt Sir Edward Denny's
castle there, with the greatest part of the town, to the number of
one hundred houses at least, also Richard Hoare of the New Manor
had his houses, to the number of four, burned by the said besiegers
at the time of the said siege, and further he cannot depose.

EDW. VAUCLIER.

Jurat. coram nobis, 21 *March*, 1642,
   PHIL. BESSE.
   BENJ. BARASTER.

CXCIII.

TIRLOGH KELLY, of the town and parish of Youghal, in the
barony of Inchiquin, within the county of Cork, gent., an Irish
Protestant, duly sworn and examined upon oath, before us, by
virtue of a commission under the broad seal of this kingdom to us
and others directed, bearing date at Dublin the 5th day of March
last, touching the losses and sufferings of his Majesty's subjects

British and Protestant, in the province of Munster, by means of the rebellion, besides divers other particulars to be inquired after by virtue of the said commission tending to the (*illegible*) of this present rebellion, deposeth and saith, that about the 1st of May last one Thomas Williams of Youghal, merchant, was appointed captain for the sea, by the late Lord President of this province, and being directed by his lordship, amongst other instructions, to go in company with Sir Edward Denny, Knight, to relieve the castle of Tralee in the county of Kerry, then in great extremity, being closely besieged by Colonel Donnel MacCarthy of Currens, in the said county of Kerry, Esquire, and his forces. The said Williams, about the last of May, having received directions touching his intended voyage, took shipping at the harbour of Youghal aforesaid, carrying with him four score men or thereabouts, part whereof lay aboard the said Williams's ship called the *Flower of Youghal*; their admiral appointed for the voyage the other part aboard the ship called the *Lion of Youghal*, whereof Thomas Bryant was captain, and being then seasonably provided, they sailed from thence to Cork and there took aboard their ship Sir Edward Denny and his foot company, which done they sailed away westward to a place called the Derries (*sic*) in O'Sullivan Bear's country, and having landed some men there, the enemy gave them a skirmish, and one of the said Sir Edward Denny's company called Philip O'Loinsy (*sic*) was there shot, and from thence, having got that resistance, they sailed to the river Kenmare, in the county of Kerry, in O'Sullivan Mor's country, and some men being there landed the enemy did likewise then skirmish with them but no men lost, we (*sic*) then set forth to sea again, but sailing to and fro in the river, and about the sea coast, put into a place called Ballinsceligs, where the inhabitants pretended themselves to be good subjects, but they having betrayed some of Captain Lee's company then in the harbour that went ashore, presuming on their loyalty, by disarming three or four of his musketeers there we landed some forces, and having exchanged some shots with the enemy, but losing no men, we took to sea again, burning the said Ballinsceligs and the country round about it, and took one (*blank*) Segerson, a gentleman of the same place, prisoner. Afterwards we came to the harbour of Dingleycooshe, where the townsmen resisted us, and made divers shots at the ships, and being thus opposed, we sailed out again to the river of Kenmare, and (*illegible*) drawing some cattle near the shore which were left on purpose to draw us on, we landed four score men or thereabouts commanded by Edward Vauclier, Esq., Ensign to the said Sir Edward Denny, having then in company with him Captain Grinfield Halce (*sic*) and one Mr. Lintoll. No sooner they came ashore, but O'Sullivan More's forces, consisting at least of seven or eight hundred men, laying in several ambushes, fell upon them, killing the said Halce in a barbarous manner, hewing and hacking his body in divers places, and cutting off his head, and likewise murdered the said Mr. Lintoll, and desperately wounded the said Mr. Vauclier, besides threescore and seventeen common soldiers, then killed, so that of all that company that went ashore not above three that escaped to come on board, this was upon Friday, the 3rd day of June last.

Upon Saturday following, the 4th of June, we set forward to sea, purposing to come to the harbour of Kinsale, our surgeon the day before being murdered, whereof we had then great necessity, but the wind altering, we put in that Saturday to a place called Kilmackillokistig (*sic*), in the county of Kerry, formerly a known place for fishing, and in the afternoon we landed some men, and took away from thence a quantity of salt, and having lain there at anchor until Monday following, the 6th of June, early in the morning the said Captain Williams, this deponent's lieutenant George Symons, Samuel Fenton of Cork, merchant, James Monsell of Youghal, butcher, John Boulger of the same, yeoman, Thomas Lyne of the same, shipwright, and two others went to fetch away more salt, but then and there Daniel O'Sullivan, *alias* O'Sullivan Mor, with six hundred men or thereabouts, lay in ambush in two companies at the town of Killmackillosta, and no sooner were the said Williams and the rest come ashore, but presently the enemy started out of the (*illegible*), which being discovered by the said Williams, he endeavouring to regain the boat, the enemy came upon him and the rest pell-mell with stones; the boat being out of sight of the ships, and the stones flying so fast that they could neither discharge muskets nor pistols, but at last regained the boat, yet had not the power to launch it forth from the shore through the multitude of stones flung upon them, until at last they were all stoned to death, excepting this deponent and one James Monsell aforesaid, but both were bruised and sorely wounded, and taken prisoner by the said O'Sullivan Mor, but the rest of them that were murdered and stoned, they stripped them in a barbarous and most inhumane manner, and threw their naked corpses upon the shore, cutting and mangling them in a piteous manner, not admitting them to have Christian burial, aftertimes the tide at ebb and flow beating upon their corpses on the beach to and again.

Upon Tuesday following, the 7th day of June, this deponent and the said Monsell, being the night before kept close prisoners and asunder, he, this deponent, was then brought before the said O'Sullivan, who then and there impannelled a jury of twelve men to pass upon the life of this deponent, and being arraigned and evidence also given against him, by the said O'Sullivan himself, that this deponent was guilty of high treason and (as he alleged) of robbing and burning the king's subjects, meaning themselves, but by God's assistance this deponent was then conveyed away out of sight by means of (*blank*) Sullivan, who knowing this deponent's father, the last war in the camp at Kinsale against Tyrone and the Spaniards, by his intercession this deponent's life was saved.

This deponent further saith, that during his abode with the said O'Sullivan, which was for six months or thereabouts, he heard him and other gentlemen confidently say, at several times, that they had a large commission from his Majesty for what they did, and he heard the said Daniel O'Sullivan oftentimes say, that they made no question but that the king was on their side, and was become a Roman Catholic; he likewise saw and observed during that time a Spanish barque out of Biscay, burthen thirty tons, come to Bearhaven about Michaelmas last, loaded with arms and powder, for the said Donnel O'Sullivan, which barque, as by credible information given to this deponent appeared, came hither about the 9th of May before with more powder and arms.

This deponent was likewise credibly informed, that they have four several councils or common meetings of their chieftains, and gentlemen, about the raising of an army to surprise and take the English garrison in the county of Cork, one in Tralee, in the county of Kerry, one in the city of Limerick, another at Cashel, and another at Kilkenny, the motives that induce him to believe this information to be true is, that about the latter end of November last, this deponent perceiving no way otherwise for him to come away, requested the said O'Sullivan to give him, this deponent, a pass to go to the county of Roscommon to his friends, where he was born, which being granted this deponent came to Limerick, accompanied by two of the said O'Sullivan's men, who had charge given them to see this deponent safely come thither, where this examt. stayed two days and two nights, and then and there observed several meetings of the gentlemen of the country (*illegible*)

DEPOSITIONS. 131

in counsel, namely Garret Barry, then called general of the Catholick forces for the province of Munster, for so they commonly styled him, Patrick Pursell of Croe, in the county of Limerick, Esquire, lieutenant-general of the said forces, Sir Daniel O'Brian of Ballykett (sic), in the county of Clare, knight, the Lord of Muskerry, Captain Charles Hennessy, master of their ordnance for the said province, the Lord Baron of Castle Connell, Pierse Creagh, mayor of the city, and divers other gentlemen of the county of Clare, and county of Limerick, whose names this deponent doth not remember; likewise he took notice at Clonmell that Captain Fennell and one Mr. (*illegible*), mayor of the said town (this deponent then coming thither from Limerick), went to the council at Cashell from Clonmell. This deponent further deposeth and saith, while he stayed at Clonmell he was credibly told that Owen Roe O'Neill came to Wexford, not long since out of the Low Countries, who brought in great store of arms and ammunition, and was made since general of all the forces of the province of Ulster; and after him came likewise into Wexford one Colonel Preston from Flanders, with more arms and powder, and soon after the same Preston's wife and children came into Wexford in another ship, loaded with arms, who were received with great joy and solemnity, and very soon after their landing Sir Phelim O'Neal married one of the Lord Preston's daughters, to whom the same Preston gave as marriage portion a thousand pounds in money, a thousand muskets, a thousand bandeliers, a thousand swords, a thousand carbines, a thousand pair of petronells, and one thousand great saddles. This deponent examined, likewise deposeth and saith, that he heard it credibly reported at Clonmell aforesaid that the said Lord Preston undertook (*illegible*) of taking the Castle of Dublin by May Day next, and therefore he was to have from the kingdom threescore pounds for his pains.

TIRLOGH KELLY,

Jurat. coram nobis, 11*th Jan.* 1642,
PHILIP BISSE.
THOMAS ELWALL.

Note,

The deponent's account of the skirmish at Ballinskelligs is somewhat different from that given by Vauclier and probably more correct. The latter as a connection of the O'Sullivan Mor would be very likely to underrate the number killed at Ballinskelligs. It is evident, however, that those killed at that place were all soldiers, well armed, surprised by well armed Irish soldiers, and that the surprise was a retaliation for the burning of Ballinskelligs a few days before. But Kelly tells us that the burning was also a retaliation for the killing of some of Captain Lee's English soldiers. The killing of the English at Kilmalochinsta was also a skirmish between open enemies at war, but the hacking and mangling of the bodies show how little O'Sullivan's followers understood the first conditions of honourable warfare. An old MS. History of Kerry in the Royal Irish Academy collections, written by an O'Sullivan of Dunkerron about a hundred and twenty years ago, gives the traditional account of the skirmish at Ballinskelligs, which does not differ materially from that in the foregoing deposition, but makes the number of the slain a hundred and thirty-five. The spot where they fell, which is on the way from Valentia or Cahir to Ballinskelligs Abbey, is to this day called *Traigh na Sassenagh*, or the Strand of the Englishman, and tradition says they were there interred, but from Kelly's deposition this seems unlikely. Tiegue MacMahon, an Irish Protestant of Stradbally, in the barony of Corcaguiny, county of Kerry, sworn before Bysse and Williamson on the 8th of May, 1642, confirmed the greater part of his neighbour William Dethick's deposition, and Marcus Evans, sworn before same on same day, deposed that he lived near Tralee when the siege began, and that he and his father went into the castle for shelter, that the latter died there, and that he, deponent, was present when the castle was surrendered. He further swore that 'the Protestants who died during the siege were not permitted to have Christian burial, some of the popish clergy affirming that their bodies ought to be burned and their ashes cast into the sea because they were heretics.' (*MSS. T. C. D., F.* 2, 17, *p.* 81.) Margaret Perry of Kilcushna, near Castle Island, sworn before Gray and Bysse that her husband and her two sons were murdered by the rebels. The Rev. Gregory Dickenson, rector of Dingle, sworn before Bysse, Wallis, and Elwall on the 6th of August, 1642, deposed that Thomas Hood of Dingle and his brother John were hung, the one at Dingle, the other at Tralee, by the rebels, and that ' Thomas Spring of Stradbally, Mrs. Rose Morley and her two sons of Ventry, William and Gilbert Bayley, and the Rev. John Connor had all turned to mass since the rebellion.'

CXCIV.

THOMAS FRITH, late Archdeacon of Ross, one of his Majesty's justices of the peace for the counties of Cork and Kerry, duly sworn and examined, deposeth and saith, that he lost, was robbed, and forcibly despoiled of his goods and chattels, and of the goods and chattels left him by his late brother, John Frith, gent., deceased, in Cork, worth 1,126*l*. 15*s*. 10*d*., part of which consisted of debts to the sum of 557*l*. 15*s*. 10*d*., which before this rebellion were esteemed good debts, but are now become desperate, by reason that some of the debtors are impoverished Protestants, such as William Russell, yeoman, Henry Bergin, gent., Edmund Wallis, clerk, all of or about Aghardowne, in the county Cork, John Bradshaw, gent., and John Grant, yeoman, of and about Ross, in the said county, John Barrett, yeoman, late of Killoyne (*sic*), in the county of Kerry, Richard Blackhall of Castlemaine, in the said county, Tiegue O'Healy of the same, gent., Thomas Spring of Stradbally, in the said county, Esquire, Edward Spring of Killahie, in the same county, gent., both of whom were accounted Protestants before the rebellion, Thomas Goodman, yeoman, Daniel Stiles, gent., William Dethick, gent., John Morris, Richard Trant, Morgan (*illegible*), yeomen, all of or about the parishes of Killiny, Kilgobbin, and Stradbally, in the barony of Corcaguiny, in the said county of Kerry, Devereux Spratt of Tralee, minister, Robert (*illegible*) of Glanerogh, in the said county, and divers others, and the rest are Papists, and are, as this deponent supposeth, out in actual rebellion, such as William ny (*illegible*), *alias* Donovan, yeoman, Maurice O'Callinan, gent., Owen MacDonnell Sullivan, gent., Connor O'Regan, gent., Donogh McConogher, gent., Tiegue O'Hogan, Fineen MacDermot Sullivan, James Neville, Donogh MacDermot MacAuliffe, Conogher O'Mahony, William O'Fiherly, John Bowler, yeoman, Fineen Oge Carty, gent., William MacTiegue, gent., Fineen MacRandal Hurly, gent., Conogher MacSammnagh, yeoman, William O'Cronin, yeoman, Melaghlin and Randal O'Regan, yeomen, with many others in the county of Cork, in and about the barony of Carberry, at the several villages and parishes of Aghadonne, Kilmacabee, Killahin, Kilfaghny, Kilton, and Ross Carberry. Also Hubert Hussey of Kilshannig, and Walter Hussey of the same, in the county of Kerry, gentlemen, Kelly FitzPatrick of Ardfert, gent., Tibbot FitzGerald, gent., Robert Oge of Listrim, gent., Edmund Stack of Ardfert, gent., John MacFineen, gent.,

James Cronin, gent., Edmund MacShane of Farrendalloge, gent., and Dermot O'Dingle, *alias* Moriarty of Ballinacourty, yeoman, for his cruelty to Protestants now advanced to be a captain amongst the rebels; also Owen MacMoriarty of Kildrum, gent., Daniel O'Dinagan, yeoman, John (*illegible*), yeoman, all of the county Kerry aforesaid. with divers others of whom he claims mortgages, debts, bills, bonds, under their hands. He likewise saith, that he hath heard that Thomas Spring of Stradbally, Esquire, in the county of Kerry aforesaid, with his wife and his only son, and Edward Spring of Killaghie, in the said county, gent., who were reputed Protestants, have since this rebellion turned Papists, as also John Gardiner of Ardfert, in the said county, minister, and his wife, he, as it is reported, would have turned friar, but the Papists refused to admit him, he is a man of so notorious, evil, and scandalous a conversation.

THOMAS FRITH.

Jurat. 3rd November, 1642,
PHILIP BISSE.
RICHARD PEISLEY.

CXCV.

ROBERT BECKET, of Carrigaline, in the county of Cork, clerk, duly sworn and examined before us, deposeth and saith, that on or about the 25th of May last he was robbed and forcibly despoiled of his goods worth 36l. He also saith that about the time above mentioned he was robbed by Captain MacSwiney and Captain Donell MacCarty's men, their names he knoweth not, except one Daniel O'B (*illegible*) of Barnahealy, in the said county of Cork, who carried this deponent and his wife prisoners to Dermot MacCarthy's house, brother to the said Donell MacCarthy, and after this deponent was released, on his way coming to Cork, he was assaulted violently by the number of sixteen of the rebels, who then and there stripped him of his clothes in a most shameful manner, and within the matter of a week afterwards this deponent's wife, Elizabeth Becket, coming to Cork after the deponent, she was assaulted in the highway between Barn (*illegible*) and Bally (*illegible*), in the said county, and was stripped and shot to death, and her throat cut by the rebels, where she lay in a most inhuman manner two days, and at last was buried in an unchristian manner in the highway.

ROBERT BECKET, *clerk*.

Jurat. 27th April, 1542,
PHIL. BISSE.
RICHARD (*illegible*).

CXCVI.

JASPER HORSEY, late of Bally (*illegible*), in the parish of Temple (*illegible*), barony of Clangibbon, county of Cork, gent., a British Protestant, duly sworn and examined, deposeth and saith, that upon the 1st of January, 1641, or thereabouts, this deponent lost or was robbed and forcibly despoiled of his goods and chattels to the value of 346*l*. 16*s*. And this deponent further deposeth, that about the 9th day of April last he, accompanied by Walter Harte and Robert Mitchel, English Protestants, both warders of old Castletown, in the said county, went to Doneraile to provide some powder for the defence of the said castle, and stayed there that night. But the next day, the 10th of April aforesaid, this deponent and the other two coming back to hold Castletown aforesaid, they were assaulted and set upon on the highway by John Roche of Ballinemony, in the said county, gent., having in company with him five horsemen and twenty armed footmen, who apprehended this deponent and the rest, and caused them to be disarmed and stripped of their clothes, calling this deponent an 'English traitor;' likewise the same John Roche then and there took from this deponent besides apparel (*illegible*) shillings in money, and a gold ring price thirteen shillings. And the said John Roche immediately caused the said Walter Harte to be hanged, but in the meantime proffered him his life if he would turn Papist, and for that purpose brought to him a mass priest to persuade him thereunto, but the said Harte utterly denying to turn, was presently executed.

This deponent further deposeth, that the same night, being the 10th of April aforesaid, he and the said Robert Mitchel were carried to Castletown, the Lord Roche's house, where he, this deponent, continued prisoner for ten weeks, during which time this deponent observed these particulars following, viz. first, he saw about the 15th or 16th of April two of the Lord of Inchiquin's troops, one was a Scotchman, the other an Irishman, both Protestants, with their horses and arms both taken prisoners by the said Lord Roche's forces, and brought to Castletown aforesaid, where, though the Scotchman was sorely wounded and shot through the back, they were without any mercy hanged. Secondly, this deponent likewise observed and saw one Donogh MacTiegue, an Irish Protestant, a man of threescore years of age and upwards, who was sometime servant to William Jephson of Mallow, Esquire, about the beginning of May last, as he went on the highway to Youghal, to be assaulted and taken by some of the said Lord Roche's company, who brought him to Castletown aforesaid, where he remained prisoner a long time till he was half starved, being allowed but a small morsel of bread in four-and-twenty hours, and day by day the priests and friars in the same (*illegible*), to this deponent's knowledge, being then in number fifteen at least, did use to come to the said Donogh Mac-Tiegue, persuading him to turn Papist; at last when they could not draw him, they gave him his choice to turn Papist and save his life, or else there was no remedy he must be hanged, he told them plainly he was persuaded in his conscience he was of a good and sound profession, and that he would not turn Papist while he lived. Being at last carried to the place of execution, one Father Roch and other friars and priests were a long time with him, at last he told them openly they might go to the devil if they would, but for his part he would never be persuaded by them, and begged heartily they would trouble him no more, and so, heartily praying upon the ladder, he was at last executed. This deponent's cause of knowledge of this is, that being a prisoner himself, he saw and observed those passages, and having his liberty to go up and down he came to the certain knowledge of these premises. During this deponent's restraint at Castletown aforesaid he saith, that he observed, about the latter end of April last, one Elizabeth (*blank*), a maidservant to Stephen Thompson, at Mitchelstown, in the said county, on the way coming for Cork, was apprehended by the said Lord Roche's forces and brought prisoner to Castletown, where she was adjudged to be hanged, if she would not turn Papist, which she utterly refused to do, but others then present thinking it a favour done to her, commanded her to be tied to a post and shot to death, and having made seven shots at her and hit either time, yet not mortally wounded her, at last she was in a tormenting way hanged. This examt. lastly deposeth and saith, that he, being a long time in prison and naked upon the (*illegible*), being stripped before and lying upon the ground with a little straw under him, at last he desired to speak in private to the Lord Roch that some course may be taken for his enlargement, and being admitted to his presence, his lordship spoke these answering words, or others like to them in effect, '*I can show you,*' quoth he, '*a Commission under the king's hand that we have gotten lately from Sir Phelimy O'Neil, whereby we* (meaning the Irish) *are authorised to strip and banish all the English and Protestants out of this kingdom, if they do not join with us and do as we do,*' and adding further in a smiling way, '*I will promise you,*' quoth he, '*the English shall eat no more fat beef in this kingdom,*' or words to that purpose, and further deposeth not.

JASPER HORSEY.

Jurat. coram nobis, 16*th May,* 1642,
PHIL. BISSE.
RICH. WILLIAMSON.

CXCVII.

(*Copy.*)

GEORGE GOULD, of Kinsale, aged thirty years or thereabouts, sworn and examined, saith, that about the first winter quarter in the year 1642 he lived in Kerry, and came thence to Blarney, to buy tobacco, and did see about sixteen English persons, men, women, and children, that he understood were sent from Macroom, by order of the Lord Muskerry, with a guard to Blarney, where they were delivered to the Commander there, viz. one Lieut. John McWilliam O'Reardon, as this deponent believes, who was to send them to Cork. This deponent did not see the said persons conveyed with a guard from Blarney towards Cork, but he saw some Irish men of the ward of Blarney, carrying divers clothes much bloodied on their backs, whereupon this deponent asked them whence they came, to whom some of them answered in Irish, that they had dispatched the said persons, they should never eat more bread, whereupon this deponent turned aside to James Nagle, now of Dingle, being in his company then, and said to him, that was no place for them to stay in, for he believed the vengeance of God would fall thereon, for such actions, and thereupon they went away together. This deponent being further examined, saith, he knoweth neither the names of those English persons, nor the names of those Irish that murdered them, neither doth he know any other person then at Blarney, but the said lieutenant and his ensign, Humphrey Callaghan, and whether these officers be living now or not he knoweth not.

GEORGE GOULD.

CXCVIII.

MARY SMYTH, of the town and parish of Castle Lyons, county of Cork, widow, duly sworn and examined, saith that she hath lost by means of the present rebellion to the value of 600*l.*, and that her husband Henry Smyth of Castle Lyons aforesaid, was cruelly murdered by the Condons on the 6th of April last, at Coole, near Castle Lyons aforesaid, who cut off his tongue and other members most inhumanly after he was dead.

MARY SMYTH +

Jurat. coram nobis, 19*th August,* 1642,
PHILIP BISSE.
JAMES WALLIS.

CXCIX.

ANNE SMYTH, of the aforesaid parish of Castle Lyons, deposeth upon oath that the contents of Mary Smyth's deposition are true. (*Signed as before on same day.*)

CC.

CATHERINE ROBERTS, the relict of George Roberts, of Gortna (*illegible*), in the barony of Duhallow, in the county of Cork, a British Protestant, duly sworn and examined, deposeth and saith, that at Christmas last, and divers times since the beginning of the present rebellion, she lost, or was robbed and forcibly despoiled of her goods and chattels to the value of 226*l.* 10*s.* She likewise deposeth, that about Whitsuntide last, her husband, George Roberts, in the way coming from Doneraile to Liscarrol, was assaulted by Redmund Barry of Lisgriffin, gent., and being taken prisoner, they first stripped him stark naked for the space of three hours, and afterwards most grievously stabbed his body in several places and cut his throat. And further deposeth not.

ELIZABETH THWAITES, of Liscarrol, in the said county, widow, this day also came before us and deposeth and saith, that the account in this bill (*sic*) concerning the murder of George Roberts is true.

KATHERINE ROBERTS +
Jurat. coram nobis, 5*th Feb.* 1642, ELIZ. THWAITES +
PHIL. BISSE.
THOS. BETTESWORTH.

CCI.

JOHN WHETCOMBE, late of Coole, in the county of Cork, gent., a British Protestant, duly sworn and examined, deposeth and saith, that upon the 2nd of February last, or thereabouts, and since the beginning of this rebellion, he lost and hath been robbed and forcibly despoiled of his goods and chattels worth 998*l*. He further saith, that John and Richard Condon of Ballymacpatrick, in the said county, gentlemen, and John and Richard Condon of Ballydurgan, in the said county, gentlemen, and their companies (as this deponent is credibly informed by his neighbours) were the parties that took away his cattle. He lastly saith, that his brother Bartholomew Whetcombe and a matter of eight-and-twenty persons more, or thereabouts, men, women, and children, whose names he cannot now remember, were cruelly murdered at Coole aforesaid by the said Condons and their companies.

JOHN WHETCOMBE.

Jurat. coram nobis, 14*th Junii*, 1642,
   THOS. BRETTRIDGE.
   PHIL. BISSE.

CCII.

CHRISTOPHER CROKER, being duly examined and sworn upon the Holy Evangelists, deposeth and saith, that upon Shrove Tuesday, 1641, Captain Edmund Fennell, with a strong party of rebels with him, came to Ballyamber, where this deponent's father, Edward Croker, James Pike and his son John, Thomas Rutter and another Englishman, servant to Captain Joshua Boyle, then lived, and saith that the rebels summoned them to deliver up their arms and the house unto them, or otherwise they would take it by force, yet notwithstanding they had been about half an hour attempting of it and failed, this deponent's father desired quarter for himself, his wife, and children, and those above-named Englishmen, and all others in the house for their lives, which was granted and promise given to convey them safe half way to Youghal or unto the town's end of Lismore, whereupon the door was opened, and as soon as the rebels came in, they began to deal very roughly and barbarously with us, and stript this deponent and his mother and brothers, whereupon this deponent's father, Edward Croker, demanded what they meant to do with him and if they meant to break their quarter; the deponent's cause of knowledge is, that he was with his father, Edward Croker, in the house, and heard when the quarter was granted, and saw his father deliver up the arms, at the same window which they attempted to enter at, and that he was by his father when he questioned them whether they meant to break the quarter, after the house was delivered up.

He further saith, that the same day they caused this deponent's father to be shot to death, and as this deponent heard, the said Fennell did with his own hand shoot this deponent's father in the head, after he had received two shots before from those that were appointed to execute him, and this deponent doth the rather believe it, for that he heard one shot a little while after the two first were discharged, and that he saw his father's corpse wounded with shot in the head, and two in the body, when it was carried to Lismore to be buried. And further saith, that he, this deponent, heard several of those rebels tell his mother that Fennell was the man who caused her husband to be put to death, and that all the others of their officers were willing to spare his life, but that the said Fennell swore that he would have it in revenge of one of his men who was hanged by Captain Croker, then governor of Cappoquin, who was kinsman to this deponent's father. And further this deponent saith, that the above-named four Englishmen were on the same day hanged upon the gate by the said Fennell's party, and this deponent standing by, saw them so executed, which is his cause of knowledge. And further this deponent saith, that in or about Midsummer, 1650, he being then in command under Colonel Sankey in Clonmell, met with one Lieut.-Colonel James Brian, who was then a prisoner there, to whom this deponent went, who told him that the above-named Fennell was the only man who caused his, this deponent's, father to be put to death, and in this the deponent doth the rather believe he told the truth, for that the said Brian used him and his mother civilly, and took care of them at the same time his (deponent's) father was murdered. And further saith not.

CHRISTOPHER CROKER.

This deposition was sworn before us,
  Ro. STANDISH,
  ED. THOMAS.

143

John Dartnell late of Ballihane ~~in the parish of the Barony of Decies~~ and County of Waterford
Carpenter ~~a British Protestant duly sworn and examined~~
~~before us by vertue of &c~~ deposeth and saith that on
or about the 29th day of December Last past and
since the beginning of this present Rebellion in Ireland
he hath was Robbed and forcibly despoyled of his
goods and Chattells to the ~~value~~ ~~following~~
~~viz~~ value of 217 – 10 – 0

~~Imprimis Cattle young and old viz Horses Mares and Sheep to the~~
~~value~~ of Threescore and eighteene pounds ten shillings
Item Corne in house and Haggard to the value of twenty
pounds Item Hay in Haggard to the value of seaven pounds
Item corne in ground which this deponent conceiveth to be
lost to the value of fourteene pounds Item Household
goods and household provision to the value of twenty
pounds Item Implements of Husbandry to the value of
five pounds Likewise this deponent saith that hee had
a farme being part of the lands of Ballihane aforesaid on wch hee
expended with his Improvements and building and fencing
and other Necessary things to the value of threescore
and twelve pounds The totall of this deponents
losses Amounts to the Summe of two hundred and seaventeene
~~pounds tenn shillings And he saith this deponent saith~~
~~that [illegible] he was Robbed & dispoyled of his afore said~~
~~goods and Chattells~~ by the hands of William O Murrey
of [illegible] in the aforesaid County Husbandman and by Rebells
in the parts whose names he knoweth not, Likewise this
deponent saith that there was Murthered at Cappoquin
the wife of Hugh Shugar and her daughter one Mr Browne
and his Mayde the wife of Robert Sandes the wife
of Henry Maner and her Child the wife of Mr William
Hill and one Richard Aylevor all wch were Murthered
Inhabitants in Cappoquin
A by the hands and Meanes of Captaine Edmond ffennell
Captaine Sharlogue and theire followers whose Names
this deponent knoweth not ~~And further he cannot depose~~

Jurat coram nobis
30th Day of Junii 1642.

John ⟨mark⟩ Dartnall marke

Hen: Brereton
Phil: Bisse.

DEPOSITIONS. 141

CCIII.

JOHN DARTNELL, late of Ballihane and county of Waterford, Carpenter, deposeth and saith, that on or about the 29th day of December last past, and since the beginning of this present rebellion in Ireland, he lost, was robbed, and forcibly despoiled of his goods and chattels to the value of 217*l*. 10*s*. by the hands of William O'Murrye of Affane, in the aforesaid county, husbandman, and by the rebels in those parts whose names he knoweth not. Likewise this deponent saith, that there was murdered at Cappoquin the wife of Hugh Sluger and her daughter, one Mrs. Brown and her maid, the wife of Robert Sanders, the wife of Henry Vance and her child, the wife of William Hill, and one Richard (*illegible*), all which were inhabitants of Cappoquin, murdered by the hands and means of Captain Edmund Fennoll, Captain Sharloge, and their followers, whose names this deponent knoweth not.

JOHN + DARTNELL, mke.

Jurat. coram nobis, 30*th day of June,* 1642,
THOS. BADNEGE.
PHIL. BISSE.

CCIV.

JOHN POLLARD, late of Carriginlira, in the barony of Fermoy, county of Cork, deposeth and saith, that upon the 26th day of February last, or thereabouts, he was robbed and forcibly despoiled of his goods and chattels to the value of 22*l*. 16*s*. He further saith, that one Henry Donn, servant of Captain Hargill of Carriginlira aforesaid, was murdered by Theobald Purcell, the baron of Loughmoe's men, and he further deposeth that John Keene of Carriginlira aforesaid, an English Protestant, was likewise murdered by the tenants and soldiers of Richard Nagle of Monnniminy in the said county, gent., now in actual rebellion.

JOHN + POLLARD.

Jurat. coram nobis, 24*th May,* 1642,
THOS. BETTESWORTH.
PHIL. BISSE.
RICH. WILLIAMSON.

142   THE IRISH MASSACRES OF 1641.

CCV.

MULRONEY O'CAROLL, late of Castledoe, in the county of Donegal, gent., sworn and examined, deposeth and saith, that since the beginning of the present rebellion, that is to say, about the last of October, 1641, this deponent was at Castledoe aforesaid, and elsewhere in Donegal and the King's County, robbed and despoiled of his estate and goods and chattels, consisting of cattle, sheep, corn, debts, benefit of leases, money, hogs, household goods, boats, fishings, and other things, amounting in all to the value of 1,500*l*., by and by the means of those notorious rebels following, viz. Sir Phelim O'Neil of Kinard, Knt., Maolmurry MacSwyne of (*illegible*), in the said county of Donegal, captain of rebels, Neil Morgagh MacSwyne, gent., Owen Roe MacPodden, gent., Henry MacSwyne of Castle Croghan, gent., Maolmurry MacSwyne of Castle Roughare, gent., Manus MacConogher of Drim, gent., Tiegue O'Swighan (*sic*), Owen MacAnally, Tulogh MacAnally, Dermot MacAnally, Shane O'Murry, Lawrence O'Murry, James and Col. O'Murry, three brothers, all of the (*illegible*), in the said county Donegal, gent., and divers others whose names he cannot now call to mind. That one Manus Bane of Doe aforesaid, and his three sons, and some of the rebels before named, most barbarously hanged and murdered one Robert Akins, a Protestant minister (who had often relieved and kindly entertained them in his house), and two of his brothers, John and (*illegible*) Akins, in their own house at Clondrohid, in the county of Donegal. And they also murdered three women, one of whom was great with child . . . and also murdered eight more Protestants in the Doe aforesaid, which cruelties and murders were exercised and done chiefly by command of the said Maolmurry MacSwyne of Magheramoynagh, who is grandchild to Sir Maolmurry MacSwyne. Those Septs being the most cruel and bloody minded people of any other in Donegal. And further saith, that Erwyn MacSwyne is greatly suspected for (being) a most close, cunning, and dangerous rebel, and to be accessory to divers bloody murders committed by his kerns and soldiers commanded by him. And this deponent was most earnestly moved by the said Maolmurry MacSwyne of Magherimagh, and by Brian Oge MacLoghlin, a popish priest, to join the rebels against the Protestants, and to deliver the castle of Doe unto them. And they told this deponent that the Scotch had petitioned the parliament house of England that there should not be a Papist left alive in England,

Ireland, or Scotland. And that some of the committee employed out of Ireland in England for Irish affairs having notice thereof writ over unto them in Ireland to rise in arms and take all the strongholds and forts here into their hands, or to that effect. And that they commanding the rebels now expected the fulfilling of Columkill's prophecy, which as they did construe it, was that the Irish should conquer Ireland again, or to that effect.

MAOLRONY CAROLL.

Jurat. 26th April, 1643,
JOHN WATSON.   HEN. BRERETON.
RANDAL ADAMS.

Note.

After the words 'most cruel and bloodyminded people of Donegal,' the following sentence is interlineated:

'And further saith, he well knoweth that county, and he verily believeth that there have been a thousand Protestants murdered and starved there, besides them that fled from it.'

For the Cromwellians' investigation into this murder see the letters and petitions given hereafter.

THE CASE OF HENRY O'NEIL OF GLASDROMIN.

In his notice of the Manuscripts in Trinity College, Dublin, which I have already referred to (*v. ante*, pp. 122-139), Mr. J. T. Gilbert says:—

"A remarkable instance of the unreliability of statements in the 'depositions' has been recently brought to light from unpublished records, in the case of Henry O'Neil, son of Sir Turlogh O'Neil. At the Court of Transplantation at Athlone in 1655, the Attorney-General produced depositions taken in 1642 in which Charity Chappell and George Littlefield of Armagh declared, with much circumstantiality, that O'Neil had been in rebellion in 1641 and had plundered to a large amount. O'Neil, however, obtained permission to have Littlefield and Chappell examined in Court. There both of them admitted that they were not acquainted with the facts from their own knowledge, but on the contrary knew O'Neil to have always assisted the English. The Court (at Athlone in 1655) consequently set aside the statements in the depositions, and decided in favour of O'Neil." (*Appendix to 8th Report of the Historical Manuscripts Commission, p.* 576, 1881.)

The substance of this passage has been repeated in Mr. Gilbert's preface to the *History of the Irish Catholic Confederation.* The 'unpublished records' on which he relies to sustain his charges against the depositions are those referred to in the following passage in Mr. Prendergast's and Dr. Russell's Report on the Carte MSS. in the Bodleian Library at Oxford, published in 1871.

"It was before the Court at Athlone, A.D. 1655, that Henry O'Neil's (claim and qualification) was heard. In the first instance will be found the extent and annual value of his lands, for by these were to be measured the lands he was to receive in Connaught, and either in fee for life or for term of years, according to the estate he held in them in Armagh. He claimed and proved his title to 10,000 acres (exact 9,805) in fee, of which 2,000 acres (exact 1,994) were unprofitable; that he held them by letters patent of King James I., dated 16th September, 1603, and of King Charles I., dated 19th Dec., 1625, made to his father, Sir Tirlogh O'Neil, Knt., and by the rent of a hawk, or 40s. Irish, and that on his father's death they descended and came to him. And this claim and title was allowed by the court at Athlone. But touching his qualification, evidence was tendered, on the part of the Commonwealth, of his delinquency from the books of Discrimination, to bar his claim. The Attorney-General produced the depositions of Charity Chappell of the city of Armagh, and of George Littlefield of Loughgall, in the county of Armagh, and others, taken thirteen years before, i.e., early in 1642, just after the outbreak, who alleged that the said Henry O'Neil, Arthur his brother, and Tirlogh his son, and others, on the 23rd of October, 1641, had stripped Sir Henry Spottiswoode of all that ever he had in the counties of Monaghan and Armagh, being over 4,000l. in value, and that they had robbed and despoiled her and her husband, deceased, and said George Littlefield of all their goods. The claimant, Henry O'Neil, begged to be allowed to call some of the witnesses, who were still alive, and to produce and re-examine them *vivâ voce* to their former depositions, and this being granted he called said Charity Chappell. She was thereupon demanded her cause of knowledge of what she had sworn in her deposition against Henry O'Neil in 1642. She then (in 1655) said she heard, when she was in prison in Armagh, the first year (of the rebellion) that he was in rebellion, and that what induced her to believe it was that all the country generally was in rebellion. And George Littlefield being re-examined *vivâ voce* to his former deposition, said that he heard said Henry O'Neil was out in action, but not a plunderer. But neither of them knew any such matter to be true of their own knowledge. On the contrary, Charity Chappell knew him of her own knowledge to be a great friend to the English, and it was proved by one Richard Lee, that the persons who so robbed Sir Henry Spottiswoode were tenants to the said Henry O'Neil. For proof of his good affection O'Neil produced the depositions of several witnesses on his behalf, that at the beginning of the rebellion he saved the lives of Mr. Thomas Taylor of the city of Armagh, his wife and family, and six more families of that town, who fled to him for protection, and sent them away to the English quarters. He saved the lives of Mr. FitzGerald, a minister, and Mr. Edward Trevor of Monaghan, and the wives and families of both of them.

He had kept altogether 200 persons in his house from the violence of the rebels, until he could send them to Dundalk and other English quarters, and as often as he heard of the approach of the rebels, into his country, he sent intelligence to the governors of Dundalk or Newry or the adjacent garrisons. For giving such intelligence General Owen O'Neil sent a party of horse and took the claimant prisoner and sent him to Kilkenny, where he was kept prisoner for three months, till the army was gone out of the county, and then he escaped. He had himself been robbed by the rebels of his horses and cows, and those at Glasdromin had been burned by order of Sir Phelim O'Neil. It was also deposed that he could not endure any of his sons to come near his castle. Once he shot at one of them, who was with a party coming to his house, because he was in rebellion. And he had been seen with weeping tears to bemoan himself, saying, what would be thought of him, his sons being gone into rebellion, he ' having been ever faithful to the crown of England.' Upon this state of facts the court found that he did not aid or promote the rebellion in the first year. It might perhaps be supposed that Mr. O'Neil would be entitled to a restoration of his estate, and to escape transplantation. But this would prove a very imperfect conception of the strictness of the rules of transplantation. Of course the commissioners could not find that he had aided or promoted the rebellion in the first year, or was ever in arms since, and they accordingly acquitted him of this. He had also exhibited much good affection to the English, but he must prove a constant, good affection to be spared from transplantation, and by contributing money or victuals, not taken by actual force, and the payment of taxes and levies in the rebel's quarters (where no person dared refuse them), he lost his claim (to be exempted from transplantation). Mr. Henry O'Neil was *probably* in this latter predicament. He was adjudged to transplant, but being within the eighth qualification to have two-thirds of his estate in Connaught. The value of the depositions taken shortly after the outbreak of 1641 is strikingly illustrated in these proceedings. Though taken on oath they were taken in the absence of the party incriminated, and without cross-examination, &c. . . . The decree which follows is believed to be the only example to be found of the decrees of the Court at Athlone." (*Report on the Carte MSS. in the Bodleian Library by Dr. Russell and Mr. Prendergast,* pp. 147, 148.)

Then follows the decree, of which more presently. Such is Mr. Prendergast's and Dr. Russell's very able statement against the Cromwellian judges of Henry O'Neil, and against the truthfulness of the depositions taken in 1642. It seems at first sight unanswerable. At the same time thoughtful readers of the Report may be inclined to doubt that even if Mrs. Chappell and Mr. Littlefield did contradict in 1655 what they had sworn in 1642, that would be sufficient ground for our believing that the eight hundred or a thousand witnesses, baronets, knights, gentlemen, clergymen, ladies, farmers, and tradesmen, who had made depositions in the latter year against the Irish Catholics were all more or less perjured. But setting this aside, let us come to the pith of the whole matter, and in the first place inquire where Mr. Prendergast and Dr. Russell found all those remarkable proofs of O'Neil's loyalty to England and the English, the tales of his refusal to allow his sons to come to his house, his tears and his threats to shoot them for their rebellion, his *vivâ voce* examinations of Mrs. Chappell and Littlefield in the Court at Athlone in 1655, which drew from them a flat contradiction of what they had sworn to in 1642, &c. What proofs have we of all those things set forth in the above passages of the Report? Any one reading those passages would naturally suppose that Dr. Russell and Mr. Prendergast had examined for themselves the records of the Court of Transplantation at Athlone in 1655, containing contemporary reports of the re-examinations of Mrs. Chappell, Littlefield, Leo, and others, as well as the first examinations of the two former in 1642, and that a comparison of the two sets of original examinations, and an exposure of their inconsistencies, was the ground (and a very good one it would be) which Dr. Russell and Mr. Prendergast had for declaring O'Neil had been wronged through the perjuries of the examinants. The confident tone of the above passages regarding their re-examinations in 1655, leaves no doubt on the reader's mind that the original contemporary reports of those re-examinations are in existence, and that those passages in the Report give us a correct abstract of them, and I was so impressed by it, that after I had copied the original examinations of 1642, from the books in the College, I at once set to work to search for those of 1655, taken in the Court at Athlone. I had not (and have not) any wish to make a 'case' out for either party, and if it could be proved that those two witnesses or any others had sworn falsely, I was sincerely desirous to expose their falsehood, and thereby serve the cause of truth, which was all

I had at heart in the investigation of the depositions from first to last. But to my surprise, when I came to search, at the Public Record Offices and the Record Tower in Dublin, for the records of the Court of Transplantation at Athlone, containing the re-examinations of Mrs. Chappell and Littlefield, which the Report on the *Carte MSS.* led me to believe were in existence, I learned that all Records of that Court, with the exception of one thin volume containing the reports of the trials of a few delinquent proprietors in the precinct of Athlone, had been burnt in the great fire of 1711, which destroyed many other valuable State papers in the Dublin collection. Still impressed with the idea that Dr. Russell and Mr. Prendergast must have in the course of their long researches somewhere seen, at least, authentic contemporary copies of those re-examinations of Mrs. Chappell and Littlefield in 1655, I asked my friend and relative Miss Rowan, who inherits the ability of her accomplished and worthy father the late Ven. Archdeacon Rowan for historical research, to examine the *Carte MSS.* at the Bodleian, the MSS. in the British Museum, and the State Papers at the Rolls House, to endeavour to discover those documents. Our united searches, with every assistance from the courteous officials in those institutions and offices, proved fruitless. In the end I reluctantly came to the conclusion that Dr. Russell and Mr. Prendergast could never have seen the re-examinations of 1655 or even authentic contemporary copies of them, and that their sole authority for the statement in favour of O'Neil and against Mrs. Chappell and Littlefield was the decree above mentioned. It is printed at length at p. 148 of their valuable Report on the *Carte MSS.*, but as three-fourths of it consist of a schedule of the different lands comprised in the 10,000 acres claimed by O'Neil, it is only necessary to give here the remaining fourth part, which is as follows:—

"Touching the qualification of the said Henry O'Neile, it appeared by the evidence produced on behalf of the Comonwealth & by the general oaths of John Corren of Drumboate aforesaid, Charity Chappell, late wife of Richard Chappell, late of the town & county of Armagh, & George Littlefield, late of Loghgall, in the county of Armagh, that on the 20th day of October, 1641, Sʳ Henry Spotswood, knight, was stripped & dispoyled of all his goods, ready money & chattells, that ever he had, in the severall counties of Monoghan & Armagh, to the value of above 4,160*l.* by Henry O'Neile of Glasdromine, Esq., Arthur O'Neile his brother, Tirlogh O'Neil his son, & divers other Rebells; that the said Charity Chappell & her late husband & the said George Littlefield were in the first yeare robbed & dispoyled of all their goods, &c., by the parties then in the present rebellion, to wit, Henry O'Neil of Glasdromine, Esq., & divers others, and whereas it was alleged by the councell on behalf of the said claymant, that some of the deponents were yett living who had deposed against the said claymant (O'Neile), to witt, Charity Chappell & George Littlefield, & therefore (he) prayed a commission to re-examine them, touching theire former depositions, against the said claymant, & the Court being desirous to be fully informed of the truth thereof, gave liberty to the claymant to produce them *vivâ voce* in Court, which accordingly he did, & this day being appointed for the re-hearing of the said cause, the Court having entered into a full and deliberate hearing thereof; and the said Mrs. Chappell being demanded upon oath the cause of knowledge of her former depositions against the said Sir Henry O'Neile, said she heard he was in rebellion the said first yeare, when she was in prison in Armagh, & the reason then induceing her to believe the same was, that all the country was generally in rebellion; & the said George Littlefield deposed upon oath, that he heard the said Henry O'Neile was out in action, but not a plunderer, but neither of them of their own knowledge did knowe any such matter to be true; but on the contrary, the said Charity Chappell did affirme her knowledge of him to bee (*sic*) a greate friend to the English; and by the oath of Richard Lee it appeared that Sʳ Henry Spotswood was robbed in the first evening of the rebellion; the persons that so robbed the said Sʳ Henry were tennants to the said Henry O'Neile; and the oaths of the said John & Samuel Corren being too generall & uncertaine to amount to convinceing proofes; and touching the good affection of the said claymant, it appeared to this Court by depositions of severall witnesses, taken in behalf of the saide claymant, that the said Henry O'Neile at the beginning of the rebellion secured & saved the lives of Mr. Thomas Taylor of Armagh, his wife and family, and six more families of the said towne which fled unto him for safeguard, & sent them away to the English quarters, & did likewise save the lives of Mr. FitzGarrett, a minister, his wife & family, & one Mr. Trevors, a minister,

& Mr. Edward Trevors of Monoghan, & both their wives & families, with severall other English, to the number of two hundred, all which persons he kept in his house, from the violence of the rebells, untill he found conveniency to send them safe to Dundalke & other places of the English quarters, & from time to time, as often as he heard of the approach of the rebells into the country, the said Henry O'Neile did send intelligence to the governor of Dundalk or Newry, or the next adjacent garrisons of the English, & that for giveing such intelligence, Generall Owen O'Neile sent a party of horse & took the said claymant prisoner, & sent him to Kilkenny, where he was kept prisoner until the army was then gone out of the country, being about a quarter of a yeare after, at which time he made his escape, & the rebells did at the same time take a great number of horses, mares, cows, and other cattle from the said claymant; that the said claymant's cattle and horses at Glasdromine were burned by Sir Phelim O'Neil's order; that the claymant could not endure any of his sonns to come neare his castle; that he once shott at one of his sonns who was with a party comeing to his house, because he was in Rebellion, & did oft with weeping teares bemoan himselfe saying, what would be thought of him, his sons being gone into rebellion, hee having ever been faithfull unto the Crown of England; so that comparing the evidence of the said claymant with the evidence against him, upon the whole matter, the Court is not judicially satisfied that the said Henry O'Neile did not aid & assist or otherwise promote rebellion in the first yeare, nor was in arms since. The Court doth therefore think fit and adjudge the said Henry O'Neil to be comprised & doth fall under the eighth qualification of the Act of Settlement of Ireland, bearing date the 20th day of August, 1652. And it is further ordered, adjudged, & decreed that the said Henry O'Neile shall have and enjoy two thirds part of his said estate to him, his heirs and assigns for ever, in Connaught or Clare, according to the true intent of the said eighth qualification of the said Act of Settlement: Saveing to his Highnesse the Lord Protector & Comonwealth of England all right and title which at any time hereafter may appear to belong or appertain to his said Highnesse, or the said Commonwealth, and saveing to all other persons all right and title which at any time hereafter may appear to belong or appertain to them or their heirs, into or out of the lands and estate claymed by the said Henry O'Neil or into or out of any part thereof in any wise. Dated at Athlone the 5th day of November, 1655."

"*Examd. by,*
Rd. Couse, *Registrar.*"

"Isaac Dobson.
Wm. Frankland.
J. Southey."

"*Compared with the Original this* 29*th December,* 1668,"
"John Taylor, *Reg*^r."   "Wm. Cooper."

Perceiving that the above as it stands in Dr. Russell's and Mr. Prendergast's Report on the *Carte MSS.* (p. 151) seemed to have been printed from a mere copy made in 1668, of an original of 1655, and knowing the suspicious character of many similar documents drawn up in the former year, I wrote to Mr. Prendergast to ask if the original decree or a certified contemporary copy of it made by the Cromwellian officials was in existence. In reply he wrote to me saying, 'the decree is an office copy made in 1668, by the officers who had official care of the Cromwellian legal papers. These being all brought together for the use of the Commissioners of the Court of Claims, were unfortunately burnt in the great fire at the Council Office in 1711, and amongst them the Athlone decrees.' Thus there is not a single original record of the proceedings at the Court of Athlone in 1655 regarding Henry O'Neil in existence.

The sole authority for all that Dr. Russell and Mr. Prendergast have stated about him and the alleged re-examinations of Littlefield and Mrs. Chappell in 1655 at Athlone, contradicting what they had sworn in 1642, is this copy said to have been made by the royalist officials of the Court of Claims in 1668 of a decree, alleged by them to have been issued by the Athlone Court of eight years before.

Now when we remember that all impartial historians of credit, and some who, like Carte, are decidedly partial to the claims of the Irish loyalists of 1660, admit that the forging of documents attempting to prove the 'nocent' Irish of 1641-2 'innocent,' in order to restore them to their forfeited lands and oust the Cromwellian grantees, was a regular branch of business in 1660-7; that Richard Talbot,[1] subsequently Duke of Tyrconnell, known even amongst his

---

[1] *V.* p. 153 of Report on the *Carte MSS.* by Dr. Russell and Mr. Prendergast, where they say with respect to the Allen estate that the old proprietors were restored through the aid of Talbot and Lord Berkely, the latter acting 'it would seem out of pity, and Colonel Talbot on promise of part of the lands for his

Cavalier associates by the sobriquet of 'lying Dick,' drove an actual trade in those frauds, receiving large sums of money or promises of large slices of the lands claimed in return for concocting them and 'floating' them by his influence at Court; that Henrietta Maria's profligate favourite Jermyn, Earl of St. Albans, also traded successfully in the same frauds, it seems quite probable that this 1663 copy made by those noblemen's friends is from beginning to end a forgery. It is to the frequency of such frauds that Brodie alludes in his observations on Dean Kerr's worthless declaration (v. Vol. I. Introduction, p. 119).

At all events before we accept this copy of a lost original against the veracity of the still extant original depositions of Chappell and Littlefield in 1642, we are surely bound to sift and test the former by the latter. This is just the contrary of the process adopted by Mr. Prendergast and Dr. Russell. They print the copy of 1663 impugning the veracity of the original depositions of 1642, without printing, or even examining the latter, and they build up a whole case against those original documents on the sole authority of a copy of a lost original.

I must ask my readers to note that I am not here concerned with the guilt or innocence of O'Neil, but with the charge made by Dr. Russell, Mr. Prendergast, and Mr. Gilbert against the veracity of Littlefield's and Chappell's depositions in 1642. For reasons to be given hereafter, I think Henry O'Neil was not deeply involved in the massacres and outrages committed by his sons and other rebels in 1641-3, but that he was a more or less passive spectator, a waiter on providence, afraid or unable to do much against them, and desirous to take his politics and his creed from the conquering party. But before we can believe, on the authority of the copy of 1663, that Littlefield and Chappell contradicted in 1655 what they had sworn in 1642, we must satisfy ourselves, by the examination

soliciting Allen's cause,' which promise was fulfilled. Carte, in his *Life of Ormond*, tells us that six Irish gentlemen, whose names he gives, paid 65,000*l*. to Jermyn to procure for them decrees of innocence, and that Antrim having no children settled the reversion of his estate on Jermyn for his influence to procure a similar decree, and to cause him (Antrim) to be released from imprisonment in the Tower, but that when Antrim was set free and restored to his estate it was found that he had, before the settlement on Jermyn, conveyed over all his said estate to his brother, so that Jermyn was baulked, and the biter bit. For a Christian and high-minded view of Jermyn's character generally and his acts, by the most eminent of living English historians, see *The Personal Government of Charles the First*, by S. R. Gardiner, F.S.A., vol. ii. p. 49.

of their original depositions made in the latter year, which fortunately still remain, what it was they actually did then swear to, and compare it with what this copy says of both those depositions, and the re-examinations of 1655. If we find that the original depositions of Littlefield and Chappell in 1642 correspond with the abstract given of them in the copy of the decree, and that they are in contradiction to the abstract the copy gives of the same witnesses' re-examinations in 1655, then Mr. Prendergast, Dr. Russell, and Mr. Gilbert have some ground whereon to maintain their particular charge against those witnesses, and their general one against all the depositions of 1642. But if, on the contrary, we find that the 1663 copy gives an untruthful abstract of the two witnesses' depositions in 1642, making them say what they did not say, and that the abstract it gives of their re-examinations in 1655 shows that they only repeated in substance what they had actually sworn to in 1642, then manifestly there is no reasonable ground for doubting their veracity, and the particular and general charges of Mr. Prendergast, Dr. Russell, and Mr. Gilbert cannot be maintained, while the copy of the decree, on the other hand, is proved to be untruthful, is self-convicted of untruthfulness, if I may be permitted to use the expression.

According to the copy and the three gentlemen who place such reliance on it, as convicting Chappell and Littlefield (and many others) of perjury, those two witnesses deposed on oath in 1642, that in the first year of the rebellion ' they were robbed and despoyled of all their goods and chattels by Henry O'Neil of Glasdromin.' George Littlefield made two depositions before the Commissioners, one of which, containing no mention of Henry O'Neil, has been already given (*v. ante*, p. 85). The second deposition of Littlefield, sworn on the same day before the same Commissioners, is as follows:—

"George Littlefield, late of Loughgall, in the county of Armagh, being sworn and examined, deposeth, that about the beginning of the present rebellion he was robbed and despoiled of his goods and chattels, viz. two horses worth 5*l*., household stuff and (*illegible*) to the value of 15*l*.; also this deponent hath lost the benefit of a lease of a house and backyard which he held in Loughgall for fourteen years to come, upon which this deponent hath bestowed lately in building 30*l*. ster., and he likewise hath lost the hereafter profits of a farm worth 7*l*. per an.

He also saith that about the 11th of May last, when the whole country about Armagh was burnt, this deponent was forced to shelter himself in an island, and being there taken by the rebels James O'Donnelly, late of (*illegible*), labourer, and Hugh Boy MacManus, late of Dromully, gent., he was constrained to give them 19*l*. for a convoy for himself and some of his friends towards Dublin, but having got the money into their hands, they did not according to their promise send a convoy with this deponent, but kept him prisoner, and would have murdered him, but he escaped that night. And this deponent saith, that the persons hereinafter named were in open rebellion in the said county of Armagh, about the beginning of March last : Sir Phelim O'Neil of Kinard, in the county of Tyrone, Turlogh O'Neil, Esq., brother to Sir Phelim, Patrick Ballagh O'Donnelly of Bally (*illegible*), yeoman, Neil O'Donnelly of the same, yeoman, Shane O'Haghie (*sic*) of Benburt, in the county of Tyrone, gent., Alexander Hovenden of Ballinbeatagh, in the county of Armagh, gent., Edmund Crawley of Armagh, gent., Murtogh O'Donnelly, late of Charlemont, gent., Henry Ogo O'Neil of Glasdromin, Esq., John Stanley, late of Drogheda, alderman, Shane O'Neil, late of Killnaman, in the county of Tyrone, gent., Art O'Neil of Mullaghmore, gent., Henry O'Neil his son of the same, gent., and several others whom this deponent cannot now remember. And further saith, that Manus O'Cahan of the Grange, near Loughgall, gent., a colonel among the rebels, Brian Kelly of Charlemont, in the county of Armagh, a captain of the rebels, Shane O'Neil, also of Charlemont aforesaid, captain of the rebels, Patrick O'Donnelly of (*illegible*), in the same county, gent., are with many others mentioned in his former deposition in actual rebellion."

"GEORGE LITTLEFIELD +"

"*Jurat. June* 1*st*, 1642,
  WM. ALDRICH.
  WM. HITCHCOCK."

It will be seen that in this, his second and last deposition, made on June 1st, 1642, George Littlefield does not accuse Henry O'Neil of having 'despoiled him of all his goods and chattels.' The deponent does not in fact accuse O'Neil of plundering any one, but merely swears in 1642 what, according to this copy of the decree, he swore in 1655, that he believed O'Neil was out in rebellion with his sons, brother, and kinsmen. Hence the whole charge made by Dr. Russell, Mr. Prendergast, and Mr. Gilbert against Littlefield's veracity, on the ground that he contradicted in the latter year what he had sworn to in the former, falls to the ground. The main question before the Court was not whether O'Neil was a rebel, for that the Court held every man to be who had sided with Charles I., but whether he had murdered or plundered Protestants, or sheltered their murderers and plunderers.

Now as regards Mrs. Chappell's evidence, it will be also seen by her deposition of 1642, here printed from the original in Trinity College, Dublin, that she never did swear in that year as the copy of 1663 alleges she did:—

"CHARITY CHAPPELL, late wife of Richard Chappell, late of the town and county of Armagh, Esq., widow, duly sworn and examined before us, deposeth and saith, that, since the beginning of the present rebellion, her late husband and she have been by the rebels forcibly expelled from their farms and grounds, which they held in lease for sixty years or thereabouts, all lying in or near Armagh aforesaid, of the yearly value of 400*l*., her own when the rebellion began, one year's value whereof they have already lost, amounting to 400*l*., and that her said husband being since dead, she is like to lose the future profits thereof until a peace be settled, and that the same farms come to their former value. And this deponent and her husband were also deprived, robbed, and otherwise despoiled, since the beginning of this rebellion, of their stocks of cattle upon their grounds, worth 961*l*., of corn and hay in the stack worth (*illegible*), corn in the ground worth 87*l*., plate and household stuff worth (*illegible*), wool worth (*illegible*), debts owing by divers persons, some in rebellion, and the rest robbed and disenabled by the rebels to make her any satisfaction, in all amounting to the sum of 2,248*l*. And further saith, that there is owing unto her by debts of English Protestants, slain and robbed by the rebels, so as they are disenabled to give her any satisfaction, amounting in all to 253*l*. And that the parties hereinafter named, being all actors in the present rebellion, are also indebted to this deponent, in several and particular sums of money, amounting in all to 131*l*., the names of which positive rebels are these, viz. Hugh Boy McDonnell of (*illegible*), in the county Antrim, captain of rebels; Alexander Hovenden of Dallin (*illegible*), another captain ; Hugh Modder

O'Quin of the same, gent.; Patrick Morgan of Armagh; Mackillduffe O'Quin of the Fews, gent.; Henry O'Neil of Glasdromin; Turlogh O'Hagan of Armagh, labourer; Patrick and Thady O'Donnell of Armagh, merchants; Edmund Kelly of (*blank*), John and James Hanlon of Armagh, millers; Patrick Donnelly of Armagh, merchant, Edmund O'Donnell of Lisduane, farmer; all of the county of Armagh, and Edmund Crelly of Armagh aforesaid, another captain of rebels. And further saith, that by means of the said rebellion she hath lost and suffered by the wasting, spoiling, and burning of her houses and improvements to the value of 700*l.*, besides many debts and other losses she cannot remember, she having had her debt books and most of her writings burnt by the rebels, and therefore their value she cannot now estimate. And further she saith, that she hath credibly heard that the rebels did slay and kill divers Protestant ministers, viz. Mr. Fullarton, minister of Loughgall, Mr. Blyth, minister of Dungannon, Mr. Robinson, minister of Kilmore, and his wife; Mr. Hudson, minister of Desert Martin, Mr. Griffin, curate of Armagh, and that at one time the rebels took away from Armagh threescore Protestants and murdered them, and a second time about forty-five were also by them murdered, and that when Armagh was burned, the rebels murdered a great many more Protestants, but how many she knoweth not; many children being seen there murdered in vaults and corners, where they fled to hide themselves. And saith, that her present losses by means of the rebellion that she can remember, cometh to 3,243*l.*, her future loss being like to be 400*l.* per an. as aforesaid. And further saith, that one Mr. Preston, son-in-law to Turlogh Oge O'Neil, uttered these words, viz. that the '*gentry of Ireland on their side did much grieve that the scum of the English should be there to overtop them.*' And that she often heard divers of the rebels say, that Sir Phelim O'Neil was by them made 'the O'Neil.' And the very morning that Armagh was burned, the said Turlogh Oge O'Neil said in her hearing, that if the English army came on behalf of the king, he would deliver to them the town of Armagh, but that if they came on behalf of the parliament of England, then he would not surrender it to such rogues, but would fight it out. Yet afterwards, when he thought the English army came near the town, both he and Sir Phelim O'Neil and the rest of the rebels there suddenly ran away from them and fled. And further saith, that Michael Dunn of Castle Dillon, in the county of Armagh, was in open rebellion."

"*Jurat.* 20*th July,* 1642,
  John Sterne.
  Wm. Aldrich.
  Hen. Brereton."

"Charity Chappell."
"John Watson.
Wm. Hitchcock."

  Mrs. Chappell was the widow of a rich merchant, and evidently a shrewd, money-loving, energetic woman of business, and a friend to the parliament even in the presence of the royalist Commissioners. Like all persons of her type and class, she may have somewhat exaggerated, with no deliberate or conscious dishonesty, the value of her stolen goods and bad debts. But she never once in this her deposition of 1642 accuses Henry O'Neil of having 'robbed and despoiled her of all her goods,' as the copy of the decree says she did. She merely says, like Littlefield, in his deposition made some six or eight weeks previously, that she believed Henry O'Neil was in actual rebellion, and that he was one of her debtors.

  Thus we have now exposed two absolute falsehoods in this copy made in 1663 of a decree alleged to have been issued in 1655. This copy tells us the two witnesses swore in 1642 that they were robbed and despoiled of their goods and chattels by Henry O'Neil of Glasdromin, but their original depositions of that year now before us prove that they swore no such thing. Therefore Mr. Prendergast's and Dr. Russell's charge against the said witnesses, based on the statement in the copy that they, when re-examined in 1655, swore, in contradiction to their evidence in 1642, that they were not plundered by O'Neil, is proved utterly groundless, as is the general charge against the rest of the depositions based on this imaginary contradiction.

  But it may be said the copy of the decree asserts that Mrs. Chappell swore in her re-examination in the Court at Athlone in 1655, that Henry O'Neil, whom she called a rebel in her first examination in 1642, was a great friend to the English, and that here at least she contradicted herself, and gave ground for Mr. Prendergast's and Dr. Russell's charges. To this I answer that our sole authority (so-called) for what Mrs. Chappell is asserted to have said in her re-examinations in 1655, our sole authority, in fact, for supposing that these re-examinations ever took place at all, is this copy of the decree in which we have already detected two great falsehoods. If such re-examinations in the case of Henry O'Neil were ever made in the Athlone Court, I do not believe the abstract of them in this copy of 1663 is correct, any more than the abstract of the examinations of 1642 which it gives is correct. We have found the latter to be false, and are therefore quite justified in believing the former would be found so, if the records of the Athlone Court had been preserved as the depositions of 1642 have been. And as to the alleged depositions of 'divers (anonymous) witnesses' which are mentioned in this untruthful copy, as bearing testimony to Henry O'Neil's tears and threats at his son's rebellion, and his having saved the lives of more than two hundred Protestants, including the family of Mr. Taylor, they may be all dismissed as myths of Dick Talbot's or his friends' invention, or at least as exaggerations containing a grain of truth with a hundredweight of falsehood. It is probable that Henry O'Neil, like Sir Phelim himself, and other rebels who actively persecuted and plundered the Protestants, and were accessory to their murder, may have protected a Protestant here and there, towards whom he had a friendly feeling. But such exceptional acts of kindness it is needless to say would not entitle him to be pronounced innocent in the Court at Athlone, where justice was impartially administered. We know from the deposition of Michael Harrison that it was Sir Phelim O'Neil himself who gave Mr. Taylor and his wife a protection, although it would appear that Henry O'Neil also had a friendly feeling towards their son, and as Harrison believed, would have saved him if possible. And it is wholly incredible that if Henry O'Neil had been such an uncompromising friend to the English and Scotch colonists, had protected them and opposed Sir Phelim and his followers to the extent asserted in this alleged copy of a decree of 1655, that those facts would not have been stated in several of the depositions taken between 1641 and 1654, the originals of which still remain. We have seen how careful the deponents generally were to mention the names of any Roman Catholic, from Owen O'Neil down to a poor labourer, layman or priest, who had done them a kindness, and the letters, orders, &c., hereafter given written in 1650-5, exempting from transplantation and forfeiture John Knight of Kerry, John O'Connell, Daniel O'Hagan, and other Roman Catholics who had been real, not pretended, friends of the persecuted Protestants in 1641-9, will show that such good deeds were always rewarded by Cromwell. Even Roman Catholic historians are obliged to admit that he rewarded the two priests who saved the lives of a few Protestants in the massacre at Cashel, a massacre which drew down on that place the terrible vengeance of Murrogh O'Brien, fourth Baron of Inchiquin. Another proof that this copy of the decree of 1663 is a more or less clumsy fraud, is to be found in the account it gives of the sworn evidence of John and Samuel Corren.[1] Both those witnesses distinctly and positively swore in 1642, that Henry O'Neil was one of the rebels who plundered the houses and lands of Sir Henry Spottiswoode. Whether they swore truly or falsely their testimony was decided and particular in marking him as a plunderer as well as a rebel in 1641. Yet this copy of the decree describes it as having been 'too generall and uncertaine to amount to convincing proofes.' How false this description is, will be seen by the following copies of the Corren's deposition in 1642, from the originals in the books in Trinity College, Dublin.

"SAMUEL CORREN, of Drumboate, in the county of Monaghan, yeoman, aged threescore and four years or thereabouts, being examined and sworn upon the Holy Evangelists, saith as followeth: that on the 22nd day of October last past, Sir Henry Spotswood, Knt., was robbed, stripped, and despoiled of all the goods, chattels, ready money, and other things that ever he had in the several counties of Monaghan and Armagh by Henry O'Neil of Glasdromin, Arthur O'Neil, his brother, and Tirlogh O'Neil, son to the said Henry O'Neil, all of them inhabiting in the county of Armagh, and their accomplices and adherents, that is to say, in ready money, plate, and household stuff to the value of 2,500l., in cows, horses, and sheep to the value of (*illegible*), and in corn and hay to the value of 100l. or thereabouts. And he further deposeth and saith, that Sir Christopher Bellew, *alias* Bedlow, of Castletown, in the county of Louth, knight, on the 25th day of October last past, being Monday, between nine and ten o'clock in the forenoon of the same day, he, this deponent, did then see him, the said Sir Christopher, accompanied with his own footman, Patrick O'Doughlin, come off and from his own lands into and upon the lands and grounds of the said Sir Henry Spotswood, lying and being within the territory of Drumboate, in the said county of Monaghan, and from thence he, the said Sir Christopher in his own person, his

[1] They were dead in 1655, if we are to believe the decree, which only mentions Chappell and Littlefield as then living.

said footman, and certain other persons, his tenants, did drive away to the number of eighty head of cows and other cattle of the proper goods of him the said Sir Henry Spotswood into the lands of him the said Sir Christopher Bedlew, *alias* Bellow, lying in the county of Louth. And further this deponent deposeth and saith, that he, being then servant to the said Sir Henry Spotswood, and tendering the goods and welfare of him the said Sir Henry, went of his own accord to Castletown, the dwelling-house of the said Sir Christopher Bedlow, *alias* Bellew, and informed him that the said Sir Henry was then before robbed of his goods and chattels to a great value, and also then and there told the said Sir Christopher that there was to the value of 200*l*. worth of the proper goods of the said Sir Henry then remaining in the houses and possession of several of the tenants of him, the said Sir Christopher, hoping by such complaint that the said Sir Henry might receive some present remedy and relief. But he, the said Sir Christopher, said he would neither meddle nor make nor give any assistance at all."

"SAM. CORREN."

"*Deposed before us, Jan.* 15*th*, 1641,
 RANDALL ADAMS.
 HEN. BRERETON."

Three days later John Corren made the following deposition:—

"JOHN CORREN, of Drumboate, in the county of Monaghan, yeoman, sworn and examined, saith, that on the 26th day of October last past, Sir Henry Spotswood, knight, was robbed, stripped, and despoiled of all the goods, ready money, and chattels that he had in the several counties of Monaghan and Armagh, which this examt. believeth to be to the sum of 4,160*l*. or thereabouts, by Henry O'Neil of Glasdromin, Esq., Arthur O'Neil, his brother, and Tirlogh O'Neil, son to the said Henry, all of them of the county of Armagh, and divers other rebels, some on horseback and some on foot under their command, and that they left the said Sir Henry nothing at all. And further saith, that on Monday next then after this deponent being escaped away from Drumboate aforesaid, where he and other of his fellow-servants were shewdly wounded, inasmuch that he believeth the other two are dead, went to one Sir Christopher Bellow, *alias* Bedlow, of Castletown, in the county of Lowth, knt., with intention to have procured a pass to Dublin from him, and

DEPOSITIONS. 161

telling the said Sir Christopher how the said Sir Henry Spotswood was robbed of his goods, the said Sir Christopher then denying to give this deponent any pass, then and there said, and confessed to this deponent that he (Sir Christopher) was present on the lands of the said Sir Henry Spotswood when his goods were taken and carried away, and that therefore this deponent need not tell him any more about it."

"JOHN CORREN +"

"*Jurat.* 18*th Jan.* 1641,
HEN. JONES.
WM. ALDRICH."

The following deposition was also made against Henry O'Neil, his sons, and tenants. I omit the long inventory of the deponent's goods and chattels stolen or destroyed.

"PAUL REED, of Blackstaff, in the county of Monaghan, clerk, sworn and examined, saith, that by means of this rebellion he was deprived and despoiled of his wife and children ; two of his children with poverty and bad usage perished, and three with his wife were murdered ; one was murdered at Blackstaff with three men and women by the rebels of Monaghan, viz. Patrick MacMahon, Art MacMahon, and their brother, whose (Christian) name he knows not, and one James MacMor MacMahon and a drummer from Ardee, whose name he knows not ; this deponent's wife and the two other children were barbarously and cruelly murdered within one mile or two of Glasdromin Castle, in the Fews, by Henry O'Neil's servants and tenants, and their bodies left to be food for dogs and fowls of the air. This deponent further saith that the rebels of the county Monaghan, Lowth, and Armagh, over and above the above-named rebels who with force of arms have used (*illegible*) and cruelties towards his Majesty's Protestant subjects of the kingdom of Ireland, whom he knows are : Ardell MacMahon, MacHugh MacMahon, Cormac Art MacMahon of (*illegible*), in the county of Monaghan, Con MacMahon, brother-in-law to Cormac Bawn MacMahon in the parish of Killeane, county Monaghan, Patrick MacLaughlin MacMahon of the (*illegible*), Henry O'Neil of Glasdromin, Art Oge O'Neil, brother to said Henry, both of the Fewes, in the county of Armagh, and the most part of the inhabitants of the (*illegible*) towns of the Fews, of the county of Lowth, and the inhabitants of Drumble (*sic*), of the county of Armagh, were at the robbing and spoiling of the inhabitants of Drumboate, being Sir Henry Spotswood's house, in the county of Monaghan. This deponent further saith, that he thinks of his conscience, that the tenth part of the British of the whole north of Ireland who were robbed and despoiled by the rebels, are not at present alive, so many being murdered and cruelly put to death, others being stripped and robbed of their clothes and all they had, through sickness and poverty miserably dying, and others for succour and relief flying the kingdom, and dying in Scotland and England although relieved there."

"PAUL REED."

"Jurat. 9th August, 1642,
JOHN WATSON.
JOHN STERNE.
HEN. BRERETON."

Sir Henry Spotswood himself made the following deposition. It is as far as I could ascertain the only one in the whole thirty-two volumes in the college in which the pen has been drawn over the relation of a murder or alleged murder. Sir Henry having left his Irish servant O'Donnelly at Drumboate after he was wounded, was in doubt about his having recovered and heard conflicting accounts on the subject. This accounts for the alteration in the MS. which was evidently made the day or week that the deposition was taken. It tells in favour of the Commissioners' impartiality, not against it, that they hastened to erase the account of the supposed murder.

"SIR HENRY SPOTSWOOD, late of Drumboate, in the county of Monaghan, sworn and examined, deposeth and saith, that about 6 or 7 o'clock in the night of the 22nd of October last past, he this deponent was robbed, stripped, and despoiled of all the goods, chattels, ready money, and other goods that ever he hath within the several counties of Monaghan and Armagh. And quickly after he was also robbed, stripped, and despoiled of all the goods and chattels that he had within the counties of Fermanagh and Tyrone, by the rebels now up in arms in those counties, viz. by Turlogh O'Neil of Lany, barony of Glasdrum, county of Armagh, Esq., Sir Phelim O'Neil, knt., of Kinard in the said county, Coll MacMahon of the barony of Dunamaine, county of Monaghan, Esq., and Rory Maguire, the Lord Maguire's brother, and divers other rebels, under their command whose names this deponent knoweth not: which said goods consisting of corn, cattle, household stuff; ready money, his interest of leases and debts due, amount in all to the sum of 5,580l., or thereabouts. And this deponent further saith that the said rebels did grievously wound that the said rebels about the same time did most cruelly and barbarously murder one Patrick O'Donnelly, this deponent's servant, and detained as prisoner Jane, this deponent's daughter, and three of his servants, by name John Morris, Richard Lee, and Anne Lee, who still, as he believeth, remaineth in prison with the said Coll MacMahon, in Carrickmacross. Beside the same rebels kept in restraint one Mr. Robert Boyle and his wife, one Mr. Magill, another minister, Mr. James Montgomery, another minister, one Ralph Seacome, gent. And this deponent hath not only suffered the losses and wrongs aforesaid, but many more in other places, whereof as yet he can give no present estimate. And further saith, he credibly heard that the rebels aforesaid, or some of them, did often wish that they had in custody this deponent's person, that they might cut him in pieces, or words to that effect."

"HEN. SPOTSWOODE."

"*Jurat.* 15*th Jan.* 1641,
    ROGER PUTTOCK.
    RANDAL ADAMS."

Another Monaghan witness made the following deposition a year later :—

"ELIZABETH CLARK, late of Peterborrow, in the county of Monaghan, widow, late wife of Thomas Clark, of same, gent., sworn and examined saith, that in the beginning of the present rebellion, and by means thereof, her said husband and she were expelled, robbed, and otherwise despoiled, of their residence, goods, and chattels of the value, and to their present loss, of 385*l.* by Patrick MacArdell MacEiver MacMahon of the Cargagh, in the said county, gent., Garret Makee (*sic*), of (*blank*), near Peterborrow aforesaid, and many other rebels, whose names she knoweth not, and saith, that most of her said goods were brought unto and received by Collo MacBrian MacMaghan (*sic*), now of Carrickmacross, Esq., Roger Whitehead of Enniskeen, in the said county, gent. And further saith, that the parties whom she saw and knoweth to be in actual rebellion, and to carry arms against his Majesty and his loyal subjects, are these that follow, viz. the said Collo MacBrian MacMahon, Roger Whitehead, Patrick

McArdell McEiver McMahon, Patrick FitzEdmund and Owen O'Murphy, two bloody rebels, Patrick Groom (*illegible*), Garret Makee, and one Art McBrian McMahon, brother to the said Coll Patrick McLoughlin McMahon, and Ross McLoughlin Mac-Mahon, Eiver MacLoughlin MacMahon, their vicar-general, a most cruel and bloody priest; Edmund McLaughlin McMahon, another priest; Pierse O'Duffy, and Turlogh O'Duffy, his eldest son, which said Turlogh O'Duffy, and Ross McTurlogh Mac-Mahon drowned seventeen men, women, and children, all Protestants, at Ballenrosse, in the said county; Patrick MacEiver Mahon, Owen MacEiver MacMahon, Rory and Hugh MacEiver Mahon, and Art MacEiver Mahon, being the sons of Collo Mac-Eiver MacMahon near Castleblaney, gent., Tirlogh Oge O'Neil and Shane O'Neil, both sons of Henry O'Neil of Glasdromin, Esq., Philip O'Calon (*sic*) of (*blank*) near Carrickmacross, gent. Donogh Roe O'Calon and Patrick Roe O'Calon, brothers and kinsmen to the said Philip O'Calon; Philip O'Duffy, popish priest, of the parish of Dunamaine. And further saith, that on New Year's Day, 1641, the aforesaid three priests, chief instigators, and the rest of the rebels caused this deponent's husband and Mr. William Williams, Mr. Ethel Jones, Mr. Gabriel Williams, Mr. James Montgomery, minister of Dunamaine, Mr. Boswell and his wife, who were so aged they both went upon staves, Thomas Osburne, Richard Hollis, Richard Taylor, John Morris, Philip Pharley, William Wood, Thomas Trann, John Jackson, Thomas Aldersley, George Green, Ralph Seacombe, Edward Ball, Edward Cudworth, Robert Ray, Richard Gates, and John (*blank*), servant to Mr. Boyle, and another that was servant to Mr. Dillon and gathered his rents, John Walmisley, Richard Musgrave, William Musgrave and his wife, Henry Wylie, George Harrison, Thomas Young and divers other Protestants, whose names she knoweth not, to be put to death; some they hanged, and some they stabbed, wounded, and cut to pieces, and one of these, the said Osburne, after they had hanged him they gave him at least forty wounds in several parts of his body. And saith further, that the said Eiver Mac-Loughlin (MacMahon), the priest, brought a warrant from Coll MacBrian, and others of the rebellious council at the siege of Drogheda, for putting to death the Protestants aforesaid, and employed and busied himself in the procuring thereof, and afterwards showed the said warrant to this deponent and others.

And further saith, that the said rebel Patrick MacLaughlin

MacMahon, and others of the rebels, often said in her hearing that if they might have their own laws, and all Lord Deputys and other great general officers, judges, and magistrates to be all of the Irish (race), then they would not forsake the King of England, but if they might not they would make a king amongst them of their own; further saying that now they had begun they would either root out all the English, or the English should root out them, for they knew if the English prevailed they (the Irish) should never be trusted, and therefore they would go on in their actions, or words to that effect. And saith also, that the said rebel, Owen O'Murphy, escaped the gallows by the means of the said Mr. Williams, and yet he was the man that caused the said Mr. Williams to be hanged."

"The mark + of ELIZABETH CLARKE."
"*Jurat.* 17th Jan. 1642,
WIL. ALDRICH.
HEN. BRERETON."

As I have already pointed out, the question with which I am here concerned is not the guilt or innocence of Henry O'Neil, but the veracity of Mr. Chappell and Mr. Littlefield in 1642. Did they swear in that year that they were robbed by Henry O'Neil as this 1663 copy of a decree alleged to have been made in 1655 tells us they did? Their original depositions made in 1642 before us prove that they did not. The falsehood of at least one portion of this copy being thus proved, are we justified in accepting as truthful the other portion of the same copy professing to give us an abstract of what the same witnesses are said to have sworn in 1655? Clearly not, the strength of the chain is its weakest link. Unless we find from other contemporary records good proof that the statements of the 1663 copy respecting the depositions (now apparently lost or destroyed) of 1655 are truthful, we are justified in believing they are as untruthful as the statements of the same copy respecting the depositions of 1642 (still in existence) are known to be. Until such contemporary records of 1655 are before us, whatever be the guilt or innocence of Henry O'Neil, the charges made against the veracity of Mr. Chappell and Mr. Littlefield fall to the ground.

After a careful search through the fifty-five volumes of Commonwealth Records now in the Public Record Office, I could only discover the following brief order concerning Henry O'Neill of

Glasdromin, directing that the 'allegations' he had made in his petition to be dispensed from transplantation to Connaught should be considered, and that his prayer should be granted if he were found to be superannuated, that is, too feeble in health, and too old to move with safety to his life. Many old, sickly persons who had been proved 'nocent' were nevertheless dispensed from transplantation on the ground of sickness or old age. The dispensation was sometimes for a given time, sometimes for a prolongation of a temporary reprieve, sometimes excusing the person from moving at all.

"*Commonwealth Books*, $\frac{A}{4}$. *P. R. O.*

"Ordered that the above petition of Henry O'Neil of Glasdromin, in the barony of the Fews, in the county of Armagh, setting forth his saving many English at the beginning of the rebellion to the hazard of his life; being therefore wounded and driven from his habitation by the rebels, his continued good affection, his former dispensation from transplantation, be referred to the Commissioners for the adjudication of claims and qualifications of Irish proprietors, to consider of the allegations therein; and if they find him superannuated, then to certify the same, that his person may be dispensed from transplantation, but his estate to be disposed of according to rule, as by his qualifications shall be distinguished by said Commissioners, according to their instructions. Dublin, 5th February, 1654. THOMAS HERBERT, *Clerk of Council.*"

All the scanty evidence we have about Henry O'Neil of the Fews or Glasdromin proves that he was at best a weak, wavering man, not an active rebel or persecutor of the English like his sons, brother, and nephews, but on the contrary willing, if not earnestly desirous, to save the lives of some of his Protestant neighbours, provided that he could do so without much trouble or danger to himself. One of the deponents in 1642 swore that Henry O'Neil had promised the mother of Brownlow or Bromley Taylor to intercede with Sir Phelim for her son's life, but that he failed to do so through timidity or dilatoriness, and that she bitterly reproached him on that account. Michael Harrison's evidence tends to confirm this. The times in which Henry O'Neil lived were unfavourable to lukewarm politicians or timid mediocrities. It is one thing to pity him as we may, may, must do, but quite another to make his weakness and wavering timidity a ground for calumniating persons who honestly swore to what they know or heard of his conduct in 1641. Had he been allowed to retain his estate he could only, at his advanced age, have enjoyed it for a few years, his brother, nephews, and sons being all indisputably active in the rebellion, mercilessly plundering the Protestants, 'nocent,' as the phrase went, in the fullest sense of the word. Nalson gives the following deposition concerning Henry O'Neil's nephews.

"The examination of RICHARD GRAVE, of Drumboate, in the county of Monaghan, taken 25th October, 1641, who saith, that on Friday last, the 22nd of this month, a little before night, a son of Art Oge O'Neil's of the Fews, whose name he knoweth not, accompanied by about a hundred of the said Art Oge's tenants, armed with swords, pitchforks, and muskets, came to Drumboate to the house of William Grave, brother to the said Richard, and having broken down the doors and windows of the said house, they rifled it and robbed him of all the money they could find there, and of sundry goods that they were able to carry away, and when they had so done they came to the house of William Grave the elder, father to this examt., and robbed him of all his money, clothes, and sundry other goods. He saith that also, the same night, they broke into the house of Sir Henry Spotswood in the same town, and took from it all the money, plate, &c., they could find there. He saith also, that about twelve o'clock the next day the same persons came again to the said town, accompanied by two or three hundred more, and robbed and spoiled it of all the goods and chattels they found there, and presently after they set fire to all the houses and burnt them to the ground. That the goods which his father, himself, and his brother did lose thereby were worth 500*l*., and that he verily believes that the goods which Sir Henry Spotswood lost were worth 1,000*l*. at least. And saith further, that on Friday aforesaid, while the said Art Oge's son was in this examt.'s father's house, he heard him, the said Art Oge's son, and one Patrick MacCadron of Dromboate, say that it was but the beginning, but that they, before they had done, would not leave one alive, rich or poor, who went to church, and saith also that the said Art Oge's son and Patrick MacCadron said there that by the next night Dublin would be too hot for any of the English dogs to live in."

"RICHARD GRAVE."
"JAMES WARE."

RECORDS

OF THE

HIGH COURT OF JUSTICE.

1652—1654.

RECORDS OF THE HIGH COURT OF JUSTICE.

THE documents from which the following extracts have been made are bound up in a small, square octavo volume, forming part of the valuable collection of MSS. bequeathed to Trinity College, Dublin, by Doctor Stearne, Bishop of Clogher, from 1717 to 1745. Considering the great interest and importance of those notes, made by one of the judges of the High Court of Justice of 1652-4, as the prisoners were on their trial before him, it is truly strange that they should have lain for more than two hundred years quite unnoticed by historians, so that no portion of them, except the speech at O'Neil's trial, which I chanced to discover in 1882,[1] and which was immediately printed by the Rev. Mr. Meehan, has ever been even quoted until now.

In the official report for the Historical MSS. Commission on the MSS. in Trinity College, those records are merely catalogued with many others, although one would have thought that a few extracts from them would have been rather more useful to the student than the many with which the report is filled from the published works of Michael Carey (which Reid says he notices only for its 'flagrant demerits') and other well-known writers. I greatly regret that the work of copying the depositions and the limits of the space at my disposal here do not allow me to give the whole of the records of the High Court of Justice in 1652-4. The trials of MacCarthy Reagh, of Colonels Fennell and Luke Toole of Castle Kevin, who was seventy-four years of age when he was brought before the court, charged with being accessory to the murder of two poor cottiers in Wicklow, are full of interest.

The long trial of the Reverend Edmund O'Reilly, the Roman Catholic Vicar-General of Dublin diocese, shows the impartiality with which the prisoners were treated, and the latitude allowed them in the preparation of their defence. The popular notion that

[1] v. Introduction, vol. i. p. 160.

neither justice nor mercy was shown to priests in the Cromwellian courts is scattered to the winds by the proceedings on this trial. It is noteworthy that the majority of the witnesses against the Vicar-General were persons of his own race and creed. Mr. and Mrs. Wolverston, members of an old Anglo-Irish Roman Catholic family of good position in Dublin and Wicklow, whose daughter was a nun, gave evidence against him. He charged two of the Irish witnesses of the O'Byrne clan with having sworn falsely against him because he had formerly punished them for immorality, but their evidence was in itself trifling, and it is impossible to believe that all the rest of the witnesses were immoral and perjured. The prisoner did not indeed venture to say that they were so. At the same time it is only fair to point out that much of their evidence was mere hearsay, and that a witness of English name, probably a Protestant, swore that O'Reilly had saved the lives of several Protestants. For these very sufficient reasons, although a verdict of guilty was found in his case, his life was spared. He himself gave a remarkable piece of evidence as to the impunity that murderers enjoyed under Lieutenant-General O'Byrne.

Carte, and other Royalist historians, assert that the real cause of the mercy shown to Vicar-General O'Reilly was that he had secretly betrayed the Irish and English troops of Ormond and Purcell at Baggotrath in 1649 to Michael Jones, the Parliamentary general, by inducing an Irishman to offer himself as a guide to the Irish Royalist troops, and to mislead them in a midnight march. Father Walsh, the Franciscan friar, who certainly had peculiar opportunities for detecting such an act of treachery, assured Carte and Ormond that O'Reilly had been guilty of it. The charge may have been true, for it is certain that about that time the Jesuits and a section of the Roman Catholic clergy were endeavouring to come to secret terms with Cromwell and the Independents, finding that Ormond could not be won over to change his religion. (v. vol. i. p. 380.) O'Reilly was appointed Archbishop of Armagh by the Pope in 1656 and died in 1669.

I would direct the reader's special attention to that passage in the judge's speech at Sir Phelim O'Neil's trial which relates to the Royal Commission. There are two reports of this speech amongst the Stearne MSS. One of them, as I have already said, has been printed by Mr. Meehan in his history, and for this reason, as well as because it is much less full than the one given hereafter, and contains only a bare allusion to the Royal Commission, I do not think it worth reprinting. The fuller report of the speech, which I do give, distinctly charges O'Neil with having *altered* the commission. This throws quite a new light on the historical puzzle, showing that the popular notion, grounded on Dean Kerr's declaration, that the judges in the High Court pressed O'Neil by threats and bribes to throw the whole burden of his guilt on Charles, is wholly erroneous. The passage hereafter reported shows that while the judges believed that the king had given O'Neil a certain commission to raise the Irish against the Parliament, that they equally believed that he, the prisoner, had altered the commission to justify crimes and outrages, for which the king had given him no license. And this is probably the true solution of the puzzle. It is consistent, too, with the revelations in Lord Antrim's 'Information,' and Lord Maguire's confession, which, as Reid observes, do not tell the *whole* truth, but a portion of it (*v.* Reid, vol. i. p. 289, *note*). I have also omitted the two reports of the trials of Sir Phelim for the murder of Bromley[1] or Brownlow Taylor, and Mr. Blaney, because the evidence in these is merely a summary of that already given at length in the depositions of Michael Harrison, Anthony Atkinson, and others. Harrison was the principal witness against Sir Phelim on the general charge of rebellion, and on the particular charges of murder.

A curious 'hitch' occurred when preparations were being made for the trials, owing to the fact that under an old law in the Irish statute books the murder of an Englishman in Ireland by an Irishman was made high treason, and a correspondence took place on the subject between the judges and the English Council. Ultimately the rebel leaders appear to have been all tried, first for the crime of rebellion, and then for being principals or accessories in the murder of one or more persons.

A deposition which I copied, but in some way mislaid, mentions that the murderer of Mrs. Maxwell said, in the deponent's hearing, that he had drowned her because Sir Phelim told him she was a witch, and the murderer added that he had never any luck since, which he ascribed to the vengeance of the devil and her sister witches still living. The almost universal belief in witchcraft in both islands in the 17th century makes this very probable. The exaggerations of the numbers murdered in the rebellion, and the language of the judge to O'Neill seem to us of course cruel if not unjust, but they were as much the result of the spirit of that age as were the accusations of witchcraft and the stories of omens and

[1] The name is spelt indifferently Bromley or Brownlow in the depositions.

apparitions. The blood which had deluged the country for ten long years, since O'Neill had begun the rebellion, had excited men's minds to the highest pitch. But, however that excitement and panic influenced the imaginations of orators and writers who had lived through those terrible years, it is clear that the judgments of the court were unbiassed, and that priests as well as laymen had fair trials. Lord Muskerry's speech after sentence shows that this was the case. A letter, printed by Mr. Gilbert, from Colonel Jones to Major Scott, dated 1st March, 1653, gives the following account of O'Neill's bearing in court and of Lord Muskerry's return to Ireland.

" Sir Phelim O'Neill was taken and yesterday tried at our High Court of Justice at Dublin, and condemned of high treason, and within a few hours a period will be given to his high titles as being created Earl of Tyrone by the Ultaghes, according to their rude solemnities, Prince of Ulster by the Pope's commission or bull, General of all the Leinster and Ulster forces by commission of the Lords of the Pale, and the prime and chief actor in the horrid massacre and rebellion by commission from the late Charles Stuart, as himself hath often confessed and published in his manifesto, all of which was made good by evidence at his trial. This course of inquisition after blood and doing exemplary justice is terrible to this nation, insomuch that the murderers' hearts faint, and their joints tremble, even to admiration, when they come to the bar. This cruel monster of men, when he first came to the bar, was scarce able to stand for trembling or to speak for tears. . . . The Lord Muskerry is lately landed at Cork, and says he will cast himself upon the Parliament's mercy, pretending that the clergy in Spain had determined to murder him, and that Portugal would not entertain him, of all of which I believe but my share. He is sent for to Dublin *in salva custodia.*"

Jones's letter must be taken *cum grano salis.* His sentiments about Muskerry were not shared by Cromwell or the judges. The writer of the 'Aphorismical Discovery,' who shared to the full and revealed the real sentiments of the nuncio and his clerical following in Spain and Ireland, leaves us no room for doubting that Lord Muskerry was regarded with the most deep-rooted hatred by them, and that he could find neither rest nor peace amongst them, although he had forfeited vast estates and risked his life a thousand times for Ireland, and for the Roman Catholic

Church. But, staunch and devout Roman Catholic as he was, he refused to sanction the extermination of his Protestant countrymen at the bidding of his priests, or to become the mere tool of their insatiate greed, and therefore his ancient royal Irish blood, his valour, his devotion were as nothing in their eyes.

Nalson has printed several depositions from the Carte MSS. of Protestants whose lives had been saved by Lord Muskerry. He was pronounced not guilty in consideration of the articles under which he had surrendered Ross Castle to the army of the Parliament in 1652, commanded by Ludlow and Waller, who besieged it for some weeks straitly by land and ships on the lake. It was the only place of strength then left to the Irish in Munster, and its fall was inevitable, but a whole fortnight was spent in debating on the articles of surrender. The following explanation was appended to these articles, which exempted from pardon all who had a share in the massacres :

"We esteem such persons only guilty of murder who, during the first year of the war, have contrived, aided, or assisted, acted or abetted, any murder or massacre upon any person or persons of the English, not in arms, but following their own occupations in their farms and freeholds. By aiding, assisting, or abetting, we understand such as have by acts of their will, either precedently advised, or commanded, such murders or massacres, or subsequently approved thereof, in sheltering such murderers and keeping them from justice.

"Since the first year of the war, we esteem those only guilty of murder who have killed any of our party after quarter given ; provided always, the person or persons who did so kill did know before, or at the said killing, the said person or persons had the quarter ; provided likewise, the person or persons so killed did not by act of hostility against the Irish, or otherwise, legally forfeit his said quarter before the said killing.

"We further esteem such to be guilty of murder who killed, or commanded to be killed, and whoso killed, any of our protected, who were protected by the Commander-in-Chief of the Irish party or by anyone authorised to give protection in the behalf of the Irish party, if the party so killing knew of the protection at the time of killing. Provided the party so killed did not legally forfeit his said protection at the time he was so killed.

"We further esteem that if any person formerly under our

protection, who shall during that time have killed, or cause to be killed, any person under our protection, and afterwards shall run to the enemy, this with any case of the like kind shall be adjudged murder. And that any countryman not in arms, nor under our protection, who has by any sleight or promise of safety drawn, or caused to be drawn, in any person under our protection, to the taking away of his life, this with any case of the like kind shall be deemed murder.

"As to religion, we do declare that it is not our intention, nor as we conceive the intention of those we serve, to force any to their worship and service contrary to their consciences.

"HUGH ROGERS.   ANDREW ELLIOTT.
FREDERICK MULLENS.   JOHN USTEAD (WELSTED?)
FRANCIS GOOLD.   HARDRESS WALLER.
AULY LEYNE.   WILLIAM ALLEN.
                                          JOHN NELSON."

In the copy of the articles of Ross, which Archdeacon Rowan has given in his 'Lake Lore,' the name of Frederick Mullens does not appear; the signatures are Hugh Rogers, Andrew Elliott, Francis Goold, Andrew Leyne, John Meade, Edmund FitzMaurice, Gerald FitzMaurice, Robert Coppinger, and Callaghan O'Callaghan. Frederick Mullens, an officer in the army of the Parliament, was ancestor of the present Lord Ventry. The Archdeacon adds in a footnote that Lord Muskerry and those under his command, had good need that the definition of 'murder should be clear and well limited,' and that 'in the University Archives (*MSS.*, *F.* iv. 16) there is a shorthand abstract of the trial of Lord Muskerry and acquittal for the murder of Mrs. Hussey at Macroom ' (' Lake Lore,' *Appendix*, p. 182). The abstracts mentioned by Archdeacon Rowan are the records, given hereafter, but he was mistaken in supposing that they are in shorthand; they are all in a very crabbed, bad, but ordinary handwriting, passages here and there are extremely difficult to read, some words quite indecipherable, but again whole pages can be read without much difficulty by any one who has long experience in such researches and patience over them. At first sight the writing does resemble shorthand, and it is in a certain sense mental shorthand, if I may use the expression, for the writer constantly omitted articles, conjunctions, and prepositions not essentially necessary to the understanding of the meaning of the sentence. I have supplied those words here and there, putting them in parentheses, so that the reader may read the notes as they stand in the original only, or with the supplementary words as he pleases.

Another highly important passage to which I would direct his special attention is that at page 199 of the report of Lord Muskerry's trial, where the depositions taken by Archdeacon Bysse at Waterford and Cork are referred to. From this passage we find that for the 'justifying' of those depositions when they were produced in court, to be used in evidence against the prisoner, that Mr. Waring, the official who had charge of them under the Council of State, 'testified upon oath' that he had 'abbreviated' them, by order of the said Council, 'as to losses but not as to murders.' I had not read those notes of the proceedings in the High Court when I came to the conclusion, mentioned in vol. i. p. 129, that those crossing-out lines in the depositions taken by Archdeacon Bysse in Waterford and Cork were marks of abbreviation, not cancellings, but if any doubt had remained on my mind that they were so, Mr. Waring's sworn statement would have at once dispelled it.

The order at page 236, confiscating the Cromwellian soldier's debenture for the benefit of the widow and orphans of Turlogh O'Byrne, the poor Irish carpenter he had murdered, and the letter of Cromwell at page 238, on behalf of Mr. Barry, are good proofs of the generous and merciful nature of the Protector, so ill understood to this day by many of his countrymen who profess to admire 'his historical greatness.'

Those English commentators on Irish history who know less of it than of the history of any other country in the civilised world, write of the crimes of Cromwell at Drogheda and Wexford, and tell us that his 'great figure cannot charm or attract though it may overawe,' and that 'sentiment and romance'[1] are all in favour of his opponents in Ireland. This may be true of that trumpery modern sentiment the late Lord Lytton describes in his 'New Timon':—

'Men in whom sentiment the bloodless shade
Of noble passion alternates with trade.'

But Cromwell's justice and mercy are alike incomprehensible to men of this stamp. A hundred poor Irishmen, like the carpenter Turlogh O'Byrne, might have perished before that hero of modern sentiment and romance, Harry Jermyn, and his associates, would

[1] V. an article on 'The Ethics of Biography' in the *Contemporary Review* for July 1883.

have wasted a thought on those waifs and strays of the 'common sort,' as the Cavalier phrase went in both islands. The Reverend John Dod, whose evidence before the English Parliament has been, as I have already said, in part printed by Mr. Gilbert, stated that he saw among the Irish officers and soldiers, high in favour with Charles and the Cavaliers at Oxford in 1643, many Irish rebels, especially one "Thomas Brady, who had been a chief actor in the massacre at Belturbet," when old men, helpless mothers, and little children, shrieking on their knees in vain for mercy, were driven in a flock to the river's side and there drowned (v. ante, vol. i. p. 303). The carnage at Drogheda, when the town, garrisoned by the English Cavaliers, who expelled impartially many Irish Protestants and Irish friars (lest they should betray it to Cromwell or O'Neil), was taken by storm, was at once a retribution for Portadown, Belturbet, and Shrule, and a preventive against the repetition of such horrors in future. Cromwell's judgment was that of the prophets of old, '*the leaders of this people cause them to err*,' and who can doubt it was a right one that knows the real facts of Irish history? The Roman Catholic Lord Castlehaven, while endeavouring to clear the Irish royalist leaders of encouraging the barbarous cruelties committed by their followers, is honest enough to add, 'Still I think them (the leaders) inexcusable, because I see no great difference whether a man kills another himself, or unchains a fierce mastiff that will tear him in pieces.' But the noble historian should have remembered that the English Cavaliers were as responsible as the Irish leaders. Cruel as Phelim O'Neil and his followers were, they had at least certain great provocations to urge in their defence, which I have been careful to record, moreover the masses of the Irish were grossly ignorant and superstitious, and the English Cavaliers who garrisoned Drogheda, while they were willing to use those masses for their own purposes, hated and despised them. So long as that garrison maintained itself and its party in Ireland, so long must the island have been stained with crimes like those at Belturbet and Portadown.

Those ill-informed English commentators on Irish history above mentioned are fond of quoting from the pages of Anthony à Wood a story which he alleges he heard from his brother, who served under Cromwell at Drogheda. Wood, according to this story, just after the town was taken in the hottest moment of the storm, met a beautiful young lady, richly dressed and covered with jewellery, who entreated him to save her life, which he was about to do, when a Cromwellian soldier dragged her away, killed her and flung her corpse over the city wall. The incident was a sad and horrible one, only too likely to have taken place then, or even at a later date, wherever an infuriated soldiery took by storm a besieged town. But when English modern sentiment and romance undertake to deliver judgment on Irish history, they ought to remember that long before this richly dressed lady was killed at the siege of Drogheda by an infuriated soldier, hundreds of helpless old men, women, and little children (poorly dressed it may be), were flung into the rivers at Portadown and Belturbet, not in the fury of battle or siege, but as they submissively fled before their Irish captors who had promised to guard and protect them to the place where they were to embark for England. The relatives of those humble victims, the brother or cousin of John Gregg (v. Deposition CLXXIX.), who saw his son cut in pieces, and had those pieces flung in his face in the church of Loughgall before he too was murdered, those who saw the Rev. Mr. Oliphant murdered in presence of his wife, and his corpse tied to a horse's tail and dragged about the roads (v. Dep. CIII.) were probably some of them assisting Cromwell at Drogheda, and they were not likely any more than John Erwyn, mentioned in Grany ny Mullan's deposition (v. ante, vol. i. p. 152), to measure out much mercy to the Cavaliers and their allies at Drogheda and Wexford.

A review of Lord Lawrence's Life, by Mr. R. B. Smith, lately appeared in a first-class English magazine. The reviewer, Mr. Eastwick, excuses the severities inflicted on the Indian mutineers of 1857, and blames Lord Lawrence's biographer for not remembering the atrocities which provoked those severities. One epitaph in the memorial church at Delhi, Mr. Eastwick says, records the 'death of thirty-one persons all of the same family, from the aged folk down to children of a few years old, ending with the murder of the baby in arms. Mr. Smith,' adds Mr. Eastwick, 'seems altogether unable to realise the feelings of Englishmen at this period.' Yet Mr. Eastwick in this very same review censures Cromwell, and revives against him the stale old worthless accusations of self-seeking and duplicity. If it were a horrible crime, deserving severest punishment, for the Hindoos and the Mahometan people of India to murder in one day thirty-one persons of one household, what shall be said of a professedly devout Christian tribe who murdered in one hour a hundred helpless unarmed men, women, and little children, believers in Jesus Christ, and many of them of the mixed English and Irish race, as were not a few of the murderers?

Let English modern commentators on Irish history judge of our forefathers as they may, the wise and true-hearted Irishman of 1883, knowing how Ireland was made the victim of English parties and the Stuart king's greed and despotism, will, like Irishmen of the same type in 1649, acknowledge that the advent of Cromwell was, as I have already said, a blessing in disguise, since it put an end to the scenes I have described in the Introduction to the Depositions (vol. i. p. 156).

Had our forefathers bearing English or Irish names, whatever their creed, been united, and by their union had they been able to fight for and maintain the freedom of the whole country, and to establish prosperity and peace within its borders, against all intruders, royalist or republican, I could wish that advent had never taken place which caused no doubt temporary suffering to so many of them. But as matters went in 1641-9, I cannot, notwithstanding my sincere and deep natural sympathy with my forefathers' sufferings, regret the inexorably stern decrees of this true High Court of Justice, or admit that Oliver Cromwell was Ireland's worst enemy.

PARTICULAR CHARGES AGAINST SIR PHELIM O'NEIL.

FEBRUARY, 1652.

I.

For the murder of Lord Caulfield.

1. MAJOR PATRICK DORY, present (in Court swears) that Sir Phelim in October, 1642, seized the Lord Caulfield and kept (*illegible*). That the Lord Caulfield desiring the examt. to be left with him as speaking the (Irish) language, being that day to be sent away, Sir Phelim told him that he (Lord Caulfield) should have better company before night. That Neil MacKenna asked Edmund Boy Hugh (as the prisoner and his escort were entering Kinard gate) '*Where is your heart now?*' who thereupon shot him, Lord Caulfield. That the Lord Caulfield was committed to Neil MacKenna and Neil Modder O'Neil. That as the Lord Caulfield was passing through the gate at Kinard the word was given to the left hand file to make ready, at which the Lord Caulfield was startled a little, but Neil Modder told him there was no danger, then Neil MacKenna said to Edmund Buoy Hugh as before ('*where is your heart now?*').

2. ALEXANDER CRICHTON, (deposed) that Edmund Buoy O'Hugh, foster-brother to Sir Phelim, shot Lord Caulfield.

3. JOHN PERKINS, (deposed) that Lord Caulfield (was) committed to Neil MacKenna and Neil Modder O'Neil ; that he was shot by Edmund Buoy O'Hugh, foster-brother to Sir Phelim.

4. MR. JOSEPH TRAVERS, present (in Court swears) that about the end of December, 1641, the examt. speaking with Sir Phelim O'Neil, he said to examt. '*they* (the English) *have Maguire prisoner with them, but if they touch the least hair of his head Caulfield shall die for him.*'

6. Mr. JOHN KERDIFFE, present (in Court swears) that at the funeral of the said Lord Caulfield Sir Phelim came to Charlemont, and alighting (from his horse) in the examt.'s hearing asked, ' Is the Lord Caulfield dead ? I would he had died seven years ago, for I am a thousand pounds the worse for him.'

The Prisoner's Defence.

That the Lord Caulfield was to be sent away to Cloughoughter by order of the Provincial Council. Denieth not but that he might say and do as to the Lord Maguire what concerns Lord Caulfield.

II.

For the murder of John Maxwell and his wife.

1. DR. MAXWELL, deposed, that by Sir Phelim's express orders James Maxwell was murdered in height of a fever, and raving so (Sir Phelim) paying him (a debt) of 260*l*. His wife murdered while in labour.

2. JOHN PARRY, deposed, John Maxwell and his wife were drowned by (order in a) letter from Sir Phelim, that letter (*illegible*) convoying.

3. MICHAEL HARRISON, present (in Court swears) that he heard that James Maxwell having lent Sir Phelim about 200*l*. sent a letter concerning him, after which (letter was received) Maxwell was murdered.

4. NICHOLAS SIMPSON, present (in Court swears) to the murder taking place, but not to Sir Phelim (ordering or being engaged) in it.

5. JOHN PERKINS deposed those two were murdered by special directions from Sir Phelim and his brother Tirlogh.

The Prisoner's Defence.

That he desired his witnesses' papers, but that they were not allowed him. Denies that any of his convoys ever sold their trust for convoy of English, but that (*illegible*) only to Moneymore, and there delivered them over to another convoy. That many English

RECORDS OF THE HIGH COURT OF JUSTICE. 183

so convoyed (by his orders) came safe, amongst them some now appearing in Court. That at the Newry the English and Scotch army put all to the sword, and not till then was any such thing done by his party. Denieth owing Maxwell any money, but he (Maxwell) gave him some money for kindness he owed him (prisoner). Denieth that he (prisoner) had a half sister unmarried before the wars, this to charge as to Cowell. Denieth his giving a warrant for hanging Maxwell, but that he (prisoner) did hang some for murders. Saith that one of the O'Hughs, a principal actor in this murder, is now in Coleraine, Art Hugh or Brian Oge O'Hugh.

THE LORD PRESIDENT'S SPEECH AT THE SENTENCE OF
SIR PHELIM O'NEIL.

March 5th, the day of Sentence.

Sir Phelim O'Neil, Mr. Attorney, hath exhibited a charge of High Treason in this Court, not one charge but several charges, accumulated treasons, rebellion, and the effusion of a sea of innocent blood (against you).

The first charge is for the Rebellion itself devised by you and acting in it. The others are particular (charges) for (murder of) James Maxwell, *etc.*

1. For the general charge it is testified that about five or six years before the rebellion the plot was in your heart, that to avoid suspicion you counterfeited yourself as a fool in all great men's company, that none might think you had in you such a contrivance, but when the tragedy began to open, then the world would know you were not a fool. But now see in the conclusion who is the fool! You fool this night (*illegible*) shall take away thy soul was said to one fool who heaped up treasures; you (Sir Phelim) heaped up treasures by pillage of Protestants, but now, oh! fool this night, etc. (shall thy soul be required of thee). But *habemus confidentio rem* (sic) he in his own examination clears (*i.e.* shows) his being guilty of raising this rebellion (saying) that he and the Lord Maguire and others met in Dublin and consulted on this plot. That for carrying on of the plot that there was an oath of secresy, that at their meetings (there was) a dividing of the shares of the work, and who was to take Dublin, Londonderry, Charlemont, etc., the last (was) your part as you acknowledge, and by the evidence (it)

appears with how much treachery that your part was acted. Next, you appear at Drogheda, at the invitation of the Lords of the Pale; there you were invested with power from them and made commander-in-chief at that siege, see your confession. But what! O'Neil to be chosen by those of English blood! Can they forget their blood? But why this? You laid not your plot like a fool (in this), for you said if they would not come (to join you) you would produce their writings under their own hands against them, thus you are chief in command. Then you came to Monaghan and met the ancient vassals of O'Neil, O'Reillys, MacMahons, etc. (They) chose you their chief in Ulster, this is another title, and all this is by your own confession. (You have) another title from the Supreme Council of Kilkenny, by whose order you are made President of Ulster, this also in your own confession. Further, by other testimony titles come yet on you, and at Tullaghoge you are made Earl of Tyrone. Now you are above your former style, you are his Excellency, not Sir Phelim, you have all at your will and command, and may grant commissions that all may be done according to your royal intents, you grant charters, power of life and death, commissions of *oyer* and *terminer*. Now state is upon you truly, and your Excellency's meat is served up with drum and trumpet. Are you yet at the highest? no, to all this is wanting the Pope's Bull, without him the work is imperfect. Now Father Paul O'Neil that went thirteen times in a half year between you and Brussels (comes in) and by a Bull from the Pope you are made Prince of Ulster, now are healths drunk on the knee to Sir Phelim O'Neil, Earl of Tyrone, Lieutenant General of the Catholic army, and King of Ireland. Are we yet at the end? No, yet is there one more title wanting (to you) *Phelimy Totane*, the last and most affecting, as sung by your Bards, none of them singing of any of your titles, but (this of) *Phelimy Totane*.

But (let us) add to all these the degrees and merits of your (other) actions.

.1. Your first action of treachery and blood was that of your surprising Charlemont, and using those there (as you did) then and after.

2. At Dungannon, Captain John Perkins, your ancient acquaintance, is surprised, and (the warder) of the castle by Patrick O'Modder, under colour of (seeking a warrant) for (recovery of stolen) sheep; see your treachery throughout, while he (the warder) is labouring to do justice he is set upon with skeans at his breasts. Did not Hugh MacPhelim Byrne do the same against Pont on the

hill of (*illegible*) under pretence of expecting justice from him a prisoner? The like was done at Mr. Arthur Champion's, in the same way he was seized and murdered with his family. But that this may not (appear to be done) by Sir Phelimy O'Neil, he cometh in (to Captain Perkins) at midnight (*illegible*) after Charlemont with a boast, '¹ *Ho! so you old Fox have I caught you all secure? like the Lord Caulfield, all is our own, all Ireland (is ours) this night!*' '*I fear*,' says Perkins, truly speaking, '*Sir Phelim, we shall have a second O'Dogherty in you for seizing and burning Derry, and killing the governor*' (great is your) anger, and there you leave him.

3. You go on (your way unchecked) and on Captain Perkins' horses you post the same night to Mountjoy, and after the same night you come to Dungannon again, and there you and your followers kill and pillage sixty families in and about Dungannon, contrary to your covenants, and now *Phelimy Totane* begins (indeed) to appear.

4. You burn (*illegible*) and all the Londoner's plantations in one morning, 1,200, 900, 1,000, 800, and many more in the counties of Antrim and Down, and murdered (*illegible*) now (you are) *Phelimy Totane*.

5. Five thousand in three days when the Scots began to march.

6. The murder of the British is so acceptable to you that Art Oge O'Neil, to please you, and to gain your good opinion (says that), he had but one Scotchman on his land, and that he killed him. Why (did he so kill this man)? To please (you) Sir Phelim O'Neil. To please you is to murder. That murdering sept of the O'Hughs and the MacModders were yours and your brother's (own) fosterers and followers.

7. Many Protestants are buried alive, otherwise they would not bury them at all, the English now are (*illegible*) denied (when dead) a grave.

8. You yourself confessed, as is testified, that you killed 680 at Scarvagh, and (that you) left neither man, woman, nor child in the barony of (*illegible*), and left none in all the plantations about you.

9. Those actions put the English on their defence in the church of Armagh, Sir Phelim comes and treats (with them) and with the fox's skin, since the lion's will not do, he offers good quarter for life, goods, estates, and to (let them) live in their own houses. They are

¹ This is a quotation from Captain John Perkins' examination, which is in the volumes in the College, but as it contains little more than Harrison's I have not copied it.

glad of this, they accept, for Sir Phelim swears (they shall have quarter), nay, you would sign it (you say) with your own blood, nay you (say to them) if you need it you shall have my son Henry (for) a pledge. They yield, now all is yours, they are oppressed, they cry, but no remedy!

10. But that is not all, after your being beaten off that siege at Drogheda, and afterwards from Dundalk, one of your bloodhounds, Manus O'Cahane, is employed to carry away the Protestants. Whither? to Coleraine? But how (does he do so, he) who murdered on the way three hundred, and these (murdered) after all those engagements (of yours)?

Things to be observed in your convoys in every treachery (said to be) safe convoys, but see the secret of it, to make them sure by murdering (those convoyed) and this appearing the English began to (*illegible*) not going with those convoys, and so were preserved.

(It is to be) observed also that in any loss (to you) or on the English army marching away, all the English about (there were) murdered (by you) in revenge, and by way of prevention (*illegible*).

To keep yet farther at Armagh (you are) now Phelimy Totane again, Armagh is fired (by you), and many in their houses and outside them (are) murdered and drowned, to the number of 580 in the country thereabouts (*illegible*), the English drawing towards the Newry.

You will not be bound to (keep faith with) heretics by your religion. '*Children are to be deceived by apples, and Heretics by oaths,*' so saith your clergy, to promise and break (your promise) is your doctrine, and in that way destroy them.

On the repulse (of your followers) at the siege of Augher, all in the way are murdered, so at Castlederego, and (your followers have for these murders) warrants under your own hand. Being beaten (again) at Lisnagarvey, you come away, Phelimy Totane, (and) you let twenty-four (Protestants) be locked up in one house (to be burnt) poor souls, whose outcries might move many (as well as) Sir Phelimy O'Neal (who) could not but hear, and yet he was not moved, and his wicked followers boasted of that fact, and delighted in the cries of the poor people. This (happened) not in one place but in many instances. Now (you are) Phelimy Totane indeed (*illegible*), so as no lustre can parallel (yours).

In the parish of Loughgall, of 4,000 communicants all are lost, murdered, or drowned.

At Portadown drowning of Protestants (goes on) by 20, 40, 60, 100, 150 at a time (*illegible*) to 1,000 at least estimated in all, (until)

God testified against it by visions affrighting the very murderers, some warrants under Sir Phelim's hands (*illegible*) these they said were but English devils. Owen Roe O'Neil detests your execrable actions and cruel villainies (*illegible*), your brother Hovendon would not join with you (in them), your very (*illegible*), and your secretary also. ' *What is that to you ?* ' say you to them all ; nay your own mother said she had never offended the English but in being mother to Sir Phelimy O'Neil.

And for particular revenges of yours, 1st, the murder of one Cowell, because he would not marry your kinswoman ; 2nd, Dr. Hodges (is murdered) because he would not make your gunpowder.

And for particular cruelties, 1st, your burning of Armagh (*illegible*), contrary to your promises. Remember Mr. Starky and his daughters, what could an old man of a hundred years old (do to) hurt you ? but blood is the thing (you want) it matters not where or how. Many are not killed outright, that is too much mercy, but they half kill them, and come again and look on them, and rejoice to see them languish, they beg for death, but that mercy is denied ; for instance a young man with his back broken is put to (lie on and eat) grass, the mercy (accorded him) is to remove him to another pasture, to live longer in that misery.

When murdering the Protestants the word was ' *your soul to the devil,*' was not the cruelty to the body enough, but will you follow the soul (with it) as far as in you is ? Mr. Allen's wife outraged before her husband's face, then they kill him and her.

But these (things) are (done by) men whose hearts are hardened (*illegible*), killing poor English, (*illegible*) *ille improbus ille puer* (sic) *tu quoque mater*, mothers and children are as bad as the men, and their children like them. That the heathen should act cruelties it is not to be wondered at so much, but here religion is the business, and for religion see (*illegible*).

At Monaghan at a festival in their drunkenness (this is one of the crying sins of Ireland) what sport have they at their feast? An Englishman is laid before them on the board bound, and at every health they stab him with a skean, but do not (kill him), and they drink and he bleeds, and they drink again, and presently, when he is all one wound, he is cast out on a dunghill.

All this on (*illegible*) of the great rebellion and the proceedings in it. Next their hatred to the English nation.

(They) destroy even the cattle because they are English, this at (*illegible*).

They destroy all the English habitations. When asked, can you not keep them for yourselves? No! (they answer) that would make the English think of returning here again, and so we will burn all to the ground (*illegible*). O'Neil cursed any of his posterity who would (take to) building houses, sowing corn, or wearing English apparel or speaking the tongue of the English nation.

This is an inherited hatred, see it in Shane O'Neil, he built a fort which he called *Fagh na Gall*, or 'to the hate' (or scorn) 'of the English,' when he burnt Armagh. Do not you inherit that? So Tirlogh Lenogh is chosen after Shane as O'Neil, the Act (of Parliament) makes it high treason to take that title, but the Parliament withal begs Tirlogh's pardon from the Queen (for having taken it), the Queen pardons him, he as soon as he returns to Ulster rebels again and burns all, and after him Hugh O'Neil is set up by the English against Tirlogh (*illegible*).

To all this is added your turning the dead Englishmen with their faces downward to look into hell, and women in like manner obscenely dealt with. Hatred to the Nation (not less than to the) Religion (of the English), the Holy Scriptures despitefully used, Bible trodden under foot, etc.

Your neighbours murdered, one of them, Blyth, being about to be murdered, held up your protection to heaven (to witness) against you (*illegible*).

Now to what end was all this? the end was to maintain the king's prerogative, the Catholic cause, and to banish all heretics. In your commissions to advance the king's prerogative, and to propagate the Catholic (*illegible*) is to murder by fire and sword. Is this the way to plant (your) religion, to beat your religion into Protestants' hearts by beating out their brains?

But they (the Protestants) had a Protector whom you saw not. He that is in heaven laughs you to scorn, He saw your red hand, you now see His, He made you scourges to His enemies, now He is casting the rod into the fire.

But by what authority was this your end to be compassed? You knew well (*illegible*), but the king's commission you altered, the copy of the commission is produced, but you deny it.

I will be brief now in the particular charges against you.

1st. For the Lord Caulfield, he invites you to his house, you enter and then betray him, but you might then have used him civilly, you had inventories of his plate and linen, which pleased you so well that you kept it yourself. The Lady (Caulfield) and her children are sent out barefoot, and after fifteen weeks the Lord Caulfield is sent away to Kinard, and, in the midst of the guard you appointed for him, he is murdered by O'Hugh, your own fosterer. You had not justice in your heart, Prince of Ulster! on other (and lesser) occasions he (O'Hugh) was clapt up in prison, now he escapes, and for him an Englishman and a Scotchman are hanged!

2ndly. Lieutenant James Maxwell and his wife (are murdered, and) this by your command; he was a gentleman to whom you were indebted, and, being in a burning fever he is taken out of his bed in a raving fit, and then murdered, he not knowing what they were doing with him. His wife, how was she used? She, being in labour, is also dragged out, the child half born, and both drowned in the Blackwater, what! this done by (order of) Sir Phelim? What! was he born of a woman who did this?

3rdly. Richard Blaney was hanged by your special command, and that without question or trial. This was not done by that law of England so scorned by you, charge him, hear him, try him legally, that is the way of our English law!

4thly. Brownlow Taylor, this is the last (particular charge) as now remembered. He was carried before you not examined, or tried, but by your orders hanged, no entreaty for him would prevail with you, notwithstanding your protection and quarter at Armagh.

All this is truly (sustained) according to the evidence (before the Court), and upon all and singular you are found guilty, and (we) have given sentence. Not such as to those on either hand of you, but as you exceeded (them) in cruelty, so is your sentence; though your actions were beyond all, that sentence is (*illegible*) by the just and honourable (*illegible*) of England.

To be hanged, drawn, and quartered, etc.

At the Sentence.

You have received the just judgment of this Court for your actions. I desire, though your bodies perish here, that you may yet have a joyful resurrection in the day of the Lord Jesus. There is a throne of Grace even for murderers, a blessed Saviour who died for you, the perfection of His sufferings is sufficient for all sins whatsoever (*illegible*), and faith in His blood will wash out every guilt, apply yourselves to Him that you may die with faith and repentance, that while your bodies shall go to the grave, your souls shall find grace, mercy, and comfort.

The Examination of Sir PHELIM O'NEIL, *taken 23rd February, 1652-3, before (blank).*[1]

Who being examined, saith, that about a quarter or half a year before the beginning of the rebellion in Ireland, that the plot of the said rebellion was discovered to him by the Lord Maguire and Roger Moore, and they two and Philip O'Reilly and this examt. several times met and discoursed of the said plot. He saith, that at other some of the said meetings, Colonel John Barry, Sir James Dillon, Anthony Preston, and Hugh MacPhelim were present. He saith, that there was an oath of secrecy administered to such persons as were made privy to the said plot, (and) that the said oath was given to the examt. at his chamber in Nelson's house in Castle Street by the Lord Maguire and the said Roger Moore. He saith, that at their meetings it was agreed that the several forts in Ireland should be taken, and to that purpose the examt. was appointed to take Charlemont, the Lord Maguire to take Enniskillen, Colonel Barry, Anthony Preston, Roger Moore, and Colonel Plunket to take the Castle of Dublin, Sir James Dillon to take the fort of Galway, Sir Morgan Kavenagh and Hugh MacPhelim to take the fort of Duncannon. That when the forts had been taken, that then the government (was) to be altered and new Lords Justices to be made and addresses to be then sent to the king.

He saith, that after the rebellion, at the time of the siege of Drogheda, the examt. with his forces in Ulster were invited to come to the said siege by several of the Lords and Gentlemen of the Pale, both by message in writing and otherwise. He saith, that the letter for his invitation was subscribed by the Earl of Fingal, the Lords of Gormanston, Slane, and Louth, and by most of the Gentlemen of the Pale then at the siege, both by message in writing and otherwise. He saith, that when he and his forces came thither, the said Lords and Gentlemen of the Pale, at a meeting at Bewly, gave a commission to the examt., signed by the persons aforesaid, appointing the examt. Commander-in-Chief of all the forces then at the said siege. He saith, that soon after the 22nd of October, 1641, at a meeting at Monaghan, the examt. was chosen Commander-in-Chief of Ulster by Philip MacHugh O'Reilly, Colonels MacMahon and Maguire, and several of the O'Neils and MacMahons, Maguires and others, and a Commission for that purpose was given to him

[1] *MSS. T.C.D.*, F. 3, 7.

by them. That afterwards, by order of the Supreme Council of Kilkenny, the examt. was made president of Ulster.

He denieth that he was chosen Earl of Tyrone at the hill of Tullaghoge, or that he ever assumed that title, or subscribed any letter or writing as Earl of Tyrone. He saith, that the said Colonel John Barry being very intimate with the Lord of Ormond, it was considered that the said Colonel Barry was at the said meetings by the privity and appointment of the said Lord of Ormond.

He saith, that it was resolved at some of the said meetings, that upon the change of the government, the said Lord of Ormond and the Lord of Gormanston were to be appointed Lords Justices of Ireland, and that the sword should be given them.

PHELIM O'NEIL.

Witnesses:

CHARLES COOTE. HEN. JONES.
ROBT. MEREDITH. ANTHONY MORGAN.
HIE. SANKEY. WM. ALLEN.

HIGH COURT OF JUSTICE, DUBLIN,

DECEMBER 1ST, 1653.

Trial of the LORD VISCOUNT MUSKERRY, *as accessory to the murder of*

I.

Mrs. Hussey,
Mrs. Crocker (*sic*) and her daughter,
George A. Miller and his wife,
Ellen Colman and her child,
Charles Vavasour and his wife and two children, and two other persons whose names are unknown, near Blarney, in the county Cork, on the 1st of August, 1642.

II.

William Deane and three others and a woman called Nora at Kilfinny, co. Limerick, on July 29th, 1642.

III.

Roger Skinner at Inniskerry, co. Cork, (*blank*), August, 1642.

Evidence.

PHILIP KING present in court swears (*illegible*), that Captain Reardon of Blarney slighted the relation of that murder when fourteen persons were slain, of whom eleven were slain near Blarney, the other three near Cork. Saith, that Gerald Barry ordered this examt. with others to serve under said Captain Reardon at Blarney, that Donogh Reardon did send out Denis Long and others from Blarney to convoy them (the fourteen English) to Cork, and that Denis Long (*illegible*).

That the convoy sent from Macroom returned and were not at the murder, and that some English did stay at Macroom Castle without constraint, that these were afterwards convoyed thence as they desired it, and that this examt. was one in those convoys.

RICHARD STABBER deposed that some English, amongst them Mrs. Hussey, etc., desired to go to Macroom, and that the Lord

Muskerry appointed Donogh Reardon to convoy them to Cork. Examt. heard not that any of the murderers were ever punished.

GEORGE SMITH, present in court, swears, that on Ash Wednesday, 1641, the Lord of Muskerry first ordered (*illegible*) that thereupon the English (prisoners) desired to be gone to Bandon, which the Lord of Muskerry would not allow of, but he assented to their going to Cork, that they were on their way thither, the most part of them, murdered, and that the Lord of Muskerry did to this examt.'s knowledge (*illegible*) for the fact.

2nd Examination. The murder of Scott (he) being under Muskerry's protection, and the murderers not punished, but some of them dwelling on his (the Lord of Muskerry's) land. Saith, that when those with Mrs. Hussey went towards Cork, orders were given by the Lord of Muskerry's steward, MacSwiney, who did (*illegible*) the examt. not (*illegible*) and advised Mrs. Baldwin in like manner not to (*illegible*) that murder. The examt. heard that the clothes of those murdered about Blarney were brought back to Macroom, and heard that MacSwiney, said steward of the Lord of Muskerry, did inquire of those that came back (from conveying the murdered) 'if that were not done,' they answering it was, (*illegible*) examt. being demanded by the Lord of Muskerry what was his cause of knowledge that said MacSwiney was his (Lord Muskerry's) steward, saith that he (MacSwiney) was commonly esteemed as such and did live in Macroom. That the *time* of this murder examt. saith he remembers not (certainly), but thinks it was about Easter, 1642. Saith, that he, the examt., did stay until August after at Macroom, and that other English did desire to stay when Mrs. Hussey went away and did stay. Saith, he knoweth not whether those murdered with Mrs. Hussey were killed by the convoy from Macroom. Saith, that the English desired to be gone, (*illegible*) that a gentleman desired the Lord Muskerry to stay the examt. and Mr. Baldwin.

4. GEORGE FIFE.[1]

5. MARY FIFE.

6. MELAGHLIN DUOHILLY, present (in court, swears) that he was one of the convoy that went with Mrs. Hussey; that he was a servant to Mrs. Hussey and by her own desire (appointed) to go with her; that the Lord Muskerry was not going from Macroom; that Mrs. Hussey desired to go to Cork, her husband and son being there.

---

[1] The witnesses whose names only are set down, appear not to have sworn to anything material, and consequently no notes of their evidence are given in the original MS.

ALICE STABBER, present (in court, swears) that the Lord Muskerry did send MacSwiney to this examt.'s mother (*illegible*), that her mother desired of the Lord Muskerry that she might stay (at Macroom), but he said, as this examt. was told by Mrs. Hussey her mother, he would not have any such wasps in his beehive; saith, that the English being gone away some of the convoy returned and left the said English and they were afterwards murdered. Saith, that one O'Keily was sent by the Lord of Muskerry to Barry, the (Irish) general, by whom he was hanged for saying that one troop of horse would rout all Muskerry's.

2nd Examination. Saith, that the Lord of Muskerry, as she heard, denied a pass to her mother desiring it.

3rd Examination. Saith, that an Irishman that came from Castletownroche was hanged by the Lord of Muskerry's directions, he being charged to be a spy, and that he (Lord Muskerry) then ordered the hanging of a woman for a spy and that she was hanged accordingly: that it was about Lammas that those were sent away with Mrs. Hussey. Saith, that Reardon, who was an Ensign at Blarney and did command the convoy, did dismiss some of the convoy and carried the English with him, after which they were murdered by four musketeers that came out of Blarney Castle; that the Lord of Muskerry did examine (*illegible*) that murder as she heard, but did not do anything against them. Saith, that Edmund Maolmor MacSwiney was the Lord of Muskerry's steward. Saith, she heard that MacSwiney did ask (the murderers) 'if that were done' as aforesaid. She further saith, that she heard of threatenings given out against the English (party) and that thereupon he (Lord Muskerry) sent them away. She had this relation (only) by hearsay.

CAPTAIN JOHN REARDON, present (in court, swears) that the next morning after the murder he went to Macroom hoping to see the Lord Muskerry, but not finding him there he did write to his Lordship, and also to General Barry giving the names of the murderers; that Donogh Reardon told him that the Lord Muskerry sent him with the convoy.

THE PRISONER'S DEFENCE.

That being then to remove out of that country, the English apprehended hurts and desired and prayed him to give way to their departure desiring to go to Cork; that (therefore) he sent to the

constable Tiegue MacDonogh Beare to appoint as many of the
neighbours as was convenient for a convoy. That Mr. Baldwin
desired to go to Bandonbridge, that there were then (*illegible*) of the
Lord President's (St. Leger's) army at Cork ; that Kilnamcaky with
his party was at Bandon, representing in or about 200 horse and 680
foot ; that he (Lord Muskerry) denied Mr. Baldwin and Smith (leave)
to go to Bandonbridge, for Baldwin was a clever and knowing guide,
he using writing, and the country (Irish) fearing prejudice by him,
they advised him (Lord Muskerry) not to let Baldwin go, therefore
he (Muskerry) desired Mr. Baldwin to stay till his return, for reasons that he had, and that (*illegible*) should be safe in the interim ;
that they (Baldwin and Smith) stayed accordingly, and were afterwards with all theirs safely conveyed away. It was the desire of all
the rest of the English to be gone, wherein the prisoner (Lord
Muskerry) said that he would not advise either their stay or their
going, but that they might go if they pleased.

Witnesses for the Defence.

1. WALTER BALDWIN (being) asked whether those going were
ordered to go, or (whether) it was of their choice (that they went),
saith that those going to Cork, as he heard, desired to be going to
Cork ; did not hear that they desired to go to Bandon, but he, the
examt., desired it, and did before that hear them desire to go to Cork,
and particularly Mrs. Hussey. That none were enforced to stay,
nor (had he) heard of any (being) forced to go.

2. EDMUND STABBER. That he lived at Macroom when Mrs.
Hussey and others came there ; that she desired him, this examt.,
to desire the Lord Muskerry that she might go to Cork with the rest
of the English going thither, that the Lord Muskerry answered he
would not either advise them to stay or to go ; that if any pleased
to go he would send to the constable for a convoy for them. Being
asked whether any of those desired to go to Bandon, saith none
desired or had occasion to go to Bandon but Mr. Baldwin, Smith,
and some others who were afterwards sent thither. That Donogh
Reardon coming to Macroom at the time of the convoy he was
desired by the Lord Muskerry to assist the constable in the convoy.
That the examt.'s brother, Richard Stabber, told him that that
convoy went as far as (*illegible*) bridge, about a mile or more from
Blarney, that he, the said Richard, went a little further (*illegible*),
and afterwards returned, after which those English were murdered
by the soldiers of Blarney, not by any of the convoy. That the

convoy was sent away the next day after the Lord Muskerry went away; that the Lord Muskerry did stay away a long time, but how long this examt. knoweth not. That the English that stayed or went were not enforced to do either.

3. TIEGUE MURPHY. (Saith) that he was in Macroom when Mrs. Hussey, the day before the Lord Muskerry went away, desired she might have liberty to go to Cork, and named some townsmen to go with her, his Lordship said she need not trouble herself, but go to the constable and he would order it. That he, this examt., was then present, and that he went away with his Lordship the next day. Being asked if his Lordship did force any to stay for his convenience, saith that his Lordship said that who would should go.

The Lord of Muskerry here added that he prosecuted those that acted in that murder. That he left the country for a time. That he did hear of that murder by letter from John Reardon, and that he did give an account thereof to the General (*illegible*). That he did also write to the (*illegible*) concerning it, desiring that it might be looked after, and to bring to justice the actors.

Witnesses for the Defence.

1. CORNELIUS MURPHY. That he, this examt., waited on the Lord Muskerry and was his secretary; that a letter was sent by his Lordship to General Barry (*illegible*) being then at Kilkenny, the substance of it was that an account might be had by him, the General, of that murder (committed by the garrison of Blarney).

2. COLONEL CALLAGHAN O'CALLAGHAN. That he, this examt., was with General Barry, either at Limerick or Kilmallock, when the General did read to Lieutenant-General Purcell a letter sent by the Lord Muskerry concerning the murder of the English sent from Macroom; the contents of it were that his Lordship was much grieved at that murder, desiring the General to prosecute the murderers to justice, but (examt.) did not hear what was then done thereupon.

The Lord of Muskerry here added that on the conclusion of the treaty of peace in 1646, among the instances of murders to be excepted he elected to offer (those concerned in) this murder now in justice, if any instances of that kind might be allowed, but that course was not thought fit, lest any should know what was intended, and so decline joining in the peace and avoiding the trial after.

For this the prisoner produced as witness,

1. SIR ROBERT TALBOT (who saith) that a Committee was appointed at Kilkenny to consider of the treaty for peace, and they considered concerning instances of murder (*illegible*) they of Leinster gave that (massacre) of Longford, those of Connaught that of Shrule, those of Munster that of Cashel and the Silver Mines. The Lord Muskerry then added that of Macroom, which he said should be punished, which paper was afterwards delivered by this examt. to the Lord of Ormond, who said that such instances would restrain justice to those few and desired rather to (*illegible*) in the general murders and massacres and the time for prosecuting them (to be limited) to two years, that the Lord Muskerry did insist on the said murder to be excepted out of the Act of October 8th.

2. JOHN GOLD (*sic*) that he waiting on the Lord of Muskerry, being one of the Commissioners for the treaty of peace, at Mr. Booth's house in Dame Street, Dublin, the examt. did hear his Lordship instance the murder of Macroom as one he would insist upon was not to be shut up (but) that it was conceived not fit to give any (such) instances fearing Sir Phelim O'Neil would fall off, this examt.'s cause of knowledge is that he was standing by at the meetings of the said Commissioners and did hear as aforesaid.

(Here) the Lord Muskerry desired that Dr. (*illegible*) might declare himself in this particular.

3. Dr. (*illegible*) saith, that at supper with the Lord of Ormond at the time of the said treaty he did hear the Lord of Muskerry desire much to insist (*illegible*) on the prosecution of murders.

Here his Lordship added that the Nuncio and his party, opposing the peace and corrupting many to join with them, made preparations against the Lord of Ormond then with a party ordered to Kilkenny; that the Lord of Ormond returned to Dublin, after which the Nuncio and his party prosecuted those, and particularly him, the Lord Muskerry, for insisting on the peace, and seized on him and Sir Robert Talbot, Dr. Fennell, Sir James Dillon, Sir Pierce Crosbie, etc., who were kept prisoners at Kilkenny and adjudged to suffer if (*illegible*), but that waiting and seeing the Lord Ormond treating (*illegible*) they hastened to close with him and the rest of the before-mentioned prisoners, and called (*illegible*) to employ some to France to the Queen and to the Prince then there and to present themselves to them, and to excuse their miscarriages with the Lord

Ormond and the Lord Muskerry, and the Lord (*illegible*) and Mr. Brown (were) chosen for it. On which they (the Council of Confederate Catholics ?) reassuming their authority at Kilkenny he, the Lord Muskerry, did write to the Council from Waterford, (he) then sailing for France, desiring them to take the said murder at Blarney into consideration.

For this the prisoner produced as witnesses :

1. JOHN GOLD (who saith) that on the Lord of Muskerry going into France he did send the examt. to Kilkenny, to take out a commission there for inquiring after the said murder, which he had, and it was sent into the country, that it related to this particular murder, Mr. (*illegible*) and Dr. Fennell's hands were to that commission among others.

2. DR. GERALD FENNELL (who saith) that the Lord Muskerry did send before going into France for the said commission, which was issued accordingly, to which the examt.'s hand was added and that John Gold had the commission to be executed.

His Lordship (here) added that on the Treaty in the last articles he did insist on the explanations, and did then instance that he would never consent that any of the actors in this murder should be pardoned, and (allowed to) pass under these articles. This testified in Court by Colonel (*illegible*). His general (course) concerning murders to be (*illegible*) testified by the Major-General, and that he (prisoner) was full in his expressions against murder (*illegible*), this murder particularly, and was equally against (all) murders in general.

COLONEL (*illegible*) did then declare that the Lord Muskerry did as was before spoken by Sir Robert Talbot and Dr. Fennell. His Lordship added his insisting on the articles.

THE COUNSEL. 1. MR. REARDON. (There is) nothing in this evidence of the Lord of Muskerry commanding or advising as in the explanation and 2nd and 7th articles. That more than one witness is necessary for life, etc. That no act of his (prisoner's) will proved (him consenting) to the act he might know of it after (it was done).

2. MR. KENNEDY. Accessory to persons unknown.

MR. REARDON. The Lord Muskerry commands a lawful thing (in commanding) them to be conveyed away, (and) if the convoy had murdered, as it appears (they did) not, it is not to be charged on him not commanding it.

3. MR. BROWNE. The 1st Explanation. Where an explana-

tion is given of an article it is to be insisted on not to give an explanation of an explanation. (*illegible*) proof not probability (of guilt necessary).

LORD MUSKERRY saith his apprehension of the meaning of the article, explanation 1st (is that the person accused as accessory must be shown to have had a share in the murder by) an act of the will either advising or commanding (it to be done) (or by) sheltering murderers knowing them to be such, and proved to be such (or by) keeping them back from justice (*illegible*). That he hath prosecuted and endeavoured to bring them (the murderers) to justice. He saith, that he never had a command till the siege of (*illegible*), and (that) when (he was) not in power he could not punish (*illegible*) not done by that civil convoy which he sent (from Macroom).

On the Private Debate.

DONOGH, VISCOUNT MUSKERRY
  for } NOT GUILTY.
MRS. HUSSEY, ETC.

DONOGH, VISCOUNT MUSKERRY, for (murder of) WILLIAM DEANE, *alias* DENE, and three others, Irish, and a woman called NORA.

Evidence.

As to generals. GEORGE SMITH, present. ALICE STABBER, present.[1]

MR. ATTORNEY, for justifying the examinations taken by Mr. Bysse in Munster, produced the warrant for the Commission for taking the examinations, from the hands of Mr. Exham, the Clerk of the Hanaper, which was endorsed by some of those who paid the (*illegible*) now in Court. Also concerning the said examinations Mr. Thomas Waring was examined in Court on oath of his receiving them by order from the Council of State to be (*illegible*), he saith further that by order he did abbreviate the said examinations as to losses (but) not[2] as to murders.

[1] George Smith and Alice Stabber merely repeated the evidence already given by them on the former trial.

[2] *v. ante*, p. 177. This passage, with the exception of two words, is unusually clear and legible. The first word marked in above as illegible is probably 'fees' or 'fines,' the second looks like 'preserved,' but it may be 'copied.' Here, at all events, is the explanation of Warner and Mr. Gilbert's (so called) 'cancellings.' They are marks of abbreviation made carefully so as not to cancel a single line, but to leave it clear and valid.

Mr. Attorney then desired that the examinations of Bird so taken should be recorded. To which the prisoner's counsel, Mr. Reardon, opposed that before the reading of the examinations it should be (*illegible*) concerning the said Bird, whether he be alive, if so, and that he may be had, that he appear, or that the truth of his examinations appear on oath.

WILLIAM BIRD (saith) that the Lord of Muskerry about February, 1641, told this examt. that the Irish had a commission from the king to do what he did.

MARY FIFE (saith) that her father having the Lord of Muskerry's protection, notwithstanding some of the Lord's soldiers did murder him, and she heard that the Lord of Muskerry had notice thereof, and of the actors, yet never heard that he punished any for it, and the examt. durst not complain to the Lord of Muskerry.

MARY AUSTIN. That the examt.'s father and her brother were murdered, that she believeth the Lord Muskerry heard of it, yet did not punish any for it; that John O'Keily, her late husband, was sent by the Lord Muskerry to General Barry, by whom he was hanged, as she heard from Alice Stabber, that the Lady Muskerry did send (him) to the Lord Muskerry, who sent him to General Barry as aforesaid.

SIMON BRIGGES (saith) that in the ward of (*illegible*) he did see (*illegible*) persons hanged by the Lord of Muskerry's command.

JOHN CRUCE, present (in court, saith) that at the siege of (*illegible*) by the Lord Muskerry, one Dermot O'Brian, an Irishman of the English party, and not a soldier, was brought before the Lord of Muskerry and hanged in his camp in his presence. The examt. heard this from others.

JOHN WARREN (saith that) John Millet and two others English (were) killed near the Lord of Muskerry's camp, that they had been prisoners the day before in the said camp, and were sent away with a convoy.

WILLIAM CARY, present (in court, saith) that John Phips, sent away by the Lord Muskerry with a convoy, he was with his wife hanged by the convoy, and the son of the said Phips also murdered afterwards by the same party. This by hearsay.

HONORA SHEA, present (in court, saith) that William Woods and William (*illegible*), who had and shared the Lord Muskerry's protection, were notwithstanding murdered, this (was) done, as (was) reported, by some of the Lord Muskerry's soldiers, others reporting them to belong to others, this (was) about three years since.

Robert Morley, present (in court, saith) as the former examt., Honora Shea, and that he did not think the Lord Muskerry careful of making good his protection.

William Eames saith, that the Lord of Muskerry was of those that besieged the Castle of Askeaton, and that after quarter was given it was broken.

December 3rd, 1653.

Evidence.

1. The prisoner's examination. (He saith) that in June or July, 1642, Kilfinny Castle was besieged by General Barry, not by this examt., that the siege continued about six (*illegible*). That he, this examt., was there but four or five days before the castle was delivered, he denieth that any were executed in his presence, or that he did then hear of any (that were) executed after quarter given, that the quarter was for the English; the Irish (*illegible*).

2. Richard Blackhall (saith) that he was besieged at Kilfinny by the Lords Muskerry, Roche, Major Purcell, etc., that William Deane was murdered (*illegible*), three Irishmen and Nora, a woman, hanged.

3. Dame Elizabeth Dowdall saith that Lieutenant-General Patrick Purcell, with an army of seven thousand, (besieged) the Castle of Kilfinny, (which) being taken July 29th, 1611, William Deane, sent out as scout, was killed. That the chiefest of the besiegers were General Barry, Lieutenant-General Purcell, and the Lord Viscount Muskerry, etc., that Nora and some others were then murdered.

4. Anthony Sheryn (*sic*), present (in court, saith) that he was (among the) besieged at Kilfinny by the Lord Muskerry, etc., that William Deane was murdered at the siege, that (*blank*) and three Irishmen were hanged, and an Irishwoman after the castle (was) delivered.

This Examinant's 3rd Examination. He names the persons of those Irish so hanged, and that he did see the day before the surrender the Lord of Muskerry ride by the castle, and did see him after the castle surrendered. That the Lord of Muskerry commanded there a regiment of foot, which he, this examt., did see (*illegible*), and on inquiry was told it was his (Lord Muskerry's). That (when) quarter was given, the Irish being to stand at mercy: that after those Irish were hanged, as before (related), the news of it was brought to the Lady Dowdall, who demanded the reason, it was answered because they stayed with the English; that two of those Irish so hanged did not bear (arms).

THE PRISONER'S DEFENCE.

(He) desired to hear all his charges before (he made) a particular defence; the reason (is) for answering the articles together with Mr. Attorney's preamble, which did not relate to this (particular) charge: yet proof was brought into it, contrary to the nature of a preamble. But, the Court desiring him to proceed to his defence on the present charge, he produced:

1. GERALD FITZ-GERALD (who saith) that he was in the Castle of Kilfinny when that place was besieged by General Barry, that the Lord Muskerry was at the siege, and that he, this examt., did not hear of any detained there, that the prisoners that were hanged did watch and ward, and did march out with others in the castle to take preys, and had arms in the place, that they did take preys in the country before the siege; so said Anthony Sherwin; that Nora or her brother did go forth as a spy, which occasioned their hanging her, whereas they spared other Irishwomen there; so said Sherwin; that the Lord of Muskerry was not present (at the execution), and that the execution was by order of General Barry and Purcell, and was (*illegible*) by the captain that carried this examt. with the rest (*illegible*).

2. CAPTAIN DAVID POER (saith) that the quarter to the castle was that the Irish (*illegible*) General Barry commanded three men and a woman to be hanged, being Irish, that the Lord Muskerry had no command at the siege, that General Barry commanded in chief.

3. JOHN GOLD (saith) that going to Limerick he went to the siege of Kilfinny, which was in the way; that the Irish (in the castle) were by the General Barry excepted from quarter, and that the woman Nora was looked upon as a spy that passed through the camp into the castle; that those hanged were executed the day after the surrender, as he remembers. He did not stay (to be present) at the execution (*illegible*), the examt. is now servant to the Lord Muskerry, and (*illegible*) since 1644; that the Lord Muskerry had no command at that siege, that he (examt.) desired General Barry to give him a convoy going away, which he refused till Newcastle were taken.

COUNCIL, MR. REARDON (*illegible*). That those hanged were (hanged) by order of the General (Barry) or of Lieutenant-General Purcell, the Lord Muskerry was there, but as a private person, none ordered by him to be hanged, and he (was) not present at the executions, and, not having command, he neither advised nor acted nor kept (*illegible*) to be charged with it.

As to the Time of the Acts.

It was in the first year (of the rebellion), a puissant army of 7,000, with a lieutenant-general, a major-general, in an orderly course of war (*illegible*), whether what was done at that time be (*illegible*) excepted in the articles.

As to the Charge.

The actors (in the murder), said to be persons unknown, and (no one can be charged as) accessory with persons unknown, the other persons murdered are unknown, the evidence is as to persons known, so as the provisions agree not to the charge.

Mr. Brown. By the articles murder excepted, (*illegible*). The prisoner challengeth the articles and the (*illegible*).

At the Private Debate.

DONOGH, VISCOUNT MUSKERRY }
for }
WILLIAM DEANE, ETC. }

As to matter of fact . . . GUILTY.
Articles considered . . . NOT GUILTY.

READ THE SENTENCE.

As now on the whole matter you are discharged, my Lord, give me leave for a word to you. You have escaped the last judgment of this Court. You had a just judgment of indemnity in the first charge, (and) of acquittal in the rest.

I only offer now to your notice this, that when you went off and joined with the rebels, if that you have not joined with all that they did, and the shedding of innocent blood, with which these wicked rebels have defiled the land, yet see if it deserves not your serious thoughts, that through you also the sword hath raged in this land and plague and famine.

We shall all one day stand before the judgment-seat of Christ to answer for all done ; and certainly, surely, for this also at that day, my Lord, you must answer, and see if you have not in that joining, joined with one of the most horrible massacres in the (world). I observe two such: 1, the Sicilian Evensong, *anno* 1282, when all the French were (cut off) by conspiracy on Easter Day at the tolling of the Evensong, which they (the Sicilians) performed without sparing any, for they intended to root out all the French (*illegible*). This was the Sicilian Vespers.

The second massacre, that of Paris (St. Bartholomew), was also very notorious, but it and the other were short of this. That of Sicily was to root out the French, this was to root out the English nation and the Protestant religion, there but 8,000 killed, only a few that escaped to a fort called (*illegible*), who were afterwards starved. But here in a short time above 300,000 British and Protestants murdered or lost in cold blood, so as that the number far exceeds Paris or Sicily, no torments, no burying alive there, only death, but here death was a mercy (*illegible*).

Now, my Lord, lay your hand on your heart when you leave us (*illegible*) that party, see how this blood comes home (to them). Go! expiate it by repentance.

Lord Muskerry's Speech after his Acquittal.

I have not much to say, although I cannot say all I feel in the way of thanks to this Honourable Court (*illegible*), I must say that I have in these whole proceedings met with justice, without any leaning to my prejudice, but that if any leaning hath been it hath been to my favour rather. It is one of the greatest providences that ever I met with this. I met many crosses in Spain and Portugal. I could get no rest till I came hither, and the crosses I met here are much affliction to me, but when I consider that in this Court I come clear out of that blackness of blood by being so sifted, it is more to me than my (lost) estate. I can live without my estate, but not without my credit.

THE CASE OF COLONEL MACSWEENY.

The first witness examined against Colonel Maolmurry [1] Mac-Sweeny appears to have been Maolrony O'Carroll, Constable of Castle Doe for the English government and a Protestant, whose deposition, taken on the 26th of April, 1643, by the three clerical commissioners, Rev. John Watson, Rev. Randal Adams, and Rev. Henry Brereton, has been given at p. 142. MacSweeny was then serving in the Irish army with many others against whom similar charges had been made. Yet the clerical commissioners have been censured by Irish writers for having taken depositions against the accused in their absence, as though the unfortunate clergymen had it in their power to compel the accused to leave the Irish army and appear before them in the midst of a fierce civil war. The marvel is how the Commissioners or Magistrates were able to move about the country at all at such a time, that they did so at peril of their lives is shown by the murder of Archdeacon Bysse, one of their number, in Waterford, on his way to Dublin with the depositions he had taken (v. vol. i. p. 123). After the reduction of the whole island by Cromwell, the relatives of Mr. Aikins revived the old charge of 1643 against MacSweeny. By that time O'Carroll was probably dead, at least he was not re-examined in 1653, and as usual, the Cromwellian Court did not rest satisfied with the depositions of ten years before, but sought in every direction for living witnesses, whose evidence might be collated with these documents.

I desire to call the reader's particular attention to this case, inasmuch as it shows how utterly incorrect is Sir Charles Gavan Duffy's account of the Commission issued under Cromwell to inquire into the murders committed between 1641-54. Sir Charles tells us that this Commission was issued to investigate the wrongs of the

[1] For the meaning of Maolmurry (called in English Myles) and Maolrony *v.* Joyce's *Irish Names*, 1st Series, p. 360.

'British in Ireland,' and that the 'maddest evidence' was received by it 'against the Irish, while no witness was heard on their behalf' (*Bird's-eye View of Irish History*, p. 100). This is surely the 'maddest assertion' that party prejudice ever put forth even in Ireland. As I have already shown, more than thirty depositions, some of them made in Irish by the Magees and other poor Irish Roman Catholics (who probably had not a drop of British blood in their veins) whose relatives were murdered in the retaliatory massacres at and near Island Magee in January, 1642 (N.S.), were taken by the Cromwellian Commissioners against the Scotch and English murderers. Some of those depositions and many others against English and Scotch murderers of Irish are now laid before the reader for the first time, after they have been neglected or deliberately suppressed from party motives, by every writer except the able and impartial historian of the Irish Presbyterian Church, Dr. Reid. We can see for ourselves, unless we prefer to be misled, as Sir C. G. Duffy has been, by the rhetoric and false statements of Burke and Curry, that the Cromwellian Commissioners took care to collect evidence against all murderers, English, Irish, and Scotch, showing no favour or partiality to any one of them, on account of his creed or nationality, or the worldly position or creed of his victims. So far did the Commissioners go in their care to punish murderers of inoffensive Irish, and to sift and test the evidence of Englishmen and Scotchmen against Irishmen, and to allow the latter to bring forward witnesses for their defence, that Carte and other royalist writers charge them (the Cromwellian Commissioners and judges) with unjustly favouring the Irish, just as in the following letters we find Mr. Aikins, a Cromwellian officer, charging Colonel Venables with unduly favouring Colonel MacSweeny. Indeed, Sir Charles Gavan Duffy, with a curious inconsistency, says that the 'only notable victim' of the Commission (which a few pages before he represents as eager to exterminate the Irish) was Sir Phelim O'Neil (*v. Bird's-eye View of Irish History*, pp. 100-118). There are birds and birds, but clearly Sir C. G. Duffy's bird is not the 'keen-eyed eagle.' The truth is that a poet seldom makes a good historian, and that in much of what Sir C. G. Duffy has written about 1641 he has been guided by that mistaken poetic maxim which he sets forth in the dedication of his brochure to the Roman Catholic bishop of Clogher, that 'traditions and memories interpret the past better than the historian.' One of the real grievances of Ireland is that writers on her past and statesmen who desire to draw instruction from it too often prefer to rely on traditions and memories more or less myths, rather than on the sober facts of history. How these latter can put an end once and for ever to the myths about the injustice of the Cromwellian Commissioners to the Irish leaders the following documents will help to show.

To the Right Honourable Sir Gerald Lowther, Knight and Baronet, Lord President of the High Court of Justice, sitting in Dublin, these,

RIGHT HONOURABLE : In observance of the Commission sent to us bearing date the 10th of January last, we have sent for Mr. Alexander Aikins, not being able to get any information of any other person in this precinct that could give evidence concerning the murders committed by Colonel Myles MacSweeny and others, and we took his (Mr. Aikins') examinations and recognizances to (*illegible*) and afterwards by virtue of your said Commission we sent unto the said Mr. Aikins unto the north, having written unto Sir George St. George to send some soldiers along with him, to endeavour the apprehending of MacSweeny and the rest, who had their hands in that murder; but after his long stay there, seeing he could not apprehend them, he sent us the enclosed letter, which with his examination and recognizance we have transmitted to you, and leave to your consideration. Having received information from Captain Pakenham, that there was one Dendy in Captain Sandford's troop, who could give evidence concerning the murders committed at Bellanleck (*sic*) in the year 1651, for which we understand Daniel Maguire is now prisoner in Dublin, we sent for him and likewise for Nangle, Darcy, and Fagan, who the said Dendy informed us, he conceived were accessory to the murder, and having taken their examinations, they confessing nothing which we could apprehend to be material, and his (Dendy's) evidence against them being but slender, we adventured, upon good bonds for their appearance upon summons, to let them have their liberty; his recognizance to prosecute the examinations, bonds, and recognizances, we likewise enclose, and having also received some information against Con Kelly about the murder of Thomas MacEgan, we took the enclosed examination, but seeing we could not apprehend his body, although we endeavoured it, we proceeded no further. We do herewith return your Commission, which if not delayed (through our not hearing from Mr. Aikins until very lately) you had received sooner, and leaving the whole to your consideration and to the guidance of the (*illegible*), we remain your assured and humble servants,

H. WADDINGTON.

Athlone, 30th March, 1653.   ALEX. BRASIER.

(*Enclosure.*)

The Examination of Alexander Aikins, gent., of the (*blank*) *in Sir George St. George's company of foot, concerning the murder of Robert Aikins, and some other English in the beginning of the rebellion at Clandehorba, in the county of Donegal, in the province of Ulster, taken by order of a Commission of the High Court of Justice, sitting at Dublin, bearing date the* 18*th of January instant, directed unto Alexander Braxfield, James Shaen, Henry Waddington, and George Southcote, Esqs., or any one of them.*

The said examt., Alexander Aikins, aged about twenty years, duly sworn and examined, deposeth and saith, that this examt.'s father, Robert Aikins, minister of God's word of the parish of Clanderhorba, in the county of Donegal, with several other persons were living in a slated house, three stories high, at Clandehorba aforesaid, in the first year of the rebellion. And that about Candlemas in the said year, in the night time, when all the people of the house were asleep, there came some persons unto the door and knocked, and this examt.'s said father awaking, inquired of one Edward Evans, advising[1] him thereof. The said Robert Aikins demanded who was at the door, and it was answered, 'I, Maolmurry MacSweeny.' Thereupon the said Robert caused a candle to be lighted, and called upon one to open the door, whereupon the said MacSweeny and five more, viz. Manus MacKonogher, Dualtagh MacGarvy, Brian Reagh Offary, Donnel MacIllbridy, and Neil O'Donnell, came rushing into the said house with their swords drawn. And the said Robert Aikins inquiring of the said Maolmurry MacSweeny what was the matter with them, the said Maolmurry answering bade him put on his clothes and he should know presently. And having caused the said Robert to put on his clothes, the said Myles MacSweeny took him and three more, viz. Marcus Aikins and John Aikins, brothers, unto the said Robert, and one Robert Buchanan out of doors, and bade them say their prayers,

[1] *i. e.* warning him or telling him of the knocking.

and then brought them into a barn, where they hanged them all four and murdered one John Adams, whom they stabbed with skeans, being all English Protestants, and afterwards the said Myles came back again into the said house and sat down upon Edward Evan's bedside, with his sword drawn, lying across his knee. And then one Janet Parbarot (*sic*), lying in bed in the same room, went down upon her knees and prayed him to save her and such of her family as were there, whereupon the said Myles (in Irish Maolmurry) promised and said, ' My life for you and yours, no harm shall come to you or to any one that belongeth unto you.' And then when news was brought that the said Robert and the other four were murdered he, MacSweeny, went out of the house, and having put this examt. and all belonging to his father out of it, he put the said Janet in possession of this examt.'s father's house and goods. And then he with those of his company went away that night; and the next morning some of the said Myles's men, but examt. cannot positively depose whether the said Myles was with them or not, came to the said house and took the widows of the said murdered persons, and hanging up ropes upon the rafters, threatened that if they would not confess their money they would hang them. Whereupon one Elizabeth Todd, the widow of the aforesaid John Aikins, confessed and gave sixteen or twenty pounds unto them, which money the said Elizabeth did lately receive satisfaction for from the said Myles. And this examt. saith, that his cause of knowledge of what he hath deposed is, that he was in that said house the night the murders were committed, and that he saw the said Myles and the other persons who came upstairs with him, with their swords drawn, and doth perfectly remember and know what he hath deposed to be true. And further saith, that one Robert Dall, who held the candle while the said persons were murdered in the barn, told the widows awhile after, in this deponent's hearing, that the said Myles cut down the said Marcus after he was hung up, and that afterwards the said Marcus was hanged up until he died. And this examt. further saith, that he is informed and verily believeth that the said Myles MacSweeny, Manus McConogher, Dualtagh McGarvey, Brian Reagh Offary, Donogh MacGilbridy, and Neil O'Donnell, the murderers aforesaid, do now lie and reside in the country of Doe, in the county of Dunangall (*sic*) and barony of Kilmacrennan, and parishes of Clandehorba, Roy, and Mullish O'Biggory (*sic*) in the province of Ulster. And being demanded who can probably give evidence on behalf of the Commonwealth concerning the matters and things aforesaid, this examt. saith, that the persons undernamed can give full information therein, viz. Margaret Walker, late wife to Mr. Robert Aikins, who was then murdered, now married to William Cumberland, living in the town of Coleraine, Elizabeth Todd, late wife to John Aikins, now widow, living in the county of Donegal, barony of Raphoe, parish of Rey, Elizabeth Morton, late wife of John Adams, who was then murdered, now married to Edward Dall, living in the parish of Clandehorba, barony of Kilmacrenan, county of Donegal, Robert Dall, husbandman, now living in the same parish, barony, and county: Janet Greenhill, married to Phelimy O'Dogherty, now living in the parish of Menagh, barony of Kilmacrenan, county of Donegal, Jane Evans, married to James Peebles, now living in the same parish, barony, and county. And further deposeth not.

ALEXANDER AIKINS.

Taken as aforesaid, 28*th January,* 1653, *before us,*
  H. WADDINGTON.
  ALEX. BRAXFIELD.

To the Honourable the Commissioners of Revenue for the precinct of Athlone, these present. Hast, hast (sic).

HONOURABLE SIRS,—By virtue of the power, authority, and order given me by your honours for to repair into the province of Ulster with a commanded party of Sir George St. George's soldiers for the apprehending of the bodies of such persons as had a hand in the murder of Robert Aikins and others who were murdered at one time with him. According to your honours' orders, I have been in the aforesaid province, and have done as much as it possibly lay in my power to do, in exercising my duty in performance of the trust laid upon me, yet could not find any of the said persons, orders having been sent to the Commissioners of the Revenue for Derry ten days before my going into those parts, viz. to Major Bolton, Ralph King, Owen Wynn, and John Reeves for the causing of the body of Colonel Myles MacSweeny to be apprehended and sent close prisoner to Dublin, the said Colonel MacSweeny, not thinking of any such thing, went, as I was informed, to the gates of Derry, and there got intelligence that if he would go into the town he would be apprehended. What way he could have been thus informed I cannot tell, unless it were by some person belonging to the Commissioners, for it is told me that none did know of it but themselves and some officers that they had given orders to for the apprehending of him: but being informed one way or the other at the very gates of Derry, he went away and could not be found, neither could I hear where he should be, he being so well beloved by all in these parts, and especially by [1] Colonel Venables, Lieut.-Col. Thomas Newburgh, and the rest of the Commissioners. They told me they were sure he was cleared of the murder laid to his charge before them already, and that they would do their endeavour that he should not suffer for it. As for the rest of the murderers, there is (*sic*) three of them in the county of Dunagall and barony of Kilmacrennan, viz. Dualtagh MacGarvey, Donell MacGilbridy, and Brian Reagh Offary, they are maintained by their friends in the said barony, yet hath this long time been upon their keeping. They were at my being there treating with one Lieutenant Matthew Foot, that they might have his safe conduct to come in and clear themselves, and lay the fact upon Colonel MacSweeny, who is guilty of it, but they would not come in so long as I was in the country. Yet they are much afraid to come in, by reason that they are informed Colonel Venables is such a great friend of Colonel MacSweeny, and would, right or wrong, have them to suffer for what MacSweeny hath done. For what they did they say they will make it appear it was by his directions and commands, he being then their commander. Colonel Venables I am confident hath written to Dublin that MacSweeny may be granted the privilege to be tried in Ulster, when, as I heard Colonel Newburgh say, he would be willing to come in and there to be tried, but as for to be sent to Dublin, he (Newburgh) considered that they were as sufficient to try him there as to send him to any other place. I know very well if they pleased they might apprehend him, but they had rather give him intelligence of any such thing than do him any such prejudice, they are all of them such friends of his, and will do all they can to clear him. I delivered your honours' letters to the Commissioners, wherein you desired that they would be pleased to give me their warrant, being within their precinct, for seizing the goods of the murderers, the which at first they granted, and wrote their warrant upon my petition, and after they had signed it they said one to another that Colonel Venables would be offended at it, and they tore it in pieces, and said they would give me no warrant for anything until they did know Colonel Venables' pleasure in it. Upon which Colonel Venables came to Derry, when I did question the Commissioners before him the reason for not granting me my

[1] Compare *Bird's-eye View of Ireland*, p. 122.

lawful request. They answered me that they would consider what they thought fitting to be done, and bade me to wait and they would give me an answer: so after having waited ten days upon them, their answer to me at last was that they would give me no order against their goods until they saw whether they (the accused) were condemned or not. Their plot for it is that I may not have any ability wherewith I may be able to pursue against MacSweeny in law, neither am I able for want of the same to pursue him, nor the others; they made me wait upon them so long that it did prove very chargeable to me, having the charges of eight soldiers to pay for the space of twelve days, while the said Commissioners kept me there, and nothing the better for my staying.

I have sent here enclosed unto your honours my petition, humbly desiring that your honours may be pleased to get me a warrant for the goods of the murderers, without which I am not able to pursue them, nor answer at any court where I shall be summoned to appear, all which I humbly desire your honours to take into consideration, and trust that they who defend the cause of murderers will be found out. There are two of the murderers, as I am informed, viz. Manus McConogher and Neil O'Donnell, in the county of Tyrone, but what place within that county I cannot tell, this being all that I can give you and account of, I take leave and rest

Your honours' in all humbleness to serve you,
ALEXANDER AIKINS.
Carrigdromask, this 25th March, 1653.

(*Enclosure.*)

The Humble Petition of ALEXANDER AIKINS *to the Rt. Hon. the Commissioners of the Revenue of Ulster,*

Humbly sheweth, unto your Honours, that in the first year of the late rebellion in Ireland Colonel Miles MacSweeny took away in his custody and keeping the value of 200*l.* worth of your petitioner's father's goods and chattels, which he converted to his own use, and refuses to give your petitioner any satisfaction for the same, pretending that his capitulation doth free him of all such like facts done by him. It is the desire of your petitioner that he (the said Colonel) might appear and first clear himself of the murder laid to his charge, which if he can free himself of that he may be the sooner freed of what robberies he hath done if his capitulation doth clear him. So it may be please your

Honours that your petitioner doth conceive that if he, Colonel MacSweeny, cannot clear himself of the murders laid against him, that he is as liable to give satisfaction for what robberies he hath done as for the murders he hath committed. May it therefore please your Honours to take the premises into consideration, and to grant your petitioner a warrant to what officer your Honours shall think fit, for the seizing upon the goods, chattels, and corn of the said Myles MacSweeny, and the same to be put upon security until the said MacSweeny appears and answers your petitioner's suit. And your petitioner shall always pray, &c. &c.—*February 1st*, 1658.

To the Rt. Hon. Sir Gerard Lowther, Knight, Lord President of the High Court of Justice at Dublin.

MY LORD,—Some public occasions drawing me at this time hither, I met with your Lordship's (order) to one Mr. Aykins (sic) for the apprehending of Colonel Miles MacSweeny with others as murderers of his father Mr. Aykins, a minister, and in regard some occurrences relating unto that matter are known to me, I thought myself obliged to give your Lordship an account of my knowledge. In September, 1652, I marched to suppress the said MacSweeny, who was in arms at that time in those parts, and hearing some reports of the said Mr. Aykins' murder, I made inquiries into the matter and examined some witnesses, Scots, Protestants and such as lost some of their nearest relatives at that time, by some of the men in your order mentioned, being some of them servants to Mr. Aykins at the time of his death and eye-witnesses of all that was done, as Robert Dall, Janet Doherty (a Scotchwoman as I am informed married to an Irishman, her daughter married to a Scottishman), and one Greenhill, who lost his mother and brother, as is related, with some others whose examinations were taken by Sir George St. George at my request, in regard I declined to enter into any treaty, much less to conclude any articles with the said MacSweeny until I were satisfied he was guilty or no; and since his articles were approved and further explanations added to them by the Rt. Hon. the Commissioners of the Commonwealth, of all which Examinations, Articles, and Explanations the enclosed are copies. This young Aykins lived a soldier under Sir George St. George when those examinations were taken and could not be ignorant of the business, and was then silent; since which time he and his mother, of whose abode at the time I could not learn anything, have sought unto MacSweeny for satisfaction, which being denied in that measure they demanded, they now prosecute him, after they have, as I am informed, taken some money which their threats and his fears extracted from him, not being guilty as I believe. Aykins' petition is herein enclosed, who being examined by us, confessed that in September last he demanded the money for his father's goods, which being refused, he, in January last, informed against the said MacSweeny, who hath lately writ to me and I believe will offer himself to trial, but is I am informed at present very sick, and very probably will give bonds to appear when recovered, if your Lordship please to allow of the same. His fidelity since his submission in discovering enemies, and assisting our forces upon all occasions which all the State's servants employed in those parts can and will testify, from whom I have this, will I hope persuade your Lordship to accept of bail (for him), which is all that is humbly offered on his behalf by, my Lord,

Your Lordship's very humble servant,

R. VENABLES.

Derry, Feb. 22nd, 1653.

(*Enclosure* 1.)

The Examination of Robert Dall, of Donraghe in the parish of Kilmacrennan, county of Donegal, taken by me, Sir George St. George, Knt., at Castledoe, by the direction of the Hon. Colonel Venables, Lt.-Col. (*torn*) *upon the last day of September,* 1652, *who being duly sworn on the Holy Evangelists,*

Saith, that he being at Mr. Robert Akin's [1] house, his then master, at the very beginning of the rebellion, there came to that house in the night, three hours before day, some men and knocked very earnestly at the door requiring to come in: they within fearing no great harm opened the door to them, when presently entered four men, viz. Manus McKonogher, Dualtagh MacGarvey, Brian Reogh Offary, and Donell MacGilbridy. The first man, Manus MacKonogher, had his sword drawn, and to the best of this examinant's remembrance there was also one Neil O'Donnell, who likewise came into the house with his sword

[1] The name is spelt indifferently in the depositions, Aikins, Aikin, Akin, and Aykins, but this is a common occurrence in old documents, where a surname is often spelt in a dozen different ways.

drawn. As soon as they came in they called earnestly for Mr. Robert Aikins and his two brothers to rise hastily, which accordingly they did, then they pressed them hard to have money from them. Mr. Aikins answered them that he had none and told them that it was well known in the country that he lived to the height of his estate, that he had newly built the house he lived in, and married one of his daughters, which would sufficiently excuse him from having any money, if they would be reasonable. They replied that they would have money or they would put him to death, he answering still as before that he had none; then they took him and his two brothers Marcus Aikins and John Aikins and led them forth of the door threatening to kill them unless they (the rebels) might get money, which the others still said they had not: then they bade them (their prisoners) prepare to die, offering them to choose what death they would die, either to be killed by a sword or bullet or to be hanged, they all chose to be hanged, so they (the rebels) carried them all into Mr. Robert Aikin's barn a little remote from the house, and first they hanged up Marcus Aikin; then presently came in Colonel Miles MacSweeny, who very much reproved them for that bloody act and presently drew his sword and cut down Marcus Aikin again, and charged them with all the earnestness he could to desist from such outrages, and not only to forbear hanging the other two, but him he had cut down, who was then recovered and walked on his feet about the house. Manus O'Konogher replied that he would not obey any of Colonel MacSweeny's commands that night, and presently the said Manus and his company took the said Colonel by the neck and thrust him out of doors and locked the door, and so they returned to their bloody business and hanged up all the three brothers and another man called Robert Buchanan, a servant of Mr. Aikins. After that they went to John Adams' house and brought him to the barn where those men lay dead and bade him prepare himself to be hanged as the rest were before him, he told them he would not, and so struggled the best he could for his life, and then Manus McKonogher drew out a long skean he had and thrust it through him and so killed him, this deponent saith they forced him to carry a candle and light them all the time they were doing these villanies, which is the cause of his certain knowledge of all that he hath here deposed. He also saith that Colonel Miles MacSweeny came not to them until seven o'clock

the next morning after he was thrust out of doors, and then he
came to the house, and this deponent could not observe that
either the night before, or in the morning when he came, that
he had any wish or desire that any should be murdered, but was
very much offended at it.

signed GEORGE ST. GEORGE.

copia vera, examined by us, this 20*th Feb.* 1653,
R. VENABLES.
RALPH KING.
JOHN REEVES.

(*Enclosure* 2.)

*The Examination of Janet O'Doherty being taken before Sir
George St. George, Knt., at Castledoe, the last of September,*
1652, *by desire and order of the Hon. Colonel Venables and
Lieut.-Col. Thomas Newburgh.*

Who being duly sworn upon the Holy Evangelists saith, that
she being in Mr. Robert Akin's house, with her husband where
they then lived about the Candlemass after these wars began,
there came some men to that house after their first sleep in the
night and called earnestly to come in (*i.e.* to be allowed to come
in). Mr. Robert Akin himself rose out of his bed opened the
door and let them in, when presently entered Colonel Miles
MacSweeny, Manus MacKonogher, Donell MacGilbridy, and
Donnell MacGarvey, Brian Reagh Offary, and Neil O'Donnell.
Upon their coming in in such a manner John Akins demanded
of them what they would have, and some of them, this deponent
knoweth not which, said they would have money: presently
another, whom she thinks was Manus O'Konogher, answered that
they would have lives and money afterwards when they had
(*torn*) them all. Robert, Marcus, John, and the servant Robert
Buchanan put on their clothes, and they (the rebels) carried them
out of the dwelling-house into the barn, this deponent and her
husband being in their (*torn*) in an upper chamber in the house
saw not further what they (*torn*). After a little while Colonel
MacSweeny came into the chamber of this deponent where she
lay and sat down at the (*torn*) side and told this deponent and
her husband that those com(*torn*) that were with him had
hanged up Marcus Akin, which he thought at the first they had
done in jest, but seeing the man was black in the face and supposing he drew near death, he drew out his sword and cut him

down, and desired them, as he told this deponent, that they would forbear to kill any of them, whereupon they took him by the shoulder and told him he was a faint-hearted fellow and thrust him out of doors, from whence he came to this deponent's lodging as aforesaid and stayed until fair (*i.e.* clear) day in the morning. This deponent further saith, that after the murderers had dispatched their murders, they came into Mr. Akin's house again, and one of them, Manus MacKonogher, having a long skean in his hand, his arm being bloody up to the elbow, sat down and called for drink; then he and the rest of his followers were boasting and bragging of what they had done, and they said that Colonel MacSweeny was but a faint-hearted, cowardly man, and that they had thrust him out of door from amongst them for that he would not have them kill the men. And further deponeth not.

signed GEORGE ST. GEORGE.

copia vera.

(*Enclosure* 3.)

The Examination of John Greenhill, of the parish of Moragh, barony of (illegible), county of Donegal, husbandman, aged forty years or thereabouts, taken before us the 2nd of October, 1652.

This deponent being duly sworn, on the day aforesaid, deposeth and saith as followeth, viz. : that in or about the month of February, 1641, this deponent being at Mr. Robert Akin's house at (*illegible*) in the county aforesaid there came thither Colonel Maolmurry MacSweeny, Manus MacKonogher, Doltagh MacGarvey, Daniel MacIlbridy, Neil O'Donnell, and Brian Reagh Offary, who, as they confessed, often stayed in the said Mr. Akin's house, and took forth Mr. Robert Akin and his brothers, Mr. John and Mr. Mark Akin, and Robert Buchanan their servant, and carried them to the said Mr. Akin's barn near his house, where they first hanged the said Mark Akin. And the said Colonel Maolmurry MacSweeny coming thither after them, and finding the said Mark Akin hanged, did threaten the said Manus MacKonogher, and the rest of his confederates, and thereupon the said Colonel MacSweeny drew out his sword and did cut the rope wherewith they hanged the said Mark, so that he fell down alive begging his life again, whereupon the said Manus and the rest of the said party did, as they said, thrust the said Colonel MacSweeny out of the door, locking the door upon him, and calling him a cowardly base fellow for not joining with them in executing and murdering the said Mark Akin and his son and servant, whom they murdered, as they told this deponent that very night, and that Colonel MacSweeny thereupon fell a weeping without doors at their killing Scotchmen as they all said. And this deponent also saith, that the said Manus MacKonogher and Doltagh MacGarvey did in this deponent's hearing in a bragging manner affirm and say, that they and the said Donell MacIlbridy, Neil O'Donnell, and Brian Reagh Offary did at the time aforesaid send for one John Adams, then living near Clonder (*blank*) aforesaid, and would have hanged him, but he struggling with them they took their skeans and stabbed him. And this deponent further saith, that he hath often afterwards seen the said Colonel MacSweeny weep and lament the murdering and killing of Mr. Akins, his son, and servant aforesaid.[1]

signed ROBERT VENABLES.
J. EDWARDS.
THOS. NEWBURGH.

copia vera, examined by us this 20*th of February,* 1653, ROBERT VENABLES, RA. KING, THOMAS NEWBURGH, JOHN REEVES, FRANCIS BOLTON, OWEN WYNN.

[1] Janet Peebles (daughter of Janet Doherty) and John Ennis also swore to the same effect.

HIGH COURT OF JUSTICE.
6TH SEP. 1654.

Trial of EDMUND O'REILLY, *priest and Vicar-General, and of* EDMUND DUFFE BIRNE, *for the murder at the Black Castle of Wicklow, 29th December,* 1642.

Evidence.

LUKE BIRNE. That before the battle of (*illegible*) Hill, he was at dinner with Edmund Birne (*illegible*). That O'Reilly advised him (witness) to kill all the English about him. That witness saying that Joyce was a person of honour, O'Reilly replied, ' I know more than you.' Edmund Duffe told witness he had a hand in that murder. O'Reilly charged witness with high treason for corresponding with the English, and got him thereupon to be questioned and committed, and that the said O'Reilly excommunicated him for favouring the English.

HUGH MCLOUGHLIN BIRNE. (It was) reported that Edmund Duffe Birne and others were principals actors in that murder.

HUGH MCLOUGHLIN BIRNE, further examined, (swore he) heard that Edmund Duffe Birne, etc., (were) actors in that murder. Heard that O'Reilly continued at Ashpole's house at Wicklow until the night of that day, and that some of the murderers were in his company before the action. He believeth that O'Reilly had a hand in the murder for the reasons aforesaid.

PETER WICKHAM, (present in court, swears) that he, being then high sheriff of Wicklow, and at Ashpole's house at Wicklow, did see Edmund O'Reilly (there). That he, this examt., ordered the empannelling a jury for inquiring of that murder; that (on his) saying they (the warders of the Black Castle) were murdered, O'Reilly said, ' *What great hurt was there if those churls were burnt accidentally ?* ' Witness was told by the inhabitants of Wicklow, that Edmund O'Reilly did lie at Ashpole's house aforesaid all the night that the murders were committed, and that Edward Birne, foreman of the said jury, saying it was murder, he was put out and another put in his place. That Edmund O'Reilly, being one of the commissioners for the county, refused to deliver the Castle of Wicklow to the English, for it would be, he said, (*illegible*) to the country to keep it. Heard that O'Reilly was present when Edward Birne was removed from the jury as aforesaid, that the said Birne said so to the examt., and (it was) so reported commonly.

EDWARD BIRNE, present (in court, swears) that he was foreman of the jury, that being of opinion that it was murder, he was sent for by Edmund O'Reilly, one of the commissioners for the county of Wicklow, and demanded why he thought it murder, and he gave his cause of knowledge therein, and he was, by the said O'Reilly and the rest of the commissioners, put out of the jury. That this inquiry was two or three days after the murder, and that another foreman was put in his place. (It was) reported that Edmund Duffe Birne did that murder. (It was) reported that O'Reilly was an advisor in that murder, and an (*illegible*) of it before the fact.

EDWARD BIRNE'S further examination. That he was by Edmund O'Reilly and the rest of the commissioners, of whom he (O'Reilly) was chief, put off the jury, for the reasons aforesaid, and committed by them for twenty-four hours, and being released that he, with Peter Wickham, desired Edmund O'Reilly and (*illegible*) to permit the persons murdered to be buried, offering twenty shillings for each of them; they (O'Reilly and the commissioners with him) refused, in that they (the murdered men) were heretics, (to bury them) in the church or churchyard, and that O'Reilly ordered examt.'s imprisonment aforesaid.

THOMAS SHERIN (*sic*). That he was then servant to Edward Birne, former examt., examined June 3rd, 1645, soon after the fact, and that Edward Birne and Peter Wickham offered twenty shillings apiece for burying each of the murdered persons, which was offered to Edmund O'Reilly and others, but it was not allowed.

ANDREW KENNY. He heard that O'Reilly said that Joyce and the rest should not be buried in the church.

COOLE TOOLE, (present in court, swears) that he heard that Edmund Duffe Birne, etc., were actors in the murder at the Black Castle in Wicklow, and that Edmund O'Reilly used to say that they had little to do that inquired after the murder of churls, meaning the commissioners taking the examinations concerning that business (had little to do), and that the said O'Reilly was busy in demolishing the Castle of Wicklow, the examt. not hearing of any direction he (O'Reilly) had for so doing.

COOLE TOOLE'S further examination. He heard that Edmund Duffe Birne, etc., were actors in that murder; heard that Edmund

O'Reilly did stand by and see the Castle of Wicklow demolished; heard that Edmund O'Reilly did find fault with the examt. and others for being inquisitive after the said murder, and that (he said) they had little to do.

NICHOLAS PASMERE. That he, dwelling at Wicklow, Edmund O'Reilly, commanded this examt. and others, about six or seven weeks after, to break down the Castle of Wicklow, on pain of hanging; that the said O'Reilly used to lodge at Thomas Ashpole's house in Wicklow, which Ashpole was agent or proctor to the said O'Reilly, and that the said O'Reilly was Governor (of Wicklow) when the inquest was taken concerning the murder, and that Edmund Birne, the foreman of the jury, was soon after committed (to prison) by Edmund O'Reilly, but wherefore this examt. knoweth not.

NICHOLAS PASMERE'S further examination. That the examt. with others, shortly after the murder, demolished the castle by order of Father O'Reilly, and, in the doing thereof, Hugh McPhelim Birne, demanding who put them on that work, and they saying Father O'Reilly, he forced them off of this design, but the next day O'Reilly did set them to work again.

TIRLOGH McDERMOT BIRNE, (present, swears) that he did see the Castle of Wicklow on fire, and about a month after (it was) reported that Edmund Duffe Birne, etc., were actors in that murder, that Edward Birne, who had been foreman at the inquest, was about a week after committed to the castle at Arklow, but for what cause he (witness) knoweth not.

LOUGHLIN QUIN, (present, swears) that about a week after the murder Cahir Cullen told this examt. that Edmund O'Reilly and Luke Toole's sons were the principal men that caused that murder, etc., and that the said Cullen and others told him that O'Reilly had his share of the arms, ammunition, and goods which were in the castle, and (it was) commonly reported that the said O'Reilly caused the castle to be demolished, and caused a cess on the country for the charge of that work.

LOUGHLIN QUIN'S further examination. That Thomas Ashpole, about a month after the murders, then proctor to the said O'Reilly, told the examt. that Edmund O'Reilly was in his, the said Ashpole's house, that day that the murder was committed, and that O'Reilly did then and there promise the said murderers that he would absolve them if they would kill all in the said castle, who did kill accordingly, and that the said persons after told the said

Ashpole that they would not have done it but by command of the said O'Reilly, and that he, the said O'Reilly, promised them absolution. And the examt. did about a month after see the said O'Reilly putting his foot on several places of the wall of the castle, and he did order and direct the pulling the same down, and the examt. was told it by James MacBrian Birne, that Garret Toole and Talbot Toole told him that they would not have committed the said murder and burnt the castle, but that they were set on by Edmund O'Reilly, who promised absolution for the same. That Edmund Duffe Birne, etc., were also actors (in it).

PHELIM MCTIRLOGH BIRNE, (present, swears) that the next day after the murder he did overtake Edmund O'Reilly and others going towards Wicklow, who being told of the murder by one they met, the said O'Reilly seemed to wonder at it. (It was) reported in the country that the said murder was contrived in the house of Thomas Ashpole, and that Edmund O'Reilly was one in the plot, and paid for the demolishing the Castle of Wicklow. Examt. also heard that some of the actors in that murder did after (*illegible*), of whom Edmund Duffe Birne was one. (It was) reported that none durst act such a murder if Edmund O'Reilly had not a hand in it, he being so leading (a man) in the country. Examt. heard that Edmund O'Reilly was the day of the murder in the town of Wicklow, and that night he went to Christopher Wolverston's house, and the next day returned to Wicklow.

CHRISTOPHER WOLVERSTON, (present, swears) that the night the Black Castle was burnt, Edmund O'Reilly did lodge in the examt.'s house at Newcastle, and having discourse the next day with the said O'Reilly, both going towards Wicklow, he, the examt., did perceive that O'Reilly was no way troubled at the news then brought him of the said murder, and that late in the night of the murder the said O'Reilly did come from Wicklow to the examt.'s house, and it was commonly reported that the said O'Reilly had a hand in advising and furthering the said murder, and examt. was told that (when) O'Reilly saw a piece of pork (being roasted) at the fire, he said it was like Joice's breech, and examt. believeth that the actors would not have done that murder but by countenance of O'Reilly, that this was a common report; that the examt.'s daughter observing Edmund O'Reilly to speak much of Joice, she told this examt. she believed he (O'Reilly) was troubled with Joice.

MARY WOLVERSTON, (present, swears) that it was reported Christopher Toole was an actor in the murder at the Black Castle, and she telling Edmund O'Reilly of the murder at Wicklow, he said it was accidental, and she pressing the contrary, he said angrily, ' *What have you to do to be so curious as to inquire after such things ?* ' Examt. was told by her daughter-in-law, Margaret Wolverston, that, discoursing of the murder, the said O'Reilly said *' there was more ado about the roasting of a company of churls than about the committal of the good Lord Herbert then committed at Dublin.*' And her said daughter told her that a piece of pork roasting at the fire and blistered, the said O'Reilly said it looked like John Joice's breech. Examt.'s said daughter is a nun.

LEWIS DAVYS. That Father O'Reilly and others of the clergy did put Tibbot Toole on the murder at Wicklow, in which they were actors, which the said Toole told this examt., he being then a proctor in the county of Wicklow.

RICHARD QUIN, (present, swears) that Edmund Duffe Birne, etc., were said to be actors (in the murder), that he, Birne, went first into the castle with Joice, drinking with him until night, and that the next day Edmund O'Reilly came to Wicklow, (and it was) reported he said that ' *it was little hurt that the churl was burnt,*' meaning John Joice. The examt. was one of the coroner's inquest, and Thomas Ashpole told him then of the persons who did the murder, who had been in the said Ashpole's house.

EDMUND WALSH. That Edmund Quin, priest, told this examt. that Edmund Duffe Birne, etc., were drinking with John Joice in the Castle of Wicklow, who made much of them on the day of the murder. That the murderers did frequent the company of Edmund O'Reilly, who never questioned them (for it), though he had power in the country, nor were they excommunicated by him or by any others. That Edmund Duffe Birne being charged by the examt. with that murder, said he made some of the clergy acquainted with it, but which of them he would not tell.

DERMOT McWILLIAM TOOLE (first examination). That Tibbot Toole told him that Edmund O'Reilly did put him (Tibbot) on to that murder, the examt. said that Edmund O'Reilly was like enough to charge him with it, to which Tibbot said he feared him not, he being in it as deep as any, (for) he did advise him.

DERMOT MACWILLIAM TOOLE (second examination).

BRIAN BIRNE, (present, swears) he heard that Edmund Duffe Birne, etc., were drinking in the Castle of Wicklow the day of the murder. (It was) reported that Edmund O'Reilly was the chief adviser and procurer of the said murder to be committed (there), and of the demolishing of the castle, that no more English garrisons should be there. A warrant (was) signed by Edmund O'Reilly and other commissioners, he first subscribing for raising the power of the country, if need be, for obedience to that order.

EDMUND DUFFE BIRNE (prisoner), his first examination. That two days before the murder he discoursed with Tibbot Toole and others at a place called (*illegible*) concerning that business, and the day of the action he was in the castle.

EDMUND DUFFE BIRNE (prisoner), his second examination. That he, with the rest, were drinking till night at the Castle of Wicklow, and that all being made prisoners, the examt. being above stairs, heard a voice below, and, going down, found Joice and the rest murdered, that he asking the rest, who brought him into that action, how they durst enter on it, they answered they were warranted by one of the chiefest men in the country, viz. Father Edmund O'Reilly : that afterwards the examt. told O'Reilly that Lieutenant-General (*illegible*) had sent to seize him, examt., and O'Reilly answered, ' *You need not fear, I warrant you.*' This was in the garden of Balligarney.

SIMON ARCHPOLE. That he was clerk and registrar to Father Edmund O'Reilly when the murder was (committed) at Wicklow, that he heard O'Reilly say he gave 3*l.* of his own money towards the breaking down of the Castle of Wicklow. Examt. heard that some of the murderers came to O'Reilly to be absolved for that fact, and that he did absolve them. That the castle was pulled down about a month after the murder.

HENRY HENY, (present, swears) that it was reported that Edmund Duffe Birne, etc., was of the actors in the murder at Wicklow Castle. That Edmund O'Reilly was in Wicklow that week that the murder was acted. That O'Reilly was at the demolishing of the castle the summer after the murder.

EDMUND O'REILLY (the prisoner's examination). That Tibbot Toole and Edmund Duffe Birne coming to him to be absolved for the murder at the Black Castle, he refused it, being forbidden by the Common Law, etc.

EDMUND O'REILLY. He demanding time for his defence until the next day, it was granted, notwithstanding that it was not usual, the evidence of the Commonwealth having been opened.

THE DEFENCE OF EDMUND O'REILLY, PRIEST,
SEPTEMBER 7TH, 1654.

He takes exception to the testimony of Luke Birne as being an enemy unto him, the prisoner, who did note that at the beginning of the rebellion he, being at Dublin resident at that time, excommunicated the said Birne for living in adultery, and not for such ends as is (sic) alleged. (In answer) to the second witness, Hugh MacLaughlin, as to the prisoner's being at Ashpole's house the day of the murder, Nicholas FitzGerald (is) produced by the prisoner, (who saith) that he is most certain (that) the day of the murder Edmund O'Reilly was then at Rathdown, ten miles from Wicklow; that the night before the murder he, O'Reilly, came to the house of Mrs. Wolverston at Newcastle, the examt. being then in his company and was his attendant at mass. He did hear Edmund O'Reilly excommunicate all that were actors in that murder about a month after.

(In answer) to Mr. Wickham's examination, (prisoner) denieth hearing anything of Joice's murder until then, that examination contradicted what was spoken by Wolverston of prisoner's being at Wicklow the night of the murder, denieth he refused delivering Wicklow Castle to Ormond, saith he was a friend to Joice and did him good offices, denieth saying '*What matter if the churls were burnt accidentally?*' (In answer) to Edward Birne's examination, prisoner saith he, Birne, was not committed for that cause (his verdict on the inquest), but that he was charged with sending his servant Sherin to Dublin with billets, and that for giving intelligence to the enemy he was committed. Denieth that Edward Birne was removed from the jury. (In support of this) Richard Quin is produced by prisoner, who having been one of that jury saith he did not see any put out of it, or put in on the putting any out, and Peter Wickham (is produced, who says) he was not present at the first inquest.

JAMES BIRNE, the examt. offered by Mr. Attorney, deposes that he was coroner, and appointed a jury of which Edmund Birne was foreman, that he, Edmund, being of a different judgment from others, was called before Edmund O'Reilly and others of the commissioners, and was put out, and another was put in his place, being Walter Birne or Richard Quin.

The prisoner (in rejoinder) allegeth that James Birne had this information from Edward Birne, and he (prisoner) laboureth to weaken Edward Birne's testimony by denying his having offered money for the burial, as was said, and if false in that, he is not to be believed in other things. Saith, that Edward Birne beareth malice to him, the prisoner, for adjudging against him in a matrimonial cause, and for living viciously, and that the prisoner therefore had put him out of employment. (In answer) to Edward Sherin (prisoner says) he was servant to Edward Birne and (in answer) to Andrew Kenny (it is) all but hearsay. (In answer) to Coole Toole as to the demolishing of the castle, he saith nothing, as nothing is now in question. He saith much inquiry was made after the murderers whom they (the witnesses against him) well know, this was the fault he found with them making ado about nothing, not doing therein what should have been done. Denieth he found fault with Toole or any for being inquisitive after the murderers. Saith, as to demolishing of the castle, it was not begun until nine months after the murder, and not altogether until March following. Richard Quin, again produced by the prisoner, (saith) that the demolishing of the castle was in October after the murder, which was in the December before; his cause of knowledge is that he was then portreeve of Wicklow, and questioning Thomas Ashpole's absence from court he excused himself as being then overseer of the work for pulling down the castle of Wicklow.

In answer to Laughlin Quin prisoner saith he is a notable thief, and that for a fact of that kind the examt. caused him to be bound with withes, but after upon meditation released him, and on that account he, Loughlin, feigns all that he hath saith.

In answer to Simon Ashpole prisoner saith that he, Simon, leaving his religion to please the enemy, he speaks against the prisoner being a priest. Denieth giving 3*l*. or any money towards the demolishing of the castle. The prisoner saith that he engaged for Thomas Ashpole, who promised to pay 3*l*. for (*illegible*) the castle.

In answer to Phelim MacTirlogh Birne denieth the contriving of the murder, and in answer to Edmund Duffe Birne, prisoner, saith that he did not speak with those that acted in the murder (*illegible*), and that if they said they had allowance from him (to commit it), why did not Edmund Duffe Birne himself ask him (O'Reilly) the question, often seeing him? He assured them he believed it.[1]

---

[1] Edmund Duffe Birne having informed against his fellow-prisoner, Father O'Reilly, and sworn that the murderers had told him, Edmund Duffe, that they had the priest's permission to commit the crime, O'Reilly asks why did not Edmund

EDMUND DUFFE BIRNE here saith that he confessed to Edmund O'Reilly that he was in the action at the Black Castle but not in the blood there spilt, and that O'Reilly absolved him and enjoined him penance by saying some prayers and fasting. O'Reilly denieth this or that he said 'I'll warrant you you need not fear,' or if he said so it was because Hugh MacPhelim did never punish any one for crime.[1]

MR. ATTORNEY GENERAL (*intervening*) offered in further evidence the examination of Tiegue MacMorrogh Birne that shortly after the murder Edmund O'Reilly did send warrants for demolishing the castle of Wicklow, and of John MacCahir Birne that he heard by common report that the castle was pulled down by direction of Edmund O'Reilly.

The prisoner Edmund O'Reilly's defence to this is that it was no difficult matter to demolish the walls of that castle next the sea, being of clay and stone easily cast down, and not needing much labour. In answer to Christopher Wolverston and his wife he denieth his coming to Newcastle from Wicklow, but he came from Rathdown to the other side of Newcastle. In answer to Lewis Davis saith that what Toole said was false, in answer to Richard Quin saith that he, prisoner, did speak those words about churls, etc., that he might gain an opportunity to prosecute the murderers more freely, and in answer to Edmund Walsh prisoner denieth keeping company with the murderers, and that they might be in the place where he was without that implying his conversing with them. And the prisoner here (further saith) he did excommunicate all the actors in that murder, and that it was a simple (*i.e.* foolish) question of Edmund Walsh to ask, '*Would you do such an action without the advice of the clergy?*'

The LORD PRESIDENT (here saith): But such things have been done by the advice of the clergy, as the powder treason and this rebellion, and this war is called (by them) *bellum religiosum*.

EDMUND DUFFE BIRNE, prisoner, being demanded of that discourse, saith that he had discourse with Edmund Walsh, but doth

Duffe ascertain from him, whom he often saw, if this was true? arguing that as he did not his evidence is inconsistent and false. There is much in this argument.

[1] *v. ante*, p. 223, where Edmund Duffe says O'Reilly spoke those words to encourage him and the rest of the murderers not to fear being punished by their Lieutenant-General, Hugh MacPhelim Byrne, for the murder. Whatever we may think of the truth or falsehood of this statement of Birne's, the admission of Father O'Reilly that the Irish Lieutenant-General never punished murderers is noteworthy for more reasons than one.

not remember the particulars, and that he did never personally speak with any of the clergy in that business, but he was told by Tibbot Toole, etc., that they had spoken with the clergy. Denieth that he was excommunicated by O'Reilly.

EDMUND O'REILLY, prisoner, saith that the excommunication was spoken at mass, and he produced for witness

ALISON BROWNE, who saith that she was present in Wicklow, when Edmund O'Reilly spoke publicly against the murderers at Wicklow, and said that he would go to Kilkenny to get them (*illegible*).

RICHARD QUIN being told by the said Alison that he was then present and heard what she hath declared, he saith he remembereth it not.

CAHIR TOOLE saith he did never hear of any such excommunication.

A letter from Kilkenny, without date, was offered by Edmund O'Reilly to the Court and read, (it saith) he did excommunicate those that burnt the Castle of Wicklow. This (was writ) with another ink and I think with another hand. In answer to Dermot O'Toole prisoner saith if Tibbot Toole said so, it is false (*illegible*). In answer to (*illegible*) Birne it is but by report and that private.

JOHN BIRNE and HUGH BIRNE said in court that they did not hear of any excommunication.

SIR ROBERT TALBOT, present, swears that on the Treaty for Peace, he being one of the Commissioners for it, Edmund O'Reilly did write to them that if a course were not taken for punishing the murder at Wicklow, God would not prosper them. Also at Kilkenny Edmund O'Reilly did solicit proceedings in it (*illegible*), who gave commissions for inquiry of it.

CAPTAIN JOHN BELLEW's letter was offered by Edmund O'Reilly in court, dated 12th June, 1652, mentioning that O'Reilly was the great prosecutor (of the parties) in that murder.

NICHOLAS FITZGERALD, produced by the prisoner, (swears) that the prisoner did solicit Nicholas Plunket the lawyer to prosecute (for) that murder.

TIRLOGH REILLY (swears) that prisoner did write by the examt. to Mr. Belling concerning that murder (*illegible*), which letter he delivered the same year the murder was committed. Examt. heard from others that the murderers were excommunicated and that prisoner was beneficial to the English, and not a murderer of them.

MR. PEMBERTON swears concerning Mr. Walworth, a minister preserved (by prisoner), also he preserved a trumpeter, Simon Bellew, George Green, William Willings, and other English about (*illegible*), he preserved an Englishman at Arklow, in *anno* 1646 he preserved a boy, *anno* 1645 he preserved some in a frigate that was cast on the coast of Wicklow, an (*illegible*) surgeon coming from Dublin, a (*illegible*) coming from Dublin, Christopher FitzWilliams and a boat at (*illegible*) belonging to (*illegible*) some cars of a company going to Wicklow, a cow taken from one, (he also) preserved Mr. Cornewall, a minister, Henry White, a minister at Arklow, another old minister and Mr. Conway, a minister, and Mr. Robert Conway. He (prisoner) was courteous to Lieut.-Colonel (*illegible*), lent him his sword and gained him the best respite he could. Lieutenant Mason had respite by his (prisoner's) means. On Captain Hewetson being wounded, and after he died would have buried him. He preserved one that would have been otherwise hanged at (*illegible*), he brought to Dublin from Trim Mr. Robert Lett's children, he preserved two soldiers of the name of (*illegible*).

EDMUND DUFFE BIRNE'S defence (is) that he was of that party but not in the murder.

TIRLOGH MACDERMOT BIRNE. This now offered by Mr. Attorney: That Edward Birne, the foreman of the jury, found it murder. But afterwards it was found chance medley, and so delivered in writing to the coroner.

VERDICTS.

EDMUND REILLY, a priest . . . GUILTY.
EDMUND DUFF BIRNE [1] . . . GUILTY.

[1] Birne's fate is uncertain, but O'Reilly, as I have said (*v.* p. 172), received a pardon and lived until 1669.

LIST OF EXAMINATIONS TAKEN AGAINST CAPTAIN
SANKEY[1] FOR THE MURDER OF ONE RORY *alias*
JAMES MACGANAN (*sic*).

Exam. of GARRETT FITZGARRETT.
Exam. of ANSTACE LOMBARD.
Exam. of EDWARD FITZGARRETT.
Exam. of GEORGE KING.
Exam. of THOMAS BOURKE.

To THOMAS HERBERT, C.C.

SIR,—This gentleman, Mr. John Farrell, is one in our order to be aprehended (*sic*) and brought to Dublin for the High Court of Justice, but these are to mind you that in the course of all the examinations or the brief of them by which your orders are drawn, you will find this gentleman had no hand in the murders, but only it was desired he might be spoke withal, but yet notwithstanding it was thought he should be sent for; now, Sir, upon his importunity and (*illegible*) having earnest occasion with Lieut.-General Farrell, his brother, Major Richardson and I have taken the boldness to give him leave to go to Dublin, where he will stay till Major Richardson come with your prisoners, which I hope will be in a few days, and I hope we shall give a good account of what we are entrusted withal. Sir, because you will have more at large very suddenly I have spared to trouble you at this instant with any particulars. I pray, Sir, that this gentleman may have all the civil respect that may be, for I am confident there is nothing against him, and by those (*illegible*) and by those which he hath kept and

---

[1] He seems to have been a nephew of Colonel Jacob Sankey, the well-known Cromwellian officer. The murdered man was probably a MacCannan or MacCan. I could ot find the verdict in this case.

delivered unto us as much as will be desired of him. And by the examination of several witnesses it appears he hath been very kind to several of the English and deserveth much respect for it. I know, Sir, you may serve him in getting him discharged with all convenient speed, after your prisoners are come to you, which I desire your favour in, and I know you will the rather do when you see the examinations which with all speed shall be sent unto you; which is all but to assure you, Sir, I am,

Your servant,

H. STOPFORD.

Feb. 2nd, 1652.

LIST OF PRISONERS TRIED FOR MURDER BEFORE THE HIGH COURT.

December, 1652.

Charles MacCarthy Reagh for the murder of John Burrows, Andrew Rackham, Owen MacDermot, and John Phipps.—NOT GUILTY.

John Oge Crowley for murder of John Phipps.—NOT GUILTY.

Dermot O'Mahony for murder of John Phipps.—GUILTY.

Colonel Bourke for murder of two English at Callan.—NOT GUILTY.

Patrick Boylan for murder of three English.—GUILTY.

John Elliott for murder of Philip Gloster.—GUILTY.

Richard Rourke, *alias* Raherty, for murder of three Englishmen, names unknown.—NOT GUILTY.

James Goodman for murder of William Behane.—GUILTY.

Edmund Brennan for murder of Christopher North, clerk, and forty persons in a church at Castlecomer, also for the murder of Anne Guest, three more English, Lewis Davis, and one Barnard.— NOT GUILTY on all counts.

Colonel E. Fennell for murder of several persons at Cappoquin, women and men.—GUILTY.

John Brukler and Tiegue O'Holohan for murder of an Englishman.—GUILTY.

John Long for murders at Belgooly.—GUILTY.

Manus MacShee for murder of Thomas Reynolds.—NOT GUILTY.

Fineen Gibbon and Donogh Keefe for the murder of John Baker and the Combes.—Gibbon, GUILTY. Keefe, NOT GUILTY.

Richard Condon for the murder of one Morris, a sawyer.— GUILTY.

David Rawleigh for the murder of the Whites.—GUILTY.

Redmond Roche and Phelimy O'Connor for the murder of Dermot (*illegible*).—NOT GUILTY.

RECORDS OF THE HIGH COURT OF JUSTICE. 233

Garret FitzGerald for the murder of William Atkins and two others.—NOT GUILTY.

David O'Connell for murder of Ensign Miles Cooke.—GUILTY.

Colonel Fennell for a murder at Ballinkeen, and for the murder of Ensign (*illegible*).—GUILTY. For two maids at Dungarvan.—NOT GUILTY.

John Lacy for the murder of Donogh O'Donoghue, Patrick Doran, and Gregory Thomas. Deferred for further evidence to Chief Justice Cooke's Session.

Dec. 14*th*, 1652.

Sentence was this day pronounced in open court, whereby twenty-four were acquitted, thirty-two condemned, and some respited.

John Tyrell for murder of Philip Carr.—GUILTY, by confession.

Edward Butler for murder of three Englishmen and two women.—GUILTY.

Charles MacCarthy for murder of Owen MacDermot, Carthy, the question put whether the prisoner did know of the articles of protection given the said Owen.—NEGATIVE.

John Barnewall for murder of an Englishman.—GUILTY.

Jan. 27*th*, 1652, *O.S.*

Gerald FitzGerald for murder of Rich. Price.—GUILTY.

Patrick Begg murder of Rich. Langford.—GUILTY.

John Talbot murder of Owen Healy.—GUILTY.

Nicholas Sweetman murder of Nich. Smith.—GUILTY.

Hugh Connor, *alias* Hugh MacDavid, for murder of John Taylor.—GUILTY.

Same for murder of Alexander Shine.—GUILTY.

Luke Toole and Donogh Oge Birne and Charles Birne for the murder of Edward Snape, Thomas Huntpage, and one Richard a carpenter.—Luke Toole and Donogh Oge Birne, NOT GUILTY. Charles Birne, GUILTY.

Ambrose Connor murder of Mary Bax.—GUILTY.

Captain Dudley Colley murder of John Brown.—NOT GUILTY.

Tiegue Molloy murder of Philip Carr.—GUILTY.

Feb. 1652.

Edward Fitz for the murder of Toby Emmett.—GUILTY.
Luke Lynam murder of Richard Gaine.—GUILTY.
Phelim MacTirlogh Birne for the murder of Dudley Birne.—GUILTY.
Sir Phelim O'Neil for the rebellion.—GUILTY.
For the murder of Lieut. James Maxwell and his wife, Richard Blaney, Brownlow Taylor, and Lord Caulfield.—GUILTY.

March, 1652.

Andrew White for the murder of John Wear.—GUILTY.
Murtogh MacEdmond Birne for murder of John Leeson.—GUILTY.
Patrick Boylan for murder of George Blundell and five others.—GUILTY.

July, 1653.

John Keane for murder of Thomas Robson.—GUILTY.
Dermot MacDonogh Birne for murders at the Black Castle of Wicklow.—GUILTY.
Donogh Magennis, *alias* Donogh the Smith, for Thomas Reade, Thomas Taylor, Henry Reade his wife and son.—GUILTY.
The Court adjourned to the 11th of August next, at nine of the clock.

August 11*th,* 1653.

Robert Pasmere and John Maguire for murder of Robert and Ambrose Burton.
(*blank*) Nugent for a person whose name is unknown; prisoner saith he is not of Drumacree as alleged but of Nugent's (*illegible*), and that John Nugent of Drumacree is the person charged. Prisoner respited till inquiries are made.
Brian Farrell for Thomas Canning in 1644.
Nicholas Archbold for Robert Pont.
John Archbold for Thomas Potts.

September, 1653.

Edmund Reilly, a priest, for murders at the Black Castle of Wicklow on Dec. 29th, 1645.—GUILTY.

Edmund Duffe Birne for same.—GUILTY.

Andrew Rafter and Bridget FitzPatrick for the murder of Mary Harding and four of her children.—Andrew Rafter, GUILTY. Bridget FitzPatrick, NOT GUILTY.

October, 1653.

Robert Passmere for murder of Thomas Cox.—GUILTY.

Same for murder of Ambrose Robert and Mr. Burton, a minister. —GUILTY.

Nov. 1653.

Michael Doyne for murder of James Hamilton.— GUILTY.

Dec. 1653.

Lord Muskerry for Mr. Deane and three others, and a woman named Nora.—As to the matter of fact, GUILTY. As to articles considered, NOT GUILTY. Same for Roger Skinner.—NOT GUILTY.

May, 1654.

Lord Muskerry for murder of a man and woman unknown.— NOT GUILTY.

June, 1654.

Brian McCooker for William Norman.—GUILTY.

Brian McRedmond for murder of Jane Leslie and her children, 20th May, 1642.—GUILTY.

Hugh McRichard Farrell for the murder of Thomas Trafford and others at Longford in 1641.—GUILTY.

Christopher Nugent for a person unknown.—NOT GUILTY.

Manus Duff MacMahon for William Williams, Gabriel Williams, Ishell Jones, Thomas (*illegible*) at Carrickmacross, county Monaghan, 2nd January, 1641.—GUILTY.[1]

---

[1] The above is only a portion of the list in the Stearne MSS., which appears to have been made out from day to day in the court by Judge Lowther. In some few cases the verdicts are not mentioned. For the murders at Carrickmacross and Longford see Depositions XXIII., XCVI., XCVII., etc.

MISCELLANEOUS.

COMMONWEALTH BOOKS. P.R.O. DUBLIN.

$\left(\text{Vol. }\frac{A}{8}\text{, p. 97.}\right)$

UPON consideration had of the report made by John Santhy (sic) and Thomas Fowler, Esquires, late Commissioners appointed for holding the assizes in the Circuit of Connaught, whereby it appears that at the assizes and gaol delivery holden at Athlone, for the counties of Longford, Westmeath, and King's County, the 10th day of April last, Jeremiah Stibbins, late a soldier in Captain William Heydon's company, being disbanded and left to due course of law, was indicted of treason for the murder of Tirlogh O'Byrne, a carpenter, and the issue being referred to the trial of a jury, they, upon the evidence before them, did return their verdict, and found the said Stibbins guilty of manslaughter, per misadventure, so that by the law he was adjudged to forfeit his goods and chattels to his Highness the Lord Protector. And whereas information hath been given to this board that the said Captain Heydon hath remaining in his custody a debenture belonging to the said Stibbins, amounting to about fifteen pounds,[1] which the said Commissioners did propound might be disposed of for the relief of the widow of the said Tirlogh O'Byrne and his four orphans. And upon consideration had of their poverty and distressed condition, it is ordered that the said Captain Heydon do cause the said debenture to be delivered to the said widow, or disposed thereof to the best advantage towards the support of her and the said children. Dublin Castle, 6th July, 1655. THOMAS HERBERT, Clerk of the Council.

[1] It is to be remembered that 15*l*. at that time was equivalent to at least 150*l*. of our present money.

(*Ibid.* P.R.O.)

Upon the petition of Daniel O'Hagan, setting forth his constant good affection to the English interest, and desiring he might be dispensed with from transplantation into Connaught or Clare; on consideration had thereof, and of the report of the Committee for transplanting, it appeared by certificates from several persons of known integrity that the petitioner did expose himself to many hazards of his life, against his kindred and relations, in the beginning of the late horrid rebellion, and was, under God, a means to preserve many of the poor English and Protestants from the bloody massacre, and hath continued always faithful to the English interest. To the end, therefore, that so singular an example of kindness and affection may not be left unrewarded, it is thought fit and ordered that the said Daniel O'Hagan be dispensed with from transplantation into Clare or Connaught, and likewise that he be recommended to those in chief authority in England for a mark of their favour unto him. And, in the meantime, that the Commissioners of Revenue at Belfast do, out of the lands of Arthur (Art) O'Neil, in the county of Antrim, set out and make and perfect a lease of some part thereof unto the said Daniel O'Hagan, for a term of seven years from May next, (paying contributions) as they shall judge to be of the clear yearly value of 50l. per annum. Dublin, 6th March, 1653. CHARLES FLEETWOOD, MILES CORBET, JOHN JONES.

(*Ibid.* P.R.O.)

To the Committee of the Commonwealth in Ireland.

GENTLEMEN,—Having received the two enclosed petitions and papers of John Prendergast and the widow Brooke, whose cases have been so represented to me, which, if true, deserve some tender regard. Wherefore I thought fit to recommend them to your consideration, that they may be permitted to reside on and enjoy their present estates and habitations, unless there be some instant cause to the contrary.

However, I would have their transplantation to be suspended until I receive from you an accompt of their particular cases and conditions, and that you receive further order therein.

Your loving friend,

Whitehall, 22*nd March*, 1653.   OLIVER P.

(*Ibid.* P.R.O.)

To the Right Hon. the Lord Deputy.[1]

DEAR CHARLES,—This poor man's case, if it be as it is represented in his petition, is very sad and deserves to be pitied. I believe him in great extremity of want and poverty, and therefore I earnestly desire you to take his condition into your consideration, and let something be effectually done for him, whereby he and his family may have a subsistence; indeed, I have been much affected with the sense of his distressed condition, and therefore pray do not forget to take some course for his relief,

Your loving father,
OLIVER P.

Whitehall, 10*th May*, 1655.

(*Ibid.* P.R.O.)

For the Right Hon. the Lord Deputy and Council in Ireland.

MY LORDS AND GENTLEMEN,—The enclosed petition being presented to us by Colonel Jephson, we could do no less than earnestly recommend the same unto you, judging it very reasonable, and a matter of great justice if what is alleged therein be made appear unto you upon the place, that the orphan Tibbot Roche be restored to the possession of his father's lands and estate, and that some other lands in Ireland not yet disposed of be assigned to those officers and soldiers to whose lot the lands of the said orphan are fallen for satisfaction of their arrears. We shall not need to use any further arguments to press you to this our desire, the case itself as represented being so just and equitable, we rest,

Your very loving friend,
OLIVER P.

Hampton Court, 16*th July*, 1655.

(*Ibid.* P.R.O.)

To Colonel Phaire.

Receiving intelligence of the return of the Lord Muskerry and Colonel Callaghan into this country, and of their declining their

---

[1] This letter was addressed to Fleetwood on behalf of one James Barry, a native of Cork or Kerry.

former intentions for the transporting of men, we have thought it fit and shall desire you immediately to send both of them up with a safe convoy to Dublin, that so we may understand something more further from themselves of their present resolution; in the doing whereof we shall desire you that all civil respects may be shown unto them, we remain, etc.,

M. C., C. F., J. J.[1]

Dublin, 19th Feb. 1652.

[1] *i.e.* Miles Corbet, Charles Fleetwood, and John Jones.

CATHOLIC ACCOUNTS OF THE MASSACRES.

I feel it is only fair to give the following hitherto unpublished accounts of the massacres at Cashel, Shrule, and other places which are amongst the Carte MSS. in the Bodleian Library. The first and fourth appear to have been drawn up by Mr. Kearney, a native of Tipperary, and the brother of a Roman Catholic ecclesiastic, for the information of the Duke of Ormond, when he was Viceroy after the Restoration, and engaged in carrying out the Act of Settlement. The rest appear to have been written by an Irish Catholic during the Commonwealth period. As all four accounts are largely composed of hearsay reports of what took place fifteen or sixteen years before, they must be received with caution and carefully compared with the sworn depositions given in vol. i. p. 388-98, vol. ii. p. 42-46. At the same time it is evident that the Catholic writers in certain cases honestly relate what they had seen for themselves, and thus we can in turn check the hearsay in the earlier depositions by their testimony and discover when it is false. On one point it will be seen that those contemporary accounts drawn up between 1650 and 1666 by Roman Catholic Irishmen are in perfect accord with the depositions and flatly contradict the declamatory assertions of certain Roman Catholic writers and orators of the eighteenth and nineteenth centuries. While these latter, as boldly imaginative on their side as Sir John Temple was on his, profess to have discovered that no massacres of Protestants took place, that the soldiers in the Irish army 'never massacred ¹ one Protestant in cold blood,' Mr. Kearney and his co-religionists who lived through the civil war never dream of denying that cruel massacres of unarmed Protestants were committed not only, as Father Walsh ² admitted, in Ulster but

---

[1] *Bird's-eye View of Irish History*, p. 117, by Sir C. G. Duffy.

[2] 'Your Grace,' says Walsh the Franciscan friar, writing to Ormond, 'knows with what horror the Irish nation looks upon the massacres and murders in the

at the Silver Mines, Shrule, Cashel, and other places, and even describe at length how, as they believe, the vengeance of God fell on the murderers, who managed to escape the arm of the law. Sir Charles Gavan Duffy draws a terribly sensational picture of the slaughter at the taking of Cashel by Murrogh O'Brian, Lord Inchiquin, but omits what the better informed Irish Catholic contemporary of Inchiquin takes care to mention, that one at least of those who fell on the 'Rock,' Tiegue O'Kennedy, had been a chief actor in the cold-blooded massacre of the thirty-two unarmed poor men, women, and children at the Silver Mines. If all of the murderous brood who committed that massacre had fallen by the swords of Inchiquin and his soldiers, it would have been, even in the judgment of not a few of their better disposed Roman Catholic contemporaries, too honourable a death for them.

I.

To His Grace the Duke of Ormond, Lord Lieutenant of Ireland.

Humbly presented : I find that the first insurrection in the county of Tipperary was on the Eve of the Presentation of the Virgin, being the 20th of November, 1641, when a great many of the common sort and many young idle fellows of the barony of Eliogarty, some of the barony of Middlethird, and some of Kilnemanagh, gathered into a body and took away a great number of cows and sheep from Mr. Kingsmill from Ballyowen, whereof notice being sent to Sir William St. Leger, then Lord President of Munster,[1] being brother-in-law to Mr. Kingsmill, he, within two or three days after, came with two troops of horse to Ballyowen, and being informed that the cattle were driven into Eliogarty he marched that way, and as he set forth he killed three persons

---

north committed at the beginning of the rebellion by the rascal multitude upon their innocent, unarmed, and unprovided neighbours . . . . all unbiassed men distinguish between the first conspirators that were a handful of hare-brained men of broken fortunes and desperate resolution, who took up arms and made the crime of rebellion more horrid by the foul actions with which the rude multitude did asperse it.'—*The Irish Colours Folded and Tracts of Irish History from 1655 to 1682.* British Museum Library. Father Walsh, it must be remembered, was here writing his own opinion, not that of his Church, which excommunicated him for his candour.

[1] v. Carte's *Life of Ormond and Letters*, vol. v. for St. Leger's own despatches relating his pursuit of the rebels on this occasion, and Appendix Y.

at Ballyowen, who were said to have stolen some mares of Mr.
Kingsmill's, and near it at Grange he killed four innocent labourers,
and at Ballygalbert he hanged eight persons, and burned several
houses there, and with much importunity and intercession the life
of Mr. Morris Magrath, a well-bred gentleman, being one of the
grandchildren of Archbishop Milerus, was saved, it being plainly
proved he had no hand in the prey. And from thence Captain Peasley
with some of the troops marched to Ardmaile (sic) and there killed
seven or eight poor men and women, and thence marched to Clonulta,
and there killed the chief farmer of the place, being Philip Ryan, a
very honest and able man, not at all concerned in that insurrection.
And thence they marched to Gowlyn (sic) and there killed and hanged
seven or eight of Dr. Fenning's tenants, and burned many houses in
that town. And in all this march the Lord President and Peasley
took up all the cattle of the inhabitants they met, being great
numbers, and sent them to the county of Cork. After this service
the President about the 25th of November went to Clonmell, where
Captain Peasley with his troop met him, and the prime nobility
and gentry of the country being surprised at this rash and bloody
proceeding of the Lord President, many of them flocked after him
to Clonmell, as James Lord Dunboyne, Thomas Butler of Kilconnell,
James Butler of Killslaugher, Theobald Butler of Ardmaile, Richard
Butler of Ballynakill, Philip O'Dwyer and divers others of good
quality, and observed to the President how he had exasperated the
people generally to run from house and home, and that they were
gathering in great numbers together, not knowing what to trust to.
And that they the aforesaid gentlemen waited upon his lordship to
be informed how affairs stood, and that they coveted nothing more
than to serve his Majesty and preserve the peace, and desired that
he would be pleased to qualify them with authority and arms, and
that they would suppress the rabble and preserve the peace. But
he, in a furious manner, answered them that they were all rebels,
and that he would not trust one soul of them, but thought it more
prudent to hang the best of them, and in that extraordinary passion
he continued, while those and divers other persons of quality, their
neighbours, waited on him. And they withdrawing returned to
their several habitations much resenting his severity and the uncertainty of their safety. And then suddenly the President marched
from Clonmell unto Waterford, hearing that some of the Irish of
Carlow, Kilkenny, and Wexford went over the river into that county
to plunder and prey some of the English. In which march his

soldiers killed many harmless poor people, not at all concerned in the rebellion, which also incensed the gentry of the county Waterford to betake themselves to their defence.

After the President returned to the county of Cork, the gentry of Tipperary considering the violence of his proceedings, and the aptness of the vulgar sort under colour thereof to plunder their English neighbours, laboured within their various jurisdictions for a while to suppress these insolences. But notwithstanding all their care the common sort grew so addicted to plunder that they found a body of about 500 of them together, and marched towards Cashel, in order to take that city and plunder the English. But several of the gentlemen of quality in that country, and some of the Catholic clergy of Cashel, hearing of their resolution met them [1] in their march, and by fair words and sermons dissuaded them from that wicked attempt, and by that means dispersed them. But soon after Philip O'Dwyer of Dundrum, alleging that he could not keep those of his country at peace, pretending that they could not sleep safely in their houses, while Cashel was a receptacle for the President's troops to come thither and rush amongst them and destroy them, as they did their neighbours, Philip Ryan and others, he, Philip Dwyer, gathered a body of people of the county together on the 30th of December, 1641, marched to Cashel and took the place. And they endeavouring, as it is said, to secure the goods of all the English inhabitants there and to put them together into a storehouse, whether with his command or against his will (I am not certain),[2] some of the rabble that went with him to Cashel, finding out some of the English there, killed thirteen of them, viz. William Bean and his servant Thomas Sadler, William Bousfield and his wife, John Banister, Mr. Carr, John Lentre, Richard Lane, John Anderson, Mr. Franklin (*illegible*), a joiner, and John Fawkes.[3]

But all the rest of the English were saved by the inhabitants, and by the Roman Catholic clergy of the town, who in the streets exposed themselves to rescue them. Some of those preserved were

[1] None of the depositions, not even that of the Catholic Mayor of Cashel in 1641-2, Nicholas Sall, mention a word of this.
[2] Gilbert Johnstone's deposition (CXLV.) says that Dwyer was looking on while some of those murders were committed.
[3] Ellish Meagher's deposition (CXLVI.) says that to her knowledge twenty-three persons, including old women and children, were murdered, and that she saw their corpses in the streets of Cashel, while a number of others were subjected to the most barbarous treatment, stripped not only of their clothes, but of the bandages and plasters they had put on their wounds.

Dr. Pullen and his wife and children, who were protected by the Jesuits,[1] (*illegible*) Darling and one Bankes by Richard Conroy, Rowland Lynch and his wife and children by William Kearney; James Hamilton, the Archbishop's son, and his mother and sister, and (*illegible*) and Daniel and Mrs. Brown and others at Mrs. Young's house. Mr. Mooney his wife and daughter, John Morewood and his wife, Mrs. Moore, Laughlin Fiske and his wife, Toby the cooper and several others whose names I yet find not.

The preservation of Dr. Pullen by the Papists is taken notice of in Sir James Ware's books *die possibilie Hiberniæ* (sic), and divers of the poor English were preserved by Joseph Everard and Redmond English, two Franciscan friars in their chapel,[2] some under its altar, which was proved in Cromwell's time upon the trial of the said Father English, whereupon he was acquitted and permitted to live in the country, and the like privilege was accorded to Father Joseph Everard, as Colonel Sankey well knows.

And soon after the said English persons so preserved were by a guard of the Irish inhabitants of Cashel safely [3] conveyed to the county of Cork as they desired. And in their march some of the convoy were wounded in preserving them from the violence of the rabble that met them on the mountains. For this murder at Cashel, at a Court at Clonmell, about the 8th of November, 1652, Colonel Tiegue O'Meagher, Lieutenant-Colonel Donogh O'Dwyer, Theobald Butler, Hugh Ryan, Ulick Bourke and others, were tried and convicted and soon after executed: some at Clonmell, some at Cashel. And at another assizes James Bourke of Scartfield was convicted and executed for the said murder. James Hamilton, the Archbishop's son, who now lives in Dublin, and was an eye-witness of

---

[1] One copy of a deposition made by a maidservant in Cashel says that a Jesuit father exerted himself to save the lives of some of his Protestant neighbours, and Dr. Pullen, a Protestant clergyman, made a deposition to the same effect. No other Jesuit is mentioned in the depositions as aiding the Cashel Protestants.

[2] I could find no mention of those Franciscans in any of the depositions or in the Records of the High Court of Justice, so far as I had time to search them. If the two friars performed such great services to the Protestants it is strange that they are not mentioned in the depositions where the Jesuits' services to Dr. Pullen are recorded. The only authority for F. Everard and F. English's services seems to be the above document amongst the Carte MSS., but the writer of it appeals so confidently to Colonel Sankey as a witness to the truth of what he states, that it is difficult to doubt him.

[3] Ellish Meagher's deposition says some of them were murdered, and others treated with atrocious cruelty. *v. ante*, p. 42.

the barbarous proceedings at Cashel, can, if he pleases, give your Grace a perfect account of them. His father Archibald and his brother William and others were gone away before Cashel was taken, and his brother Lewis was left with Edward Sall of Cashel. The 1st day of January, 1641-2, a rabble of people flocked into Fethard and seized on the keys of the gate, there being but few English inhabitants in this town, such as Mr. Loe, the minister, and his family, Mr. Robert Hamilton, a minister, and his family, Robert Powell and John Lobb, and their families; they were all secured and preserved, but such of their goods as they had not before placed by way of trust in the custody of their Irish neighbours were seized upon and put up in a castle or tower, and James Lord Dunboyne hearing of the violence committed at Fethard, did the next day go thither and dispersed the rebels, and set the English at liberty, and at their request sent Mr. Hamilton and his family safe to the Lady, then Countess, now Duchess of Ormond, who took them with Mrs. Loe and her children, and divers other English families, soon after safe to Dublin. The Powells and Lobbs and their family were safely conveyed where they desired, and Mr. Loe preferred to be left at his landlord's, Geoffrey Mockler's, house of Mocklerstown, in hopes the times would grow calmer, but unfortunately he afterwards went in Mr. Mockler's company to Fethard, and Mr. Mockler having unfortunately left him there, as he thought in safe hands, his own occasions calling him to Clonmell, Mr. Loe most inhumanly and barbarously was at nighttime taken out of his lodgings and cruelly murdered by a company of rebellious rogues, which were discovered to be Thomas Quigley, James MacHugh, Richard Nagle, Donogh Markey, and others. And afterwards the first three of the murderers were, by the inquiry and care of Mr. Mockler, Mr. Loe's son, and by some of the inhabitants of Fethard, brought to judgment and executed.

In the month of December, 1641, the English in the towns of Clonmell and Carrick were preserved, and no blood spilt or plunder suffered, and so was Waterford, Dungarvan, Kilkenny, Callan, and Gowran, only that some of the rebels fell to plunder at Kilkenny, which when the Lord Mountgarret heard he rushed among them and shot one Richard Cantwell to death, which stopped their fury. I find that Sir George Hamilton the elder, having kept several families to work the Silver Mines at Doonally, in the county Tipperary, several of the Kennedys and others in their company most inhumanly and cruelly murdered sixteen[1] of these poor people. I cannot yet find certainly in what month this murder was committed, but have sent to know, and hope soon to be directly informed, and though these murderers were not brought to justice according to the due course of law, yet by the just judgment of God they all came to very sad ends.

After the taking of Cashel, as before mentioned, several of the prime gentry of the county Tipperary had several meetings in January, 1641, and agreed to raise several foot companies, and appointed officers over them, and invited the Lord Viscount Mountgarret, whom they heard had a commission from the justices to raise men, to be their general, upon which his lordship, about the latter end of January, 1641, came with fifteen companies of foot to Cashel, where, and in his rendezvous at Menenerla, in Clanwilliam, some of those of Tipperary joined him. In his march he appointed a company to block John Wise, one White, and others, who kept the castle of Ballyowen, and used to plunder some of the neighbours at night, and in the day-time appeared on the roads in women's apparel and robbed and killed some. Wise happened to be shot as he was going out of the castle, and afterwards White delivered it up to the Irish. And then also Lord Mountgarret ordered a company to block in a company of the English that had got together into the castle of Goelyn, who also burned and plundered some of their neighbours. From his rendezvous at Menenerla, Lord Mountgarret marched to the castle of Cnockardan, kept by the sons and servants of one Thomas Groves; he summoned them to yield, which they refusing, after two days' resistance, they surrendered upon a promise of life and arms, which was performed to them, and their goods given to the soldiers. In the taking of this castle the second son of Mr. FitzGerald of Burntchurch was killed.

. . . .

Before Mountgarret returned from the west, the poor English at Goelyn Castle being straitened for want of victuals, and despairing to be relieved, such of them as were able to march went on a dark

---

[1] Anna Sherring's deposition says that thirty-two persons, including her husband, ten women, and four children, were murdered at the Silver Mines on this occasion. v. Deposition CXLIV. For the fate of their Kennedy murderers v. p. 251. The Kilkenny depositions prove that cruel murders took place in that county, and that Cantwell was active in committing them, notwithstanding Lord Mountgarret's exertions. The proofs that he shot Cantwell, however, are slender.

night unawares to the besiegers, and made their escape with their arms, but they were met the next day in the mountains by James Butler of Ruskeagh, who killed some of them[1] and took others prisoners, whereof he hanged a Scotsman, for which the said James Butler was tried, convicted, and hanged at Clonmell, at a gaol delivery before Colonel Sankey and others. And for the poor men, women, and children left behind at Goolyn Castle, that were not able to go, the barbarous fellows that blocked them in most traitorously and inhumanly murdered them, the certain number of these murdered I find not, but I hope soon to know it. And because the company that did besiege the castle did belong to Pierse Butler of Shanballyduffe, and James Butler of Boytonrath, the said James and Pierse, Thomas the eldest son of Pierse, and one Patrick Keane, were in Cromwell's time, *anno* 1653, tried, convicted, and executed at Clonmell for the same barbarous butchery, though they were not present at it, yet their being officers of the company was sufficient to convict them. One George Cooke and his brother Robert kept the castle at Breakstown, and Robert being upon the battlement in September, 1642, was shot by one of the soldiers that blocked them up, and the castle surrendered in October, 1642.

These are the chiefest and all the violent actions I can find to have been done in the county of Tipperary in the first year of the rebellion.

And I do find that several of the English were preserved by some of the Irish there, as Sir Richard Everard, Bart.,[2] before the rebellion had planted the most part of his estate with English tenants, and at the beginning of it, observing the force and violence of the Irish to be so great that he was not able to protect all the English from the violence of the rabble, at first he sent away such of them as were able and rich with all their stock and other goods to the English quarters, and there being families of them that were poor and unable to remove, as many as 88 persons, the said Sir Richard kept and maintained them until the middle of June, 1642, at his own charges, and not being able to protect them longer against the violence of the storm, he conveyed them and their goods safely to the English garrison at Mitchelstown. And when that garrison was taken by the Irish, Sir Richard sent to some of the

[1] For these murders *v*. Deposition CXLV.
[2] Several depositions confirm the account here given of Sir Richard Everard's conduct. He was, I believe, the brother of the friar already mentioned as having saved some lives at Cashel. His daughter married the son of the Knight of Kerry.

families there that were very poor to come to him, whom he kept and maintained a long time, and then sent them away to the place they desired to go to. And as soon as the Cessation was made some of those poor tenants came back to him, and he settled and maintained them till Cromwell came to the country. All which was sufficiently proved by several persons in the Court at Athlone, when Sir Richard was upon his trial of qualifications, and that he was a common harbourer of the poor English in their distress, and that he was neuter for the first two years, and that several of his houses were rifled and burnt for his opposing the Irish, and that they took away from him 160 cows, 33 stud mares, and 2,000 sheep, all which can be fully proved if material. The Lady Viscountess of Thurles preserved some English. Thomas Tobin of Kilgenemanagh preserved many English families at Clorhane, John Hackett of Ballyskittane preserved two or three English families, as Ruth Hope's, John Moore's, (*blank*) Fiske's. And John Campbell of Ballynakeady preserved some, as did Dr. Fennell.—(*Carte MSS.*)

II.

On January 1st, 1641, Fethard was surprised by Theobald Butler, commonly called the Baron of Ardmayle, by drawing thither in small parties, such as he intrusted, of the vulgar sort of the barony of Middlethird, without any suspicion had by Martin Hacket, the governor of the town, or any of the burgesses or inhabitants. The honest and simple magistrate was seized in his own house, the keys forced from him by the Baron, who opened the gates and let in a throng of his adherents, about 1,000, armed some with swords and skeans, most with clubs and pikes. The lower sort of them, and especially one Theobald Butler FitzTheobald, fell to plundering the English inhabitants, viz. Robert Hamilton, minister of the town, a Scot, G. Loe, minister of Clonyn and three parishes, Robert Powell, John Lobb, and five others, in which Theobald Butler had the greatest share, pretending to be an old soldier and to have served in Ulster in the disbanded army of the Lord Strafford, and usurping the office and name of Quartermaster-General. Hamilton was kept in restraint some days, and also minister Loe, and then Hamilton was sent with his wife and children under a safe-conduct to Carrickmagrissy (*sic*), where the Countess of Ormond then resided, and went thence in her ladyship's company to Dublin, where he deposed before the mayor impious falsehoods, and several gentlemen of Tipperary with being at the surprisal who were not there, particularly one Mr. St. John of St. Johnstown (who died yesterday, being 6th of February, 1656, at Kilbride, at the house of his second son, Oliver St. John [1]), and whom he, Hamilton, calls a colonel and puts at the head of 500 men bearing the name of soldiers, in the market-place of that town upon its surprisal. Whereas it is generally known to the chief inhabitants of Fethard that Mr. Robert St. John was not there at all, and was of so temperate a disposition that he scarce ever wore so much as a defensive sword, and loved his ease so well that he scarcely ever appeared at any public meeting of the barony of Middlethird, and had no ambition but to enjoy his estate, which he derived from his ancestors many centuries ago, and all his discourse to me, who was one of his nearest neighbours, was, that he would have nothing to do in those wars, and that whoever had Cashel, Clonmell, and Fethard he would submit to him, and to my own special knowledge he had no personal intermeddling with that war, otherwise than in paying his contributions. Yet upon Hamilton's false information, against which no appeal or traverse would be admitted without a bribe, he was by the Commission lately sitting at Athlone declared a 'nocent,' and deprived of two-thirds of his estate, and was so harassed with his own and his son's, John St. John's fruitless attendance for redress, that he died before his time of grief and want.

James Butler, the now unfortunate Baron of Dunboyne, lying the night that Cashel was taken at Ballyshiaghane, overslept himself luckily in the morning, and a gentleman, a neighbour intimate with him, sprinkling him with some drops of water as he lay in his bed, he resented it, rose in a passion, and would not go to the surprise of Cashel, but returned to his house of Kiltynane. In his return passing near Fethard, and hearing the town was surprised by the Baron of Ardmayle, his lordship being chief commander of the barony of Middlethird, by special grant made to some of his ancestors for services performed to the Crown of England, took on him the command of Fethard, and made his brother, Mr. Thomas Butler, governor of it, and sent out the disorderly rabble that came with the Baron of Ardmayle, and Mr. Piers Butler of Rathcoole (next the baron the chiefest of the surprisers) placed in it a garrison and guard of the ablest persons, protected the British inhabitants

---

[1] A note to this says: 'Robert St. John died at Kilbryde, February 6th, 1656, and was buried the next day at St. Augustine's Abbey near Fethard.'

from further plundering, freed them from restraint, sent Mr. Loe to his landlord, Mr. Geoffrey Mockler of Mocklerstown, with his wife and family, as also the Powells and John Lobb to a place of safety as they desired, towards Youghal. And so ordered the matter that there was not one man, woman, or child killed in that enterprise, and the goods pillaged were returned with little or no charges, and satisfaction fully made to the sufferers, not by the actors, but by the better sort of people in the town; only Pierse Butler, as he pretended, out of friendship to Hamilton, kept all his cattle that he possessed in Ballynteample, parcel of Rathcoole, and at Myletonne (*sic*). G. Loe, Vicar of Clonyn, coming a pretty while after from Myletonne to Fethard, was murdered in his bed (as he lay there) by one James MacHae, a carpenter, and another, while he was fast asleep, and carried out folded in a coverlet, or forced to walk with them, to Crump's Bridge (a pretty distance to the east of Fethard), and there they threw his body into the river. Great search was made after the murderers by Mr. Geoffrey Mockler, and by Robert Bysset, in whose house the murder was committed, and James MacHae being suspected, Mr. Mockler gave information against him to the Lord Ikerrin, then Lieut.-General to Lord Mountgarret, who committed him to prison to the county gaol, whence escaping he lived in Leinster, and coming to Kilkenny was known by an inhabitant of Fethard and committed by the governor. But denying himself to be MacHae, he was sent to Clonmell to have the fact cleared, denied the murder at first, but at last owned it, and discovered his accomplice, who was drawn and quartered at Clonmell, as MacHae was at Fethard on a gibbet erected near the place of the murder. Before he was imprisoned by Lord Ikerrin he had been taken up at Fethard, but an officer, pretending he was one of his soldiers, took him out of prison, and, marching with the other Tipperary forces, he was then known and seized.

In December, 1641, the city of Kilkenny was surprised by the Lord Mountgarret, who fortunately died soon after the yielding up of Galway, thereby preventing the execution intended him. He never thought of permitting plunder, yet the vulgar sort flocking after him plundered English, Irish, Papist and Puritan alike, without distinction, which all the generals with him could do could not prevent, though they did the shedding of blood. His lordship published prohibitions against pillaging, and one Richard Cantwell (descended from Mr. Richard Cantwell of Paynestown, in the barony of Slieveardagh, a gentleman while he lived of great esteem for his hospitality and good parts) transgressing his inhibition he (Lord Mountgarret) shot him dead with his pistol, having no respect of persons, or regard to friendship and dependency in such a public concernment, though he would not for 500*l.* have lost that person so killed, being an able and very active young man, and a brother of Mr. John Cantwell, the late abbot of the abbey of Holy Cross, whom his lordship for sundry respects much favoured and respected.

.   .   .   .   .

Dermot O'Kennedy of Dounarieke (*sic*) in the barony of Upper Ormond, dying before these distempers, happened to have seven sons. These seven combining together, without any provocation, came suddenly into the dwelling-houses of Dounarieke aforesaid, and massacred sixteen [1] honest and civil miners, and refiners, hired to work at the Silver Mines, under the oversight of Sir George Hamilton, who not submitting until near his decease to the course of government established by the confederate Catholics, and the poor man having no near relation to prosecute, the murderers escaped a legal punishment, for which the magistrates appointed by the confederate Catholics are not to be excused; yet they escaped not the judgment of God, for 1st, John O'Kennedy, the elder brother of the seven, having attempted several ways of preferment in Munster, Leinster, and Ulster, where he bore the name of a colonel to uphold himself, and received the profits of his estate of Duneally, and the lead of that mine, all could not maintain him in any decency, so debasely addicted (was he) to swearing, tippling, and plundering, that with a party of thieves and tories he wasted his native country, and cruelly oppressed Upper Ormond, and at last was killed in an action and beheaded, his head put upon a stake, and his body left to the fowls of the air.

2ndly. Henry O'Kennedy, the second brother, followed the outrageous courses of his elder John in rapine, troubled in conscience for it, ran headlong desperately into the Shannon and was drowned.

3rdly. Kenny, the third brother, not inferior to the former in mischief, being committed to the shire gaol at Limerick, did indeed before his trial make his escape, but so odious was he to his neighbours that he has not been inquired after, nor is it known what has become of him.

[1] *v.* note to p. 216, and Deposition CXLIV., showing that thirty-two persons, of whom ten were women, and four children, were murdered at the Silver Mines.

4th. Donogh, the fourth brother, though a Franciscan by vocation, yet joining with his brothers, so infectious is iniquity, was of late unfortunately killed.

5th. Edmond, the fifth brother, a Franciscan too, but an associate, died lately, I pray God that he ended his days like a good Christian.

6th. Tiegue, the sixth brother, was killed at St. Patrick's rock, when surrounded by Lord Inchiquin's forces.

7th. William O'Kennedy, the seventh brother, though yet living, is credibly believed to have in the first year of the late civil war killed sixteen innocent persons by treachery, besides what he did at the Silver Mines.

A like cruel massacre upon the poor English men, women, and some young children was committed at the Castle of Goellyn (*sic*) Bridge in the barony of Clanwilliam, in the county of Tipperary, after that the English warders, having formerly by burning and spoiling much injured their neighbours, ran away from there, those weak, feeble persons not able to go after them, being found there the next day, as the report then was, is since continued, and by the English especially accepted for truth, some of whom were killed, and others cast alive into a deep hole or pit and covered with earth and stones, and some young children, at least one infant of a goodly aspect, cast over the bridge into the river Suir and drowned . . . the actors in this crime were never since nor in Cromwell's time called to account for it . . . but James and Pyers Butler, Thomas Oge Butler, and Patrick Keane (leaders in the siege of the castle) were condemned and executed at Clonmell, 10th May, 1653. Thomas Butler FitzJohn and Richard Bourke were acquitted on proof that, they being of the company that blocked the castle, yet out of their affection to the English interests and government relieved the warders with ammunition and victuals. Piers Butler, who was (*illegible*) just before the deserting of the castle, was at his trial so weak that he could hardly stand or speak, he died a Roman Catholic. His son Thomas, idly talking at his trial of his and Patrick Kean's being wounded at the siege of the castle as they were viewing the outworks (for the evidence did not go so far), occasioned their conviction. James Bourke, the informer against them, was descended of good parents in the county Limerick, and married one of the Hacketts of Cashel, widow of Mr. Bourke of Scartviefoyle (*sic*), in Clanwilliam, whose estate and means he lavished, and then following unruly courses, fell upon a poor tenant residing at Ballyshiaghnine, and charging him with the massacre at Cashel, seized the poor man's goods without warrant, and being questioned for it before Major Green, it fell out that he was himself impeached as concerned in that massacre, and he was arraigned at the next assizes before Judge Donellan, convicted, and executed.—(*Carte MSS.* vol. lxiv. pp. 435-461.)

III.

When Cashel was, on St. Nicholas' Day, attempted by Theobald Purcell, Baron of Loghmoo, since deceased, with a party of 1,500 foot, who came to the gates of the town with intent to surprise it, the intercessions of Father Dan Kearney, Friar Joseph Everard, and Father Sall, who went out with the Roman Catholic clergy in procession[1] to meet them, prevailed with them (the rebels) to desist from their enterprise without doing violence to the city or any English or Irish there, which gave them respite to remove themselves and goods to places of safety, as Archibald Hamilton and his Dean Dr. Pullen did, who went away with their wives and families, and such as tarried till O'Dwyer's coming had their goods, which they confided to the Roman Catholic clergy, re-delivered to them. Philip O'Dwyer died of a languishing disease at his house Doundromore, on the 3rd of May, 1648, Mr. Theobald Butler, Mr. Tiegue O'Meagher, Lieut.-Colonel O'Dwyer, brother to Philip, with one Brian Kearney FitzJohn of Ballybegg, Ulick Bourke of Lis (*illegible*), Hugh Ryan, and others were executed for the Cashel massacre, being condemned at the greatest trial held for the county Tipperary under Cromwell. Mr. Richard Butler of Ballynekill and Mr. Charles O'Dwyer were fortunately acquitted at the great trial held at Clonmell before Justice Donnellan, who sat as president a day or two before the feast of St. Martin, in November, 1652. Redmond English, a Franciscan, was so zealous to save the English, he hid some of them under the altar, which being proved at his trial saved his life. Mr. R. Butler of Ballynakelly was the youngest son of James, sometime Baron of Dunboyne, and was saved by the English jury on the general good report of his noble carriage and civility in all his actions, and so was Charles O'Dwyer of Crul (*illegible*) for the like character, and his love of quietness, though the evidence was as full against them as against the others, who, except Ulick Burke, whom I cannot specially accuse, and will not attempt to excuse, were all free from shedding of blood, and so

[1] *v. ante*, p. 213, *note*.

254   THE IRISH MASSACRES OF 1641.

Tiegue Oge O'Meara, Lt.-Col. Dwyer, and Brian Kearney protested at their examination at Clonmell, on November 23rd, 1652.

Theobald Butler, Ulick Bourke, and Hugh Ryan were executed at Cashel on the gibbet in the wall against the Court House, November 24th, 1625. Fr. Joseph Everard when he could not stop the massacre left his maledictions on the actors of it.—(*Carte MSS.* vol. lxiv. pp. 432-458.)

IV.

As concerning the murders committed at Shrule, in Connaught, I live at such a distance from that place that I cannot yet exactly learn the precise time, manner, or number of the murders there committed, and can only at present as to that particular observe to your Grace, what I remember to have read in a printed collection by R. S.[1] of some murders committed on the Irish with observations on falsifications of some murders said to be committed by the Irish. I say that it is confessed that a barbarous murder was committed by one Edmund Atlea,[2] an irreligious, profane fellow of the county of Mayo and his wicked accomplices at Shrule on about thirty[3] persons. And that the neighbouring gentry came with all expedition to the rescue of the said Protestants. And that they did rescue the Bishop of Killala (who was said to have been murdered in that place) and his wife and children and most of the Protestants there, and that one Brian Killery, a friar, the guardian of the abbey of Ross, near Shrule, was one of the first that made haste to that rescue, and brought the said bishop and his wife and children with

[1] The pamphlet or paper containing this collection by R. S. is in the British Museum Library, and has been often quoted by Irish writers, but a comparison of its statements as given in the above account with the sworn depositions of the survivors at Shrule and others, will show how little the vague stories of this anonymous pamphleteer are to be trusted.

[2] This Edmund Atlea, probably Edmund of the Hills (*v.* Deposition CLXXXIX.), could have been no other than the Edmund Bourke with whom Lord Mayo 'covenanted' to convey the Protestants to Shrule, and who was the first to begin the massacre at the bridge (*v.* vol. i. p. 382-394). The choice of such a man for the convoy renders Lord Mayo suspect, although it is probable he could have found no trustworthy person, had he really wished to do so.

[3] Dean Fargy's widow swore (*v.* p. 7) that there were a party of fifty-five Protestants, besides the Bishop, the Dean, and six other clergymen (in all sixty-three), and that all the men of this party except the Bishop and two others were murdered at Shrule. Several women, she also swore, two of them being *enceinte*, were murdered there.

several others of the said distressed Protestants into his monastery, where he civilly treated them for several nights, until Mr. Bourke of Castle Hacket brought the said bishop, his wife and children into his own house, where they wanted nothing for several weeks, the like being done by several other neighbouring gentlemen to the rest of the said Protestants, until they were sent into places of security by the Marquis of Clanricarde's orders. That paper (written by R. S.) observes that the Lord Viscount Mayo, upon pretence of having a hand in that murder, was in Cromwell's time put to death, though it is said he proved at his trial that he was a Protestant at that time that the murders were committed, and that it was a great providence he escaped to be killed by them [1] (the Irish). That paper also takes notice that though he who writ the collection of the murders committed upon the English, said in his first and second pages that in 1642 many Protestants were murdered in a barbarous manner at Kilkenny, and likewise that at Graigue, in the county Kilkenny, seventy Protestants were murdered with most horrible circumstances, whereas at Kilkenny there was but one woman smothered in a tumult in 1641, for which the Lord Mountgarret shot Cantwell dead, and that at Graigue there were not any murdered during the rebellion. The truth of this is so confidently affirmed by persons of honour and quality as that they are content to allow the whole abstract of murders of English for truth if the author can prove that any Protestant was murdered in Kilkenny or Graigue but the said single woman.[2]

[1] The Viscount Mayo of 1641-2 died before Cromwell arrived in Ireland. His son Theobald or Tibbot, according to his own deposition, given in vol. i. p. 396, was forced away from Shrule by John Garvey, the sheriff of the county, to save his life, while he was attempting to stop the massacre. Lord Mayo's Protestantism was doubtful, he became a Roman Catholic three days after the massacre (Deposition CIX.), and his son the Viscount, executed by Cromwell, was, I believe, a Roman Catholic. In his examination, however, he charges the Roman Catholic Archbishop and priests with having failed to keep their promise of remaining with the convoy to ensure its safety. There is not a particle of good evidence to show that the gentry generally made any efforts to save the fugitives. John Brown, Esq., of the Neale admits that he, like the Roman Catholic Archbishop and priests, fled away from Shrule and left the Protestants to their fate. (v. Depositions CIX. to CXVII.)

[2] If this rash challenge were accepted all Sir John Temple's abstracts would pass for truth, inasmuch as the murders of several Protestants at Graigue are proved by the depositions of the widows and relatives of the murdered men, and by those of Sir Edward and Lady Butler. The oaths of those 'two persons of honour and quality' must certainly be preferred to R. S.'s anonymous report of

And R. S. also observes that in the county of Galway all the war time, several Protestant ministers, viz. Dean York, Mr. Carryn (*sic*), MacNeil and other ministers and their flocks had meetings there without interruption, living amongst the Irish. If your Grace think fit to speak to the Earl of Clanricarde, he may persuade Colonel Kelly to give your Grace a true account, as well of that murder at Shrule, as of all other notable transactions in Connaught in the beginning of the rebellion, and to read the collections of murders on both sides would do your Grace no harm.[1]—(*Carte MSS.* vol. ii. pp. 122-215. *Bodleian Library*.)

the parole evidence of anonymous persons, who for aught we know never existed at all. R. S.'s observations as to the safety of the Protestant clergy in Galway are proved worthless by the depositions of the few of them who survived. See also Mr. Goldsmith's account of Lord Mayo's remarks to the Archbishop when he wished to have that clergyman given up to him.

[1] The above is endorsed by Carte, 'This seems to me to be Mr. Kearney of Fethard's handwriting.'

APPENDIX.

A.

(*v.* vol. i. p. 17.)

EXAMINATION OF DERMOT OGE MCDONNE, TAKEN BEFORE THE LORD OF MEATH, SIR TOBY CAULFIELD, CAPTAIN DODDINGTON, AND FRANCIS ANNESLEY, THE 8RD OF APRIL, 1615.[1]

"ABOUT a fortnight after the summer assizes held at Dungannon, A.D. 1614, this deponent, with one Dermot McRedmond Moyle in his company, came to the house of Art Oge McDonnel O'Neil chanceably at a time when those therein were at mass. They found the door shut, and two men keeping it, called Hugh Moyna McGillpatrick and Hugh Moyna MacArt, who knows this deponent and his companion, and let them into the house, where they found the friar O'Mullarky saying mass, who was lately come thither out of Tyrconnell. The hearers were Brian Crossagh O'Neil, Art Oge O'Neil McDonnel, and his two brothers; Owen McPhelimy, Sheely ny Hosye, wife to the said Art, 'Ould' Donnel O'Neil, father to the said Art, and the priest MacMurphew. Examt. only stayed within while he said his prayers, and came out of the house within a little while, and Cormac MacRedmond Moyle followed him soon after.

At this examt.'s going out of the house the priest MacMurphew called after him, saying, '*Dermot, you are making great haste out of the house.*' To which this examt. answered him that he had some business without, and that he could stay no longer in the company. The priest then said to this examt., '*It is no matter whether we ever see any of your master's men or not,*' meaning the king's, as this deponent expounded it. Then said Brian Crossagh to the priest, which words this deponent overheard, '*He shall answer for this another day.*'

[1] *MSS. T.C.D. Fol.* 3, 15.

Then this exant. went on his way with Cormac McRedmond Moyle towards the house of Brian Crossagh, and on the way met Owen McFerdoragh Ony Maguire, who, after holding some short communication with them, they telling him what they were doing at Art Oge's house, went along with them to Brian Crossagh's house, but before they got there Brian himself overtook them, and said to this examt. that '*they did ill to flee from God's service,*' to which this examt. answered, that '*they did not flee from God's service, but from the troubles of this world, which he had lately tasted enough of.*' And this the examt. said further to Brian, '*If thou wilt give me a buieng*[1] *to be thy friend, I will give thee a buieng to be my friend.*' Then Brian Crossagh answered, he would take no *buieng* of this examt., but then presently after gave him his sword, bidding this examt. say, if he were asked how he came by it, that he got it at play: whereupon this examt., taking the sword, said he would refuse nothing that came to him in God's name.

And so taking his leave this examt., with Cormac McRedmond Moyle and Owen McFerdoragh Boy, went to the house of one Brian Maguire, which was not far off, where they had not stayed long when Brian Crossagh O'Neil sent for them to come back again, and on their way back this examt. said to his companion, '*I am afraid Brian will take back the sword from me, and therefore I will hide it,*' and so this examt. left it in a farmer's house called Gillenef MacRogan, who can witness it, telling him he won it at play.

At his return to Brian's house he found Brian and his wife on a bed of rushes, and Brian called to him and bade him sit down, which he this examt. did, leaning his back on a *speere* or division of wattles made in the house, which looking through he espied Friar O'Mullarky on the other side of the said wattles, and when Brian perceived that this examt. had espied the friar, he said in jest to him, '*Take care, there is something there that will hurt thee,*' to which this examt. answered, he would not willingly be hurt. Then the friar spoke likewise in jest, saying, '*If I were a bull beggar I would eat thee,*' and then, turning his speech into earnest, said, '*If I did not think thou wouldst be of my counsel I would cut off thy head.*' Then Brian rose from his bed and said, '*Tarry until I have talked with him,*' and so went out of doors, taking this examt. with him, and said unto him, '*Dermot, thou hast been a servitor for the king, and hast brought many men to great trouble and some to their deaths. Let me see what thou hast got by it. If thou shouldest*

---

[1] *Bieng*, a gift to win favour and pledge friendship. See vocab. of Irish terms, Calendar of Irish State Papers, Hen. VIII. vol. iii. p. 588.

serve for five years more, and cut off as many more, thou shouldest have nothing but in the end to be hanged for thy labour. I was at the assizes the other day, and Justice Aungier was ready to revile me like a churl if I did but look awry, and the other black judge would lean his head upon one shoulder to see if he could espy any occasion to hang me. By my good will I will never go among them any more, and if thou wilt take my counsel I shall have no occasion to think my sword ill bestowed.'

Upon these speeches Art Ogo O'Neil came out, and with him Owen McFerdoragh Boy and Cormac McRedmond Moyle, and then Brian said to this exaint. and the rest that they had been servitors formerly, but now if they would take his counsel he would bring them to better service, and if they would take his counsel he would take theirs. And he further said, ' You are all gentlemen; I know if you give me your word you will not break with me, and if you will be of my counsel we will get many more of our party, and for your better assurance Edward O'Mullarkey shall make the order of your reward.'

Then said this examt., ' Let me know first what you mean to do, and then it may be we would be of your counsel.' Then said Owen McFerdoragh Boy, ' I love my own Lord well (meaning Con Roe Maguire), yet I love thee far better, and I have cause to love thee because thou marriedst my Lord's daughter.[1] Therefore if thou canst work with these gentlemen (meaning this examt. and Cormac MacRedmond Moyle), thou mayest be sure of me.'

Then said Art Ogo O'Neil, ' If I durst trust thee I would quickly tell thee what we would have thee do. But I am afraid you would betray us,' and with that he went into the house where the Friar Edward O'Mullarkey was ; and the said Art, plucking out a little red box, wished all the men that were where that box came from were there betwixt that and the church well armed, which church stood about half a mile off, called Tullyakteyne, and with that pulled out a large paper out of the box, saying that if they knew what was written in that paper they would not be afraid to take their party in the business they went about, for, said he, ' there is not a gentleman in the country but his hand is set to this paper to take our parts.'

Then they drank aqua vitæ out of a little bottle, which the friar had of extraordinary good aqua vitæ. Having drank, this examt. said to Owen MacFerdoragh Boy, and Cormac McRedmond Moyle asked, what business was that they so earnestly demanded help in,

[1] Brian Crossagh O'Neil, himself illegitimate, was married to the illegitimate daughter of Con Roe Maguire, chief of his sept.

and what aid or warrant they had to hope to bring it to pass. Then said Brian Crossagh, '*Is not Sir Toby's fosterer a good warrant?*' This examt. replying, asked, '*What fosterer has Sir Toby?*' They answered it was Con Roe MacNeil. And Art said further that, howsoever long Sir Toby had that fosterer, he had much need to have him. Then this examt. asked, '*Why how do you think you can get Sir Toby's fosterer that he is so careful of?*'

Then Brian Crossagh said he was sure to have him, whensoever he liked, and that he had a friend in Sir Toby's house that was most of his counsel, which had promised to deliver the boy unto us. Cormac asked, '*Who was that that was so near Sir Toby and so much their friend?*' Art Oge said it was Ned Drumane. Then, said Brian McFerdoragh Boy, it is true that if you have Ned Drumane to your friend you may be sure to have the boy, for Sir Toby trusts him as much as any man about him. And then Art Oge said that in a few days he would go to Charlemont to see how soon Sir Toby was to go to Dublin, meaning not to take away Con McGrogy until Sir Toby were gone to Parliament, and that then Ned Drumane should bring the boy unto them, and they would keep Ned Drumane prisoner with them two days, and then send him back to Sir Toby, as if he were in no fault. And further Art Oge said, '*If our fortune be to speed well you shall have good commands under us: if not, we can all go to Spain with the boy, and be welcome there.*' Saying further, '*Do not you see that William Steward, who married my sister, if he take our parts, he being of the best blood of the Scots, you may be sure that the best of the Scots will be with us, and we make no question of William Steward but he will join with us whensoever we shall call for him, either in Ireland or to get us a ship to convey us away.*'

Then this examt., making a doubt that William Steward was not on their side (as they boasted), Brian Crossagh took a book and swore by it that William Steward was promised to them. Art O'Neil took the book and swore the like, and so did Owen O'Neil, brother to said Art, and that William Steward's hand was to the writing, further telling and assuring them that within one month they should hear of wars in Scotland, and that Alexander MacJames MacSurly Buy had set his hand also to the writing, and those of Scotland should begin the war first.

Brian Crossagh said further, that if it had not been for three of his friends that counselled him, he had not been at the last assizes at Dungannon. Then this examt. and his companions asked Brian how long it would be before the plot was put into execution, and Brian answered that they would stay no longer than to receive an answer to a letter which the Friar O'Mullarkey was then writing to Alexander McSurley Buy, which letter being written, they all four signed it before their faces, viz. the Friar O'Mullarkey, Brian Crossagh O'Neil, Art Oge O'Neil, and Owen O'Neil, brother to the said Art, and then Brian Crossagh put the letter in his pocket. By this it was supper time, and Brian swore that he would eat no meat until the friar had made friends between them and Art Oge, for there had been unkindness between them and Art Oge upon a matter they had discovered to the Bishop of Meath of Art Oge having an intention to take him prisoner. Then the Friar O'Mullarkey ordered that Brian Crossagh and Art Oge should give this examt. and Owen McFerdoragh Boy 5l. apiece, and that they should both go to Sir Toby Caulfield to deny the truth of the information they had before given to the Bishop of Meath of Art Oge's intention to take him prisoner. Owen McFerdoragh Buy said he durst not go without a protection, so that Art Oge sent one Hugh Moynagh McArt to the said Sir Toby for the said warrant and protection, promising they should discover some good service for his Majesty. As soon as Hugh was returned with the protection and warrant, they both went to Dungannon, where they found Sir Toby, and Owen Boy did then and there make his denial (of his former information) touching the taking of the Bishop of Meath.

But this examt., being as he said moved in conscience, stole out of town, and performed not the like as he had promised, for which Art Oge grew very much displeased, and devised to murder him, or do him some mischief, as hereafter shall be shown,

About a fortnight afterwards, this examt. was by the devices of Brian Crossagh O'Neil decoyed to the house of one Shane O'Dowey and Owen O'Dowey under false pretences, and having gone about a stone's cast within a wood near the house, being led by one Pholimy McGillrowney, one Patrick Oge O'Murphew, that was lying in waiting for him, fell upon this examt., and then the aforesaid Phelimy, that enticed him into the wood, took him by the leg and pulled him down to the ground, and instantly Art Oge came in with Mahon McGillegroom, Hugh Moynagh McArt, Owen McFerdoragh Boy, and Owen O'Neil, brother to Art, all falling upon this examt. First they searched him and took away from him his ticket of pardon, and the warrant that the judge had given him for his safe coming to the assizes at Dungannon. Having taken those things from him, Art Oge drew his *skean* to have killed him, but Patrick Oge MacMurphew stayed him, wishing him not to draw his blood, but rather to sew him up in his mantle and leave him there. So they tied him up with withes and stames, and then fell to council whether they should kill him or not. And he thinketh they had killed him but that his gossip Owen McFerdoragh Boy dissuaded them, wishing them rather to send him to the gaol and lay treason to his charge. With which course Art Oge was at the last contented, making full account Sir Toby would have hanged him as soon as he had brought him to him. And so this examt. was sent to the jail, and there remains."

(*Signed*) GEORGE MIDENSIS.
TOBY CAULFIELD.
FRAN. ANNESLEY.

In order to understand Brian Crossagh's account of the criticising glances of 'Justice Aungier,' and the '*other black judge*' (probably the counsel or serjeant-at-law) at the Ulster Assizes, which so disgusted him, we must remember that the government of 1609-20 professed a wish that the Irish chiefs should attend the courts of justice, and take part in their proceedings, at least manifest an interest in them, and a preference for English law over the Brehon system. Thus in 1609, the Solicitor-General, Sir R. Jacob, describing the Ulster Assizes, writes to Salisbury, that 'Mac Sweeny Fanagh came and sat with the judges in Court, though he came in an uncivil fashion in his mantle.' The Irish chief's preference for the Irish mantle (a graceful covering enough) was believed to betoken that he had still a suspicious hankering after his native fashions, if not native laws.

The Alexander MacJames MacSurly Buy or Buie, *i.e.* Alexander the son of James, the son of Charles the Yellow, or yellow haired, mentioned in this deposition, was, I believe, the son of Sir James MacDonnell, brother of the first Earl of Antrim, but the genealogy of this family has been much confused (*v. ante*, vol. i. p. 21).

B.

(*v.* vol. i. p. 25.)

PETITION OF WEXFORD FREEHOLDERS AGAINST PLANTATIONS.[1]

To the Rt. Hon. Lords and others of his Majesty's most honourable Privy Council.

The humble petition of Redmond McDamore, gent., in the behalf of himself and of divers gentlemen and freeholders of Mac-Damore's country of Wexford in the realms of Ireland,

Humbly shewing unto your Lordships that your petitioners, according to his Majesty's gracious commission of defective titles for the settling of the subjects of that kingdom in their estates, and his Highness's proclamation thereupon, and the Lords Justices of assizes in that county, their publication thereof at the general assizes there holden, and according to an order of the late Lord Deputy and other commissioners on the 8th of February, 1609, did, in the year 1609, surrender their lands unto his Majesty, assuring themselves of re-grants of them to themselves and their heirs by letters patent. After which surrenders the petitioners seeking to have re-grants accordingly from his Highness of the said lands, Sir Edward Fisher, Knight, William Parsons, surveyor, and others having obtained letters patent as undertakers of the petitioner's said lands did set on foot an ancient pretended title to the said lands for his Majesty, derived from the Lord Viscount Beaumont, never before heard of in the memory of man, and thereupon suddenly in term time (your petitioners then being destitute of counsel) procured a commission to return commissioners, some of them being undertakers, for finding of an office at the town of Wexford to entitle his Majesty to the premises by colour of the said supposed title, for the finding thereof there was impannelled a jury of the great freeholders of the said county, some of them being near of kin to Sir Lawrence Esmond, Knt. (who was a principal undertaker of other lands in the said county of Wexford upon the same ancient pretended title) to

[1] *S. P. I. Vol.* 204, 10*A, Rolls House.*

inquire of the said petitioner's title. Yet after full evidence given the said jury would not find the pretended title for his Majesty, whereupon the said jurors in the winter vacation were advised (called before) to the Exchequer at Dublin, and there urged to inquire further into the said title. And the said jurors, insisting upon their first verdict, were thereupon examined separately, and some of them for their intractability were there publicly committed to the Marshalsea, and afterwards censured in the Star Chamber without allowance of counsel, and some others, whereof one was an undertaker, and another who was employed in the said commission, were joined with the other yielding jurors, who found the long-slept title for his Majesty to these lands.

And whereas heretofore, upon humble petition and complaint made unto your Lordships of the said proceedings, it pleased your Lordships, among other directions, to direct that if the petitioners and the natives did not conform themselves to your Lordships' directions, that then all parties should be left to be tried by the due course of the common law, and that the possession in the meantime should be left in the natives until (lawful) eviction.

Yet notwithstanding, so it is, Right Honourables, that the said Sir Edward Fisher, William Parsons, and others, in Michaelmas time last, preferred an English bill into the Exchequer against the petitioners, setting forth no other title but that the king was seized and granted the same by letters patent, dated the 17th of February, in the 9th year of his reign, to the said Sir Edward Fisher and his heirs, yielding 8*l*. Irish per annum, where the petitioners paid yearly 10*l*. for the same, and suggested that by reason the petitioners held the same by force he could not make his entry into the said lands to enable him to have an action at the common law. Unto which the petitioners made answer, that they held their lands by descent for many hundred years together, and that they were ready to answer the petitioner at the common law, and in the same term a Latin information was exhibited in the same Court of Exchequer against your petitioners for the same cause, and before they answered the said informations, the said Sir Edward Fisher obtained an injunction to dispose of the petitioners' said lands, which they and their ancestors held by descent time out of mind. The which was executed accordingly in March last in a most injurious manner by soldiers with force and arms, to the great annoyance and utter ruin of the petitioners, their wives and families, being many thousand souls, if their Lordships did not yield speedy relief unto them.

The petitioners most humbly beseech your Lordships to consider their poor estates being utterly ruinated and impoverished by the aforesaid courses, and for that they did hold their said lands by course of descent and not by tanistry, as was said, that therefore your Lordships would be vouchsafed to further their suit, and that his Majesty may be graciously pleased to direct his Highness's letters to the Lords Justices of the said realm of Ireland, requiring them thereby to grant by letters patent unto the petitioners and their heirs respectively, their said several lands, surrendered as aforesaid, according to his Majesty's said commission, proclamation, and order in that behalf, under such rents, terms, and service as to his Majesty shall be thought fit. And that such distresses as have been taken on their lands by the said Sir Edward Fisher may be restored.

And also that order may be taken for the enlargement of such of the petitioners as remained in prison upon attainder, by reason of their suit concerning the said lands. And your petitioners shall be bound to pray for your Lordships' long lives, &c.—(*No date, calendared under May*, 1616.)

C.

(v. vol. i. p. 26.)

THE COMMISSIONERS' RETURN AND CERTIFICATE CONCERNING THE GRIEVANCES OF THE NATIVES IN THE PLANTATION OF WEXFORD, A.D. 1614.[1]

The new plantation intended in the county of Wexford, in the province of Leinster, is to be made in the two baronies of Gowrie (sic) and Ballykenny in the half barony of Skerrywalshe, which contain, as they are estimated by survey, 66,800 acres of land and certain tracts of wood, boggy land and mountain, all lying together in one continent betwixt the river of Slane on the south, the river of Arklow north, and the sea on the east, and the bounds of the counties Carlow and Kildare on the west, whereof the profits and occupations have been for many years in the several septs of the Kavenaghs, Kinsellas, MacSaddocs, MacDamores, and Murroghs, and other of the Irish septs, and to some of ancient English that not long since obtained part of those lands from the Irish. The possessioners claimed and pretended to hold those lands as their freehold by descent, after the custom of Irish gavelkind, and have been impannelled since the king's time on juries as freeholders, whereof the number presented to be freeholders and who offered their surrenders were 440 or thereabouts, as appeareth by the books delivered to us for surrenders, but now affirmed by the natives to be 667, of which fourteen had letters patent for part of their lands from the Crown, all which countries yielded yearly to his Majesty in rents and compositions only 179*l*. 3*s*. 4*d*., besides 90*l*. yearly which Sir Richard Masterson, Knight, had anciently granted him, and 20*l*. yearly which Walter Synnot had in lieu of Irish chiefries to them granted by the Crown; by several letters patent, upon evidence given at the Exchequer bar, in a trial betwixt the said Richard Masterson and one of the sept of the Kavanaghs, in the term of Easter and in the seventh year of his highness's reign, some overture was made for a title to his Majesty to these lands, after which and before the said title was made known to the Lord Deputy and commissioners such as claimed to be freeholders obtained from the

[1] *Harris's Hibernica.*

commission of surrenders, orders, according to the usual form, for their several surrenders, and for effecting thereof procured out three several commissions to the king's escheator, and others, to inquire what lands and tenements they hold either by descent or tanistry and thereupon to accept their surrenders. Upon two of which commissions nothing was done, but upon the third commission directed to his Majesty's said escheator and others, the commissioners on the 27th of January, 1609, received the several surrenders of all such as then claimed to be freeholders within those limits of all their lands, tenements, and hereditaments, comprised and specified in two several books then delivered to the escheator: the which surrenders the escheator confessed he did show to the Lord Deputy, and some other the commissioners for surrenders sitting upon the commission; but for that the time by proclamation limited for the natives to proceed with their surrenders was then past, the escheator was by the commissioners desired to return and keep the surrenders, and not to make return thereof, until his Majesty's pleasure was further known; for that the king's learned counsel affirmed, they had discovered a good title for the king to all those lands, and that the commission warranted not them to accept those surrenders: according to which direction the escheator detained still the commission surrenders and books not yet returned, after which the Lord Deputy, *anno* 1610, certified his Majesty and some of the Privy Council in England of his highness's title, and that the natives offered to surrender and to take new estates upon the commission of surrenders, and defective titles, and thereupon several directions were given to his lordship for the proceeding unto plantation, as by his Majesty's letters, and letters from some of his Privy Council, doth appear.

After which, the Lord Deputy resolved on a project for the division and plantation of those countries, whereof he hath sent to his highness by us a copy subscribed by his lordship, since which, on the 27th of July, 1611, his lordship sent Sir Lawrence Esmond, knt., Sir Edward Fisher, knt., William Parsons, Esq., and Nicholas Kenny, Esq., his Majesty's surveyor and escheator, to make known to the inhabitants of those countries that nothing was intended unto them by that plantation but good, for albeit the whole country was the king's to dispose of as he pleased, yet he was pleased to accept of their surrenders, and to repass to such as were worthy and fit to be made freeholders, convenient portions in fee simple at reasonable rents, and to others of the inferior sort competent portions for lives and years, and that the civilising of the country was the chief thing aimed at, with some increase of revenue to the king, and that if any man were obstinate and opposed against the general good intended, they should have justice, which is the benefit of subjects, but were to look for no favour. According to these directions the said commissioners treated with the inhabitants, and divers of the principal of these pretended freeholders yielded to accept the Lord Deputy's offers, and by several writings, dated in August in the ninth year of his highness's reign, did give up and surrender their lands to his Majesty, upon hope to have re-granted to them convenient portions in the new plantation, his lordship thereupon assigned unto 57 of the natives, to be divided into several portions, 35,210 acres, to be granted in fee simple, which 57 were by a jury of that country presented to be the fittest men in those limits to be made freeholders. The particulars of these proportions, together with the names of those natives, are hereinafter expressed, of which 35,210 acres there were assigned to the said Sir Richard Masterson 10,169; for his said chiefries 2,120; the residue for his land in the Morrogh's country. Of the natives which agreed to the new plantation 16 of them accepted estates of their proportions from Sir Richard Cooke, Sir Lawrence Esmond, Sir Edward Fisher, knights, the first patentees made of that country in trust. Of these 57 natives 21 are still to retain their ancient houses and habitations, with their grounds adjoining. Some of their lands lying remote from them being laid to the new undertakers' proportions are to be taken from them, in lieu whereof some allowances are to be made of lands lying nearer their dwellings, with which they are not contented, for that they are not sufficiently recompensed for the lands taken from them as they affirm. To the residue which claim to be freeholders, being for the most part possessed of but small portions, no allowance of land or recompense is assigned or given, but all they, in number 990 or thereabouts, and all the residue of the inhabitants, tenants, and cottiers, estimated to be 14,500 men, women, and children, may be removed at the will of the patentees, which notwithstanding few are yet removed, and it is offered by the new undertakers, as formerly by the Lord Deputy, it was appointed that all those to whom no portions by this new division are assigned, and all the under tenants inhabiting within their proportions, may, if they will, reside and dwell in these countries, as tenants to the English and native undertakers, without removing of any but such as dwell on those grounds, which the patentees shall use for their necessary demesnes to their castles and houses, and that they will be bound to let and set to those natives that want proportions lands at easy rents and rates as they held them before, all rents, charges, and exactions being considered which they paid to his Majesty, Sir Richard Masterson, Walter Synnot, and others.

APPENDIX. 269

The proceedings against the natives have been in this manner: in June, 1611, upon motion of the king's learned counsel, a writ of seizure was awarded out of the Court of Chancery, to take into his Majesty's hands all the said lands and tenements, which was grounded upon some ancient records remaining in that court, mentioned in the inquisition hereinafter specified, which was returned and executed by the sheriff, but no proceedings thereupon. After which a commission under the great seal of Ireland was directed to the Lord Bishop of Ferns, Sir Thomas Colclough, knt., Sir Dudley Loftus, knt., John Beere, Esq., his Majesty's sergeant-at-law, William Parsons and Nicholas Kenny, his Majesty's surveyor and escheator, to inquire of his Majesty's title to those lands. The commissioners, on the 26th of November, 1611, met at Wexford for the execution of the said commission, where after divers adjournments until the 4th of December, the jury then offered their verdict of *ignoramus* to the king's title, the which the commissioners refused to accept, and bound the jury to appear before them in the Exchequer Court, the Thursday s'ennight next following, but the jury, upon their petition to the Lord Deputy, had their appearance respited until the 18th of January following, at which day the jury appeared in the Exchequer before the said commissioners and Sir John Denham, knt., then Lord Chief Baron, Sir Francis Aungier, knt., Master of the Rolls, Baron Hassett, and Justice Lowther, associated by commission to the former commissioners. After long time spent in the evidence on both sides, eleven of that jury agreed to find his Majesty's title, but five others of them refused to join with those eleven in that verdict, who were then by the commissioners committed to prison, and afterwards censured in the Castle Chamber for refusing to join with their fellows to find his Majesty's title according to their evidence, and the rest of the jury were discharged. Then the Court of Exchequer directed a writ to the sheriff of Wexford, to summon a jury to appear at the Exchequer bar in Hilary Term next following for the said inquiry. The sheriffs returned Sir Thomas Colclough, one of the former commissioners, and those eleven of the former jury that had agreed to find his Majesty's title, and some others, which eleven, so formerly sworn with Sir Thomas Colclough and John Murchoe, now a patentee in the new plantation, found an inquisition to this effect, the copy whereof we are ready to show, namely ; That upon the submission of Art MacMurrogh and Mallogh O'Murrogh, chief of their septs, and David Moore and Manus MacGerald of the Kinsellas, and divers others of the Irish, unto King Richard the Second, by indentures dated the 7th of January, in the 12th year of the reign of the

same king, the said parties did covenant with Thomas, Earl of
Nottingham, then Marshal of England, and Deputy of this kingdom, that they and every one of them before the first Sunday in
Lent then next following, would relinquish and surrender to the
said king the full possession of all the lands, tenements, castles,
woods, forts, and pastures, with their appurtenances, which by
them and all others of the Kinsellas and every of them, their companions, men, or adherents, late were occupied within the province of
Leinster in Ireland, *sine aliquo retinement, sibi reservato, sine reser-
vando quocunque modo, sine dolo et absque fraude,* (sic) their move-
able goods only excepted, and that they before the said day would
leave the whole country of Leinster to the true obedience, use, and
disposition of the said king, his heirs and successors; and that the
said earl, on the part of the king, covenanted that these chief men
and their soldiers or men of war, during their lives shall have pay
in the king's wars, and should enjoy them to these and their heirs
all such lands as they should conquer from any rebels in this kingdom. The said Earl also agreed that the king should grant to Art
MacMurrogh, the chief of the Kavenaghs, a yearly annuity of eighty
marks, and restore to him his wife's inheritance in the county of
Kildare, which annuity was paid divers years, as appears by some
records: they also find that on the 12th of February next ensuing
a commission was granted unto the said Earl Marshal to receive
the homage of MacMurrogh and all the Irish of Leinster, and to
take their homages and submissions, which was done, and to dis-
tribute the lands of the chieftains and men of war who were to
depart to others of the king's subjects. They further found that on
the 28th of April then following, King Richard the Second granted
to Sir John Beaumont, knt., and his heirs all and singular the
castles, manors, lands, tenements, and hereditaments within the
meares and bounds following, namely, from the bank of the water
of Slane, on the part of the south, to the black water of Arklow, of
the part of the north, and from the main sea on the east unto the
bounds of the counties of Carlow and Kildare on the part of the
west, excepting the lands of the Earl of Ormond, if he had any
within these bounds, to be holden by knight service *in capite*; and
that the said Sir John Beaumont, by virtue of these letters patents,
was seized of all the lands within these meares (excepting the Earl
of Ormond's lands, Roches' lands, Synott's lands, Wadding's lands,
the lands of the Bishop of Ferns, advowsons of churches, and some
other things in the said inquisition excepted), and that the said
Sir John Beaumont died seized thereof, and that after his death
the same lands (except the before excepted ones) descended to

Henry Beaumont, his son and heir, who, 1, Henry V., died thereof so seized, and that all the premises, except before excepted, descended to John Beaumont, his son and heir, being an infant, after whose death an office was found accordingly, and livery used by which it appeareth that seven manors, namely Farringmall O'Felmigh, Shemall, Lymalagoughe, Shelala, Gory, and Dipps (*sic*) were all the lands and dominions within those meares and bounds which were granted by virtue of that office seized into the king's hands, and so remained until the said John Beaumont sued his livery the 3rd of September, 13, Hen. VI., and that the said John, on the 7th of August, 24, Hen. VI., made a warrant of attorney unto John Cornwalleys, chief baron of the Exchequer, and John Townley, Esq., to let and set his lands within those meares and bounds, and all other his lands in Ireland and that he thereof died seized, and had issue two sons, John the eldest and William the second, both viscounts, and one daughter named Joan, which two sons died without issue of their bodies, and that the said Joan their sister was heir to William, who last died, and was married to John, Lord Viscount Lovell of Titchmarche, and that they had issue Francis, Viscount Lovell, attainted of treason by Act of Parliament in England, 1, Henry VII., and confirmed in Ireland: by which acts all his lands in England and Ireland were vested in the actual and real possession of the Crown, and so descended by mesne descents to Queen Elizabeth, and after her Majesty granted the manor of Dipps to the Earl of Ormond and the manor of Shilela to Sir Henry Harrington: and that the rest descended to our sovereign lord the king, as by the copy of the said office and inquisition ready to be shown doth appear.

On the 12th of February, in the 9th year of his Majesty's reign, upon motion of his Majesty's Council, before any patent was granted of these lands, it was ordered by the Court of Chancery that such as should be patentees from the king should be put into possession by injunction out of that court, without further motion of all those lands, within those meares and bounds, when the same shall be granted and the sheriff to continue them in possession from time to time, in which order the king's title and the seizure is expressed; after which the said inquisition so found at the Exchequer bar was transmitted into the Chancery and then several patents granted of several portions as followeth, namely,

	Acres.
To Sir Richard Cooke, knt., his Majesty's secretary	1,500
To Sir Lau. Esmond, knt., a servitor native of Wexford	1,500
To Sir Edwd. Fisher, knt., a servitor	1,500

To Francis Blundell, Esq. 1,000
To Conway Brady, the queen's footman 600
To Nicholas Kenny, escheator 500
To Wm. Parsons, surveyor. 1,000
To Sir Roger Jones, knt. 1,000
To Sir James Carroll, knt., Remembrancer in the Exchequer 1,000
To John Wingfield, Esq., servitor 1,000
To Sir Adam Loftus, knt. 1,000
To Sir R. Jacob, knt., his Majesty's solicitor . . . 1,000
To Fergus Græme 800
To Sir Rich. Wingfield, knt., marshal of the army . . 1,000
To William Marwood, Dep. Remembrancer . . . 1,000
To John Loghorn, Esq. 1,000
To Francis Blundell, Esq. 1,000
To Capt. Trevillian and Capt. Fortescue 2,000
To Thomas Hibbots, Esq. 1,000

Total 19,900

Proportions of the ancient possessioners, how many acres they formerly enjoyed, and how many are assigned unto them in the plot of the new plantation, and which of them had formerly patents from the Crown.

Ancient.	Acres.	Newly Assigned.
Sir Richard Masterson . .	7,060	Whereof of native lands 3,800, of crown lands 2,800, by collation of patent 460, and 2,400 assigned for his chiefries.
Michael Synnot . . .	300	240 of his former possessions.
Dowlin MacBrien, patent Morgan MacBrian, patent Edward MacDowlin, patent Dowlin MacMurrogh, patent	2,800	2,400 removed.
Griffin MacDonnel, patent .	350	200 of his former possessions.
Walter Plunket . . .	350	300 of his former possessions.
Donnel Spaniagh, patent .	400	300 of his former possessions, besides 320 by former patents.
Patrick Peppard . . .	1,400	1,252, whereof his former possessions about 700 acres, a place taken from him wherein he had made provision to build.
Dermot Cune	100	100, to hold his former lands.
Capt. Denis Vale . . .	400	900, whereof 400 old possessions.
Walter Synnot . . .	1,960	1,967, whereof 1,567 old possessions, and for his rents newly added 2,120.

APPENDIX. 273

Ancient.	Acres.	Newly Assigned.
James Synnot	865	865, whereof old 567.
John Synnot FitzRichard	545	005, whereof old 545.
John FitzPierce	556	410, whereof old 360.
Jasper Synnot	975	730, whereof old 390.
Robert Codd [1]	960	840 of his former possessions.
John Malone	486	486 of his former possessions.
Henry FitzPierce	340	240 of his former possessions.
William FitzWalter Synnot	120	240, whereof 120 former possessions.
Donnel Vally	525	370, whereof former 229.
Tiegue MacArt	330	220, whereof former 134.
Patrick Walsh	126	126 removed.
Tiegue O'Bolger	120	120 former possessions.
Ferdoragh McDermot	382	240 removed.
George O'Murchoe	200	100 of former possessions.
Donnel O'Doran	480	300 of former possessions.
Felix McDermot, patent	565	1,206 removed.
Murrogh McPharson	250	204 removed.
Gerard McJames	160	120 removed.
Phelim Mc da Moore	240	200 removed.
Redmond Mc da Moore	240	200 removed.
Tirlogh McMoriertagh		
Donogh McMoriertagh	400	300 removed.
Donnel McMoriertagh		
Owen McHugh, Ballach McDermot	300	300 removed.
John Esmond	100	100 removed.
Cullogh McBragh	120	100 removed.
Francis Wasser	200	187 removed.
Donnel McDonogh Enteskin (sic)	196	208, whereof formerly 80.
Owen McGerrald	200	127 removed.
Anthony Brisket	120	120 removed.
Edmund Duff McDermot	206	120 removed.
Owen MacHugh		
Ballagh McDonogh Oge	450	300 removed.
Donogh Oge	120	60 removed.
John Brazil	120	166 removed.
Mr. Browne	840	840 removed.
Nicholas Netterville	500	500 former possessions.
Thomas McKeogh	200	200.
Richard Cromwell (patentee)	300	300 former possessions.
Henry Walsh	220	130 former possessions.
Sir H. Wallop	1,010	1,100, whereof formerly 1,040.
Patrick Esmond	400	500.
John Murchoe	—	700.
Art McDermot	1,200	1,000 removed, but not yet set out.

[1] Anastatia Codd, the mother of Thomas Moore, was a member of this Wexford family. (V. Lord John Russell's Life of Moore.)

VOL. II. T

Edmond MacArt and Richard MacArt, patentees, have no allowance in this new plantation from the lands taken from them.

There are within the limits aforesaid more than the said proportions about 12,000 acres not yet granted, intended to be passed to martial men, who are to build upon the borders and fastnesses but cannot until some of the patentees be removed unto the lands assigned to them. The names of these martial men are Captain Dorrington, Captain Meares, Captain Pikeman, Captain Cawell, Captain Ackland, Captain Henry Fisher, Lieutenant John Fisher, Lieutenant Burroughs, Mr. Gillet, Mr. Waldrond, Lieutenant Stratford, Mr. Sherlock, Mr. Hashwell (*sic*). After the before mentioned patents granted the said patentees this 7th of May last obtained several injunctions to the sheriff of Wexford to put and continue them in their several portions of lands specified in these patents, which the sheriff accordingly performed, and did break open the doors of such as resisted and turned them out: yet, notwithstanding, upon submission divers of them were permitted to return to their houses again. And in harvest last the said sheriff by warrant from the Lord Deputy was assisted by the bailiffs of the new patentees to take up the fourth sheaf of their corn for the Michaelmas rent, in regard they were then to pay the king's rent; which fourth sheaf the patentees still detain, the natives being allowed to take the rest to their own use. Many such of the natives as formerly agreed to this new plantation now absolutely dislike thereof, and of the proportions assigned to them in lieu of their other possessions taken from them because that, as they affirm, their proportions assigned are not so many acres as they are rated to them, and because the acres taken from them are far more in number than they are surveyed at, which difference cannot be decided without a new survey, which some of the natives desire. All the ancient possessioners of the English race, and divers of the Irish have been always faithful to the Crown of England; but most of the Irish were rebels in the time of the great rebellion of Tyrone. Several of those to whom proportions are assigned are of the septs of the Kavenaghs and Murroghs, which held land in these limits before; Walter Synnot, Patrick Peppard, and Art MacDermot offer for themselves and the rest of the countries that they will pay such rents and perform the buildings and covenants to the king's majesty that these new un-undertakers are to perform, but they do altogether refuse to repay to the undertakers their charges disbursed about this plantation, which are rated at 9,000*l*. Every undertaker of 1,500 acres is to build a castle or stone house of 30 feet in length, 24 in breadth, and 30 feet high besides the battlements. Every undertaker of

APPENDIX. 275

1,000 acres is to build a castle or stone house of 24 feet square, and 30 feet high besides the battlements; and every undertaker of 500 acres is to build a strong bawn of lime and stone, these buildings to be made within four years after the patentees have quiet possession. The yearly rent reserved to the king is five pounds for every thousand acres granted to the English, and 6$l.$ 6$s.$ 8$d.$ for every thousand acres granted to the natives, except for those lands assigned to Sir Richard Masterson and Walter Synnot in lieu of their rents and chiefries out of the whole.

The rents yearly reserved and to be reserved to his Majesty if the plantation proceed will be 426$l.$ 18$s.$ 10½$d.$, and the country is discharged of the rents and chiefries granted to Sir Richard Masterson and Synnot, which are 210$l.$ per annum.

   Signed and sealed by
     Arthur Chichester. Humphrey Winche.
     Charles Cornwaleys. Roger Wilbraham.
     George Calvert.

D.

(*v.* vol. i. p. 29.)

PROJECT FOR THE PLANTATION OF LONGFORD, BY SIR OLIVER
ST. JOHN, LORD DEPUTY, SENT TO THE ENGLISH COUNCIL
MAY, 1618.[1]

The time of the year wearing away in the employment of the measurers in the county of Longford, I thought it agreeable to my duty at this time to make known to his Majesty and your Lordships what I conceive will be the issue of the work of that plantation, so honourable for his Majesty and so profitable for the present condition of this poor kingdom; preserving a more full relation thereof until the finishing of the advancement, at which time I shall be able to acquaint his Majesty and your Lordships with a more particular knowledge of the state thereof. The work being great and requiring a careful deliberation in the proceedings thereof, mine opinion is that the best (plan) is to settle Longford this year, and if the time will permit O'Carrol's country, and to leave the county of Leitrim, MacCoghlan's and O'Molloy's countries, being more factions than the first two, for the work of next year.

Concerning the county of Longford, of which I will now only make mention, having carefully looked into the former proceedings and the inquisitions and surveys of that county, I find that the whole consisteth of six baronies, esteemed at 50,000 acres. But I hope when the exact measure is taken it will come to more. I find that the lands of the bishops and clergy, the old globes and churches, the abbey lands and some patentees who have obtained grants in fee farm, will not come within the compact of the escheated lands, but must for the most part be set apart from all distributions. I find also two rents payable by that county, the one of 200*l.* to the heirs of Sir Nicholas Malby, being the ancient composition of that county, the other of 120 beeves, being the ancient rent payable to the castle of Granard. These two rents are needful to be compounded for and a compensation of land for them taken out of the whole county, otherwise the undertakers will be

[1] *Carew MSS. Lambeth, vol.* 613, *p.* 83.

subject to the exactions and distresses of other men, which would be very inconvenient.

It will be needful also, that there be taken out some quantity of land, to be bestowed by his Majesty for the bettering of the livings of the poor incumbents of the parish churches, according to that which was allowed in the plantation of Wexford. And in like sort a portion of lands to be bestowed upon a corporate town and for the creating and maintenance of free schools; all which must be deducted before I can give a guess what the remainder will be, that shall be left for the distribution. For albeit the king's advisers are of opinion that some of the grants of the patentees are questionable, yet I suppose his Majesty's purpose is not to have them for the most part questioned, but either to let each of them have their lands, or to give them other lands in lieu thereof.

The general contents of the whole country and the deductions formerly mentioned being thus compared, I am of opinion as well upon the consideration of the former surveys taken in the late Lord Deputy's government, and by the former judgment of this begun advancement, that out of the remainder there may be set by for the placing of undertakers 12,000 acres, being, as I guess, a fourth part or somewhat more; in the distribution whereof, I humbly propound to his Majesty and the Lords, how needful it will be that the natives of all those lands as are so to be disposed of to undertakers may be bestowed upon such servitors remaining in this kingdom as have well served in the wars, and have had no land at all given them, and those to be chosen and nominated by the Lord Deputy, not in great quantities, as was done in Ulster, and in the late plantation of Wexford, but in smaller proportions, as in 200, or 300, or 400 acres. By which manner of plantation the buildings will be more, the bodies of men in greater quantities, and consequently they and their posterity, by their continual residence, be a sure continuance of the plantation, and a strong instrument for the settling of peace and civility in those parts, and become more profitable for the commonwealth, and yet his Majesty's rents continue the same; whereas if those lands should be distributed in greater proportions, as 1,000, or 2,000, or 3,000 acres, the building would go on more slowly, the country would be left more weak, by reason of the large wastes, the freeholders more scarce and the Irish less kept in awe by them. And for the residue to be bestowed upon the British undertakers, I humbly propound that their portions may be smaller, and the undertakers more in number than they were in Ulster and Wexford. For now Irish land is more valuable, and the county of Longford adjoining on the English pale more safe and commodious to be planted. And experience hath taught us that in Ulster the undertakers' buildings have not been so readily performed as was expected, nor the British brought over in sufficient numbers to inhabit those great scopes, neither hath the number of freeholders been planted in those lands that was covenanted by those undertakers, and such as have been made freeholders were held at such high rents as they are not left able to do the service of freeholders. And this way of making smaller undertakers holding only of the Crown was the ancient manner of planting Irish countries, as may appear by the multitude of castles in the English pale, and the counties of Tipperary, Limerick, Kilkenny, and all the counties where the old English do yet keep their footing; that course was held in the late plantation of Leix and Offaly, where many English undertakers had freeholds granted unto them from the Crown of small quantities of land. And their posterity continued there freeholders still, and are very useful, as well in times of war as in times of peace, and it is very probable that in this very county of Longford the granting of great proportions to the English at their first planting there was the principal cause it was so soon overcome by the Irish. I do also humbly propound as a matter of special consideration in this work, that the undertakers may be placed in the most uninhabited parts of the country, as towards the county of Leitrim, Cavan, and Roscommon, and so to leave the natives to inhabit that part that lieth nearest the English pale, where their ancient borders do still remain, and the rather for that the natives now inhabiting that part are reasonably reclaimed by civil education, and many of them have built good stone houses where they dwell. And for the full setting of those lands I humbly propound that I may be warranted to grant estates in fee farm as well to natives as to undertakers, receiving from the natives for every acre of twenty-one foot to the pole twopence sterling, and from the undertaker one penny sterling, in respect of the charges of his building, and that where the towns or cartrons do consist for the most part of bogs, barren mountains, and unprofitable wood, the surveyor to have power in the making up of their particulars to lay those bogs as an addition to the towns, and to set a rent upon the same by the acre, at one rate to the natives, and at a lesser rate to the undertakers, according to the goodness and quality thereof.

That every proportion of under 1,000 acres may hold of the castle in Dublin of free and common soccage, and every proportion of 1,000 acres, or above to hold of the king's majesty *in capite*, for in the old plantation of the pale all the undertakers and their heirs do hold of the king their proportions by the greater or smaller *capite*.

That every undertaker and native of 1,000 acres and above be bound within three years to build a castle of 30 feet in length, 20 feet in breadth, and 25 feet in height; the castle to be built of stone and lime or brick and lime, and compassed in with a bawn of 300 feet in compass of stone and lime or brick and lime. And every undertaker of two acres, and so to 1,000 acres, to be bound to build a strong house of stone and lime or brick and lime, within a bawn of 200 feet in compass. And every undertaker of quantities under 600 acres to build a good house of stone and lime or brick with lime, the natives of those two last named proportions to be left to themselves.

That every proportion of 1,000 acres and above may have a manor with a Court Baron and power to create tenures and a (*illegible*). And every proportion of 600 acres, and so to 1,000, to have a manor with a Court Baron, and power to create tenures. The proportions under 600 acres to have neither.

That among all the undertakers and natives there may be grants made of six market-towns in the most convenient places, and no more; and fairs in so moderate a number as may stand with respect and convenience, and rents to be reserved upon both. That no native shall have granted unto him less than 100 acres, except very few, and upon good consideration, and none at all under 60 acres. That every undertaker and native that is bound to build may have liberty to take a proportionable quantity of timber and other material for his building in any place within the plantation, by warrant from the Lord Deputy, with a limitation of the time of that liberty.

That every ancient pretended possessor who shall be now made a freeholder shall depart with at least a fourth of the lands he formerly possessed, for the accommodation of the plantation, besides a rateable proportion towards the compounding of the two rents before mentioned, of Sir Nicholas Malby and Sir Francis Shaen. That every undertaker and native shall content himself to enjoy his proportion, according to the number of acres laid down by the new admeasurement, without any questioning of the old measures. That every undertaker and native shall be bound to make his undertenants build together in townships, with a *nomine penæ* for those that shall suffer their tenants to build dispersedly.

That the tenants may be tied with a proviso of forfeiture not to sell their lands in fee simple or fee tail, or lease them above forty years or their lives to any of the Irish, lest the old lords should grow great again. That the State may have power to place such of the (*illegible*) natives of the country as shall not have lands attached unto them upon the lands of any undertakers or natives, who are to have leases for 21 years or for their lives, at such reasonable rents as shall be set down by the Lord Deputy and Council, whereby such as cannot be made freeholders may be provided for here to remain.

That every undertaker and native be bound to sow yearly a quantity of hemp, according to his Majesty's directions in that behalf, and that proportionally according to the quantity of each man's proportion. That the Lord Deputy may be warranted to grant a quantity of lands to each parish church for the bettering of the living of the poor incumbents, as was done in Wexford. That a corporate town be established in some convenient place within the plantation, and 100 acres to be allowed to the burgesses that shall undertake it, with warrant to make a grant of a corporation with such name and such immunities and privileges as were granted to the corporations in the escheated lands of Ulster, and that some lands may be allotted for the maintenance of free schools. That the natives be tied by a proviso of forfeiture neither to take upon them the name of O'Farrell, nor to yield or maintain or set up that name by giving it rent, cutting, or service, nor to divide their lands by gavelkind.

That the whole charge of admeasuring the country and other necessary accounts for the finishing and settling of those lands be borne by the natives and undertakers by equal contributions.

E.

(*v.* vol. i. p. 30.)

ARGUMENTS OF NATIVES AGAINST LONGFORD PLANTATION.[1]

Motives to prove that it is more for his Majesty's honour, profit, and service to confer the lands in the county of Longford on the natives than to dispose thereof by way of plantation.

1. For his honour : It will be taken most grievous, not only by the inhabitants of the said county, but by all the subjects of Ireland, that a title of 300 years ago should be now discovered to take away any man's land, by which course no man can be secure of his estate, for in that space their patents and credences might be lost.

2. The composition by her late Majesty in the 13th year of her reign with the said natives, that in compensation of 400 marks to be yearly paid to her and her successors that the said county should by this patent pass to them and their heirs, by this plantation will be violated. And if it were with a common person the covenant had been made in law and honour, he had been bound to perform it. And the like covenant now made with all the rest of the subjects of the said realm was performed unto them. And to exclude only Longford were most injurious. And for further proof of this assertion his Majesty in July last sent his letters to the Lord Deputy of Ireland, commanding him to pass to all his subjects of Connaught and Thomond all their land by letters patent, according the like indentures of composition, signifying by his said letters that he was bound by law and in honour to perform with them, and so by a like reason with Longford.

3. The Earl of Devonshire's word, being then Lord Deputy, given to the natives for their lives, will be by this disposal of a plantation not performed, and the meanest undergovernor's word in the kingdom heretofore hath been inviolably kept, and now, if it be broken, it must make us distrustful, and be a touch of dishonour.

4. The benefits of his Majesty's Council several letters for passing the land to the natives, wherein he specially noted that he was

[1] *S. P. I. vol.* 233, *p.* 50, *Rolls House.*

bound to convey it to them, is not performed. Yet those letters were granted upon great deliberation of the Lords of the Council, and after consultation and a full debate of the matter were drawn up by Sir Thomas Lake, Sir Robert Gardiner, and Sir Roger Wilbraham by direction of the Lords.

5. James O'Farrell, one of the chiefest men in the country, who hath great possessions there, and hath served the Crown in France, Flanders, and Ireland, died; his son is very young, and his Majesty's ward, under his protection, and derives his estate by letters patent. His Majesty in honour cannot dispose of the land during his ward's minority, to dispose of others and to take part of their land for rent, where the ward ought to contribute, is not just but ruinous.

Secondly, to confer the land upon the natives is most for his Majesty's profit.

1. It is to be considered what rent his Majesty is to get by the plantation: which it will appear is not more than 100*l.* per an., which also must be laid upon the natives as more aggravation.

2. Lands according to Lord Chichester's project must be taken from the natives to buy the rent beeves of Granard, being 120 beeves per annum, to the assignees of Sir Francis Shaen nominally. But the truth, as it shall appear, is that the assignees of Sir Francis are not known and are uncertain, but that this land is intended for Sir James Hamilton, who ought not to have it. And if he ought, yet there is but a lease for thirty years yet to come thereof, and of the manor of Granard, yielding to his Majesty 87*l.* per annum. And the portion in the Crown (*illegible*) a small recompense to be given for the lease, yet his Majesty will lose the inheritance of the manor of Granard, and the said rent by the plantation. It will be objected that Sir Francis Shaen had his Majesty's letters to have the fee farm. To this we answer that the letters never took effect, and that his highness was deceived in the grant. And even if the grant did pass to Sir Francis his heirs ought to have it, for whom it is not now intended, neither do his heirs sue for it, or know of it, but it is Sir James Hamilton that must have it all.

Admitting that the fee farm was passed to Sir Francis, yet that no recompense was given for it, for it shall be proved it was ever had by coercion or distress, by bringing of soldiers hither, and there is no account to prove that his Majesty or his lessor ought to have it, and it can be proved that the inhabitants brought several actions at the common law to try the title, but they were not suffered to proceed in them. And although the rent were lawfully taken, yet if the last office taken before the Lord Chichester be of force, and that it entitleth his Majesty to the land, it shall be made most apparent that the lessor or his assignee hath no right to the rent beeves, and therefore ought to have no right to the land.

3. Land according to the plantation project must be taken from the natives and given to Malby to buy up 200*l.* rent per annum. But it is to be noted that the rent was only entailed to the heirs male of the body of Sir Nicholas Malby, of whom there is only (*illegible*) and the reversion is in the Crown, so that the (*illegible*) recompense ought to be given, and the king may (*illegible*) to give a fee simple for an estate in tail. And it can be proved that about the 6th year of the king's reign this rent was sold unto his Majesty and surrendered in his Chancery in England, for which his highness gave valuable consideration, yet never received the rent. If those that then sold it had no estate therein, they deceived his Majesty, and ought to restore the recompense.

Admitting his Majesty hath no right to the rent by the conveyance, yet if the last office be of force, wherein Malby was one of the jury, it can be made most apparent that he hath no right to the rent, and by consequence ought to have no land in recompense. And furthermore, as the Lord Chichester hath been careful to give the opinion of the king's counsel of his Majesty's right to the said county, it were expedient to have their opinion whether the king also ought not to have the said rent.

4. The Lord of Delvin must have land, and it is most apparent that the letters patent granted unto him by his Majesty of lands in the said county were surrendered, and that his Majesty gave him Crown lands in lieu of them which he enjoyeth. And these Crown lands were granted unto him to the intent he should restore the lands contained in his former patent to the natives, and now to demand them again is most strange. And if he sues for other land not contained in the former patent, it is for others besides himself, from whom he hath private compensation, and by his countenance seeketh to serve them. Abbey lands he hath by letters patent which he ought to enjoy.

5. Five hundred acres of land shall be discovered to lie in his Majesty's grant by good apparent title lately accrued that shall not offend any native, and that his Majesty by the indenture of composition, letters, or otherwise is not tied to give away, but undoubtedly hath in his own grant which may be granted to satisfy the (*illegible*) of his service.

6. The project of Lord Chichester intendeth to have land given to buy up this rent, whereby great possessions are to be taken from the natives, is fully satisfied by the observations aforesaid, for as there was no rent there is no land needed to buy it, and also his

project to take land from them for service is supplied (shown that it can be satisfied another way). By these means the benefit of his Majesty's indentures, his Majesty's word and letters, and all things else are performed to the natives to their full contentment and settlement, and his Majesty's revenues will be increased 800*l*. per annum (which was the old rent intended) by reserving so much upon the new patent to the natives. His Majesty in right ought to have that, and it was nimbly paid formerly to others.

Thirdly, it is most for his Majesty's service to confer the land on the natives.

1. By giving the land to undertakers his Majesty preserveth but some servitors, and will lose the love and hearts of many of his poor subjects.

2. By taking the land from those that served him truly all through the last rebellion, and not performing his covenant and promise with them, he will make them desperate.

3. If these lands be taken from them, they being no tradesmen or having any other means to exist, they will commit all manner of villanies.

4. All the natives of the North are discontented by the last plantation amongst them, and it is much to be feared that upon the least occasion and advantage they will do mischief. It were therefore not convenient that those in the west should also be discontented, and the eyes of all the nation are fixed on this business of Longford and on the usage of its natives, that ever for the most part have done the king good service.

No date. Endorsed 'Lord Deputy Chichester revoked Nov. 29th, 1615.'

PLANTATIONS OF LONGFORD AND ELY O'CARROL.

Lord Deputy and Council to the Lords (E.P.C.),
November 8th, 1619.[1]

It may please your most Honourable Lordships. So soon as we received his Majesty's pleasure and directions for the intended plantations of Longford and Ely O'Carrol we fell into consideration how we might begin and proceed with the care and diligence the work required, but find some present interruption, partly through want of a competent number of the principal commissioners who

[1] *S. P. I. vol.* 235, *p.* 44, *Rolls House.*

were not resident here in the late time of vacation and specially because we could not draw together the chief men of those parts until the finishing of their harvest, which in this country is seldom done until towards All Hallowtide. But upon summons given them they have lately presented themselves before us; since the 28th of last (month) those of Longford submitted by an instrument under their hands and some four days after those of Ely O'Carrol did the like.

The O'Farrells, who are those of Longford, at the first made show of backwardness, not in dislike of the deduction of a fourth part of their lands, which they all knew to be his Majesty's pleasure and full resolution, but in that they complained the remaining three parts were not only subject to bear the whole charge of the composition for the 120 beeves belonging to the manor of Granard and 200*l.* a year claimed by Malby, but they also doubted that some other persons of quality each pretending to lands in that country might procure favour and exemption from bearing (a share of it) with them.

We treated as fairly as we could, and bestowing much good language upon them in the end they yielded and with cheerfulness. But not without a promise from us to become suitors for them to his Majesty that no more charges might be imposed on them nor land taken from them than is contained in his Majesty's instructions. Now may it please your Lordships to understand that there are several letters are now come to me the Deputy, for lands to be passed to some that have obtained the special favour not only to have them freed from the deduction of a fourth part, but with a direction that the undertakers shall nevertheless be fully provided for, according unto the quantities assigned unto them, and the supply of this bounty is to fall upon the natives' three-fourths, which will become the more grievous unto them. These letters I have hitherto concealed from the people, and the truth is, that as the letters preceded the instructions in date, his Majesty is as yet at liberty to do as he pleases, and they beseech him to mention their engagement to the natives to his Majesty and to let them know his pleasure therein.

As for Ely O'Carrol, the same is not liable to such charges as Longford is, being free from any compositions or burdens more than the deduction of the fourth part, and the assignment for glebes, allowances, and admeasurements and the necessary expenses for settlement of the plantation for all which the undertakers are to contribute with them. Therefore for his Majesty's service and their own good, considering it, Ely O'Carrol, a county far separated from Longford, we would wish the erection of a corporation amongst them, as well as in Longford, with the same privileges and assignments of 100 acres of land, the place to be at Ballendoragh, which is a narrow passage or strait that openeth out of that part of Leinster into Ormond and Tipperary; parts of so evil haunts as that it hath been found necessary to lay a garrison at the said Ballindoragh, which hath this two years been commanded by Francis Acland, lieutenant to Sir Henry Docwra, who is a sufficient active man, and hath been so fortunate in his employment that he has well abated the number of malefactors in those parts, whereof divers have been by him cut off and many forced into the hands of justice, to the great contentment of the country and preservation of the poor thereof. And if his Majesty and your Lordships shall approve of this proposition for a corporation, we would also wish that it were countenanced by the residence of some commander that might continue there in command of a company, there is there already a little strong castle, which may be to great good purpose maintained and preserved without charge to his Majesty, if 500 acres of land were laid to it, and a lease thereof granted (at the same rent the undertakers pay) to the commander of the fort for twenty-one years if he live so long. And now that the natives have made their submission, we will enter into the main work, one of the first parts thereof being to compound for the 120 beeves and the 200*l.* rentcharge. The one we shall soon do, but the other is encumbered with difficulty, by reason of young Malby's nonage, and his mother the Lady Sidley's absence in England, who hath an estate for life in the said rent. Besides we have no means to inform ourselves of the facts of the composition that is said to have been already made by his Majesty for the same. Because it was made in England and the several pensions given in lieu thereof are paid out of the Exchequer there (as we hear) to Sir James Crichton, Sir James Hamilton, and Sir James Sempill, who are now in England or some of them, for whom it may please your Lordships to send or cause such other as you shall think fit to confer with them and give your Lordships satisfaction therein.

In the meantime for clearing the way to our present proceedings, which might otherwise be hindered by this particular, we have resolved to set apart a proportion of land equivalent for the redemption of this 200*l.* per annum which may be hereafter disposed of according to occasion.

These things we have esteemed it our duty to acquaint your Lordships with, and do beseech your (*illegible*) for his Majesty's and your Lordships' further pleasure in the same. And so craving pardon we humbly take our leave from his Majesty's castle of Dublin, this 8th of November, 1619, your honourable Lordships in humbleness to be commanded,

OLIVER ST. JOHN.
AD. LOFTUS. *Canc.*
POWERSCOURT.
HEN. DOCWRA.
WM. JONES.

DOM. SARSFIELD.
WM. METHWOLD.
JOHN KING.
DUDLEY NORTON.
FR. ANNESLEY.

F.

(v. vol. i. p. 31.)

THERE ARE IN THIS COUNTY OF LONGFORD 142 NATIVES UNTO WHOM LANDS ARE ASSIGNED, THEIR NAMES AND PROPORTIONS ARE AS FOLLOWS.[1]

Earl of Westmeath	2917
Roger Farrall	2148
Faghney Farrall	2605
James Farrall	2458
Robert Farrall	1451
Fergus Farrall	1400
Lisagh Duffe Farrell	682
William Farrell	1039
Edmund Reogh Farrell	606
Sir Christopher Nugent	1102
John Farrell	768
Maurice FitzGerald	687
Thomas Nugent	618
Richard Nugent	609
Gerrott Nugent	644
Oliver FitzGerald	732
Kearagh MacLisagh	637
Faghney MacCormack and Gerrot Farrell	785
Gerald FitzGerald	697
Edmund Nugent	701
Nathaniel Fox	947
Edward Dowdall	718
Lisagh McJames	519
Lisagh McGillemor	561
Brian Melaghlin	120
Patrick McHubert	99
Gerrot MacShane	216
Gerald MacRory	379

[1] *Harris MSS. Library of Royal Dublin Society.*

APPENDIX. 289

Richard MacJames	236
Connell MacMorragh	192
Lisagh MacCormac and Daniel MacCormac McBrian	160
Gerald MacKedy	208
Tiegue MacConnell	110
Donnell MacWilliam	64
Brian MacEdmund	311
Gerrot MacHubbert	111
Cahill MacHubbert	86
Gillernauer O'Kenny	62
Tirlogh MacVry	63
Edmund Nugent MacEdward	163
Donogh Farrell	164
Gerrot MacMelaghlin	124
Brian Duie MacHubbert	100
Connell MacMoragh Moyle	115
Shane McHubbert and Faghney McHubbert	180
Pierse McMelaghlin	89
James McMelaghlin	136
Maha MacShane	83
Brian O'Quin	115
Edmund McHubbert	127
Gerrot Murtagh	493
Patrick MacKedy	200
James Buie MacMorogh	219
William Oge Farrell	60
Morgan Farrall	263
Tirlogh McDonnell	65
Brian McTiegue and Donogh MacBrian	155
Edmund MacHubbert	77
Hugh McEdmund	92
Donnell MacJames	74
Nicholas Archbold	411
Robert Gayner	420
William McDermott	400
Thomas McTiegue	151
James Nugent	124
Nicholas McDermott	92
Earl of Kildare	424
Keadagh MacLisagh	482
Hubert Dillon	853
Robert Dillon	406
Morrogh McMelaghlin	100

VOL. II. U

Geoffrey McBrian	119
Donogh McTiegue	107
William Ferrall	106
Donnell McDermott	80
Thomas Nugent	62
Edmund MacBuie and Richard MacTirlagh	97
Edmund MacRichard	92
Edmund MacMorogh	60
John MacEdmund	83
Cahil MacFergus	80
Hugh MacCormack O'Duffe	90
Geoffrey MacRichard	60
Fergus MacCahil	70
Lisagh Oge O'Farrel	60
Shane MacHugh	79
James MacHubbert	158
Connell MacMorrogh McEdmund	108
Bryan McKay	70
Fergus McPhelim and Hugh McGenor	231
John Quin	60
Robert and Phelim Quin	100
Lord Dillon	415
Christopher Brown	101
James Nangle	98
William MacVry	116
Thomas Kearnon	323
Richard McDonogh	85
Shane McTirlagh	215
William McDonnell	179
Edmund Dillon	599
Edmund MacCormack	278
Conell MacIrell	420
James MacWilliam	313
Tiegue MacCormack	265
Garratt Nugent	577
Oliver Nugent	162
Cahill MacHugh	280
John Farrell	120
Tirlogh Farrell	162
James MacTirlogh Cormac O'Farrell	120
Edward MacBrian	106
Rory MacCahil	95
Theobald Delamore (*sic*)	210

APPENDIX. 291

Maurice Dillon	800
James McTiegue	50
Connor Farrell	811
Carberry McShane	207
Richard FitzGerald	171
Richard Delamare	166
Hugh MacTirlogh	160
James FitzGerrott	214
Edward Nugent	892
Anlon MacKegan and Patrick MacKegan	173
Patrick O'Heiraght	180
Cormac MacKay	119
Faghney MacRory	107
Shane MacRichard	199
Kedagh McConnell	128
Andrew Nugent	885
Walter Nugent	120
Gerrott McJames	103
William McDonnogh	156
Murrogh McTirlogh	104
Daniel McDermott	110

Both the natives and the undertakers complain that the measurers have abused (*i.e.* deceived) them in giving up their survey of more acres in every proportion than there are to be found.

The case of one Tirlogh Farrell is much to be pitied, being the only Protestant of his name, and having, as is said, lands sufficient to make him a freeholder, all deductions being made, hath notwithstanding no lands assigned to him, as his own petition will show, which we offer to your consideration on his behalf.

There is no hemp sown by any in this county or in Leitrim, though his Majesty directed it by his instructions.

THE ARTICLES AND CONDITIONS TO BE INSERTED IN THE LEASES WHICH ARE TO BE MADE TO THE LESSEES IN THE PLANTATION OF LONGFORD, APRIL 5, 1620.[1]

1. The demises or leases are to be for three lives, or for one-and-twenty years, at the election and choice of the lessees, and no longer.

[1] *Harris MSS., Library of Royal Dublin Society.*

2. The lessors and lessees are to treat together for the rents of every acre, and in case they cannot agree, then two commissioners are to repair to the land to be demised, and are upon view thereof to assess the rent, near to the value of the land as it may be, *bonâ fide*, to be let for: and the lessors and lessees are to contribute equally for the commissioners' trouble and charges, while they shall be at that business.

3. For non-payments of rents at the feasts of Easter and Michaelmas, or within fifteen days after the said feasts, the lessor may distrain, and for non-payment after forty days the lessor may, at his election, re-enter to avoid the lease.

4. The lessees shall build their houses in town roods or streetways, and not dispersed, and each lessee to build a chimney in his dwelling-house, and to make a convenient garden and plant an orchard.

5. Each lessee to sow a quantity of hempseed proportionally to the number of acres he shall hold.

6. The demises or leases to be only of acres, without making mention of cartrons.

7. Every lessee holding sixty acres shall within four years enclose ten acres of his portion, and set in the banks of the enclosure quicksetts or frith, and so rateably each lessee of lesser proportion.

8. No lessee is to hold any parcel of land where he makes any claim or title, or whereof he was formerly possessed, unless the lessor himself will admit the same.

9. No lessee shall alien or do away his interest in his lease without the lessor's consent.

G.

(*v.* vol. i. p. 32.)

To the Right Honourable the Commissioners authorised by his Majesty to hear the Grievances of Ireland.[1]

A Memorial and true Information to their Honours of part of their grievances and the destruction done upon the most part of the poor natives and inhabitants of the county of Longford, in the time of the late plantation thereof, by the comitties and surveyors appointed for the said county as followeth:—

First, some of these comitties (*sic*) were their own carvers, implotting land for themselves and others, contrary to his Majesty's instructions.

Item, one Robert Kenedy, that was clerk to Sir William Parsons, Knt., Bart., chief surveyor and one of the said comitties, hath three cartrons of land in the barony of Maidower in the said county, viz. the cartron of Lymfaighter,[2] the cartron of Boherbay, the cartron of More, the two cartrons of Bernenuer, and the cartron of Belladrama, and the wood called Grillaghgarda and Clonfraigh, that containeth forty acres of arable land, or thereabouts, in these woods.

Item, the said Robert's brother, John Kennedy, clerk in the king's receipt, hath six cartrons in the quadrat of the county called Moitragh near the town of Longford.

Item, one Robert Dillon of Kanerstown, in the county of Westmeath, one of the aforesaid comitties for the county of Longford, having before the plantation but one cartron of land there, hath now four large cartrons, in the barony of Rathcline, as more at large shall appear by the said Robert's patent past of it, and other parcels of land, every cartron thereof he setteth at 10*l.* yearly rent.

Item, one Mr. Hubert Dillon, of Killireninen, in the county of Westmeath, gent., being not a native or undertaker, nor having any

---

[1] *Harris MSS., Library of Royal Dublin Society.*

[2] The spelling of Irish names and words, always bad in documents written by Englishmen in old times, is in this petition so bad and absurd as to make any attempt to correct it useless.

land by inheritance or purchase within that county of Longford, but one demi-cartron, hath obtained of the said comitties four good cartrons in the said county of Longford; Mr. Robert Dillon, the aforesaid comittie, gave the said Hubert an exchange in a town called Bruenmore, in the county Westmeath.

Item, Sir Christopher Nugent, Knt., deceased, that was one of the said comitties, hath applotted for himself a thousand acres of arable land within Longford county, as more at large shall appear, by the said Sir Christopher's particular of the premises, notwithstanding the said Sir Christopher's continual oath before divers gentlemen of the said county, that he would never demand or take a foot of the said natives' lands for himself, or his posterity, but one cartron he had before the plantation there, the which thousand acres he passed as inheritance to his second son.

Item, Mr. Harry Crofton, one of the said comitties, having never a foot of land in that county before the plantation thereof, hath now the cartron of Clonsherin, the cartron of Agheneskiagh, the demi-cartron of Turcowagh, in the barony of Moydore, also he hath the cartron of Kiltevriavagh, as shall appear more at large by his particular that he hath, every cartron of the premises he setteth at 8*l.* a year besides duties.

Item, Mr. Thomas Nugent of Collamber, Esq., one of the said comitties, hath an augmentation of four or five cartrons of the poor natives' lands, in a quadrat of the county called Killecowara, in the barony of Ardagh, and in Clinhena, in the barony of Longford, as may appear more at large by the said Thomas's patent of the premises (if any by) (*sic*).

Item, it is so that at the time of the meeting, or making acres of the whole county of Longford by survey, the eight or nine surveyors that continued more than a quarter of a year in performing that service, accompanied all that time to the number of thirty-six soldiers, who live together, and the said soldiers with their horses and four men, or horseboys, with every one of the said surveyors, lived at the charge of the poor country, taking meat and drink and lodging, and 8*d.* per day sterling beside for every one of the said soldiers, notwithstanding that the king's majesty did give the said surveyors their charges in ready money all that time; moreover, when all the natives and undertakers had their patents out of all the lands in the county, every one paid according to his proportion of land a penny ster. for every acre he had, in lieu of the charge of the said surveyors, and in recompense of the charge and service of the comitties appointed by my Lord Deputy for the said county, which charge was named the admeasurement money.

APPENDIX. 295

Item, at the second time the said surveyors returned to the said county to apportion the lands between party and party, besides their meat and drink and lodging for themselves, their horses and horse-boys, took 3*d.* an acre from each party.

Item, the whole number of the poor natives of this country do find themselves grieved in manner following, viz. where they have been formerly charged with 200*l.* ster., composition rent to her late Majesty Queen Elizabeth, that resigned the same to Malby and his heirs, and with another rentcharge of the king's that Sir Francis Shaen in his lifetime did hold, viz. 100*l.* or twenty-six towns, named of the manor of Granard: for all which rentcharge at the planting of the county there was plotted and given of the natives' land the number of one hundred cartrons, or thereabouts, which I doubt not is set, or may be set,[1] at above 400*l.* yearly rent, besides that the glebe lands and lands plotted for corporations and forts, comes to near a hundred more cartrons or above; notwithstanding that the said poor natives had not left them, for the most part, the fourth part of their former possessions, of all the whole county, the which course, as they conceive by all credible accounts, is contrary to the king's gracious meaning, to take any more of their lands from the natives of the county but the fourth part. In regard thereof, they feel it grievous and too great a charge, after the losses aforesaid, and more that comes not yet in this reckoning, to be charged with 2½*d.* in every acre of arable land they have left them, and a halfpenny in every acre of unprofitable land, and that the said lands being given unto the Lord of Longford and Mr. Malby for the said composition, the said inhabitants do find themselves nothing eased thereby, but all charged upon them, as well as upon them that got the said allowance and their rent raised to the sum of 800*l.* or 900*l.*, and odd money, beside the land given in lieu of the said old rents aforesaid.

Item, James MacWilliam O'Farrell of Ballinathan of the said county, gent. and native, having a good scope of lands of his own there by inheritance, made means to Robert Dillon, aforesaid comittie, by whose means he, the said James, lost no part of the said lands in any of the deductions aforesaid. And by the recital of the said James's wife her husband paid the said Robert 20*l.* for the same.

Item, one Edmund MacHobert O'Farrell, gent. and native, had by inheritance eight or nine cartrons of land in the said county, in a quadrat thereof called Callo, and was driven to give the said Mr.

---

[1] In Ireland the word 'set' was, and often is still used for 'let' by landlords and tenants treating about farms and houses. The same expression was used in Lancashire.

Robert Dillon, comittie, a house and other private gratifications in money, having gotten but three small cartrons in lieu of the said eight.

Item, Gillernowe O'Kenny of Gurteenbuie, in the said county, having but a cartron of land in mortgage, which was divided between him and three of his brethren, he got a cartron and one quarter of a cartron of land augmentation by the means of the foresaid comittie Robert Dillon, who received by other private gratifications of the said Gillernowe two beefs and two vessels called Cans of Honey.

Item, Sir Richard Browne, knight, baronet, being not a native undertaker, nor having any land in the said county but what he holdeth by his lady wife's jointure, hath gotten by favour or other means the following lands there, the two cartrons of Bellanathmor, the cartron of Corelaggan in the barony of Moydaner, more in the barony of Longford, the cartron of Briskill, the cartron of Clonnethlie, the cartron of Clonalsan, in Literkiragh one quarter of a cartron, in (*illegible*) and Enane two quarters of a cartron, and the third part of a cartron in Crodrum, the which lands the said Sir Richard did pass in a native's name in a patent, who had but one quarter of a cartron, which native was his gossip called Kedagh McConnell O'Farrell of Brekagh in the said county, gent. Every cartron of the aforesaid land the said Sir Richard doth set for 8*l.* ster. yearly rent.

Item, Morogh MacIriel O'Farrell, native, had but five cartrons of land before the plantation in a quandrat of the county called Callo, viz. in Castlebegg, and by whatever struggling he came thereto hath now an augmentation of five more, the which ten that he now hath is plotted to him in a choice land in the said county called Montergeolgan.

Item, Thomas McTiegue O'Farrell, a base born, that was never born to have any land, and a traitor in the late great rebellion, hath gotten one cartron of land, about the town of Granard in the said county, containing above six score acres by survey.

Item, one Pierse McMelaghlin O'Farrell, that had never a foot of land before the plantation, hath gotten four cartrons in the quandrate of the county called Moitra, the said Pierse being a traitor in the late great rebellion. Four cartrons granted thus a traitor.

Item, one Nathaniel Fox of Rathrenagh, within the said county of Longford, hath gotten an augmentation of the natives' lands about the said town of Rathrenagh, to the number of ten or fifteen cartrons over and above his former possessions in that county.

Item, one Robert MacIessiagh O'Farrell of Glyn, within the said county, Esquire, hath gotten of the poor natives' lands there, and an augmentation allowed him to the number of 800 acres of arable land, and a watercourse of a mill in Ballincaso in the said county, the inheritance of one William Farrell of Ballintobber, Esquire, without giving any allowance for it to the said William.

Item, one Robert McLisagh O'Farrell of Ballicor, in the said county, gent., hath gotten allowance of the said committies of the poor natives' lands to the number of six cartrons, without any deduction thereout, he being in open rebellion in the great general rebellion in Captain Farrell's company.

Item, Connell MacMergagh O'Farrell of Balleclare, within the said county, gent., having by inheritance there but one cartron, had allowance gotten him by the said committies of two cartrons more and two woods without any deduction, he having been also in open rebellion aforesaid.

Item, one Rory MacCahil O'Farrell of Ballinbuien, a poor freeholder, having but three quarters of a cartron before the plantation, hath gotten of the said committies an augmentation of two of the best cartrons and the largest in the territory of Moitra or Clanhue over and above within the said county.

Item, one Donough Duff McBrian of the territories of Clanhue, in the barony of Longford, in the said county, a poor freeholder, having but three demi-quarters of a cartron in the said quandrat, got of the said committies half a cartron and a demi-quarter augmentation over and above his said demi-quarters.

Item, one Edmund MacHubert O'Farrell of Moniskelagh, in the barony of Granard, within the said county, a poor freeholder, having but one cartron of twenty-four acres by survey, hath the same of the said committies without any deduction, he being in actual rebellion in the general revolt.

Item, one Richard McDonogh O'Farrell of Kilnemaddagh, in the aforesaid barony, having but one cartron in the said town of Kilnemaddagh of eighty-five acres by survey, did obtain the said cartron of the said committies without any deduction, he being also in actual rebellion in the last revolt.

Item, one Tirlogh McDonogh O'Farrell of Cavan, in the said barony of Granard and county of Longford, having by inheritance but as much as sixty acres within that barony, did obtain of the said committies the number of thirty-three acres in addition to his said three score acres without any deduction.

Item, it is so that one Edmund Nugent of Roconellan, in the county of Westmeath, gent., learned in the law, lately deceased; in the plantation time of the said county of Longford did in his rental name two cartrons, the which two Faghny O'Farrell of the

Moat, in the said county Longford, did also name in his rentals; so as it came to pass, in order to give them both satisfaction, or for some better cause known to the committies, where the (*illegible*) was but for two cartrons, either (*i.e.* each) of them had two, by which, or some other means, one Donogh MacOwen O'Farrell of Cnockaha and a brother of his that had an inheritance of two cartrons in the said county, in Cnockahabeg (which was surveyed as 200 acres of arable land, though in such cases the surveyors who gave allowances to some others, to the said Donogh and his brother gave none at all), had these said two cartrons of 200 acres quite taken away from them and given to the said Faghney O'Farrell for his part of the aforesaid satisfaction, as more at large shall appear by the said Donogh's bill of computation of the premises.

Item, it is so that the surveyors or measurers of the said county of Longford did at the time of their survey to discharge the surveyor of some remiss in his accounts in England upon the making up of his books there, for that surveyor accounting for more lands than the county containeth, surveyed and admeasured the lands of the natives next to their chief houses unreasonably and above admeasurement, and the lands of the undertakers and other favourites admeasured a far less number of acres than could stand with reason, by which many of the freeholders of that county lost their livelihoods.

Item, Mr. Edward Dowdall, learned in the law and one of the committies of the said county, hath in Clanhue, in the barony of Longford, the demi-cartron of Aghinmadder, the demi-cartron of Mogherdran, the two cartrons of Ardcullen in the barony of Granard, the cartron of Tonfinlissinbanardagh, the cartrons of Kilco and Kill (*illegible*) in the barony of Ardagh within the said county, he having no lands by purchase or by inheritance there before, and now having upwards of 1,000 acres.

Item, one John McIriell O'Farrell of Ardenragh, in the said county, gent., having only two cartrons of land in possession, to which there was a claim made by his elder brother's son, hath gotten an augmentation of a castle and twenty cartrons, he having been in actual and open rebellion in the company of Captain Richard Farrell in the heat of the last great rebellion.

Item, one Lisagh Oge O'Farrell of Leitherie in the barony of Rathclonie, in the said county, having never a foot of land before, hath gotten three score acres of arable land in Leitherie aforesaid, he being in actual rebellion in the heat of the last general revolt.

Item, one Owney McFarrelly O'Farrell of Carnagh in the barony of Moidaune, within the said county, being seised as his inheritance as of one cartron of land, called Corremore, the largest scope of all the cartrons within that territory, was not surveyed; but about four score acres of arable land, which is, by all reason, and further sixty acres over and above that reckoning, in regard that the cartron next adjoining the same near the bigness of it is found to be eight score acres arable; notwithstanding that the said Owny hath been a good servitor in the late wars, under the leading of Captain Lawrence Esmond, one of his Majesty's Privy Council, who not only wrote in commendation and behalf of the said Owny to Sir William Parsons, knight and baronet, one of the said comities, for passing the said Owny the said land, but also came in person to entreat for him to the said Sir William and the rest of the comities, nevertheless that they faithfully promised the said Lawrence to give the said servitor his own land, he being for half a year in (*illegible*) charges (*illegible*) them for the same, was nothing the more regarded by the said committees, but quite forgotten, and cast out of his said land without any manner of allowance.

Item, it fell out so that divers of the poor natives or former freeholders of that county, after the loss of all their possessions or inheritance there, some ran mad, and others died instantly for very grief, as one James McWilliam O'Farrell of Clangrad, and Donogh McGerrot O'Farrell of Cuillagh, and others whose names for brevity I leave out, who on their death-beds were in such a taking that they by earnest persuasions caused some of their family and friends to bring them out of their said beds to have abroad the last sight of the hills and fields they lost in the said plantations, every one of them dying instantly after.

Item, all the natives and poor freeholders of the said county, that lost their former possessions and inheritance, doth most humbly desire your Lordships that all the plans and rentals of the whole county be brought in one place before your honour, and the same and the grand office taken at Longford compared together, by which and the testimony of the inhabitants of the county shall be known what land and demesne belong to every native and in his possession before and at the taking of the said grand office, for it did appear that some lands at the taking of the said office that were then in possession of some of the said natives was then left out unmemorable or called upon; some others by the collectors of that county, either from mere malice or negligence, by which course, or one better known to your honours shall be known and sifted out what was done in the plantation of that county contrary to his Majesty's intentions.

II.

(*v.* vol. i. p. 30.)

THE KING'S IRISH WARDS.

"*To the Honourable the Lords and others of his Majesty's Most Honourable Privy Council,*

"*The Humble Petition of Brian O'Rourke, prisoner in his Majesty's Tower of London,*

"Most humbly sheweth that, as your Lordships well knoweth, your suppliant's whole estate is detained in his Majesty's hands, since and during your petitioner's minority, he having as yet nothing left to live on but bare (*illegible*) for his allowance, during his wardship, whereof your suppliant not having received a penny for these four years last past, he hath been forced to go naked, had he not asked some poor friend's credit for his poor clothes, which, resting unpaid, hath left both him and them utterly void of all further supply. In which extremity his Majesty was most graciously pleased to give his reference to the Right Honble. the Lord Treasurer for the payment of your suppliant's arrearages, yet his Lordship excusing the delay upon his Majesty's other occasions, your suppliant is enforced most humbly to beseech your Lordships to mediate with my Lord Treasurer for the present payment unto your suppliant of the said arrearages, and the preventing of any such future extremities as he hath now long time suffered. It being a pitiful thing that a man whose whole estate is detained should thus miserably starve in prison, which your Lordships taking into your gracious consideration, he shall (as nevertheless bound) daily pray for your Lordships' present and eternal happiness."

There is no date to the above petition, but it has been calendared by Dr. Russell and Mr. Prendergast under 1620. A second petition from the same to the same, bearing date January, 1619, runs as follows:—

" *To the Right Hon. the Lords of his Majesty's Privy Council,*

" *The Humble Petition of Brian O'Rourke, prisoner in the King's Bench,*

" In all submission humbling himself unto your Lordships that, whereas your petitioner, being ward unto his Majesty, is every way by himself disabled to take up such sums of money as may give content unto his court charges, in that the laws of this realm admit not his act to be of authority, by means whereof your petitioner is likely to remain with tedious and miserable imprisonment, to the hindrance of his ensuing preferment and present money without your honours afford him some speedy redress.

" May it therefore please your Lordships, out of your accustomed pity to a distressed prisoner, to mediate, by letters or otherwise as seemeth best to your noble persons, with my Lord of Clanricard, that he would furnish your petitioner with such sums as may purchase his freedom, which your petitioner, God permitting him to attain to maturity, would faithfully repay.

" And your petitioner, as in all duty bound, shall implore Heaven for all your honours, and (*illegible*) eternal glory upon ye all."

Two more dateless petitions, one in prose and one in verse, give us further glimpses of the life of his Majesty's Irish wards in London.

" *To the Honble. Lords and others of his Majesty's Privy Council,*

" The humble petition of Brian O'Rourke, Francis Congleton, and Christopher Phillipson, humbly shewing that, whereas your petitioners have understood that Aquila Weekes, keeper of the Gatehouse of Westminster, hath informed your honours of divers misdemeanours committed by your petitioners against him and his servants, which his reports are but mere suggestions and false surmises, as we will make manifest before your honourable Lordships : In tender consideration thereof we most humbly beseech your Lordships to be pleased to command both our appearances before your honourable table, that your Lordships may be better satisfied of the truth in this business. And your petitioners shall ever pray for your Lordships' happy preservation."

On May 1st, 1621, he again petitioned to be released from the Gatehouse prison in Westminster.

"*To the King's Most Excellent Majesty,*

"*The Humble Petition of Brian O'Rourke.*

Oh! enlight thy hart with a sakred fire!
Glorious great kinge, grant but my desier.
Oh! doe but grante that most gracious faver,
Now in my miserie prove my Savior;
Libertie, sweet Sir, is all I crave,
Oh! grant but that, and then my life you have.
In the meantime I am bound to pray
For thee my Soverayn long to bear sway,
And from your enemies may you always be
Guarded by Heaven's great polisy!"

Mr. Lemon has left the following note on the above documents (*v. Calendar of Irish State Papers*, 1614-25, p. 264).

"On the 8th of October, 1619, the Privy Council wrote to the Lord Chief Justice that Brian O'Rourke, being brought over hither to be brought up in religion, and to 'have that education that is meet for a gentleman of his fashion and means,' was in the first instance sent to the university, and from thence removed and admitted into the Middle Temple, where he continued until it happened, on St. Patrick's day last, coming from supper with some of his countrymen, he fell into a brawl, wherein some were hurt, and O'Rourke thereupon committed to the Gatehouse.' He was then indicted and removed to the King's Bench, and is there detained unless he can pay 800*l.*, for the charges and damages ' about a broken pate,' desiring his Lordship to take order for his release. It seems that the above letter was ineffectual, for on the 28th of November, 1619, they wrote again to the Lord Chief Justice to release Brian O'Rourke from the imprisonment he had so long endured, as the parties had since procured a verdict against him for 280*l.*, and praying and requiring his lordship to give order for 'stay of execution of that verdict,' and to mediate ' some reasonable and indifferent composition between the parties.' It is not improbable that the subjoined rude verses interested the king in his favour and caused the interference of the Privy Council on his behalf.

"He appears, however, to have been a very troublesome fellow, for on the 24th of January, 1621, the Privy Council themselves committed him to the Marshalsea, for what offence is not stated." (*Calendar I. S. P.* 1614-25, p. 265.)

I.

(v. vol. i. p. 37.)

LORDS JUSTICES AND COUNCIL TO PRIVY COUNCIL,
JUNE 22, 1622.[1]

May it please your honourable Lordships. We hold it our duty to advertise your Lordships, that not only the Lords and gentlemen here in a great assembly have complained to us of abuses in the plantations in this kingdom, but now many of the natives of Longford, Ely O'Carrol, and Leitrim, and the lesser territories, with daily importunities did so press upon us, that we thought best, in regard of his knowledge of the Irish language, to entreat Mr. Hadsor to peruse the matter of their complaints, but with this caution, that if any of them did oppose his Majesty's title to that land, the great inquisition or the instructions given by his Majesty for settling of those several plantations, that they should be (*illegible*) by him; who accordingly has taken note of those which he conceiveth to be just complaints within the limits prescribed, and by our direction, advised the petitioners to return into their several countries with the assurance that, if there were cause, care should be taken to inform his gracious Majesty, whereon they all returned, well satisfied, as he assures us. Since their departure we have examined two particular cases (of grievance), those of Shane MacBryan O'Farrell and Sir John MacCoghlan. Shane MacBrian O'Farrell, as we conceive, had wrong in not having any land at all assigned him in the plantation, seeing that of the lands found (by the inquisition) to be his in the county of Longford after all deductions, or anything that we hear or can be said, he had left (as it was passed to other men) 106 acres of profitable and 348 of unprofitable lands, and by the king's instructions all that had above 60 or 100 acres were only to lose a fourth, or if they would not submit, a third part of their freeholds. And likewise we find that Sir John MacCoghlan was wronged in his loss of his lands in the King's County, which he had truly purchased of Sir John King, and held by patent from his

[1] *S. P. I. vol.* 236, 23, *Rolls House.*

Majesty. To omit other particulars, and because we hoped that those two were but singular cases, that might in so great a work as these plantations easily slip in, we advised that the commissioners for plantations should propose some satisfaction to these men, Sir John MacCoghlan and Shane MacBrian O'Farrell, out of the lands yet unbestowed, and that the proportion might be so good, that the new patentees might be willing to take them, and leave the petitioners their own land, which would be to their full content.

This moderation we the rather advised, for that we find, although for Sir John MacCoghlan's obstinacy and refusal to submit, order was sent from England to take away a third part of his land, yet your Lordships had formerly written in his favour, and his complaint is, that much more than a third was taken away from him, besides his patent lands. And my Lord Justice Powerscourt, my Lord President Wilmot, and other ancient servitors here, give great testimony of the valour and fidelity of Sir John MacCoghlan, fighting for the English Crown against the rebels, in the places and lands now taken away from him. We did likewise order that Mr. Hadsor should communicate the rest of his complaints (which are many) to Mr. Surveyor Sir William Parsons to be examined, whether, in truth, the instructions his Majesty gave were broken, and they wronged or not; but it hath pleased God that the continued sickness of Sir William Parsons, best acquainted with that business, hath hindered our hopes of success and expedition in these our directions, and now the Lady McCoghlan again importunes us, and we are advertised that the natives prepare to come up by multitudes out of those parts (to urge in person their grievances). To prevent this, we have written letters to the several sheriffs to wish them for saving of their charge rather to send a few agents to deal for them, and in the meantime we, for (the sake of) his Majesty's service, humbly entreat your Lordships to give some speedy directions what answer may be given to those petitioners, whose case or complaint in general is this: they had all lands found to be theirs by the great office, but when the glebes and other public lands were deducted they were esteemed in the survey to be under 60 or 100 acres, and yet sometimes they were passed to others for more. All of the natives thus dispossessed (of their small freeholds) were by the instructions to be made lessees for three lives, or some years at reasonable rents, but by the instructions for that plantation (the case of Wexford may differ from the rest, yet wherein we know not, the instructions for its plantation not appearing unto us) they, the dispossessed natives, could not be lessees to the king, but to some of the undertakers or other natives, and the commissioners here in their discretion do not think fit to let them be lessees of their own land taken from them, and the undertaker's rents and fines and (*illegible*) and charges are so great that they cannot afford to take only a reasonable rent, so that the poor (dispossessed) men have in truth nothing, yet seem to be so reasonable that divers of them offer to take satisfaction out of the mountain, wood, bog, and unprofitable lands given to others, and to pay rent to his Majesty for them (as Mr. Hadsor tells us), but this would make a new work of these plantations, like that of Wexford, undone after the patents were sealed, and new made again. Now for the satisfaction of those poor men, or suppressing of their claims, what course your Lordship shall please to direct by the new Lord Deputy, or to the Lords Justices here, we will dutifully expect, having discharged ourselves and our duties, we hope, as far as we can see.

J.

THE FIRST REMONSTRANCE OF PHELIM MacFEAGH BYRNE.[1]

This remonstrance is made by Phelim MacFeagh Byrne, in the behalf of himself and his five sons, now close prisoners in his Majesty's castle of Dublin, of a few of those many exceptions which might be taken against the proceedings which have been of late held against them; wherein, though the said Phelim should be silent, and conceal his grievances against them, yet the whole kingdom is so full and sensible of it, and the echo thereof doth so fill all places, as your Lordships who are appointed commissioners to inquire of this matter, cannot but take notice thereof. But yet that the said Phelim may not seem to sleep in so dread an hour, he doth most humbly offer your Lordships these matters following:

First, the nature and quality of the Grand Jury which did lately pass upon the said Phelim and his sons at Wicklow, (within most men's opinion) was packed of purpose, to take away the life and estate of the said Phelim and his sons, as will easily appear by taking these jurors by the roll and considering of them, wherein Sir James FitzPierse was the foreman, whose father, brother, mother and sister, or the most of them, were at one time burned or killed by Walter Reagh FitzGerald, who was accompanied by Turlogh MacPheagh, brother to the said Phelim, and others of near alliance to the said Phelim, in that bloody action, in those late troublesome times of this kingdom. Since which time the said Sir James hath borne a secret and mortal hatred unto the said Phelim and his family, as might be instanced in many particulars. And yet to this man's judgment was the life of Phelim and all his children committed, that he might likewise cut off root and branch at one blow.

Sir Henry Bellings was the next man of the said jury, a man generally known to be the only informer against the said Phelim

[1] *MSS. T.C.D. F. 3, 17.*

and his sons, as will appear more plainly by the subsequent matters with which he standeth charged. And the said Phelim is ready to prove that the said Sir Henry Bellings used these or the like words, to the said Sir James FitzPierse in George Sherlock's house at Wicklow at the time of the trial; '*Now is the time for you, Sir James, to be revenged on Phelim MacPheagh and his sons, for the blood of your friends spilt by them.*'

George Sherlock, at whose house these words were spoken, was one of the said jury (appointed to try Phelim's case), and is a man who is altogether ruled by the said Sir James, who doth lodge at the said Sherlock's house at Wicklow at all assizes and quarter sessions, where the said Sir James being a Justice of the Peace doth duly attend, and by that means bringeth great profit to the said Sherlock. William Pluck, who is servant to the said Sir Henry Bellings, attended his said master in this service and was one of the jury.

And as for the rest of the said jurors, they are either allied or have dependency on the Lord Esmond, and some other of the undertakers, who have in a manner divided that whole county between them, and were to have proportions in the said Phelim's lands; as namely Mr. Robert Walker, and Mr. Matthews of the Rath, were and are tenants unto the said Lord Esmond, and Roger Wickam, who was likewise of the said jury, is nephew unto the said Lord Esmond, and as for Mr. Fenton, William Pluck, John Fitz-Gerald and the rest, they are known to be dependants on the said undertakers.

And this is the first thing which the said Phelim doth offer unto the consideration of the said Commissioners, to consider whether these men thus excepted against, can be competent judges of the said Phelim's life and estate, and the lives and fortunes of his children; or whether they be such men (in regard the most of them have no freehold in the said county, but are bare dependants on the said Phelim's adversaries) which his Majesty's writ doth command to be summoned, which runneth in this form, '*Præceptum fuit vicecomiti quod venire faciat coram nobis* 24 *probos et legales homines comitatus predicti, quorum quilibet habeat per se x lib. ster. vel redditus ad minus per annum, ad inquirendum, etc.*'

And the said Phelim doth not doubt but if the sheriff were examined upon oath, but that he would confess that the said jurors, or the principal of them, were nominated by the means of some great persons, or by direction from authority, and so against the laws and statutes of this kingdom. The next thing which the said Phelim doth offer unto the consideration of the said Commissioners is, the violent and undue proceeding of the said Grand Jury after they were sworn, which will appear by these particulars.

First, it will be found if matters be examined into upon oath that no evidence was delivered to the Grand Jury against the said Phelim but the examination of Nicholas Notter, a man that hath been a common and notorious thief, and who was prosecuted so hard by the said Phelim for stealing of seven cows and five garrons from his tenants, as he was forced to fly that country, and being further pursued by the said Phelim, had no way to secure himself but by accusing of the said Phelim. And this was the fit man found out to give evidence against him to such a foreman of the jury as Sir James FitzPierse.

Secondly, if Sir Henry Bellings were here to be examined upon oath, he could not deny but that the Right Honourable the Lord Chief Justice, being doubtful of what credit this evidence would be to the jury, the said Sir Henry desired the Lord Chief Justice to sign the bill and he would undertake the finding of it, which the said Phelim doth hope that the Lord Chief Justice cannot forget, being so fresh in his memory. And as for the former words spoken by him to Sir James FitzPierse, the said Phelim will not trouble your Lordship with repetition of them.

Thirdly, the eyes of great men were so fixed upon the success of this business that two several pacquets were dispatched to Wicklow about it, during the time of the trial, and these were sent for the more expedition by William Greame, one of the Right Honourable the Lord Deputy's chamber, and who is a professed enemy to the said Phelim and his family; and the said William had two or three horses set by the way to return with more expedition with the news of the said verdict.

The third thing which the said Phelim doth offer unto the consideration of the said Commissioners is, the proceedings which were held after the bill was found, which will be seen in these particulars.

The first thing which happened after the bill was found by the said Grand Jury, was the sudden death of the said Phelim's wife, who, though in perfect health at the time of the said trial, yet when she perceived the courses which were taken against her said husband and her five sons, and that their professed and known enemies were the prime and leading men of the said jury, she was so overwhelmed with grief that her heartstrings brake, and she died within some two days after. And after she was interred for the space of three weeks thereabouts, the body (contrary to all law and justice) was digged up in the presence of Mr. Fox, who is vicar of Wicklow, and taken out of the ground in a most barbarous and inhuman manner. And this shameful act, which is without example, was done, as the authors pretend, by direction from public authority, which the said Phelim doth humbly desire may be inquired after.

Secondly, the adversaries of the said Phelim were so thirsty after his blood and so impatient of delay that the term was hastened before the usual time, to no other end, as is conceived by the most of that kingdom, but to make a quick dispatch of the said Phelim and his sons; for the Courts did sit some seven or eight days before the return of any writ, except it was the *venire facias* which was for the trial of the said Phelim and his sons, which being stayed by his Majesty's most gracious commission, the said Courts had nothing to do until the ordinary time of the return of writs was come.

Thirdly, there have been some (which is a fearful thing to be thought of) executed in this city of Dublin by martial law, in or about term time, when the Courts of Justice have been open, who were never brought to public trial, to the shame of justice. And some of these have declared in the hearing of thousands at the time of their death, which was not an hour to dissemble with God or the world, that they could not do that service against Phelim or any of his sons which was desired of them, and that they knew nothing whereof to accuse Phelim nor his sons, concerning Morrogh Baccagh, as John Toole, who was lately executed here in town by martial law, and divers others who suffered in the country.

And what do these extraordinary courses portend but that the ruin of the said Phelim and his posterity was intended by the Lord Deputy? whose master piece hath been for these two last years to rack matter against the said Phelim and his sons out of prisons and dungeons, as will appear more particularly by that which followeth.

The fourth thing which the said Phelim doth offer unto the consideration of the Courts is the preparing of convicted or attainted persons for that trial to accuse Phelim and his sons. And these will be found to be either those who have refused to be drawn by promises and rewards to accuse them, or who are of that base and tainted condition that the law and justice doth reject their testimony.

The following are the names of such as could not be drawn to accuse Phelim and his sons:

Cahir McBrien of Ballydonnellstown was committed by the above named Sir Henry Bellings for not accusing them, and when the said Sir Henry could not draw him thereto neither by threats nor promises of reward, the said Sir Henry set him at liberty for a nag of four pounds price.

Donogh Corren of Tighcullen, in the county of Carlow, being apprehended by the said Sir Henry and brought before the Lord Deputy, was set at liberty when he could not persuade him to accuse Phelim or his sons.

Melaghlin McDonogh Oge of Fyana, in Ranelagh, was examined and promised great matters by Sir Henry Bellings if that he would accuse Phelim and his sons, but the said Sir Henry not being able to tempt him, he set him at liberty on some equivalent reward.

Edmund McDermot was in like sort tempted by the said Sir Henry Bellings, and released for a nag, when he could not be drawn to accuse Phelim and his sons. Tirlogh McGarret was used in the same nature by Sir Henry, who likewise received a nag from him, as will be proved. Donogh McPhilip was likewise in durance for the same cause, until he purchased his enlargement of the said Sir Henry for a garran.

Lysagh McMurtagh Byrne, being apprehended by the aforesaid William Graham, who offered him rewards and the favour of the Lord Deputy, if that he would accuse Phelim and his sons; but the said Lysagh, protesting that he knew nothing by them, purchased his peace of the said Graham for seven pounds, which he paid unto him.

Tirlogh McFardorogh, being apprehended by the said William Graham and his servants, was promised the favour of the Lord Deputy, and that his Lordship would make him a man, if that he would join with his brother Gerald in accusing Phelim and his sons; but being not able to persuade with him, he suffered him to go at large; and with this the said Phelim did charge the said Graham before the Lord Deputy at the Council table, but little notice was taken thereof at the time.

And whether this be not a poisoning of justice, contrary to the wholesome laws and justice of this kingdom at the very fountain head, where nothing but bitter waters can be expected, the said Phelim doth humbly leave to the consideration of the said Commissioners.

The names of those that have been drawn by promises of rewards to accuse the said Phelim and his sons are:

Nicholas Notter, whose examination was the only evidence which was given to the Grand Jury as aforesaid, he was furnished with apparel and other necessaries for doing that service, and this as the said Phelim had good cause to think from some such tempter.

Lysagh Duffe MacLoughlin hath been a common thief, and

being prosecuted at the last assizes at Wicklow, by Luke Byrne, who is nephew to the said Phelim, for stealing a horse, and condemned for the same, did in malice and to save his life undertake to accuse the said Phelim ; for which service he was set at liberty and well clothed, with allowance of meat and drink.

Gerald McFerdoragh is brother-in-law to Shane Bane, who was apprehended by Hugh MacPhelim, being in rebellion, and thereupon executed ; for which he doth charge Phelim and his sons. And for pretending this service the said Gerald hath the liberty of the castle and his diet.

Edmund McDowall Ena hath been a common thief, and several times indicted and tried for the same, as may appear by the several records thereof ready to be produced, and he being found guilty of several offences at the last assizes at Wicklow, desired the benefit of his book, which being tendered unto him, he could not read, and was thereupon adjudged to die ; but the said Edmund promising to do service against Phelim and his sons, his book was tendered unto him the next day, and he had the benefit thereof, though he could not read therein, nor cannot at this time.

And how dangerous it may be to the subject that they who shall undertake to accuse others should receive countenance from him who represents the person of the king, the said Phelim leaveth to the consideration of the said Commissioners. The exceptions of the said Phelim against the rest are as just, for they are exceptions which the law doth take, and not of the said Phelim's framing, as will appear by that which followeth. Edmund Duffe being presented by the wife of John Wolverston for burglary committed since the said John went last into England, and being brought to the gallows by her prosecution, it was demanded of him whether he would do service, and to have his life, being then ready to be turned off the gibbet, he undertook to accuse Phelim and his sons, or some of them. Tiegue MacWalter hath been a common and notorious thief, and arraigned four several times at one sessions and kept in close prison, until hope of a pardon did draw him to accuse Phelim and his sons.

Dermot O'Toole hath been a common thief, and these three years hath been in prison, and questioned for several stealths and robberies, and had no way to save his life but to accuse Phelim and his sons or some of them.

Walter Butler is a man that hath been in rebellion, and to save his life hath accused Phelim and his sons or some of them.

Shane Duffe MacTiegue, who is one of Phelim's accusers, is a man of an ill and lascivious life, having compacted with the devil, and was many times in familiar correspondence with the devil, as the said Shane hath confessed before many. And of as ill and notorious a life is Brian Albanagh, his son, who is another that doth pretend to do service, as they term it, on the said Phelim and his sons.

Cahir Reogh of Kilballow is one who hath been always maliciously bent against the said Phelim, and brought in Sir Richard Graham, the father of the said William Graham, into that territory, and procured the said Richard to pass a great proportion of the said Phelim's lands; a part whereof the said Cahir hath now in his possession, and to that end would be glad that Phelim and his sons were cut off, lest in time they might question him for the said lands.

Owen, alias Owny McMurrogh Byrne, having fled the kingdom for some criminal offence, was apprehended upon his return, and being brought before the Lord Deputy was committed by his Lordship's directions, and soon after put upon a rack, which he endured at that time with much torture ; but in his weakness remembering his former tortures, did yield in the end to accuse the said Phelim and his sons or some of them.

And whether these be fit or competent witnesses to convict the said Phelim and his sons, or whether it is likely that the said Phelim should commit the great designs and ill purposes he is charged with to the secresy of such ministers as these, and should not labour to draw into his faction a more likely party, the said Phelim doth humbly offer to the consideration of the said Commissioners, before whom he doth protest, as in the presence of Him who knoweth all secrets, that he never harboured a thought of those horrible offences which he is charged with : neither was there any provocation to him thereto, his late Majesty having signified his pleasure by four several letters that the said Phelim should entirely enjoy all such lands as his father died seised of, or was reputed to die seised of ; and his Majesty that now is, having by the advice of all his Lords of his council and the opinion of the Commissioners for Irish affairs, signed two several bills for the settling of all the said lands on Phelim and his sons, which being altered on the information of those great persons who have desired to make themselves lords of the said territory, they thought themselves engaged to cast what aspersions they could upon the said Phelim and his sons, who since the time that the heir of Sir Terence O'Dempsey (whose daughter was questioned for her life by the said Phelim's son) was married to the Rt. Hon. the Lord Deputy's daughter, they found an eclipse of those favours which they were formerly wont to receive from his Lordship.

And this storm hath been increased by reason of the late grant which the Rt. Hon. the Earl of Carlisle did pass of the Byrne's country in England, the envy whereof doth now fall heavy upon the said Phelim and his said sons, who are supposed to be the chief instruments used by the said earl therein. But now the said Phelim and his sons do thank God that their great master hath taken these matters into his own royal consideration, and appointed your Lordships to be his delegates, to inform yourself of the premises, and to make such a return as the whole kingdom may have cause to bless you and your posterity for it.

And in regard it will be impossible for the said Phelim or his friends to make proof of the former particulars, if that the same be divulged and come to the knowledge of their adversaries, the said Phelim doth desire your Lordships upon his bended knees to seal up the same in secrecy, until he shall make proof of those matters which your Lordships do most doubt of, and in the meantime to protect the said Phelim and his friends from the greatness of their said adversaries, who, as in other things, so in this, will labour to suppress them. And they shall pray, etc.

K.

DECEMBER 1ST, 1028; PRESENT, LORD CHANCELLOR (ADAM LOFTUS), LORD CHIEF JUSTICE (SIR G. SHIRLEY), LORD ARCHBISHOP OF DUBLIN (LANCELOT BULKELY), SIR ARTHUR SAVAGE.[1]

Seventh Deponent. Hugh MacGerrald, being duly sworn and examined, deposeth that he was apprehended by William Græme, the Provost Marshal, who kept him seven days in his custody, tied with a handlock, and two several times the said Graham threatened to hang this examt. if he would not do service against Phelim Mac-Pheagh, one time sending for a ladder, and another time shewing a tree, whereupon he would hang him, and the ropes and withes, but the examt. making protestation of having no matter to lay to the said Phelim's charge did choose rather to suffer than to impeach him without a cause. He saith that there were present at one time Mr. Calcott Chamber the older and younger, and Mr. Sandford, when the said Græme threatened to hang this examt., and at that time the examt. verily believeth he had been hanged if Mr. Chamber, observing the examt. to be on his knees, to prepare himself by prayer for death, had not dissuaded the said Graham from it for that time, the examt. being told by some present who interpreted to him Mr. Chamber's speeches, that Mr. Chamber would not have the examt. hanged on his land without better ground (of his guilt). He further saith, that after he was committed to prison, where he hath remained twenty-two weeks, he was divers times solicited by Sir Henry Bellings and Mr. William Græme promising him that he should have from the Lord Deputy much favour, means of livelihood, and his liberty, if he would do service against Phelim MacPheagh and his sons, which he refused, having nothing whereof to accuse them. He saith that he was several times brought to the Rt. Hon. the Lord Deputy to be examined, many fair promises being made him

[1] *MSS. T.C.D.*

by the said Sir Henry and Mr. Graham, so as he would do service against the said Phelim and his sons, which he this examt. was not able to do.

Dec. 1, 1628. Present, Lord Chancellor, Lord Chief Justice, Lord Archbishop of Dublin, Sir Arthur Savage.

Tenth Deponent. Ludowick Ponten, gentleman, being duly sworn and examined saith, that in the beginning of the last term he was going down St. Patrick Street, and that one Lysagh Duffe McMelaghlin, standing within a shop, called the said Lodowick by his name and asked an alms of him. The said Lodowick answered and told him that he did not think he wanted any alms by reason he was very fat in flesh, and well clothed, whereupon Lysagh said that he thanked the Lord Deputy for his clothes, for they were given him by the Lord Deputy, and a better thing. The said Lodowick then answered that he was happy that the Deputy was so well-affected towards him to give him the like. Then the said Lysagh said that the cause why he had that reward was for accusing Phelim Mac-Pheagh and his sons for the relieving of Murrogh Baccagh. The said Lodowick said it was well done of him so to do if he might with truth accuse them. Then the said Lysagh said that he could not accuse them justly of anything, but that he belied them to save his own life, he being formerly condemned for the stealing of a horse: and also said that every man that he was acquainted withal was beholding unto him for not accusing them with the like lies, and said that there was no man that was in his case but would do the like to save his own life: and withal that he would rather do it because Luke Birne, Redmond McPheagh's son, presented against him the last assizes for stealing a horse. And at another time the said Lodowick, standing at Sergeant Catlin's door waiting for Mr. Francis Sandford's coming out of the office, this Lysagh Duffe passing by, he wearing of a mantle, the said Lodowick asked him where he had that mantle, and he answered that he borrowed that mantle, and said that the Lord Deputy bought a blue mantle for him that cost ten shillings. Whereupon the said Lodowick said that he (Lisagh) was beholding to the Lord Deputy. Then Lisagh said that the Lord Deputy promised him to release his brother that was committed for Murrogh Baccagh's cause, for the service that he, the said Lysagh, did in accusing Phelim MacPheagh and his sons, and then the said Lysagh went away.[1]

[1] Compare Phelim's account of Lysagh Duffe at p. 310.

Further the said Lodowick saith, that Sir James FitzPierse FitzGerald told him several times that Walter Reogh, and Phelim MacPheagh, and Redmond MacPheagh burned his (Sir James') father and mother.

Further the said Lodowick saith, he knoweth William Pluke, one that was in the Grand Jury finding the indictments against Phelim MacPheagh and his sons, to be servant in livery to Sir Henry Bellings.

Further the said Lodowick saith, that he knoweth John Fitz-Gerald, one that was in the Grand Jury, to be a dependant on the undertakers in the Ranelaghs, and a sergeant inlooking to their woods, and now dwelling in the plantation.

LODOWICK PONTEN.

2ND DECEMBER, 1628. PRESENT, LORD CHANCELLOR, LORD PRIMATE (USHER), LORD ARCHBISHOP OF DUBLIN, LORD CHIEF JUSTICE, SIR ARTHUR SAVAGE.

Fourteenth Deponent. Murtogh MacTiegue O'Doyle being duly sworn and examined saith, that Sir Henry Bellings having sent some of his people to the examt.'s house to apprehend him, the examt. was not then at home, wherefore his wife was taken and carried to Limerick to the Lord Esmond, which so soon as the examt. heard at his return home from a fair where he had been to buy hogs, he immediately departed from home and came to this city to Sir Henry Bellings a fortnight before Lammas Day last, who brought him to the Lord Deputy, where he was examined and committed to prison, where he hath hitherto remained. He saith that no man hath dealt with him by promising reward, release, or other recompense for accusing any or doing service against any.

Fifteenth Deponent. Gerrald Owny being duly sworn and examined saith, that he hath remained in restraint this half year wanting only a fortnight, being charged with stealing cattle for Phelim MacPheagh. He saith that no man hath dealt with him by promising him any reward or recompense for accusing or doing service against any man.

December 6th, 1628. Thirty-fifth Deponent. William Eustace of Castlemartin, in the county of Kildare, Esquire, being duly sworn to set down in writing under his hand what he can say or hath heard and known concerning Phelim MacPheagh and his sons now prisoners, and others, for cause of hatred, or malice, or otherwise, of any other matters known to him that may concern the said Phelim or his sons, doth declare his knowledge as followeth: 1st, I do well remember and know that Sir Piers FitzGerald of Ballysonan, in the county of Kildare, knt., was taken prisoner by Pheagh MacHugh Birne, father to this Phelim now prisoner, and some of their followers killed on both sides, as also that Pheagh MacHugh kept Sir Piers prisoner until such time as there was a consideration given for his enlargement.

2ndly, I do well remember and know, that the said Pheagh married one of his daughters to Walter Reogh FitzGerald, when he was banished by the said Sir Pierse's means out of the county of Kildare.

3rdly, I do well remember and know, for that banishment and other occasions that the said Walter Reogh FitzGerald, accompanied by his brothers-in-law, this Phelim now prisoner, and Redmond MacPheagh now living, and divers others of their adherents, went afterwards to a place in the county Kildare called Ardrio, where finding the said Sir Pierse FitzGerald in a little castle that was thatched with but straw or sedge, set fire to the same and burnt him and his wife, and one of his daughters there.

4thly, I do well remember and know, that after these occasions and after the death of the said Pheagh MacHugh that Sir James FitzPierse FitzGerald now living, did go into England to procure letters for passing the said Phelim's lands of Ranclagh, or part thereof, as also that he did prosecute and endeavour all he could to pass the said lands according to the effect of his said letters, until he was crossed by reason of a general instruction sent soon after by the State of England after the last great rebellion, for settling of divers of the Irish of the province of Leinster, and this Phelim and his brother Redmond were by special name inserted therein for their ancient estate and lands.

5thly, I do well remember and know, that after the settlement of the said Phelim and his brother Redmond in their own possessions, it happened upon their going homewards from Dublin, that they and their company met with the aforesaid Sir James FitzPierse FitzGerald and others in his company in the county of Wicklow, taking away certain stud mares by force from them, or from some of their friends, and then did take the said Sir James prisoner and killed one of his horsemen, and took him home along with them to his house of Ballynecorr.

6thly, I do well remember and know, that within a few years after the aforesaid Sir James did entertain and countenance with all his endeavours certain of the said Phelim's followers and tenants, that pretended title to part of the said Phelim's lands, and by that means did often trouble the said Phelim, and give cause of offence to him and his tenants, and soon after gained a proportion of the said Phelim's lands by that means, and afterwards Sir James fell into a great league of friendship with Sir Richard Græme, knt., being then one of the greatest adversaries that the said Phelim had, as appeareth by the countenancing of divers of his followers and supposed freeholders against the said Phelim, by which means and otherwise he gained a great part of the said Phelim's estate, and sought by all endeavours, as well to the State as otherwise, to procure as much harm and hindrance as possibly he could to the said Phelim.

7thly, I do well remember and know, that the said Sir James's near kinswoman, Mary Dempsey, was supposed to be prosecuted by Phelim and his sons, or by their means, for her life, which was ill taken by the said Sir James and Sir Terence Dempsey, knt., father of the said Mary.

8thly, I do well remember and know, that now lately by reason of the late plantation there, Ballymoroghroe and other the lands which the said Sir James got into his possession being taken from him, that he petitioned soon after to the Rt. Hon. the Lord Deputy for recompense for the same, of some other lands of the plantation there, in regard he had been one of the first that moved for a plantation in Ranelagh, and whether this and the rest do show first and last to be causes of hatred and malice (to Phelim and his brothers) I humbly leave to your honourable censure.

9thly, I do well remember and know, that since the time that Phelim MacPheagh procured letters out of England for confirmation of the first instructions formerly mentioned to pass the whole territory of Ranelagh to him, because his own patent first past did not extend to the true meaning of the first settlement, and letters sent out of England in that behalf, that his own brother Redmond and all the natives of the territory of Ranelagh and Cosha that were supposed freeholders by gavelkind of the most part of the said Ranelagh and Cosha, did always join together to do the said Phelim and his sons all the mischief they could, as well appeareth by their working to hinder him from passing a new patent in all the time of the Lord Grandison's government, and the now Lord Deputy's time, and part of the same natives do now also accuse the said Phelim and his sons more than any others, and have all their depending upon none but such as have got part of the said Phelim's estate or patrimony, or others that are known adversaries to the said Phelim.

10thly, I do well remember and know, that the said Phelim

before his late imprisonment did publicly tax William Græme, son to Sir Richard Græme, knt., and inheritor of such lands as his father got from the said Phelim, that he sought to procure and draw one Tirlogh Bane, tenant to the said Phelim to Dublin, for concurring and agreeing with what his brother Garret Bane then and now prisoner could say against the said Phelim by way of accusation; at which time the said Phelim offered to prove the same by witnesses; and the said William doth also maintain and countenance one Cahir Reagh, being one of the aforesaid natives, who hath been these thirty years or more factiously bent for a pretended title to part of the said Phelim's lands, to do the said Phelim all the harm he could, by the countenance and supporting of the said William Greame's father, and liveth now upon the said lands under the said William free from imprisonment, for that which he accuseth Brian MacPhelim withal concealing the same as the other did. If it be treason I humbly leave it to consideration.

11thly, I do know all the Grand Jury that found the Bills of Indictment against Phelim at Wicklow for the most part not to be freeholders, except a few that were not indifferent, and the rest who had no freehold had altogether their dependancies as tenants or otherwise upon such persons as have got a great part of Phelim's estate in their hands.

12thly and lastly, I do well know that Pierse Sexton, late sheriff of the county Wicklow, had not a freehold answerable to a statute in that case provided to be sheriff, but by the favour and means of my Lord Esmond, who hath gotten part of the said Phelim's lands, Pierse Sexton's wife being a near kinswoman to the said Lord Esmond.

WILLIAM EUSTACE.

Twenty-seventh Deponent. Walter Butler being duly sworn and examined saith, that about a fortnight after May last, he was apprehended as having converse with Murrogh Baccagh, being this examt.'s uncle. He saith that he was brought before the Rt. Hon. the Lord Deputy to be examined several times, and that the Lord Deputy told him, that three or four witnesses had proved his being privy to the confederacy of Murrogh Baccagh and Phelim MacPheagh or his sons, and when the examt. denied to have any such knowledge, the Lord Deputy told him he should be hanged. He saith also that Sir Henry Bellings and Mr. William Graham did promise the examt. his pardon and his life, if he should concur with the rest, in doing service against Phelim MacPheagh and his sons; and that if he would not do it he should be hanged; whereupon he answered that if he had service he would do it to save his life. And he also saith that to save his own life he would do service against his father.

27th November, 1628. Francis Sandford deposeth, that all he knoweth concerning the prosecution against Phelim MacPheagh is, that there was one Edmund MacDonall this last assizes condemned at Wicklow who was afterwards saved, and as this examt. heard it was because the said Edmund could do some service against Phelim MacPheagh and his children in a plot, whereof Murrogh Baccagh had been the principal plotter, and as this examt. heard Sir Henry Bellings was a principal cause of his saving.

Seventeenth Deponent. Grace Pont, widow, duly sworn and examined saith, that when Phelim MacPheagh's wife died, there was a report that she was not dead: wherefore the parish clerk and some others, the examt. being present, did dig open a grave, in the church of Rathdrum, where they found no body, and close by that digged another grave, where they found the body of the said Phelim's wife, and presently closed up the ground again, but by what warrant that was done she knoweth not.

Twelfth Deponent. Teige MacWalter being duly sworn and examined saith, that he was committed to prison some three weeks before Lammas Day past (1628) by one of William Graham's servants, where he hath ever since remained; he saith that the occasion of his committal was an accusation made against him by one Dermot Toole and others, that he was privy to some concern between Phelim MacPheagh and his sons and Morrogh Baccagh. And the examt. affirmed that he neither know the man, nor to his knowledge did at any time see him, saving, as he formerly declared to the Lord Deputy at his examination, that one time he had occasion to come into the house of Elizabeth ny Shane in Ballynecorr, where he saw a stranger unknown to him, together with the said Dermot and others. And the examt. demanding who it was, he was told by those who were present, that the said stranger was one of the sheriff's men; but since this examt. hath heard that his accusers pretend that that stranger was Murrogh Baccagh, and other knowledge than that he hath none of him. He complaineth that since his restraint, he hath been very severely used, having been oppressed with grievous irons on his neck and legs, and having been kept five weeks in a dark dungeon, without fire or candlelight. By occasion of which hard terms wherein he stood, he saith that he was brought to that extremity, that he had purposed to say anything that would be demanded of him, and that he thinketh there is no man but would do so.

Ninth Deponent. Dermot O'Toole being duly sworn and examined saith, that some seventeen or eighteen weeks since, he was sent for by the Rt. Hon. the Lord Deputy, whereupon he came and immediately presented himself before his lordship, at which time he was committed upon false accusations, as he affirmeth, made against him of having knowledge of some concerns between Murrogh Baccagh and Phelim MacPheagh and his sons. And he saith that since his committal, he hath been solicited by Sir Henry Belling to do service against Phelim MacPheagh and his sons, in accusing them to have had converse or dealings with Murrogh Baccagh, with promise that in recompense thereof he should be enlarged, and have his pardon, and that if he did not yield to do such service he should be hanged. He deposeth also that the said Sir Henry dealt with him in like manner with the like promises for accusing Phelim MacFeagh with the death of Mr. Pont. All which the examt. denied, being unable to accuse them thereof. He saith also that being examined before the Lord Deputy touching the said matters of Morrogh Baccagh and Mr. Pont, when this examt. did not declare anything in accusation of any man, the Lord Deputy wished him to choose whether of those three provosts-marshal he would be hanged by, viz. Mr. Bowen, Mr. Graham, or Sir Henry Bellings, whereunto this examt. answered that he was innocent of any crime and therefore hoped not to be hanged by any man.

Twenty-fourth Deponent. William Duffe McLaghlin being duly sworn and examined saith, that he was committed to prison twenty weeks since, where he hath ever since remained, upon an accusation made against him by Dermot Toole, that the examt. had some confederacy with Morrogh Baccagh whereof he is in no way guilty. He this examt. saith there was no reward or recompense offered him to accuse Phelim or his sons.

Twenty-fifth Deponent. Morris O'Mulconry being duly sworn and examined saith, that about eight weeks since he was committed upon an accusation made against him (as he understandeth) by Gerald MacFerdorogh, who accuseth this examt. to have been a confederate with Morrogh Baccagh. He saith that the examt. having been brought before the Lord Deputy and Mr. Serjeant Brereton to be examined, the Lord Deputy told this examt. that if he did not declare what he knew of the confederacy between Morrogh Baccagh and Phelim MacFeagh and his sons, that he, this examt., should be put into bolts. He saith also that some five or six years since he was in company with and assisting Hugh McPhelim when he apprehended Shane Bane and Tirlogh Archbold, who were in rebellion, and brought them to the assizes at Wicklow, where they were executed. He saith also that Shane Bane was brother-in-law to the said Gerald MacFedoragh. He saith also that one Murrogh MacHugh, who as this examt. heard accuseth Phelim, is uncle to the said Shane, and that Tirlogh Archbold and Gerald's wife are cousins german. And he saith that Tirlogh Archbold is sister's son to Murrogh MacHugh.

Thirty-sixth Deponent. MAY IT PLEASE YOUR HONOURS,—In accomplishment of your Lordships' warrant of the 21st of this month, I have made search for the causes against the persons named in the said warrant, and do find that Nicholas Nottery, one of the said persons, stands indicted of two several felonies, the one being found against him at the assizes held at Wicklow, the 14th of August, 1626, for the felonious stealing of two cows, of the goods of one unknown, and the other at the assizes held in the same county, the 28th of March, 1627, for the stealing of one garron, of the goods of one unknown. Also I find that Lysagh Duffe McLoughlin, another of the persons mentioned in the said warrant, was, at the last assizes held at Wicklow, condemned and adjudged for the felonious stealing of a horse, of the goods of Philip MacLaughlin, of Killorclogherman. I find also that Gerald MacFerdoragh was bound over to the assizes, the 14th of March, 1626-7, for felony, viz. for the felonious stealing of a certain quantity of aqua vitæ and other goods out of the dwelling-house of Phelim MacPheagh, Esq., but was discharged the same sessions thereof, and bound to appear upon ten days' warning. It appeareth likewise that Edmond MacDonall Ena, another of the said parties, hath been twice indicted for several felonies in the same county, the first was for stealing one horse and one mantle, of the goods of Thomas O'Murgho of Ballyellan, which indictment still remains against him in the King's Bench, being returned thither by me upon a writ of *certiorari*; and the other was for stealing of a cow, of the goods of William Murrogh, for which he was at the last assizes condemned and adjudged. I find also that Edmund MacDonogh Byrne, who is alleged to be Edmund Duffe mentioned in the warrant, was at the last assizes in Wicklow, condemned and judged for breaking a trunk of Mrs. Sara Wolferston's in Newcastle, and thereout one silver bowl and four pair of sheets value vii. lib. It likewise appeareth that Tiegue Mac-Walter at the assizes held the 19th of August, 1628, was charged with the felonious stealing of one mare, of the goods of James Mac-Thomas of Roxagh; but the bill being found *ignoramus* he was discharged the said sessions. And also I find that Dermot O'Toole, another of the said parties, was amongst others indicted at the assizes held in the county of Kildare, the 2nd of March, 1626-7, for committing a burglary and stealing divers goods from Murrogh Smith, of Kill, and was afterwards acquitted thereof.

And these be all the indictments and causes that I can find against the said parties. As for Shane Duffe MacTeige I find no indictment, which I humbly certify the 25th of November, 1628. *Copia vera.* Per Henry Warren, Deputy Clerk of the Crown.

Those who wish to read the whole of the depositions and many documents, including Lord Falkland's 'Apology,' relating to the O'Byrne case will find them in the appendix to Mr. Gilbert's last work before mentioned. They are far too voluminous to be inserted here, but the above selection will give a fair outline of the whole. As I have already said, the original documents have nearly all been lost or destroyed, and we have nothing to rely upon for Phelim's case but the copies of his remonstrance and petition, and the copies of the depositions, many of them uncertified and none of them official, merely second, or perhaps third hand copies, made by some private person unknown, for his own purposes. They have no doubt a certain value, but a much less one than the official certified copies of depositions in the 1641-1654 collections, which Mr. Gilbert and others reject because they are official copies while accepting all the foregoing copies of copies in the O'Byrne's favour.

L.

The Established Church. Tithes.

(*v.* vol. i. p. 75.)

Lord Deputy Chichester to Privy Council.[1]

MAY IT PLEASE YOUR LORDSHIPS,—I lately received your letter of the 20th of last month, imparting the substance of a declaration there made unto your Lordships concerning the order which I made a little before here in favour of the British undertakers and the rest of the inhabitants of the escheated lands in the province of Ulster, for non-payment of certain tithes in kind, together with certain directions for me how to demean myself in that business. Therein I have observed, that as the reporters endeavoured to possess your Lordships with an opinion that I stood not so well-affected on the Church's behalf as was expedient, so your Lordships are pleased to make a more benign and honourable construction of my doings or good intentions therein; which I will lay up in a faithful remembrance among the other manifold debts and obligations which I owe unto your good Lordships.

But now by way of answer I may truly say this much of myself, that as I know it to be a service most pleasing to God and to the king our sovereign to have this poor Church of Ireland planted with ministers of the gospel, so the world will witness with me, I doubt not, that I have always cherished their profession, and done more for the same than for any other sort of men besides. And I have most commonly accommodated or applied the rule of justice unto all their occasions whensoever I saw it requisite. Yet it is an easy matter I know, and usual for persons who live here at their own ease, looking for awhile not beyond the exterior of some thing, to find fault in many things which they possibly cannot redress though they have power and liberty to make essay. If I had known that some had not been sufficiently satisfied here with my doings in that behalf, and that your Lordships had been pleased to take notice of the cause and the proceedings in that business, I would undoubtedly

---

[1] *Philadelphia Papers,* vol. 2, p. 399, *No.* 176A, *Rolls House.*

have given you the just account thereof, as now I must. I do confess it unto your Lordships that when I first heard it maintained by some of the prelates of Ulster here that by the project of plantation the tithe-milk, among some other innovations, was due and payable to the ministers there, truly I held it a position more zealous and sharp than moderate and cautious, and I will here trouble your Lordships with those few reasons out of many more that might be truly alleged on that behalf.

First, I know by experience, and had heard, that this manner of tithing was not general in all the king's dominions, no more was it ever heard of or ever exacted in this realm until now. Besides, if your Lordships had a prospect of this country you would easily see that it never was possible for it to be otherwise than it is at this day, (divided) in parishes of great extent, without any townredes, or certain habitations of people generally (except what some of the new planters have lately made for themselves), and those also so broken in sunder many times with rivers, bogs, woods, and mountains as are not easily passable.

Again, the ministers there are non resident for the most part, as having few churches in repair to serve God in, nor any houses to dwell in; neither do they endeavour to build any. Yet nevertheless, intending to still make their profits most among the Irish, who first felt and complained of this new tithing (and were thereto animated by some of the undertakers no doubt), they did farm their said tithe-milk unto certain kern, bailiffs-errant, and such like extortionate people, who, either by immoderate avarice or malice infused, did exact and take away the same rudely, to the extreme displeasure of the poor people, whose daily food and blood it is, and with like envy (*i.e.* prejudice) to the ministers of the gospel and their (Christian) profession.

When I first heard of those violent courses, and how they were being taken, I thought it very doubtful whether that manner of tithing in kind before the people were persuaded to conformity could be fitly called a planting of religion, and an advancement of the (Protestant) church, as many do, and sure I am that whilst some of them (the clergy and their tithe collectors) strove inconsiderately to get those tithes into their hands they foresaw not the peril they engaged themselves and others in, for one minister was pitifully murdered with forty-four wounds about him for that cause, and another lay person was slain in defence of a minister his master, and divers have been sought for, as I have formerly written unto your Lordships.

Again, of late I have been advertised of other sundry outrages committed by priests and their abettors against the ministers in other places ; also, so far hath hatred increased against them that there are some six or seven score people engaged in these villainies, who have taken to the woods and mountains upon their keeping in several parties.

On the other hand, seminary priests and Jesuits, waiting upon doubtful chances and changes of time, are still ready to work on the ill-affected multitude, incensing them to entrap and oppress the ministers how they can ; insomuch that it is no more safe for them, especially in Ulster, to stray much abroad without guards and convoys if they have occasion to travel.

Soon after the first noise and advertisement of these things, there came unto me Captain Tirlogh, the son of Sir Arthur O'Neil, and Con McTurlogh O'Neil, two principal gentlemen of their sept, one of the county of Tyrone, and the other of Armagh, expressly employed by the country to complain of this grievance they felt and to get redress, and on their own behalf also to show how one of them had been committed to prison, with many other men, by one Danson and others, the Lord Primate's officers (but without his Lordship's knowledge) for light causes to wring money out of them, etc.

Now these things, and greater, being considered of, I will leave it to your Lordships' wisdom to judge whether it were not high time, and more necessary for me, to make some good provisions for the honour of this cause with moderation and justice, and for the safety of the whole ministry, than to please the avarice of the few, in things not to be accomplished without general displeasure and danger, as experience did teach. These things I meant not to reveal unto your Lordships at this time, but I have been urged to do so, and I herewith send you the copy of the order I made for the observance of a milder temper hereafter in tithing, by which it will appear that it is but temporary, and that, howsoever they may hereafter be able to enjoy the benefit thereof, the church and clergy of Ulster is, at this day, far otherwise provided for than this kingdom hath ever known before, an everlasting monument of his Majesty's bounty and beneficence.

If I have erred in anything, I pray your Lordships to believe it proceeded of a good intention, and I will hereafter duteously observe your commandments in all things, as I am otherwise bound to do, in assurance whereof I will here cease, and humbly commit your Lordships to God's holy preservation. *From his Majesty's castle of Dublin, this 22nd day of March,* 1614, etc.

M.

A Discourse concerning the Settlement of the Natives in Ulster, A.D. 1628.[1]

(v. vol. i. p. 76.)

All British undertakers, by the articles of the plantation of the province of Ulster, are bound to bring households out of England and Scotland to people their lands, which, unless they do, that can never be a good plantation, and they will never do it, as long as they may keep an Irish native on their lands, for these reasons:—

First, because the bringing of such families thither out of England and Scotland would be very chargeable unto them, as the natives will not be, being already found there.

Secondly, because the undertakers are not willing to make estates for lives or years, as they must do to the British tenants, until such time as they have improved their lands to as great a value as they can.

Thirdly, because the Irish tenant is more servile than the British, will give more custom,[2] and pay more rent.

Now because that plantation can have no good progress, if the natives be still permitted to stay upon the British undertakers' lands, and that the forcing of the poor people from thence, before they are otherwise provided for, would breed an exceeding great clamour and confusion, if not a present rebellion, it were fit that such a course were taken for them, that they themselves might, with all willingness, leave the lands of the British undertakers', which may be done in this manner. His Majesty hath given large scopes of land to—(1) the bishops of Ulster; (2) the servitors; (3) some of the natives; none of which three sorts of men are to perform the same conditions as the British undertakers are, but may all retain the Irishry upon their lands; nay, to say truth, their lands were chiefly given them to that purpose, and their lands

[1] Carte MSS., vol. 30, pp. 53-58, Bodleian Library.
[2] By custom is meant the uncertain amount of butter, pigs, fowl, turf and manual labour which the Irish were willing to give in addition to money rent to the undertaker.

would, if not altogether, yet within very little, require as well those natives which are now upon them as the others which do not yet inhabit the British undertakers' proportions, if care be taken in the well disposing thereof amongst them, and no man have a larger scope assigned him than he can conveniently manure and stock. For the better performance of which service his Majesty may be pleased to give authority to certain discreet Commissioners, to whom both the country and people are well known, as well to view what lands are yet unplanted amongst the said bishops, servitors, and natives ; as to take notice what number of people are now unplaced and do live upon the British undertakers' lands. After which several surveys so made then and there, to have places assigned them by the said Commissioners, some of them greater, some of them lesser, according to every man's quality and means. And the natives, servitors, and bishops should be commanded expressly from his Majesty to admit the natives upon their lands so assigned to them by the said Commissioners, and to make them either leases thereof for years, or estates for lives, at such rents as are now reserved, or such as shall be thought reasonable by the Commissioners, for that plantation. Which when the people shall understand they are already so bitten with the tyranny of their landlords, the uncertainty of their abiding in any place, having no residence but at pleasure, and their expense and continual vexation in seeking new habitations, and fearing to lose their old, that they shall not need to be compelled to leave the British undertakers' lands, for they will go of themselves to their newly-assigned lands, whereof they may be assured to have estates. Or if any of them should be so senseless as to refuse so great a good, yet most of them will cheerfully embrace it, and such as are obstinate amongst them may then be compelled to leave the said lands, with more colour of justice, when there is care had for their settlement, rather than now to turn them from their habitations, before any provision be made for them, or course taken where they shall plant themselves. And because this will be a work of great pains and expense to the Commissioners that shall undertake it, whose charge there is no reason his Majesty should defray, considering that it doth principally tend to the good of others. His Majesty therefore may be pleased to give directions, that the said Commissioners may require from the natives, that are to be settled as aforesaid, for every ballyboe, quarter, poll, or (*illegible*) of land, six shillings and eight pence, sterling, and so rateably for life, or greater proportions as they shall be estated in them, or if this shall seem too much, it may be left to the Commissioners of that plantation to appoint what reward every native that is to be settled should give to the Commissioners that are to take the pains in it. It will be a work of great piety and honour for his Majesty to command a settlement of the natives (by certainty of estates under the undertakers there, bishops, natives, and servitors), who have humbly and quietly submitted themselves and their possessions to be disposed of by his Majesty, whereby they are utterly destitute of all habitation or abode other than the will of others. It will be a means of bringing great profit to his Majesty, for, as now the case standeth, if all the natives of Ulster who have no lands should go into rebellion and be attainted, his Majesty must be at the charge to reduce them into obedience, and yet gain nothing by the attainder; whereas if they were estated by long lease, or freehold for lives, his Majesty should have many forfeitures thereby, besides his usual revenues, as well in subsidies, as fines, amercements, the profits of (*illegible*) and other benefits of law proceedings, according to the course of England, which amongst those Irish can never be raised, as long as they live this vagrant and uncertain course of life. It will assure the peace of that country, for when they who had hitherto no places of residence, but were accustomed upon all occasions to run into rebellion with their lords, upon whom they did depend, shall by this settlement be drawn from them, and find the contentment of a civil life, they will then endeavour to improve their lands, increase their stocks, and get goods about them, which upon any ill-attempt they will be loth to lose. His Majesty shall by this means be the author of that great work of uniting the English and Irish together, which yet could never be done, because they never live together as landlord and tenant either in perpetuity or long leases. It will be an assured means of peace and good order to reclaim that people to civility, religion, and obedience, which will be a work of greater glory to his Majesty than if he had brought a new people into their places.

The ancient tyranny of holding them in slavish tenancy-at-will shall be thereby removed, and the minds of the people set at liberty, which were heretofore burdened with the fear of being put out of their lands, which fear always made them follow their lords into all desperate and disloyal conspiracies. It is a matter of necessity for his Majesty's service in juries and other country occasions, in which case the service is now often supplied with tenants-at-will, and those such as are barbarous and unskilful, who must do as their lords command them, though against the known truth, which, though it be much complained of by the justice and justices, yet it cannot be remedied, the British undertakers and tenants being so few. By this course his Majesty shall do that peaceably, and with comfort and prayers of the people, which hitherto could not be done nor carried, but with contention, clamour, and grave grievances, both of the British undertakers and the Irish inhabitants, if they are compelled to leave their lands, before they are in law provided for. By this removo of the Irish from the undertaker's lands, the great work of the plantation will be made perfect, which is to bring British inhabitants thither, and for which only end his Majesty gave away such large possessions for so small a value by the year. If his Majesty will endeavour a reformation in religion, that work will be of less difficulty when the people are gathered together into townships, and settled in separate parishes, whereby the minister may know his parishioners, and they him, by his having a residence amongst them, which, as long as they continue this wandering course of life, can never be done, but after the settlement it may not be doubted it will—for, to say the truth, most of the people are not unwilling to go to church if they might be so provided for—that they need not fear their lord's disfavour for so doing.

Whosoever doth know Ulster and will deal truly with his Majesty must make this report of it; that in the general appearance of it, it is yet no other than a very wilderness. For although in many of the proportions, I mean of all kinds, there is one small township, made by the undertakers which is all, yet, the proportions being wide and large, the habitation of all the province is scarce visible. For the Irish, of whom many townships might be formed, do not dwell together in any orderly form, but wander with their cattle all the summer in the mountains, and all the winter in the woods. And until those Irish are settled, the English dare not live in those parts, for there is no safety either for their goods or lives, which is the main cause, though other reasons may be given, why they do not plentifully go thither, and cheerfully plant themselves in the province.

At the time of the plantation many of the best blood of the people of that province were settled, yet for the most part they were such as in time of war had relation to this State, and for their inclining that way, neither had nor have any power with the Irish, to bring them into any civil order, though they should endeavour it. But there are others, some of them heads of Septs, some of them chief of *creaghtes*,[1] and some principal followers to the rebellious lords, in whom alone the power of those lords consisted, and who did support them in their wars. For the lords themselves had little

---

[1] V. vol. i. p. 314, for M. H. P. Hore's description of the Ulster creaghts of the 17th century.

APPENDIX. 331

benefit out of their lands, and no goods at all, but those men enjoyed or at least commanded all there were, and are they which have power over the bodies of the people and can command their dependency on whom they please. And these men have no lands, but are left at large with their followers, who now, when they see the times fall out so contrary to their expectations, would willingly settle themselves, and for the good of the country it were requisite that they should. For by them the rest of the people shall be assured, for no stealth can be done but they know it, nor any mischief plotted but they can discover it. Yet in this settlement their own dependants would be scattered from them, as much as may be, and others mingled among them.

By this settlement the Irish gentlemen who had lands assigned them in the plantation shall be rid of their multitude of idle followers, which yet do hang upon them, of whom they have neither corn or money; which is the cause that for their present relief given to these followers, they do sell away their lands by pieces, and so in a short time, all being sold, they will become rebels again. For nothing doth contain them so much in obedience as the certainty of their estate. And therefore it was one of the greatest policies that ever his Majesty put in practice in this kingdom, when he granted his commissions for surrender and settling of the Irish in their ancient estates, as by a law letter he hath been graciously pleased to do for the poor inhabitants of Connaught.

Lastly, both the habits, manners, and language of the English shall by this means be in time brought in amongst them, which, until it be done, they can never be a civil people, or any good expected out of that province, notwithstanding the plantation as it now is.

N.

LORDS JUSTICES TO (*no name given*).[1]

(v. vol. i. p. 98.)

The letter whereof you last wrote, that Sir Henry Vane would send us concerning the Lord Chancellor and Lord Lowther, is come, and therewith we have made pretty shift to work their quiet for a time and reasonable hope it will so continue, we having in a good measure calmed both Houses towards them and yet not used the power given us, threatening a rough fit of disturbance. We have now sent over all the Acts required by the King's letter brought over by the Agents, and amongst the rest that of Connaught, wherein we have sent such necessary explanations as I hope with what we formerly sent will acquit us from betraying our Master's cause. We have also now agreed upon very earnest solicitation to send over an Act against Monopolies, and an Act to take away felony, for transportation of native commodities, and in that Act we have made the four towns of Dublin, Drogheda, Waterford, and Galway subject to poundage wherefrom they were formerly freed by Parliament or Charter, and paid it only by imposition, as you may remember, which hath no ground of law, and this is a benefit to the king; on the other side we lose for the present 3 or 4,000*l.* a year, which came to his Majesty by imposition and additions in the book of rates, which I confess was hard and I think cannot hold; and besides we let loose a tie which we have on the merchants to bend them to reasonable impositions if the King will take that course.

It is true the Act will be pleasing to the people and perhaps increase trade, which is good, only one thing I would wish to be added in the return which I durst not press here, which is, that as we have got poundage upon the four towns for these native commodities, so I would have the same put in for importations specially in those four towns, and perhaps the desire of the rest will help that to pass with the other.

Now, Sir, another thing I would have presently cared for, which

[1] *MSS. Rolls House.*

is the matter of proxies of the lords now there, the names of whom I have sent unto you; they have ordered here not to allow them voices unless proxies do come, and the King's licences also for their absence, which are to be entered here, and it is most necessary that they should have voices as things stand, the whole house being now swayed by Papists : specially if they take upon them judicature in causes capital, which I see the King is not willing to allow them, and if he can keep it from them is most necessary, though they seem resolved to have it, whether precedents can be found or no, which we yet cannot find, I pray you be careful in this : I have here sent you the names of the lords here to whom I wish the proxies distributed some more and some less.

The most to come Ormond, Kerry, Thomond and Ards.

The agents of the Byrnes are now gone or going over; I pray be careful to prevent their designs, you know how it concerns the King and that country. They intend to reverse the whole plantation, which certainly will be a great mischief to the people, for they cannot be better settled both for accommodation and for rents and tenures.

This kingdom is most fearfully robbed and harassed by the soldier in every part where they come. They go six or seven miles from their garrisons, and rob houses, take away all they meet with on the way, and do all the mischief that can be, we have not had a penny these four weeks to give them. There is no martial law to govern them, which they knowing do what they list.

The people suffer much because they are Papists, wherein there is some mystery, but certainly no good to us : at least they waste many places and will bring a great destruction. I marvel they there do not send us some directions for the ' Queres.' The parliament do extremely press the Judges and they are like to be in an ill case, I beseech you urge some directions from thence with speed for it is a business of great moment.

12th of May, 1641.

Endorsed :—12 May, 1641.

Extract of a letter from the Lords Justices concerning the Chancellor and others impeached.

O.

SIR WILLIAM PARSONS TO (*name not given*).[1]

I do here inclosed send you another petition or declaration of the two Houses sent to his Majesty, which perhaps is delivered, for I hear the delivery of it is left to the discretion of their agents. By it you see with what vehemency and a kind of eager postulation they pressed for judicature, wherein his Majesty most wisely makes a stay. The danger threatened to the English and his Majesty's servants in allowing them judicature in capital causes doth daily more and more appear here, and I doubt not is foreseen there; and therefore I assure myself, his Majesty will be very weary in assenting to it. First they have not precedents for it; and secondly it is barred by an express law made in England in the first year of King Henry IV. and afterwards (amongst others, authorised, and confirmed as laws in Ireland) anno 10 Henry VII. c. 22. Besides if you please to look into the Statute Book of Ireland in a session of parliament held 11 *Reginæ Elizabethæ* c. 1. you will find it there declared in parliament, that by occasion of Poyning's Act, this parliament could not make any ordinance, provision, or order, to bind this people but such as must be first certified into England, and returned hither; whereupon some such things were done for that parliament only. And in another Act in another session of that parliament c. 8, they did esteem that Act a repeal of Poyning's Act, for so much but never to be so done again, whereby it is plain they then conceived that Poyning's Act had taken from them all immediate judicature, so as for his Majesty to grant that which can be used to no purpose but the prejudice of himself and his servants in this place (where they most need support) I submit to his high care. Touching the extenuations they seem to set forth for their two orders which we formerly sent unto you I forbear to give reply, the things being so plain in themselves only where they

[1] *MSS. Rolls House.*

APPENDIX. 335

say their order for seven days' secresy was not exclusive to the justices. It is most apparent it was, inasmuch as we could not have the copies in less than two days after demand and both Houses consultation which took up that time.

Endorsed :—12 *July*, 1641.

Sir William Parsons
out of Ireland touching
Judicature and Poyning's
Law.

P.

Irish Council to Vane, 30th June, 1641.[1]

(v. vol. i. p. 99.)

(*Extract.*)

Sir,—Since our last despatch to you of the seventh of this month, Colonel Belling (who brought us warrant from thence for exporting out of this kingdom one thousand soldiers of the new army lately disbanded here) departed hence with that regiment very quietly, although we are informed that there was great underhand labouring among the Priests, Friars, and Jesuits, to dissuade the disbanded soldiers from departing the kingdom, which also you may partly observe by the enclosed examinations.

No other of the persons licenced to export those soldiers hence have as yet come unto us, but when any of them shall come we will give them such assistance therein as his Majesty's pleasure shall be obeyed.

Upon receipt of your letters dated the eighth day of June last, we sent away our letters immediately to all the ports of the kingdom for seizing all Popish books that shall be there brought in, as also to inform us what books of that kind have been brought in and by whom within one year last past, what numbers of Jesuits, Friars, or Priests, have this last half year arrived here, and what numbers of the like or of soldiers who have had command abroad shall hereafter arrive here.

We lately received a petition in the name of the Archbishops, Bishops, and the rest of the clergy now assembled in this city of Dublin, and subscribed by two archbishops and sundry other bishops, wherein they complain that they see (with sorrow) in their several dioceses and places of residence a foreign jurisdiction publicly exercised, and swarms of Popish priests and friars openly professing themselves by their words and habits to the outdaring of the laws established, the infinite pressure of the subject, and

[1] *MSS. Rolls House*

APPENDIX. 337

the vast charge and impoverishing of the whole kingdom, as you may observe by a copy of their petition which we send you here enclosed.

Some of the archbishops and bishops have lately made known unto us in writing under their hands (copies whereof we send you here enclosed) some particulars of the excess of Popery and the public and bold exercise of that foreign jurisdiction in their several dioceses.

And seeing instead of that due obedience which the Popish pretended clergy ought to have rendered to the laws, they thus break out contrary to the laws into such insolencies and inordinate assemblies, and innovation holding of public conventions, exercising publicly foreign jurisdiction, burdening his Majesty's subjects with the heavy weight of a double jurisdiction, and double payments to clergy, labouring to erect a dependence on the See of Rome, laying hold as you may see not only on the spiritual but also on the temporal power, extending in the consequences thereof as far as in them lies even to the violent rending out of his Majesty's hands a part of his royal authority, under which all his subjects do gather the blessed fruits of his justice and the safety of his protection, as from other evils so from all foreign jurisdictions, we may not be silent, it being very apparent that such bold and insolent beginnings may proceed to further and so general mischiefs as may prove the originals of dangerous alterations if they be not seasonably prevented. Wherefore to acquit ourselves towards the duty we owe to his Majesty and this government wherewith we are entrusted, we humbly crave leave to acquaint his Majesty therewith, as a matter of high and important consideration which we humbly submit to his excellent justice.

We have also lately received information from Drogheda that there is a house there for a nunnery opened with great charge, which is so spacious it hath four score windows of a side and is not yet finished but great expectation there is of it being so soon.

We are informed likewise that of late there have been and are yet supposed to be in and about Dublin many hundreds of Jesuits, friars, and priests, which extraordinary convention of so many of them cannot be for any good purpose. And that in Whitsun-week last there was a very great assembly of them gathered together at the wood of Maynooth, within ten miles of this city, that divers gentlemen were solicited to meet at that assembly, and that some refused to be there, which particulars also we humbly offer to his Majesty's royal consideration.

We send you here enclosed a copy of a declaration and suppli-

VOL. II. z

cation made to his Majesty by the Lords Spiritual and Temporal and Commons in this Parliament assembled, dated the tenth day of this month.

Notwithstanding his Majesty's letters dated the 28th of April last concerning the Lord Chancellor, the Lord Chief Justice of the Common Pleas, and others, the House of Commons on the nineteenth of this month ordered and appointed a Committee to prepare and draw up particular and several charges against those persons, and on the 22nd of this month ordered a Committee of the Commons house to have conference with a Committee of the Lords house concerning the manner of examination of witnesses upon oath, as you may perceive by copies of both the said orders herewith sent.

Q.

PARSONS TO VANE.[1]

(v. vol. i. p. 99.)

Sir,—I lately wrote to you of several things sent by the running post which I hope is come to your hands: amongst other things I wrote to you of the bill sent thither for repealing the two Acts of Queen Elizabeth concerning certain of our native commodities. Now you see it is become the suit of the whole kingdom, and therefore now you may be confident to make the alteration which I there moved, for it will doubtless pass, which I take to be a very strong assurance of that part of his Majesty's revenue, which is the best he hath here, as it may be carried, and therefore I beseech you neglect it not. Yet as I then wrote, let not his Majesty suppose that the stay of that only will bring on the despatch of all his other business with the rest, if they come, for certainly they are much more greedily set upon the Connaught act and the act of limitation for divers main ends, than on this. Therefore let all go, *equali gradu*, which will make sure work. His Majesty runs hazard enough in passing those two acts admitting his revenue were in all the parts at the same time restored and settled; and if those acts were passed without concurrence of his business, I dare say he shall not easily obtain anything afterwards to his advantage, either in this parliament or another. I know what I say, I dare say no more, only I beseech you disrespect not this caveat.

We send you also the suit of parliament and reasons for stay of the men to be sent over seas. We formerly wrote to you how the priests had laboured in that business. Now you see the strong influence of those priests upon all public actions here, insomuch as they are able to guide the whole parliament (the Papists' votes being now strongest) to such a motion, quite cross to his Majesty's commands, which we often declared unto them, specially in a business which really is rather against than for the public peace and safety, and which few men of understanding are not so persuaded

[1] *MSS. Rolls House.*

of save that they desire to keep as strong a party here as they can for other ends, chiefly if anything touching religion or the government should be in earnest pressed upon them; herein his Majesty may please to let us have his resolution as soon as may be, for that though we make no stay of the men, but have given the colonel's warrant, and all the helps we can, yet this obstacle of parliament may much retard their despatch if his Majesty intend to send them. One thing in their reasons may be of some use, you see they speak in shew of disaffection to the king of Spain, whom inwardly they too much honour. This may be so placed in the ears and apprehension of the ambassadors and others of the Spanish side there, as may gain so ill a relish of that people against these priests and their proselytes, as may have an operation for good in the intercourse between Spain and them, and a sense of these men's ill nature and ingratitude, whose youth for matter of nurture in religion and other ways have had great and favourable acceptations in Spain, in their colleges and elsewhere.

We have with much ado drawn the parliament now to agree upon a bill for assuring a revenue out of the tobacco of 6d. upon the pound or 9d. if his Majesty will have it so. They have not yet presented to us the bill, when they do we will be as careful as we can, that it shall contain all the means both of punishment and other provisions to prevent frauds and keep up that revenue: a profit well gained upon so paltry and needless a thing. I formerly also wrote unto you of the queres which have been voted in the Commons house and now remain with the Lords. They were once there ordered to stay till next session, now by plurality of votes of the Papist party and much urgency of some of the Commons are again there in agitation and like to pass. They contain very dangerous matter both against the government in general and all the English here, whereof I can but give you notice, being the office of your poor watchman and

most humble servant,

8 *Aug.* 1641. W. PARSONS.
Mr. Secretary Vane.
Endorsed :—' *From the Lord Justice*
    Parsons. 8 *August*, 1641.
    For yourself.'

The passage in the above letter referring to the Connaught Act and the 'Grace' limiting the king's title, seems unquestionably to show that there was some secret design between Parsons and the king to, at least, delay the latter until the Irish session was over.

R.

(v. vol. i. p. 105.)

THE RELATION OF THE LORD MAGUIRE WRITTEN WITH HIS OWN
HAND IN THE TOWER, AND DELIVERED BY HIM TO SIR
JOHN CONYERS, THEN LIEUTENANT, TO PRESENT TO THE
LORDS IN PARLIAMENT.

Being in Dublin, Candlemas term last was a twelvemonth, (1640) the parliament then sitting, Mr. Roger Moore did write to me desiring me that if I could in that spare time, I would come to his house, for there the parliament did nothing but sit and adjourn, expecting a commission for that continuance thereof, their former commission being expired, and that some things he had to say unto me that did nearly concern me. And on receipt of his letter the new Commission for continuing the parliament landed, I did return him an answer that I could not fulfil his request for that present, and thereupon he himself came to town presently after, and sending to me, I went to see him at his lodging. After some little time spent in salutations, he began to discourse of the many afflictions and sufferings of the natives of this kingdom, and particularly in those late times of my Lord Strafford's Government, which gave distaste to the whole kingdom. And then he began to particularise the sufferings of them that were the more ancient natives, as were the Irish; how that on several plantations they were all put out of their ancestor's estates. All which sufferings, he said, did beget a general discontent over all the whole kingdom, in both the natives to wit, the old and new Irish. And that if the gentry of the kingdom were disposed to free themselves furtherly from the like inconvenience, and get good conditions for themselves for regaining their ancestor's estates, they could never desire a more convenient time than that time, the distempers of Scotland being then on foot, and did ask me what I thought of it. I made him answer I could not tell what to think of it; such matters being altogether out of my element. Then he would needs have an Oath of Secresy from me, which I gave him, and thereupon he told me that he spoke to the best gentry of quality in Leinster, and a great part of Connaught, touching that matter, and he found all of them willing thereunto, if so be they could draw to them the gentry of Ulster, for which cause, said he, I came to speak to you. Then he began to lay down to me the case that I was in there, overwhelmed in debt, the smallness of my now estate, the greatness of the estate my ancestors had, and how I should be sure to get it again, or at least a good part thereof, and moreover how the welfare and maintaining of the Catholic religion, which he said the parliament of England will now undoubtedly suppress, doth depend on it. For said he, it is to be feared and so much I hear from every understanding man, the parliament intends the utter subversion of our religion, by which persuasions he obtained my consent. And so he demanded, whether any more of the Ulster gentry were in town, I told him that Philip Reilly, Mr. Turlogh O'Neil, brother to Sir Phelim, and Mr. Costello MacMahon were in town, so for that time we parted. The next day he invited me and Mr. Reilly to dine with him, and after dinner he sent for those other gentlemen, Mr. Neil and Mr. MacMahon, and when they were come he began the discourse formerly used to me to them, and with the same persuasions he obtained their consent. And then he began to discourse of the matter, how it ought to be done, of the feasibility and easiness of the attempt considering how matters then stood in England, the troubles of Scotland; the great numbers of able men in Ireland, what succours there were (more then) to hope for from abroad and the army then raised, all Irishmen, and well armed, meaning the army raised by my Lord Strafford against Scotland. First, that everyone should endeavour to draw his own friends into that act, and at least those that did live in one county with them, and when they had done so to send to the Irish in the Low Countries and Spain, to let them know of the day and resolution, so that they be over with them by that day, or as soon after with a supply of arms and ammunition, as they could: that there should be a set day appointed, and everyone in his own quarter should rise out that day, and seize on all the arms he could get in his county and this day to be near winter so that England could not send forces into Ireland before May, and by that time there was no doubt to be made but that they themselves should be supplied by the Irish beyond seas, who he said could not fail of help from either Spain or the Pope, but that his resolutions were not in all things allowed. For first it was resolved that nothing should be done until they had first sent to the Irish over seas to know their advice, and what hope of success they could give; for in them, as they said, all their hope of relief was, and they would have both their advice and resolution before any further proceedings more than to speak to and try gentlemen of the kingdom everyone, as they could conveniently, to see, in case they would at any time grow to a resolution, what to be, and what strength they must trust to. Then Mr. Moore told them that it was to no purpose to spend much time in speaking to the gentry. For there was no doubt to be made of the Irish, that they would be ready at any time. But that all the doubt was in the gentry of the Pale, but he said that for his own part he was well assured that when they had risen out, the gentry of the Pale would not stay (quiet) long after, at least that they would not oppose the Irish in anything, but be neuters, and if in case they did, that the Irish had men enough in the kingdom without them. Moreover he said he had spoke to a great man (who then should be nameless) that would not fail at the appointed day of rising out to appear and to be soon in the Act. But that until then, he was sworn not to reveal him; and that was all that was done at that meeting, only that Mr. Moore should at the next Lent following make a journey down into the north, to know what was done there, and that he also might inform them what he had done, and so on parting Mr. Philip Reilly and I did importune Mr. Moore for the knowledge of that great man that he spake of, and on long entreaty, after binding us to new secresy, not to discover him until the day should be appointed, he told that it was the Lord of Mayo, who was very powerful in command of men in those parts of Connaught where he lived, and that there was no doubt to be made of him, no more than of himself, and so we parted.

The next Lent following, Mr. Moore, according to his promise, came into Ulster, by reason it was the time of assizes in several counties; there he met only with Mr. Reilly, and nothing was then done, but all matters put off till May following, when we or most of us should meet in Dublin, it being both parliament and term time. In the meantime there landed one Neil O'Neil, sent by the Earl of Tyrone out of Spain, to speak with the gentry of his name and kindred, to let them know that he had treated with Cardinal Richelieu for obtaining succour to come to Ireland, and that he only expected a convenient time to come away, and to desire them to be in readiness and to procure all others whom they could to be so likewise, which message did set on those proceedings very much, so that Mr. Moore, Mr. Reilly, my brother and I, meeting the next May at Dublin and the same messenger there too, it was resolved that he should return to the Earl into Spain with their resolution, which was, that they would rise out twelve or fourteen days before or after All Hallowtide, as they should see cause, and that he should not fail to be with them by that time. There was a report at that time and before, that the Earl of Tyrone was killed, which was not believed, by reason of many such reports formerly which we found to be false, and so the messenger departed with directions, that if the Earl's death were true he should repair into the Low Countries unto Colonel Owen O'Neil, and acquaint him with his commission from the Earl, whereof it was thought he was not ignorant and to return an answer sent by him and to see what he would advise or do himself therein. But presently after the messenger's departure, the certainty of the Earl's death was known, and on further resolution it was agreed that an express messenger should be sent to the colonel to make all the resolutions known to him, and to return speedily with his answer. And so one Toole O'Connolly, a priest, (parish priest as I think to Mr. Moore) was sent away to Colonel O'Neil. In the interim there came several news and letters and news out of England to Dublin of proclamation against the Catholics in England, and also that the army raised in Ireland should be disbanded and conveyed into Scotland. And presently after several colonels and captains landed with directions to carry away those men, amongst whom Colonel Plunket, Colonel Byrne, and Colonel Bryan O'Neil came, but did not all come together, for Plunkett landed before my coming out of town and the other two after; whereon a great fear of the suppressing of our religion was conceived and especially by the gentry of the Pale, and it was very common amongst them that it would be very inconvenient to suffer so many men to be conveyed out of the kingdom, it being as was said very confidently reported, that the Scottish army did threaten never to lay down arms until an uniformity of religion were in the three kingdoms and the Catholic religion suppressed. And thereupon both Houses of Parliament began to oppose their going and the Houses were divided in their opinion, some would have them to go, others not, but what the definite conclusion of the Houses was touching the point I cannot tell, for by leave of the House of Lords I departed the county before the prorogation. But before my departure I was informed by one John Barnowall, a friar, that those gentlemen of the Pale and some other members of the House of Commons had several meetings and consultations, how they might make stay of the soldiers in the kingdom, and likewise to arm them in defence of the king, being much injured both of England and Scotland then, as they were informed, and to prevent any attempt against religion : presently after I departed into the country, and Mr. Reilly being a member of the House of Commons stayed for the prorogation, and on his coming into the country sent for me to meet him. I came to his house, when he told me for certain that the former narration of Barnewall to me was true, and that he heard it from several there; also Ever MacMahon made firmly privy to all our proceedings at Mr. Reilly's was come lately out of the Pale, where he met with the aforesaid John Barnewall, who told him as much as he formerly told me and said, moreover, that those Colonels that lately came over did proffer their service and industry in that act, and so would raise their men, under colour to convey them into Spain and then seize on Dublin Castle, and with the arms therein arm the soldiers, and have them ready for any occasion that should be commanded them; but that they had not concluded anything, because they were not assured how the gentlemen in the remote parts of the kingdom and especially Ulster would stand affected to that act, and the assurance of that doubt was all their impediment. Then we three began to think how we might assure them help and the assistance of Ulster gentlemen. It was thought that one should be sent to them to acquaint them therewith, and they made choice of me to go by reason they said that my wife was allied to them and their countrywoman and they would believe and trust me sooner than others of the party, they or most of them being of the Pale. And so without as much as to return home to furnish myself for the journey nolens volens they prevailed or rather forced me to come to Dublin to confer with those Colonels, that was the last August twelvemonth.

Coming to town I met Sir James Dillon accidentally before I came to my lodging, who was one of those Colonels; and after salutations he demanded of me where my lodging was, which when I told him we parted. The next day being abroad about some other occasions in town, I met him as he said coming to wait on me in my chamber, but being a good way from it he wished me to go into his own chamber, being near at hand. And then he began to discourse of the present sufferings and afflictions of this kingdom, and particularly of religion, and how they were to expect no redress, the Parliament in England intending, and the Scots resolving, never to lay down arms until the Catholic religion was suppressed. Then he likewise began to lay down what danger it would be to suffer so many able men as were to go with them to depart the kingdom at such a time. 'Neither,' said he, ' do the other gentlemen that are Colonels and myself affect our own private profit, so as to prefer it before the general good of the kingdom, and knowing you are well affected thereunto, and I hope' (said he) 'ready to put your helping hand to it upon occasion, I will let you know the

resolution of those other gentlemen and mine, which is, if we are
ready, to raise our men and then to seize on the castle, where there
is great store of arms, and to arm ourselves.' This was the first
motion that ever I heard of taking the castle; for it never came
into our thoughts formerly, nor am I persuaded ever would if it
had not proceeded from those Colonels, who were the first motioners
and contrivers thereof for aught known to me, and then, to be
ready to prevent and resist any danger, that the gentlemen of the
kingdom like thereof, and help us, for we ourselves are neither able
nor willing to do anything therein without their assistance. I
began, according to the directions that were sent to me, to approve
of their resolution and also to let him know how sure he might be
of the assistance of those of Ulster. Then he told us that for my
more satisfaction I should confer with the rest of the Colonels
themselves as many as were privy to the action, and accordingly a
place of meeting was appointed that afternoon, and at the time and
place appointed there met Sir James himself, Colonel Byrne, and
Colonel Plunket. And that former discourse being renewed they
began to lay down the obstacles to that enterprise and how they
should be redressed. First, if there should war ensue how there
should be money found to pay the soldiers, secondly, how and
where they should procure succour from foreign parts, thirdly, how
to draw in the Pale gentlemen, fourthly, who should undertake to
surprise the castle and how it should be done. To the first it was
answered, that the rents in the kingdom everywhere, not having
any respect whose they should be, due to the Lords and gentlemen
thereof, should be collected to pay the soldiers. And moreover
they might be sure, nay, there was no doubt thereof, to procure
money from the Pope, who gave several promises formerly to my
Lord of Tyrone (in case he could make way to come into Ireland)
to maintain six thousand men yearly at his own charge, and that
notwithstanding my Lord of Tyrone was dead, yet that he the Pope
would continue the same forwardness now. To the second it was
answered by Colonel Byrne that help from abroad could not fail
them, 'For,' said he, 'Colonel O'Neil told me that he had or would
procure in readiness, I do not remember which, arms for 10,000
men. And moreover,' said he, 'I make no great question that if
we send into Spain we shall not miss of aid, for I being in London
the last year in the Scots troubles, I was in conference with one of
the Spanish Ambassadors there then, and talking of their troubles
then afoot he said, that if the Irish did then rise too their messengers
would be received under canopies of gold.' These last words he
told me and some one man of those that were present privately,

whose name I cannot call to mind, neither do I well remember whether he spoke to them all or no, that it was thought when they were both in arms for the Catholic cause they would be succoured by the Catholic princes of Christendom. To the third, it was answered by Colonel Plunket, that he was as morally certain (those were his words) as he could be of anything, that the gentlemen of the Pale would join with and assist them, 'For,' he said, 'I have spoke to several of them since my landing in this kingdom and I find them very ready and willing, and I have at London spoke to some of the Committees, and particularly to my Lord of Gormanston, to let them know his resolution and they approved it very well.' All this was not done at the first meeting but at three or four meetings. And at the last meeting it was resolved to the last doubt touching seizing the castle that Colonel Plunket and Colonel Byrne should undertake that task, because they were nearer to it than any other, and also seize on the forts, garrisons, and other places, where they think any arms should be, and in particular at Londonderry, which should be undertaken by those of Ulster, and then there was a set day appointed for the execution thereof, that was the 5th of October ensuing (it being then the latter end of August, or the beginning of September, 1641, I do not know whether). And everyone should make provision to rise out that day and those were named that should first succour them, that would take the castle with men presently, namely Sir James Dillon, who did undertake to be with them in three or at the most four days with a thousand men and as much more should come to them out of the north. For these two Colonels did not intend to use above a hundred men in the surprisal, whereof they were to have twenty good able gentlemen, for they made account, that having the castle, they with the artillery would master all the town, until they were relieved by men from the country. And because there was a doubt made how all this should be done in so short a time, they did appoint that all that were there present should not fail to meet again there on the 20th of September, to give an account of all things, hopes as well as impediments. And if on that interview all things should happen to be well, that they go forward, if otherwise that they prolong the execution of it to a more convenient time, and so we parted, every man into the country about his own task.

And I in my way home came to Mr. Reilly's house and there I received a letter from Sir Phelim O'Neil that his lady was dead and to be buried on the Sunday following, this being on the Saturday, and desiring me in all kindness to come to the burial, and Mr. Reilly having received another letter to the same effect would needs have me go thither (whereunto I was very unwilling, being weary and withal not provided to go to such a meeting), as well said he to prevent any jealousy from the Lady's friends as also to confer with Sir Phelim touching all those proceedings, for neither he, Mr. Reilly, nor I spoke to Sir Phelim concerning the matters before, but to his brother Turlogh O'Neil. And coming thither we found Captain Brian O'Neil lately come out of the Low Countries, sent over by Colonel O'Neil to speak to and provoke those of Ulster to rise in arms and that he would be with them on notice of their day the same day or soon after it. And it was asked the said Captain what aid he could send or procure being but a private Colonel, or where he could get any. He replied, that the said Colonel O'Neil told him he had sent to several places that summer to demand aid, and in particular to Cardinal Richelieu into France, to whom he had sent twice that year and had comfortable and very hopeful promises from them, and especially from the Cardinal, on whom he thought the Colonel did most depend; so that there was no doubt to be made of succour from him, and especially when they had risen out, that would be a means to make the Cardinal give aid. We did the more credit him in regard of the former treaty between the said Cardinal and the Earl of Tyrone as formerly is said.

For my own part I did and do believe that Colonel O'Neil doth depend on France for aid more than on any other place, as well for those reasons, as also that Ever MacMahon formerly mentioned told me that presently after the Isle of Rhé's enterprise, he, being then in the Low Country, did hear for certain, that the Earl of Tyrone together with the Colonel did send unto France to the Marshal of France, that was general of the French forces at the Isle of Rhé, to deal with him for procuring of aid to come then for Ireland, and that he received an answer from the said Marshal, that he was most willing and ready to contribute his endeavours for his furtherance therein, but that he could not for the present answer my Lord's expectations, by reason that the king had wars in Italy which he thought would be at an end within half a year or little more, and then my Lord should not doubt of anything that he could do for his assistance, but these wars continued a great deal longer, so for that time the enterprise failed. So after the burial was done, I gave those gentlemen knowledge of what I had done in Dublin and how I was to return thither, and then they began to think how they should surprise Londonderry, they being near it, but could not then agree in the manner; so Sir Phelim desired me to take his house in my way going to Dublin and that I should have a resolution to carry

with me touching Londonderry, and thereon I parted home, but
soon after came to Dublin to the before appointed meeting of the
Colonels. But first, I took on my way Sir Phelim O'Neil's house to
be certain what he had done, and his answer was, that he knew the
matter could not be put into execution by the 5th of October, as
was appointed, and that they must make another longer day for it,
and that he would provide for the taking of Londonderry by that
day, and so I came to Dublin to give an account of what was done
and also to know what further should be done. I was not two
hours in my lodging when Mr. Moore came to me, who knew what
was done formerly by those Colonels from Colonel Byrne, and told
me that the messenger sent by Colonel O'Neil was come with an
answer, desiring us not to delay any time in rising out, and to let
him know of that day beforehand, and that he would not fail to be
with us within fourteen days of that day with good aid; also desiring
us by any means to seize the castle of Dublin, if we could, for he
heard that there was great provision in it for war. And Mr. Moore
moreover said that time was not to be overslipped, and desired me
to be very pressing with the Colonels to go on in their resolution,
but on meeting the Colonels I found they were fallen from their
resolution, because those of the Pale would do nothing therein first,
but when it was done they would not fail to assist us Colonel
Plunket did affirm, and so by several meetings it was resolved on by
them to desist from that enterprise for that time, and to expect a
more convenient time. But before that their resolution, Sir Phelim
O'Neil and the aforesaid Captain Bryan O'Neil followed me to
Dublin, as they said to assist and advise me how to proceed with
Colonel Plunket, but neither they nor Mr. Moore would be seen
therein themselves, but would meet me privately and ask me what
what was done at every meeting, alleging for excuse that I being
first employed in that matter, it would not be expedient that they
should be seen in it. And moreover they would not be known to be
in the town, but by a few of their friends, until they were ready to
depart from it, at least as long as I was in town, for I left them
there. But when I made them acquainted with their determination
of desisting from that enterprise they thought it convenient that we
should meet with Mr. Moore and Colonel Byrne to see what was
further to be done concerning the further intention of their own,
and accordingly we did send to them that they should meet us, and
at that meeting there was only Sir Phelim, Mr. Moore, Colonel
Byrne, Captain Neil and myself. After a long debate it was resolved
that we, with all those that were of our faction, should go on with
that determination that was formerly made to rise out. Moreover

it was determined to seize on the castle as the Colonels purposed, for if it were not for their project and the advice sent by Colonel Neil, we would never venture to surprise it, neither was it ever thought on in all the meetings and resolutions between us, before those Colonels did resolve on it; but by reason that the other gentlemen that were privy to these proceedings were not present, the certainty of the time and the manner how to execute it, was put off to a further meeting in the country; and this was resolved in Dublin upon the Sunday at night, being the 26th or 27th of September, and the meeting was appointed on the Saturday following at MacCallogh (*sic*) MacMahon's house at Farney in the county Monaghan. And thereupon we all left the town, only Sir Phelim stayed about some one of his private occasions, but did assure his being there at that day, and by reason of that at that meeting the gentry of Leinster could not be, considering the remoteness of the place from them, it was thought fit that Mr. Moore should there wait to receive their final resolution and should acquaint the rest therewith. And in the meantime Colonel Byrne who had undertaken for Colonel Plunket should inform them of all the intention conceived, and dispose them in readiness against the day that should be appointed.

On Saturday I came to Mr. MacMahon's house; there met only Mr. MacMahon himself, Captain Neil, Ever MacMahon and myself, and thither that same day came the messenger that was sent to Colonel Neil and did report the Colonel's answer and advice *verbatim* as I have formerly repeated from Mr. Moore, and by reason that Sir Phelim, his brother, or Mr. Phillip Reilly, that were desired to meet, did not meet, we stayed that night to expect them, and that night I received a letter from Sir Phelim entreating us not by any means to expect him until the Monday following, for he had some occasions to dispatch concerning himself, but whatever became of them he would not fail on the Monday. And the next day after the receipt of the letter being Sunday (by Mr. Moore's advice) we departed from Colonel MacMahon's house (to prevent, as he said, the suspicion of the English, there many living near) to Loghrosse (*sic*) in the county of Armagh to Mr. Turlogh O'Neil's house, not Sir Phelim's brother, but son to Mr. Henry O'Neil of the Fewes, son-in-law to Mr. Moore, and left word that if Sir Phelim or any of those gentlemen did come in the meantime they should follow us thither, whither only went Mr. Moore, Captain O'Neil and myself, and there we expected until the Tuesday subsequent before any of those did come. On the Tuesday came Sir Phelim and Ever MacMahon, all the rest failing to come; Mr. MacMahon's wife was dead the night before, which was the cause that he was not there, but I gave his assent to what should be concluded to therein and his promise to execute what should be appointed him; and then we five, viz. Sir Phelim, Mr. Moore, Captain O'Neil, Ever MacMahon and myself, assuring ourselves, that those gentlemen absent should both allow and join to what we should determine, did grow into a final resolution, grounding all or the most part of our hope and confidence on the succours from Colonel O'Neil to seize on the castle and rise out all in one day, and the day was appointed on the 23rd of that month, it being then the 5th day of October, having regard therein to the day of the week on which the 23rd did fall, which was Saturday, being the market day, so that there would be less notice of people up and down the streets. Then began a question who should be deputed for the surprisal of the castle, and then Mr. Moore said he would be one of them himself and that Colonel Byrne should be another, and what other gentlemen of Leinster they could procure to join with them, and seeing the castle had two gates, the one the great, the other the little gate, going down to my Lord Lieutenant's stables, hard by which stables without the castle was the store-house for arms; they of Leinster were to undertake one gate and that should be the little gate, and the great gate should be undertaken by those of Ulster, and said he, 'of necessity one of you both,' meaning Sir Phelim and me, 'must be there, for the mere countenance of the matter, it being the glory of all our proceedings,' and this speech was liked by all then present. But Sir Phelim wished to be exempted from that employment and so did I, but then all of them set on me, desiring me to be one, alleging for reason, that their proceedings and resolutions were very honourable and glorious, it being for religion and for to procure more liberty to their country, as did they said those of Scotland of late, and that in taking the castle consisted all the glory and honour of the said act, all which should be attributed to them employed therein, and so in consequence, all or most part to be there, being as they said the chief in that enterprise. And moreover Sir Phelim said that he would endeavour to take or to procure others to take Londonderry the same day, and if he should be away that place would not be taken; with these and many other persuasions they obtained my consent, and then the Captain offered himself. They then began to think what number should be employed in that act, and they concluded two hundred men, one hundred from each province for those gates which they seized on, of which number Sir Phelim should send forty, with an able sufficient gentleman to conduct them. And likewise Captain Neil twenty, Mr. MacMahon and Mr. Reilly ten more, and I should bring twenty-two. Then began a doubt how they should raise those men and convey them to Dublin without suspicion, and it was answered that under pretence of carrying them to those Colonels that were conveying soldiers into the kingdom it might be safely done, and to that purpose Sir Phelim O'Neil, Mr. Moore, and the Captain had several blank patents to make Captains, sent to those Colonels which they sent to those that were to send men to Dublin for the more colour they bethought them of what was to be done in the country that day; and it was resolved that every one privy to that matter in every part of the kingdom should rise up that day, and seize on all the forts and arms in the several counties, to make all the gentry prisoners, the more to assure themselves against any adverse fortune, and not to kill any but where of necessity they were forced to do so by opposition, and that rule those that were appointed for the taking of Dublin Castle should observe and in particular the gentry. All their army in Ulster were that day to take Londonderry, which Sir Phelim did undertake, and Knockfergus, which they thought Sir Henry MacO'Neil would do, and to that end Sir Phelim's brother Turlogh should be sent to him, and the Newry was to be taken by Sir Con Magennis and his brothers, for whom Sir Phelim, in regard they were his brothers-in-law, his deceased lady being their sister, did undertake. Moreover it was agreed, that Sir Phelim, Mr. Reilly, Mr. Coll MacMahon, and my brother should with all the speed they could after that day raise all the forces they could and follow us to Dublin to arm the men and succour and attend and garrison the town and castle. And likewise that Mr. Moore should appoint Leinster gentlemen to send a like supply of men. Then there was a fear conceived of the Scots that they should oppose us, and that would make the matter more difficult, to avoid which danger it was resolved not to meddle with them or anything belonging to them and to demean ourselves towards them as if they were of ourselves, which we thought would pacify them from any opposition. And if the Scots would not accept of that offer of amity and would oppose us there was a good hope to cause a stir in Scotland that might divert them from us. I believe the ground for that hope was that two years before in or about the beginning of the Scots' troubles my Lord of Tyrone sent one Turlogh O'Neil, a priest, out of Spain, and that this, I take it, was the time that he was in treaty with Cardinal Richelieu to my Lord of Argyle, to treat with him for help from my Lord, for him to come into Ireland as was said for marriage between the said Earl and my Lord of Argyle's daughter or sister I know not which, and this messenger was in Ireland, with whom Mr. Turlogh O'Neil, Sir Phelim's brother, had conference, from whom this relation was had. That said messenger went into Scotland, as I did hear from the said Mr. Neil or from Ever MacMahon before named, I know not from which of them, but what he did there I never could hear by reason that my Lord of Tyrone was presently after killed. They were the more confirmed in this hope hearing that my Lord of Argyle did say (near to the same time as I guess and when the army was raised in Ireland as I think) to a great lady in Scotland, I know not her name, but did hear that she was much embarqued in the troubles of that kingdom, when she questioned how they the Scots could subsist against the two kingdoms of England and Ireland, that if the king did endeavour to stir Ireland against them, he would kindle such a fire in Ireland as would hardly ever be quenched. And moreover they, the Irish, knew my Lord of Argyle to be powerful with the Highlander Redshanks in Scotland, whom they thought would be prone and ready to such actions; they the Highlander Redshanks being for the most part descended out of Ireland, holding the Irish manners and language still. And so we all parted.

The next day being Wednesday at Leghrose (*sic*), every man went about his own task, and so when I came home I acquainted my brother with all that was done and what they had appointed him to do, and did also as they had appointed me to do, I sent to Mr. Reilly to let him know as much, and the 18th of the same month I began my journey to Dublin. And when I came to Dublin, being the day before the appointed day for putting that resolution into execution there, I met with Captain Con O'Neil, sent out of the Low Countries by Colonel O'Neil (after the messenger formerly sent by us to the said Colonel was by him (*illegible*) with his answer) to encourage us in our resolution and a speedy performance of it, with assurance of succour which he said would not fail of the Colonel's behalf and from the more certainty of help from him and to assure us, that the Colonel had good hopes to procure aid from others; he said that it was he himself that was employed from the Colonel to Cardinal Richelieu twice and that some men gave very fair promises to assure the Colonel's expectations, and that the Colonel was really himself assured of the Cardinal's aid. And he said that he was likewise commanded by the Colonel upon our resolution of the day to give notice thereof to him and that he would be over in fourteen days with aid. But he (the messenger) landed nine or ten days before and meeting with Captain Brian O'Neil, who made him acquainted with what was resolved, he did write all the matter to Colonel O'Neil so as he was sure of his speedy coming. And so that evening he and I came to meet the other gentlemen, and there were met Mr. Moore, Colonel Byrne, Colonel Plunkett, Captain Fox, and other Leinster gentlemen, (a Captain I think of the Byrnes or the Tooles but I am not sure of which) and Captain Brian O'Neil, and taking an account of those that should ha   been there it was found that Sir Phelim O'Neil and Mr. Collo MacMahon did fail of sending their men, and Colonel Byrne did miss Sir Morgan Cavenagh, that had promised him to be there, but he, the Colonel, said he was sure Sir Morgan would not fail to be that night or the next morning in town. And of the 200 men that were appointed to come there were only 80 present, yet notwithstanding they were resolved to go on with their enterprise, and all the difference was at what time of the day they should set on the castle, and after some debate it was resolved in the afternoon, and the rather hoping to meet the Colonels there then. For they said that if they should take the castle and be enforced by any extremity for not receiving timely succour out of the country (having that they could not want) . . . And so parted that night, but to meet in the morning to see further what was to be done. And immediately thereupon I came to my chamber, and about nine of the clock Mr. Moore and Captain Fox came to me, and told me all was discovered, that the city was in arms and the gates shut up and so departed from me. And what became of them and the rest I know not, yet think that they escaped, but how and at what time I do not know, because I myself was taken that morning.

S.

COUNCIL OF THE REBELS AT MULTIFARNHAM ABBEY.

(*v. ante*, vol. i. p. 106.)

After detailing the suspicious movements of the disaffected in Ireland for some months preceding October, 1641, the circulation of seditious books, and unfounded rumours of the intention of the English parliament to imprison all the chief Roman Catholic peers and members of the Irish houses, and to compel all Roman Catholics to conform to Protestantism on pain of death, Dr. Jones proceeds to give the following account of the meeting of the rebel leaders lay and clerical at Multifarnham Abbey in Westmeath a few weeks before the outbreak, as he heard it from the guardian of the Franciscan friars who was there present.[1]

"A great meeting was appointed of the heads of the Romish clergy, and other laymen of the faction, said to be at the abbey of Multifarnham, in the county of Westmeath, where a convent of Franciscan friars being openly and peaceably possessed of the monastery, the day of their meeting being also St. Francis' day, early in October, but the time and place I cannot confidently affirm, yet whatsoever their several opinions and discussions were as follows: like as I have received them from a friar, a Franciscan, and present there, being a guardian of that order. Thereupon a man and many others there agitated and the question was, what course should be taken with the English and all others that were found in the whole kingdom to be Protestants. The Council was thereon divided, some were for their banishment without attempting their lives, for this course was given (for example) the King of Spain's expelling out of Granada, and other parts of his dominions the Moors, to the number of many hundreds of thousands, all of them being dismissed with their lives, wives, and children, with some of their goods, if not the most part, and that this way of proceeding redounded much to the credit of the house of Spain, whereas the slaughter of many innocents would have been everlasting blemish of cruelty on that state; that the usage of the English, their neighbours, and to whom

[1] *MSS T.C.D.*

many then present owed if no more their education would gain much to the cause both in England and other parts. That their goods and estates seized upon would be sufficient without meddling with their persons, that if the contrary course were taken, and their blood spilt, besides the curse it would draw from heaven upon their cause, it might withal incense and provoke the neighbouring kingdom of England to the taking a more severe revenge on them and theirs, even to extirpation, if it had the upper hand.

On the other side there was urged, a contrary proceeding, the utter cutting off of them and theirs, and to the instance of the dismissed Moors it was answered that that was the sole act of the King and Queen of Spain, contrary to the advice of the Council, which howsoever it might gain that prince a name of mercy, yet therein the event showed him to be most hurtful not only to his own nation, but to all Christendom besides. That this was evident in the great excessive charge Spain hath been since that time put to by the Moors, and their posterity to this day, all Christendom also doth still groan under the misery it doth suffer by the piracy of Algiers, Sallee, and the like dens of thieves. That all this might have been prevented in one hour by a general massacre, applying that it was no less dangerous to expel the English, whose robbed and banished men might again return, with their swords in their hands, who by their hard usage of spoiling might be exasperated, and by the hope of recovering their former estates would be animated far more than strangers, that would be sent against them, being neither in their persons injured nor grieved in their estates; that therefore a general massacre were the safest and readiest way for freeing the kingdom of any such fears. In which diversity of opinion, however, the first prevailed with some for which the Franciscans saith, their guardian did stand, yet others inclining to the second, some again leaning to a middle way, neither to dismiss all nor kill all. And according to this do we find the event and course of their proceedings. In some places they are generally put to the sword or other miserable end. Some restrained their (the Protestants') persons in durance, knowing it to be in their power to dispatch them at their leisure, in the meantime they being preserved, either for profit of their ransom, or for exchange of prisoners, or gaining their own pardons by the lives of these prisoners if time would serve, or by their death if the worst did happen to satisfy their fury (*illegible*) at the first dismissed their prisoners, having spoiled them of their goods and raiment, exposing the miserable wretches to cold and famine, whereby many have perished by death, more than by the sword or halter.

So much for their councils and the effect of them, now for their intentions, all being reduced, which God forbid, to their power. And therefore do they as by a law give such peremptory conclusions, that it may be well wondered the thoughts of men, professing themselves wise, should be so vain. And herein do I still follow mine informer the Franciscan aforesaid.

1st, Their loyalty to his Majesty shall be thus reserved, thus say they of the modest sort, but both his revenue and government must be reduced to certain bounds, his rents to be none other than the ancient reservations before the plantations, and the customs so ordered as to them shall be thought fitting.

2ndly, For the government; such of them as would be esteemed loyal would have it committed to the hands of two lords justices, one of the ancient Irish race, the other of the ancient British inhabitants of Ireland, provided that they both be of the Romish profession.

3rdly, That a parliament be forthwith called consisting of whom they shall think fit, wherein their own religious men, bishops, priests, and friars, shall be assistants.

4thly, Poyning's act must be repealed, and Ireland declared to be a kingdom independent of England, and without any reference to it in any case whatsoever.

5thly, All acts prejudicial to the Romish religion shall be abolished, and it be enacted that there be no other profession in the kingdom but the Romish.

6thly, That only the ancient nobility of the kingdom shall stand, and of them such as shall refuse to conform to the Romish religion to be removed, and others put in their room. Howsoever the present Earl of Kildare must be put out and another put in his place.

7thly, All plantation lands to be recalled and the ancient proprietary to be re-invested in their former estates, with the limitations in their covenants expressed, that they had not formerly sold their interests for valuable considerations.

8thly, That the respective counties of the kingdom are to be subdivided at certain bounds or baronies assigned to the chief septs, and others of the nobility, who are to be answerable for the government thereof, and that a standing army may be still in being, the respective governors keeping a certain number of men to be ready at all risings out, as they term it; they also to build and maintain certain fortresses in places most convenient within their precincts. And that these governors be of absolute power and only responsible to the parliament.

Lastly, For maintaining a correspondence with other nations, and for securing the coasts, that also they may be rendered considerable in the sight of others, a navy of a certain number of ships is to be maintained; that to this end five houses are to be accompted, one in each province, accompting Meath for one of them, that to these houses shall be allotted an annual pension of certain thousands of pounds, to be made up of lands appropriate to abbeys. And a further contribution to be raised in the respective provinces to that end. And these houses are to be assigned to a certain order of knights answerable to that of Malta, who are to be seamen and to maintain the fleet, that all prizes are to be apportioned, some part for a common bank, the rest to be divided, for which purpose the felling of wood suitable for use is to be forbidden. The house for this purpose to be assigned to Leinster in Kilmainham, or rather Howth, provided Lord Howth join with them, his house being esteemed most convenient in respect of situation.

That this kingdom being thus settled, there are thirty thousand men to be sent into England to join with the French and Spanish forces and these jointly to fall upon Scotland, for the reducing both England and Scotland to the obedience of the Pope, which being finished, they have engaged themselves to the King of Spain for assisting him against the Hollanders and giving their (the Dutch) rebellion, as they term it, its due correction. And thus I have laid down all that I heard related, omitting what I find others more largely to insist upon. All which treacherous, vain, and airy projects God disappointed."

HEN. JONES.

Jurat. 3rd May, 1641,

    Cora. ROGER PUTTOCK.   WM. ALDRICH.
           JOHN STERNE.   WM. HITCHCOCK.
           JOHN WATSON.

From the above it will be seen that according to the Franciscan guardian (Jones's informant) his order was desirous to spare the lives of the colonists.

T.

Sir W. Cole to the Lords Justices Enniskillen, 11th October, 1641.[1]

(v. vol. i. p. 108.)

Right Honourable,—Upon Friday last two of the natives of this country, men of good credit, came to my house and informed me that Hugh Boy McTirlogh McHenry O'Neil, a captain who came from Flanders about May last, hath since that time had the chiefest part of his residence in Tyrone, at or near Sir Phelim Roe O'Neil's house, to which place it hath been observed there hath been more than an ordinary or former usual resort of people, so frequent that it hath bred some suspicion of evil intendments in the minds of sundry men of honest inclinations, and these gentlemen, my informants do say, they hold no good opinion of it, rather construing an evil intention to be the cause thereof. For my own part I cannot tell what to make or think of it. The Lord Maguire in all that time, as they also inform me, hath been noted to have made many very private journeys to Dublin, to the Pale, into Tyrone, to Sir Phelim O'Neil and many other places this year, which likewise gives divers in the country cause to doubt that something is in agitation tending to no good ends. Upon Saturday last one of the same gentlemen came again to me, and told me that as he was going home the day before, he sent his footman a nearer way than the horseway, who met with one of the Lord Inniskillin's footmen and demanded of him from whence he came? Who made answer that he came from home that morning, and the other replying 'you have made good haste to be here so soon,' to which he answered that his Lord came home late last night, and writ letters all that night and left not a man in or about his house, but he hath dispatched in several ways, and that he hath sent him [the footman] this way to Tirlagh Oge McHugh, and others, also with letters charging them to be with his Lordship this night at his house. Of which passage I would have given your Honours sooner

[1] *MSS. Rolls House.*

notice but that I deemed it fit to be silent, in expectation that a little time would produce some better ground to afford me more matter to acquaint your honours withal. Whereupon this day I understood by one Hugh Maguire that the said Tirlagh Oge Mac-Hugh, Cuconnaght MacShane Maguire and Oghie O'Hosey reported themselves to have been appointed Captains by his Lordship (Lord Maguire) to raise men, and that he had the nomination of seven other Captains to do the like for to serve the King of Spain in Portugal, and that one of the said Captains entertained twelve men. What authority or commission there is for this is not here known, but it makes some of us that are British to stand in many doubts and opinions, concerning the same, and the rather for that those three men so named to be Captains are broken men in their estates and fortunes, two of them being his Lordship's near kinsmen, and that if any evil be intended, they are conceived to be as apt men to embrace and help therein as any of their degree in this country. These matters seem the more strange unto me, for that they are so privately carried and that upon Friday last I heard Sir Frederick Hamilton say, that the Colonels that at my last being in Dublin were raising men to go to Spain were since stayed by command out of England. I have now therefore sent this bearer purposely by these to make known to your Lordships what I have heard in this business, which I humbly leave unto your Honours' consideration, and desiring to know your pleasure herein, with remembrance of my most humble service unto your Lordships, I will end these and be ever your Lordships' in all duty to be commanded,

WILLIAM COLE.

APPENDIX. 361

U.

THE LORDS JUSTICES AND COUNCIL TO THE LORD LIEUTENANT,[1]
25TH OCTOBER, 1641, DUBLIN.

(v. vol. i. p. 111.)

MAY IT PLEASE YOUR LORDSHIP,—On Friday the 22nd of this month, after nine of the night, the bearer, Owen Connolly, servant to Sir John Clotworthy, knight, came to me, the Lord Chief Justice Parsons, to my house in great secresy, as indeed the case did require, and discovered unto me a most wicked and damnable conspiracy, plotted and contrived and intended to be also acted by some evil affected Irish Papists here. The plot was on the then next morning being Ignatius (Loyola's) day about nine of the clock, to surprise his Majesty's castle of Dublin, his Majesty's chiefest strength in this kingdom, wherein is also the principal magazine of his arms and munition. And it was agreed, it seems among them, that at the same hour all other his Majesty's forts and magazines in this kingdom should be surprised, by others of the conspirators. And further, that all the Protestants and English throughout the whole kingdom that would not join with them should be cut off, and so all those Papists should then be possessed of the government and kingdom at the same instant. As soon as I had that intelligence, I then immediately repaired to the Lord Justice Borlase, and thereupon we instantly assembled the Council, and having sat in Council all night, as also all the next day the 23rd of October, in regard of the short time left us for the consultation of so great and weighty a matter, although it was not possible for us, on so few hours' warning, to prevent those other great mischiefs which were to be acted, even at that same hour, and that at so great a distance in all the other parts of the kingdom; yet such was our industry therein, having caused the castle that night to be strengthened with armed men and the city guarded as the wicked councils of these evil persons by the great mercy of God to us became defeated, so as they were not able to act that part of their

[1] Nalson, vol. ii.

treachery which indeed was principally intended, and which if they could have effected, would have rendered the rest of their purposes more easy. Having so secured this castle, we forthwith laid about for the apprehension of as many of the offenders as we could, many of them having come to this city that night, intending it seems the next morning to act their parts in those treacherous and bloody crimes. The first man apprehended was one Hugh MacMahon, Esq., grandson to the traitor Tyrone, a gentleman of good fortune in the county of Monaghan, who was with others that morning taken in Dublin, having at the time of their apprehension offered a little resistance with their swords drawn, but finding those employed against them more in number and better armed yielded. He, upon examination before us, denied all, but in the end, when he saw we laid it home to him, he confessed enough to destroy himself and impeach some others, as by a copy of his examination herewith sent may appear to your Lordship. We have committed him until we might have further time to examine him again, our time being become more needful to be employed in action for securing the place than in examining. This Mr. MacMahon had been abroad and served under the King of Spain as a Lieutenant-Colonel; upon conference with him (MacMahon) and others and calling to mind a letter which we received before from Sir William Cole, a copy whereof we send your Lordship here enclosed, we gathered that the Lord Maguire was to be an actor in surprising the castle of Dublin, wherefore we held it necessary to secure him immediately, thereby also to startle and deter the rest when they found him laid fast. His Lordship observing what we had done, and the city in arms, fled from his lodging early before day, it seems disguised, for we had laid a watch about his lodging so as he could not pass without disguising himself, yet he could not get forth of the city so surely guarded were all the gates. There was found hidden at his lodging some hatchets with the helves newly cut off and many skeans and some hammers. In the end the sheriffs of the city who were employed in a strict search for his Lordship, found him hidden in a cockloft in an obscure house far from his lodging, where they apprehended him and brought him before us. He denied all, yet so as he could not deny he had heard of it in the country, though he would not tell us when or from whom, and he confessed he had not advertised us thereof as in duty he ought to have done. But we were so well satisfied of his guilt by all circumstances, that we doubted not upon further examination, when we could spare time for it, to find it apparent. Wherefore we held it of absolute necessity to commit him close prisoner as we had formerly done MacMahon and others, where we left them on the 23rd of this month in the morning, about the same hour they had intended to be masters of that place and the city. That morning we laid wait for all strangers that came the night before into town, and so many were apprehended, whom we find reason to believe had hands in this conspiracy, that we were forced to disperse them into several gaols, and since we found that there came many horsemen into the suburbs that night, who finding the plot discovered dispersed themselves immediately. When the hour approached which was designed for the surprising of the castle, great numbers of strangers were observed to come to the town in great parties several ways, who not finding admittance at the gates stayed in the suburbs, and there grew numerous to the terror of the inhabitants. We therefore to help that, drew up and instantly signed a proclamation commanding all men not dwellers in the city or suburbs to depart within an hour upon pain of death; and made it penal to those that should harbour them, which proclamation the sheriff instantly proclaimed in all the suburbs by our commandment, which being accompanied by the committal of those two eminent men and others occasioned the departure of those multitudes; and in this case all our lives and fortunes and above all his Majesty's regal power and authority being still at stake, we must vary from ordinary proceedings, not only in executing martial law, as we see cause, but also in putting some to the rack to find out the bottom of this treason and the contrivers thereof, which we foresee will not otherwise be done. On the 23rd of this month we, conceiving that as soon as it should be known that the plot for seizing the castle of Dublin was disappointed, all the conspirators in remote parts might be somewhat disheartened, as on the other side the good subjects would be comforted and would then with the more confidence stand on their guard, did prepare to send abroad to all parts of the kingdom this proclamation which we send you here enclosed, and so, having provided that the city and castle should be so well guarded as upon a sudden we could, we concluded that long council.

On Saturday, at twelve o'clock of the night, the Lord Blayney came to town and brought us the ill news of the rebels seizing with 200 men his house at Castle Blayney, in the county of Monaghan, as also a house of the Earl of Essex's called Carrickmacross, with 200 men and a house of Sir Henry Spotswood's in the same county with 200 men, where there being a little plantation of British, the rebels plundered the town and burnt divers other villages and robbed and spoiled many English, and none but Protestants, leaving the English Papists untouched as well as the Irish. On Sunday morning at three of the clock we had intelligence from Sir Arthur Terringham that the Irish in the town had that day also broken up the king's store of arms and munition at Newry, where the store for arms hath been ever since the peace, and where they found seventy barrels of powder and armed themselves under the command of Sir Con Magennis, knt., and one Crelly a monk, and plundered the English there and disarmed the garrison. And this, although too much, is all that we yet hear is done by them, however, we shall stand upon our guard the best we may to defend the castle and city principally, those being the places of most importance. But if the conspiracy be so universal as Mr. MacMahon saith in his examination it is, namely that all the counties of the kingdom have conspired in it, which we admire (wonder) should so fall out in this time of universal peace, and carry with them that secresy that none of the English could have any friend among them to disclose it, then indeed we shall be in high extremity, and the kingdom in the greatest danger that ever it underwent, considering our want of men, money and arms, to enable us to encounter such great multitudes as they can make if all should so join against us; the rather because we have pregnant cause to doubt that the combination hath taken force by the incitement of the Jesuits, priests and friars. All the hope we have here is that the English of the Pale and some other parts will continue constant to the king in their fidelity, as they did in former rebellions. And now in these our straits, we must under God depend on aid coming forth of England for our present supply with all speed, especially money, we having none, and arms which we shall exceedingly want, without which we are exceedingly doubtful what account we shall give to the king of this kingdom. But if the conspiracy be only of Maguire and some other Irish of the kindred and friends of the rebel Tyrone and other Irish of the counties of Down, Monaghan, Cavan, Fermanagh, and Armagh and no general revolt follow thereon, we hope then to make head against them in a reasonable measure, if we be enabled with money from thence, without which we can raise no forces; so great is our want of money as we have formerly written and our debt so great to the army; nor is money to be borrowed here, and if it were we would engage all our estates for it; neither have we any hope to get in his Majesty's rents and subsidies in these disturbances, which adds extremely to our necessities. On Sunday morning, the 24th of October, we met again in council, and sent to all parts of the kingdom the enclosed proclamation and issued patents to draw hither seven horse troops as a further strength to this place, and to be with us, in case the rebels should make head and march hitherward, so as that we may be necessitated to give them battle. We also

APPENDIX. 365

then sent away our letters to the presidents of both the provinces of Munster and Connaught, as also to the sheriffs of five counties of the Pale to consult the best way and means of their own preservation. That day the Lord Viscount Gormanston, the Lord Viscount Netterville, the Lord Viscount FitzWilliams, and the Lord of Lowth, and since then the Earls of Kildare and Fingal, and the Lords of Dunsany and Slane, all noblemen of the English Pale, came unto us declaring that they then and not before heard of the matter and professed all loyalty to his Majesty and concurrence with the State; but said they wanted arms, whereof they desired to be supplied by us, which we told them we would willingly do, as relying much on their faithfulness to the Crown, but we were not yet certain whether or no we had enough to arm our strengths for the guarding of our city and castle; yet we supplied such of them as lay in most danger with a small proportion of arms and ammunition for their houses, lest they should conceive we entertained any jealousy of them, and we commanded them to be very diligent in sending out watches, and making all the discoveries they could and thereof to advertise us, which they readily promised to do. And if it fall out that the Irish generally rise, which we have cause to suspect, then we must of necessity put arms into the hands of the English Pale, in present and others as fast as we can, to fight for the defence of the State and themselves. Your Lordship now sees the condition wherein we stand, and how necessary it is, first, that we enjoy your presence speedily for the better guiding of these and other public affairs of the king and kingdom, and 2ndly that the parliament of England be moved immediately to advance to us a good sum of money, which being now speedily sent hither may prevent the expense of very much treasure and blood in a long continued war. And if your Lordship shall happen to stay on that side any long time, we must then desire your Lordship to appoint a Lieutenant-General to discharge the great and weighty burden of commanding the forces here. Amidst these confusions and disorders fallen upon us, we bethought us of the parliament which was formerly adjourned to November next, and the term now also at hand which will draw such a concourse of people hither, and give opportunity under that pretence of assembling and taking new councils, seeing the former seems to be in some part disappointed, and of contriving further danger to this state and people. We therefore found it an unavoidable necessity to prorogue the parliament to the 24th day of February next, and therefore we did by proclamation prorogue it accordingly, and do direct the term to be adjourned to the 1st of Hillary term, excepting only the Court of Exchequer, for the hastening in of the king's money. We desire that upon this occasion your Lordship will be pleased to view our letters concerning the plantation of Connaught dated the 24th of April last, directed to Mr. Secretary Vane in that part thereof which concerns the county Monaghan, where now those fires do first break out. In the last place we must make known to your Lordship that the army we have, consisting but of 2,000 foot and 1,000 horse, are so dispersed in garrisons, in several parts of the four provinces, for the security of these parts, as continually they have been since they were reduced, as if they be all sent for to be drawn together, not only the places where they are to be drawn from and for whose safety they lie there, must be by their absence distressed but also the companies themselves coming in so small numbers may be in danger to be cut off in their march; nor indeed have we any money to enable the soldiers to enable them to march. And so we take leave and remain your Lordship's to be commanded,

                      WILLIAM PARSONS.
                      JOHN BORLASE.
                      ROBERT BOLTON. *Canc.*

J. DILLON.	THOMAS ROTHERHAM.
A. *Midensis.*	ADAM LOFTUS.
J. RAPHOE.	J. TEMPLE.
R. DIGBY.	G. LOWTHER.
F. WILLOUGHBY.	G. WENTWORTH.
J. WARE.	R. MEREDITH.

V.

THE EXAMINATION OF OWEN CONNOLLY, GENT., TAKEN BEFORE US WHOSE NAMES ENSUE, THE 22ND OF OCTOBER, 1641, AT DUBLIN.[1]

(*v.* vol. i. p. 108.)

Who being duly sworn and examined, saith, that being at Moneymore in the county of Londonderry on Tuesday last, he received a letter from Colonel Hugh Oge MacMahon desiring him to come to him to Connagh in the county of Monaghan and to be with him on Wednesday or Thursday last. Whereupon he this examt. came to Connagh on Wednesday at night last and finding the said Hugh come to Dublin followed him hither. He (the examt.) came to Dublin about 6 of the clock this evening and forthwith went to the lodging of the said Hugh to the house near the Boot in Oxmantown,[2] and there he found the said Hugh and came with him into the town near the pillory to the lodging of the Lord Maguire, where they found not the Lord within and there they drank a cup of beer and then went back to the said Hugh's lodging. He saith that at the said Maguire's lodging the said Hugh told him that there were and would be this night great numbers of noblemen and gentlemen of the Irish and Papists from all parts of the kingdom in this town, who with himself had determined to take the castle of Dublin and possess themselves of all his Majesty's ammunition there to-morrow morning being Saturday, and that they intended first to batter the chimnies of the town and if the city would not yield then to batter the houses, and to cut off all the Protestants that would not join with them. He further saith that the said Hugh told him that the Irish had prepared men in all parts of the kingdom to destroy all the English inhabitants there to-morrow morning by 10 of the clock, and that in all the seaports and other towns of the kingdom all the Protestants should be killed this

[1] *Nalson, vol. ii.*
[2] Oxmantown, originally Ostmen'stown, from the Ostmen or Danes, is now covered by the Four Courts and buildings around them, but was in 1641 a suburb of Dublin.

night and that all the posts that could be could not prevent it. And he further saith, that he moved the said Hugh to forbear the executing of that business and to discover it to the State for the saving of his own estate, who said that he could not help it, but said that they did own due allegiance to the king and would pay him all his rights, but that they did this against the tyrannical government that was over them and to imitate Scotland who got a privilege by that course. And he saith further, that when he was with the said Hugh in his lodging the second time, the said Hugh swore he should not go out of his lodging that night, but told him that he should go with him the next morning to the castle and said that if that matter were discovered somebody should die for it; whereupon this examt. feigned some necessity for his casement and went down out of the chamber and left his sword in pawn, and the said Hugh sent his man down with him, and when this examt. came down into the yard, finding an opportunity, he leaped over a wall and two pales and so came to the Lord Justice Parsons.

              OWEN O'CONNELLY.

W. PARSONS.
THOS. ROTHERAM.
ROBT. MEREDITH.

THE EXAMINATION OF HUGH OGE MACMAHON OF CONNAGH, ESQUIRE, AGED 35 YEARS OR THEREABOUTS, TAKEN BEFORE THE RT. HON. LORDS JUSTICES AND COUNCIL.[1]

The said examt. saith that he thinks there will be trouble this day throughout all the kingdom of Ireland and that all the fortifications of Ireland will be taken as he thinks. And he saith that he thinks that it is so far gone by this time that Ireland cannot help it; he saith he was told this by Captain Brian O'Neil and that he and Captain Hugh Byrne were designed for the surprising of the castle of Dublin, and that if this examt. were one for that surprising, those captains were the principals therein. He saith that the place of meeting was to be at this examt.'s lodging, and that twenty prime men of every county in Ireland were to be at Dublin this last night concerning this matter, and that they were to consult of it this morning at his lodging, their weapons were to be swords and skeans and that the captains that were raising men in the Irish countries were they that should bring men hither to second the business. He

[1] *Nalson, vol. ii.*

APPENDIX.

further saith, that when they had Dublin they made sure of the rest, and expected to be furnished with more arms at Dublin. He said, 'I am now in your hands, use me as you will, but I am sure I shall be shortly revenged.' And being demanded whether the Lord Maguire was one appointed to this business he said he thought he was.

Tho. Rotherham.
R. Meredith.

William Parsons.
R. Dillon.
Ad. Loftus.
J. Temple.

W.

DECLARATION OF DEAN KER.[1]

(r. vol. i. pp. 117, 118.)

"I, John Ker, Dean of Ardagh, having occasionally discoursed with the Rt. Hon. George, Lord Viscount Lanesborough, concerning the late Rebellion in Ireland, and his lordship at that time having desired me to certify the said discourse under my hand and seal, I do declare as followeth : That I was present in Court when the rebel Sir Phelim O'Neil was brought to his trial in Dublin, and that he was tried in that Court, which is now the High Court of Chancery, and that his judges were Judge Donellan, afterwards Sir James Donnellan, Sir Edward Bolton, knt., some time Lord Chief Baron of the Exchequer and Dungan, then called Judge Dungan, and another judge whose name I do not now remember. And that amongst other witnesses then brought in against the prisoner there was one Joseph Travers clerk and one Mr. Michael Harrison, if I mistake not the Christian name : and that I heard several robberies and murders proved against him the said Sir Phelim, he having nothing material to plead in his own defence. And that the said Judge whose name I remember not as abovesaid examined the said Sir Phelim about a commission that he should have (*i.e.* was said to have had) had from Charles Stuart (as the said Judge called the late king) for levying the said war; and that the said Sir Phelim made answer that he never had such a commission and that it was then proved in Court by the testimony of the said Joseph Travers, and others, that the said Sir Phelim had such a commission, and did then in the beginning of the said Irish rebellion shew the same unto the said Joseph and several others then in Court. Upon which the said Sir Phelim confessed, that when he surprised the Castle of Charlemont and the Lord Caulfield that he ordered the said Mr. Harrison and another gentleman, whose

[1] *Nalson. Carte MSS., Bodleian.*

APPENDIX. 371

name I do not now remember, to cut off the king's broad seal from a patent of the said Lord's they then found in Charlemont, and to affix it to a commission which he the said Sir Phelim had ordered to be drawn up. And that the said Mr. Harrison did, in the face of the whole Court, confess that by the said Sir Phelim's order, he did stitch the silk cord or label of that seal with silk of the colours of the said label and so fixed the label and seal to the said commission, and that the said Sir Edward Bolton and Judge Donelan urging the said Sir Phelim to declare why he did so deceive the people, he did answer that no man could blame him to promote that cause he had so far engaged in. And that upon the second day of his trial, some of the said judges told him that if he could produce any material proof that he had such a commission from the said Charles Stuart to declare and prove it before sentence passed against him, and that then he the said Sir Phelim should be restored to his estate and liberty. But he answered, that he could prove no such thing, nevertheless they gave him time to consider of it until next day, which was the third and last day of his trial. Upon which day, the said Sir Phelim being brought into Court and urged again, he declared again that he never could prove any such thing as a commission from the king. And added that there were several outrages committed by officers and others his aiders and abettors in the management of that war, contrary to his intention, and which now pressed his conscience very much ; and that he could not in conscience add to them the injustice of calumniating the king, though he had been frequently solicited to do so by fair promises and great rewards while he was in prison. And proceeding further in this discourse, he was immediately stopt, and before he had ended further what he had to say, sentence of death was pronounced on him. And I do further declare that I was present and very near to the said Sir Phelim, when he was upon the ladder at his execution, and that one Marshal Peake and another Marshal before the said Sir Phelim was cast, came riding towards the place in great haste and called aloud ' Stop a' little ! ' and having passed through the throng of spectators and guards, one of them whispered a little while with the said Sir Phelim, and that the said Sir Phelim answered in the hearing of several hundred people of whom I myself was one, I thank the Lieutenant-General for his intended mercy, but I declare, good people, before God and his holy angels, and all of you that hear me, that I never had any commission from the king for what I have done, in the levying or prosecution of this war, and I do heartily beg your prayers, all good Catholics and

Christians, that God may be merciful unto me and forgive me my sins. More of his speech I could not hear, which continued not long, the guards beating off those that stood near the place of execution. All that I have written here I declare to be true, and am ready, if thereunto required upon my corporal oath, to attest the truth of every word of it. And in testimony thereof I do subscribe my hand and affix my seal this 28th day of February, 1681."

JOHN KER (*Locus Sigilli*).

APPENDIX. 373

X.

BRODIE'S NOTE ON THE COMMISSION TO O'NEIL.[1]

(v. vol. i. p. 115.)

"The Commission with instructions was supposed to have been carried to Ireland by Lord Dillon of Costellogh, who when the Irish Committee left the king in August accompanied his Majesty by the queen's orders to Scotland and was remarked at Court to be an uncommon favourite. He left the king about the beginning of October and carried letters to Ireland to be sworn a privy councillor of that kingdom. Now the Commission is dated on the 1st of October, while the Incident[2] occurred on the 11th, and the Commission contained a particular clause in favour of the Scotch, whom it was imagined the Incident should as a people have put under the royal management against all their former measures. See letter from Sir Patrick Wemyss to the Earl of Ormond about Dillon, &c., and which appears by comparing the matter contained in it, with the Scottish parliamentary records and acts lately published, to have been written between the 1st and 8th of October, while the postscript shows that it was carried by Dillon. (*Carte's Letters*, vol. i.) Dillon afterwards avowed himself a Papist and soon became active for the confederated Irish. Another remarkable coincidence regards the Scottish great seal, which prior to the 2nd of October, 1641, had been for 'those years begane,' to use the language of the Scots Acts (see late publication of *Scots Acts*, vol. v. for 30th September, and 1st and 2nd of October, and *Appendix*, p. 676 *et seq.*), in the possession of the Marquis Hamilton and his underkeeper John

[1] *Hist. of the British Empire*, by Brodie, vol. ii. p. 378, *note*.
[2] The Incident, as it is called by the Scotch historians, was a plot said to have been devised by Montrose and the king to seize and imprison or put to death Argyle, Hamilton and his brother the Earl of Lanerick. They were to be invited to attend Charles at a drawing-room in Holyrood on the 11th of October, and were to be there arrested by the Earl of Cranford, Colonels Stewart, Hume and Cochrane. *Hardwicke's State Papers*, vol. ii. p. 299; *Burton, vol. vii*.

Hamilton, advocate; but which on the appointment of Loudon as chancellor, with the approbation of the States on the 1st of October, was ordered to be produced in parliament by the Marquis, and the underkeeper, on the following day, that it might with all formality be delivered in parliament by the king to the newly appointed chancellor. This was accordingly done, and an act of exoneration which had been previously prepared in favour of the Marquis and the underkeeper was passed that very day. Now the supple character of the Marquis is well known, and the underkeeper was likewise a keen royalist and indeed the other's creature. Though therefore it may be inferred from the Incident that they knew nothing of any intention to grant a commission to the Irish, it does not follow that the seal, which was not confided to the Marquis as chancellor or regular keeper, was not at all times at the king's service. Indeed it might easily be required or might easily be given up as a test of loyalty without suspicion of any foul purpose either on his or his underkeeper's part; and it was alleged to have been occasionally in the possession of Endymion Porter, one of the king's attendants who had formerly accompanied him into Spain. (*Mystery of Iniquity*, ed. 1643, p. 37, 8.) Now it is remarkable that Burnet in his *Lives of the Hamiltons*, and he was at that time a keen royalist, though he takes notice of this passage in the above pamphlet, and denies the charge about the commission, says nothing about the seal's having been occasionally in the custody of Porter. See p. 250 and compare it with Carte's pretended reference to this work for his statements in his *Life of Ormond*, vol. i. p. 180. See also Charles' own offer in his answer to the declaration of no more addresses. Was not this answer originally drawn by Clarendon without the king's knowledge? Yes, and that without communication with Charles, though his Majesty afterwards approved and thus in a manner adopted it. See *Clarendon's Letters*, vol. i. p. 244, ed. 1662, p. 280, to prove by witnesses that the Scottish seal had not for many months previous to the date of the alleged commission sealed anything, without mentioning the only witnesses who could possibly have been admitted. The fact is that the Marquis and the underkeeper soon engaged for the king and that the act of exoneration closed both their mouths, since without renouncing the benefits of it, they could not allege that they had not faithfully kept the seal, the ground on which the exoneration was granted them. Now if there were a coincidence between the date of the alleged commission, the departure of Dillon and others; for presently after its date we are told Butler and divers Irish commanders of whom the court was then full were as well as Dillon dispatched for

Ireland with his Majesty's license; (*Mystery of Iniquity*, pp. 87, 88) if I say there was a coincidence between these and the Incident, surely there was a greater between the date of the commission and the delivery of the great seal to Loudon when it was put beyond the king's reach. Parliament then met early in the morning, and Friday the 1st of October was consequently the last day on which Charles could command the seal. But it is said that no true copy of the pretended commission was ever produced, that in Milton and Rushworth, being an evident fabrication, as it relates to events which did not happen until some months afterwards. Now it will be curious if this should turn out to be a perfect mistake. The commission states, that for the preservation of his person, the king had been enforced to make his abode for a long time in Scotland, in consequence of the disobedient and obstinate carriage of the English parliament, which had not only presumed to take upon them the government and disposing, &c., but had also possessed themselves of the whole strength of the kingdom, in appointing governors, commanders and officers in all parts and places therein, &c.

This commission is said in regard to the question about the power of the militia to relate to events which did not occur for some months afterwards, but Hume, who in this follows Rapin, had not much studied the subject, otherwise he never could have made such a statement. For as early as the 10th of May, 1641, the very day on which the bill was passed for continuing the parliament, a report was made in the lower house 'from a committee that was appointed to prepare heads for a conference' with the lords, 'that one have power to command in chief on this side of the Trent, and such power to choose officers as the now general hath, and to bring a list of their names to both houses of parliament.' (*Journals for 10th May*.) Again in the ten propositions to be presented to the king before his going to Scotland, there was one, that his Majesty might be petitioned to remove evil counsellors, and to commit the business and affairs of the kingdom to such councillors and officers as the parliament may have cause to confide in, another regarded lord lieutenants, and their deputies, and there is one expressed thus — 'That the cinque ports and other ports of the kingdom may be put into good hands, and a list of those who govern them may be presented to parliament, and that those persons may be altered upon reason, and that especial care be taken for reparation and provision of forts' (*Nalson*, vol. ii. p. 311, 313). In addition to this, we may remind the reader of Haselrig's bill, all which is the more astonishing that Mr. Hume should have overlooked, since Mr. Carte, from whom he borrows so liberally, has distinctly stated it. But the Commons were not content with all this, for they actually interfered with the forts, as may be seen by the Journals for the 14th, 21st, and 25th of August. What had occurred in Scotland prior to the date of the Commission confirmed their purposes. A publication of original correspondence shows, that Charles was apprised by Secretary Nicholas of the intention of the English parliament to make the concessions in Scotland a precedent for themselves. Nicholas' letters were sent back apostiled and therefore we shall present them in the original form. On the 28th of August, he writes from Westminster, 'All things are now likely to be very still here, every man's expectation being fixed upon your majesty's and the parliament's proceedings there.' On the 24th September he writes from Thorpe:

(*Nicholas' Letter.*)	(*The King's Remarks.*)
"This enclosed from my Lord Keeper was brought to me last night to be conveyed to your majesty and will I hope give your majesty an account of your last letter to his lordship. Your majesty may be pleased to procure from your parliament there some further reiteration of their declaration that what your majesty hath consented to concerning your election of officers there may not be drawn into example to your majesty's prejudice here, for if I am not misinformed there will be some attempt to procure the like act here, concerning officers, before the act of tonnage and poundage be passed to your majesty for lief. I hear that the committee of the commons hath appointed to take into consideration on your majesty's revenue next week, and that then they will sit at least twice a week. I am unwilling to give your majesty in your great affairs there too long an interruption, with the tedious lines of your Sacred Majesty's, &c. *App. to Evelyn's Memoirs,* p. 24.	"It is so and likes me well. "I like your proposition and shall get as much as I may however I thank you for your advertisement. "I pray God it be to a good purpose, and no knavery in it. "I command you to send in my name to all those Lords that my wife shall tell you of, that they fail not to attend at the down sitting of the parliament.

On the 27th of September, Nicholas writes from Thorpe, that the parliament had by its unusual proceedings begun to lose the reverence it had before the adjournment, and then proceeds thus:—

APPENDIX. 377

(*Nicholas' Letter.*)

" I hear there are divers meetings at Chelsea at the Lord Mandeville's house and elsewhere by Pym and others, to consult what is best to be done at their next meeting in parliament, and I believe they will in the first place fall upon some plausible thing that may reindegrate them in the people's good opinion, which is their anchor hold and only interest, and if I am not much misinformed, it will be either upon Papists or upon some act for expunging of officers and counsellors here, according to the Scottish precedent, or on both together and therefore it will import your majesty by some serious and faithful advice to do something to anticipate or prevent them before their next meeting.

(*The King's Remarks.*)

" It were not amiss that some of my servants met likewise to countermine their plots, to which end speak with my wife and receive her directions."

The apostiles to this letter are dated 2nd October. On the 29th of September, Nicholas writes from Westminster:

(*Nicholas' Letter.*)

" By letters to particular persons which I have seen dated 25th September it is advertised from Edinburgh that your Majesty hath nominated the Lord Lothian to be your chancellor. Whatsoever the news that is come hither amongst the party of the protesters, they are observed to be here of late, very jocund and cheerful, and it is conceived to arise from some advertisements out of Scotland, from whose actions and successes they intend as I hear to take a pattern for their proceedings here at their meeting.

(*The King's Remarks.*)

" It is not Lothian yet.

" I believe that before all be done, they will not have such great cause for joy.

This was apostiled on the 5th of October, but his Majesty mentions that he had that day also received one dated the 1st (*Ibid.* p. 28). . . It has been well observed that Charles never very pointedly denied the commission. . . The Earl of Essex told Bishop Burnet that " he had taken all the pains he could to enquire into the origin of the Irish massacre, but he could see no reason to believe the king was accessory to it; but he did believe that the queen did hearken to the propositions made by the Irish, who undertook to take the government of Ireland into their own hands, which they thought they could perform and then they promised to assist the king against the hot spirits in Westminster (Burnet's *Hist. of his own Times*, vol. i. p. 41). I cannot distinguish between the king and queen considering their dark correspondence and joint plots. . . But here a distinction must be again pointed out between the massacre and the proposition by the Irish to take the government of that island into their own hands. Of being accessory to the first the king must be acquitted. The last is in a different predicament."

Y.

OUTBREAK OF THE REBELLION IN CORK.[1]

(v. vol. i. p. 111.)

"The misery and wretched calamity that now befals the English nation, was first bruited at Cork on the 25th of April, 1641, that there should be a massacre of all the English in the city on May Day following, upon which report the priniest of the English in St. Finbarry's betook themselves to the Fort on May Eve, whereupon the mayor forbade the bringing in of the May, (an ancient custom of that rich city) whereby no suspicion might be embarked in the hearts of the English, and his fair court made him and us seemingly secure.

That day being May Eve, I came from Cork to my own house at Ross Carberry, where I met with Dominick Coppinger, Esquire, who came to entreat me to dine with him the morrow after, at his house in Ballinvreine, and desired that my man might bring a musket to help to bring home the May, and set up a May Pole at his new intended plantation by the Powry bridge, where he had begun the foundation of a market house a mile from Ross. The former I refused, the latter I sent him. This being past, all things were quiet and the raisers of that report were censured. But about the 20th of November, McCarthy Reagh, O'Donovan, Tiegue O'Downy, Dominick Coppinger, justice of the peace, his brother Thomas Coppinger of the commission, also Tiegue O'Driscol who married their sister, Dermot *Glas alias* Carthy, brother to Tiegue O'Downy, Tiegue MacFineen Carthy son of Finneen Carthy of Gortnaclough, Donoghe Carrogh alias O'Driscol, Keife O'Keife, Florence MacCarthy of Benduffe, Murrogh O'Donovan, Rickard O'Donovan, Dermot O'Donovan, Donogh O'Donovan, Cade O'Donovan, all brothers of O'Donovan, and their sons with Daniel MacOwny O'Donovan of the Freugt (*sic*), and Monartagh (*sic*) O'Donovan and his sons and Rickard O'Donovan of Kilfinian, and all the rest of the Irish gentry of East and West Carberry, were summoned by McCarthy, Lord of the country, to appear

[1] *MSS. T.C.D.*

at (*illegible*) the Friday following by virtue of a commission granted from the Lord President of Munster to the said MacCarthy to impress and raise according to his ability as many soldiers as could be provided by them to defend the western parts, they hearing that there was a rebellion in the eastern parts of Munster.

On Friday, being the 7th of January, the gentry before named with their freeholders and tenants that day met, and after their treacherous meeting was dissolved, they went to Mr. Edward Nowman's house, and there told me that they would over stand for our defence against the rebels in Tipperary and Limerick. In the very interim there came in the constable of Ross, to desire Dominick Coppinger, or his brother Thomas, commissioners of the peace, to examine one Dermot O'Brinny and six others who had stolen divers cows from an Englishman the night before, but they utterly refused it, saying that they were on the king's business already, so that in the churchyard before them all, there fled away four of the robbers, and none of the Irish would lay hands on them, though the constable in the king's name commanded them to do so.

The 2nd of January, at 12 of the clock at night, word came to us from Tiegue O'Downy, that we must shift for our lives, otherwise we should all be killed on a sudden, whereupon we all fled presently to Rathbarry Castle, a mile from the town, being in great danger of our lives, which by God's help we did, they seizing our goods without doors and within. The governor of Bandon hearing of those troubles sent on the (*illegible*) day of that inst., one Captain Hoop, a Scotsman, to Ross, who coming to the town found nothing there of any value and the rebels fled so he returned. Upon the 24th day of January, the Lord of Kinalmeaky came from Bandon to Clonakilty, where he lay all night, being most tempestuous weather, and but six troopers to Rathbarry Castle that night, who (*illegible*) on purpose to know the strength of the town of Ross, answer was returned we could not tell, but we saw numbers of people resorting thither, yet Lord Kinalmeaky came half the way from Clonakilty towards (*illegible*), but the weather being so tempestuous and the enemy strong he returned to Bandon. About the 3rd of February, Mr. Joseph Salmon, Mr. Henry Hull and John Vincent, servant to Mr. Samuel Salmon, who kept Glandore Castle, ventured to come to Rathbarry Castle three miles distant, the very day all the barony of Ibawne rose and showed themselves before the castle of Rathbarry, yet their (*illegible*) would (*illegible*) home to Glandore, but as they were riding home they were set upon, two of them then taken being sore wounded, and John Vincent was shot, who falling down, they presently came in upon him, stripped him stark naked not being

APPENDIX.   381

yet dead, presently threw a heap of stones upon him, which while they were doing as long as he had breath he called them rebels and murderers. Those were the first men of the English that were slain in those parts. And that very same night the rebels took the castle of Donnemeas, where Mr. Richard Hungerford, his two sons, and his daughter-in-law, were taken prisoners, with three men and eight women and children, who were afterwards ransomed by my Lord of Kinalmeaky. Upon the 7th of February Florence Mac-Carthy of Benduffe and his rebellious crew took two of the Rathbarry Castle men who were gone out to fetch some furze for firing, who being carried to Ross, one was cut in divers pieces and the other upon much entreaty was first stripped naked and then hanged. About the 17th day of February, the Down (*illegible*) Castle was yielded upon quarter to the rebels, that they the besieged should have what goods they could carry and be conducted safe to Castlehaven, where Rickard O'Donovan, as they were on their journey, met them and stripped them contrary to their quarter, some were wounded and part came all safe to Castlehaven. Upon the 14th of March eight men and eleven women of the castle of Donnmahon, as they were washing clothes, were taken by the rebels, none were slain but all ransomed by the Lord of Kinalmeaky, and that night the rebels cast a trench, before the castle gate, by which means they kept Mr. Barham who was the owner of the castle from water; whereupon before ten days' siege he surrendered the castle upon quarter, but as eight of the (*illegible*) of the rebels were in the castle with him delivering the orders of their agreement, one of the king's ships called the Buonaventure shot at the rebels from 14 or 15 pieces of ordnance, which made them fly, and sent the longboat on oars with a small prize in her and 60 musketeers, who marched to the castle and brought Mr. Barham and a great many women and children who were then with him out of the castle, aboard the ship, and set fire to it, thinking to burn all the goods therein, which were of great value, but presently after Mr. Barham's departure an Englishwoman, that was hid in the cliff's thinking to remain until Mr. Barham came back, went into the castle quenched the fire and saved all the goods; and the next day John Barry, captain of the rebels, his brother Edmund and his brother William Barry and Thomas MacMahony O'Hea came to the castle, seeing the coast clear and entered upon all the goods, whereupon they sent to the Lady O' (*illegible*) to Timoleague who came thither herself, and to her the goods were delivered; she had for her part eight (*illegible*) loads of bedding and clothes, and other provision which was supposed to be third part of the goods in the castle. The other two parts Captain John Barry and his brothers divided.

Upon Palm Sunday eve about half an hour before sun setting, the sun was encompassed about with a circle as red as blood, and presently after there went a stroke throughout it, like blood, part of the sun appearing on one side and part on the other side, which continued for the space of a quarter of an hour, at last it seemed all blood which was fearful and terrible to behold, and a little after the sun appeared bright. Upon Trinity Sunday there came fifty pikemen and thirty musketeers of the rebels to a meadow near adjoining the castle of Rathbarry, where 18 horses were feeding, which they thought to have taken away, but six of our musketeers and four pikemen went forth and turned the horses into the castle, and then fought with the rebels and killed six of them, only one of our men was shot in the thigh; there was on the top of the hill some half a mile from the castle 1,200 of the rebels, who showed themselves to the castle and sent unto us to yield upon quarter. Answer was returned that we scorned to take quarter at their hands. The 9th day of July, a boat being made in the castle of barrel boards, by one John Sellers, a miller, it was carried on men's shoulders in the dead of the night to the sea, being a quarter of a mile from the castle, wherein four men were put who rowed that night to Castlehaven, thinking to find there one of the king's ships to acquaint the castle with the great distress for victuals of those within the castle, but finding none there, they came away the 13th day of that instant July in another great boat to Glandore at midnight, with 12 men where they found the Elizabeth of Plymouth; the captain thereof being one Captain Brown, who had done great service in the western parts in burning the Irish dwellings and killing all that he met, withall bringing off many distressed English, and the boatsmen acquainting him with the misery of the castle, he came the next morning about 8 of the clock and sent two longboats ashore, and so there came from the castle 75 men, women, and children, who were like all to be cut off by (the rebels of) the baronies of Carberry and Ibawne, had he, Captain Brown, not kept them off with his ordnance. And he brought us that night safe to Kinsale, whereupon some of us going aboard to the Admiral in the Swallow, acquainted him with the distress of those that were left behind, upon which the next morning he went himself aboard of the Lord Forbes' ship, who was general of the army then newly come into Kinsale harbour, who called a council of war, and that afternoon went towards Bandon Bridge, the true relation whereof hereafter followeth."

The anonymous fragment breaks off here, but from the following letter it would appear that the rebels at Kinsale began their work earlier than those in the city of Cork. Lord Kinalmeaky mentioned in the above narrative was the fourth son of Richard, Earl of Cork. He married in 1639 Lady Elizabeth Fielding, daughter of the Earl of Denbigh, but was killed at the battle of Liscarrol on the 3rd of September, 1642, leaving no issue.

SIR HENRY STRADLING FROM KINSALE TO SIR JOHN PENNINGTON.[1]

HONOURED SIR,—I arrived here on the second present. This country, which I ever thought most free from disloyalty of any in Ireland, is at this instant in a general revolt, and the English in a very miserable condition, fallen from much plenty on a sudden to so much poverty that they own nothing. Every Irishman now declares himself a rebel and of all this province only the towns of Kinsale, Cork, and Youghal, (a little kept in awe by the castles) stand out for the king; and Bandon-Bridge inhabited only by English. On Tuesday last there was a meeting of the chief men in these parts, most of which pretended to be good subjects, and they have all taken oath and entered into confederacy to extirpate the English; the names of some I can remember, My Lord of Muscroe (*Muskerry*), Macartie (a man of much power) Macartie Rey (*Reagh*), Teg O'Doney, and some ten more; and they have appointed one Colonel Barry (Lieutenant-Colonel to my Lord Barrymore last year in the north) to be their general of these forces. There is very little quarter given of either side and nothing to be expected but destruction. When I shall have the happiness of an opportunity I shall take the boldness to tender my service to you and Sir, as long as I live, endeavour to express myself to my power,

Your faithful servant,

Kinsale, *March* 6th, 1641.　　　　　HEN. STRADLINGE,

Addressed :—" For my honourable friend SIR JOHN PENNINGTON, " knight, these."
Endorsed :—" March 6th from SIR HENRY STRADLING,"

[1] *MSS. Rolls House.*

Z.

The following proffer of testimony against an Irish rebel by two of his countrymen (seventeenth century " Careys ") appears to have been preserved by the royalist or republican commissioners as an etymological curiosity. The original MS. is carefully bound up with the other documents in one of the volumes of depositions in Trinity College.

"Theise ar to sertif that i Knogher ma guire and Loghlin O furnegan, that in regard wee have not goode Englis wee could not expres our minds to the ful. Therefore all that wee both can saye is that in regard wee cannot seure that wee did here him Cohonaght o garvey say that hee did kil the woman, but wee did here many others that was pressent and before his fase and hee himselfe did never doncye it, but wee can bring in too that can instifie that they hard himselef confes seueral times that he did murder an Engliswoman and did produse his skene and did show the nix that her hed did make in it, the names of these tow witnessies ar Hugh O Farrele of Magestown in the barrinny of Nannin and Turlogh Mac Carran of Tooltoilne near Keles."

The proffered testimony was rejected by the Commissioners, who had more than enough of trustworthy witnesses to hear.

The following extract from the MS. autobiography of a clergyman who was with the besieged in the Castle of Tralee in 1642, has I believe been already published by one of his descendants, an English admiral, author of Travels in Greece and Asia Minor. Some account of the Rev. Devereux Spratt will be found in the Clerical Records of Cork, Cloyne, and Ross, edited by the Rev. Dr. Maziere Brady.

" May 1st, 1620. I was born in a parish called Stratton on Vosse, in the county of Somerset, where I was religiously educated by my parents, Mr. Thomas Spratt and Elizabeth his wife, my father being a reverend, godly divine, whom God made instrumental in the conversion of many souls. When I was fourteen years old my

APPENDIX.

father died, afterwards I was sent to Maudlin Hall in the University of Oxford, where I took my degree, after which I removed to Ireland, my mother Elizabeth being called there by her father Mr. Robert Cooke, a reverend divine, pastor of the parish called the Island of Kerry in the county of Kerry, where I remained not long, but was called to the head town of the county named Tralee, where I was tutor to Sir Edward Denny's three sons. After, by persuasion of friends, I entered into the functions of the ministry. In October, 1641, the horrid rebellion of Ireland broke forth, and in it God's severe judgments on the English Protestants, there being no less than 100,000 murdered, as by public records appeareth. In February, 1641, it reached us (in Tralee), the whole county being up in rebellion, and the two companies besieging us in two castles, when I saw the miserable destruction of 120 men, women, and children, by sword and famine and many diseases, among whom fell my mother Elizabeth and my youngest brother Joseph, both of whom lie interred there. This was a sad affliction, yet I was comforted by the good end my brother made, being but eight years old, yet he begged me to pray for him and gave good assurance of dying in the Lord. After (*illegible*) months' siege both castles were surrendered upon articles into the hands of the Irish rebels. Then the Lord removed me to Ballybeggan garrison, where I preached the gospel to the poor stripped Protestants there, and passing thence to Ballingarry, an island near the Shannon, I fell sick of fever, out of which the Lord delivered me. Then having an opportunity I returned to Ballybeggan, Captain Ferriter being my convoy, where I remained in the discharge of my calling until the English army came to carry us off. At which time the enemy burnt both the castle and town of Tralee, and twice set upon us on our march to Cork, but with the power of God we still beat them. Then at Cork I petitioned the Lord Inchiquin, who gave me a pass for England, and coming to Youghal in a boat, I embarked there in one John Filmer's vessel, which set sail with about six score passengers, but before we were out of sight of land we were all taken prisoners by an Algerine pirate, who put the men in chains and stocks. This thing was so grievous that I began to question Providence and to accuse Him of injustice in His dealings with me, until He made it appear otherwise by extending mercy to me. Upon my arrival in Algiers, I found some fellow-Christians who changed my former thoughts of God that He dealt more hardly with me than with others of His servants. God was pleased to guide me and those relations of mine taken with me in a providential ordering of civil patrons for us, who gave us more liberty than ordinary, especially to me, so that I preached the gospel to my poor countrymen amongst whom it pleased God to make me an instrument of much good. I had not stayed long there when I was like to be freed by one Captain Wilde, a pious Christian, but on a sudden I was sold and delivered over to a Mussulman dwelling with his family in the town, upon which sudden disappointment I was very sad. My patron asked me the reason, and withal uttered those comfortable words 'God is great,' which took such an impression as strengthened my faith in God, considering with myself 'Shall this Mahometan teach me who am a Christian my duty of faith and dependence upon God?' After this a bond of 1,000*l.*, preserved in my pocket at sea when all else was lost, was now like to be lost, the chest wherein it lay being broken up by thieves. After this God stirred up the heart of Captain Wilde to be an active instrument for me at Leagurno (*sic*) in Italy, amongst the merchants there to contribute liberally towards my ransom, which amounted to 200 cols, which after the Captain returned to Algiers he paid. Upon this a petition was presented by the English captives for my staying amongst them, that he showed me and asked me what I would do in such a case. I told him he was an instrument under God of my liberty and I would be at his disposal; he answered, 'no,' I was a free man and should be at my own disposing. Then I replied 'I will stay,' considering that I might be more serviceable to my country by my continuing in enduring affliction with the people of God than to enjoy liberty at home. Two years afterwards a proclamation was issued that all free men must be gone. I then got my free card, which cost fifty cols, and departed with several of my countrymen to Provence, where I found the English merchants very civil to me. At (*illegible*) I embarked in a vessel bound to London, we touched at Malaga, where I went ashore to refresh myself. From thence we put to sea again, and coming on the coast of Cornwall, the Vice-Admiral Batten invited me on board his ship, and kept me a time as chaplain to his squadron, and going to the Downs I parted from him and went to London, thence to a kinsman, one Mr. Thomas Spratt, Minister of Greenwich. After a time the Lord opened a door of settlement for me in a place in the county of Cork called Mitchelstown."

He was appointed rector of Mitchelstown parish, in which I believe he died late in the reign of Charles II. Sir Edward Denny, in whose family he was living as tutor when the rebellion began, was the great grandson of Sir Anthony Denny (the favourite of

Henry VIII. and one of his executors) and his wife Joan Champernown, the aunt of Raleigh, and therefore the cousin of Edward Denny, Earl of Norwich, mentioned at p. 81, vol. i. Sir Edward married the Hon. Ruth Roper, daughter of Roper Lord Baltinglass by his wife Anna Harrington, of the Exton family, and had with other issue Sir Arthur his heir, Edward and John, the three sons to whom the Rev. Devereux Spratt was tutor in 1641. From the eldest of the three descends the present Sir Edward Denny, Bart. An interesting relic, an old English black-letter Bible, which was in Tralee church during the two rebellions of 1641 and 1688, when the town was burnt, escaped the flames, and is still preserved in the Denny family. It retains the old covers, with metal loops at the edges for fastening it with chains to the lectern or reading-desk in the church. It is probably the oldest English Protestant Bible in Ireland.

ADDENDA.

THE EXAMINATION OF GEORGE CREICHTON, OF VIRGINIA, IN THE
COUNTY OF CAVAN, CLERK.

(*Harleian MSS.* 5,999.)

  This examt., duly sworn, deposeth (*inter alia*) that Turlogh MacShane MacPhillip O'Reilly, captain of rebels in the county of Cavan, this 23rd of October, 1641, told this deponent that there was a general insurrection through the whole kingdom, that the castle of Dublin and all the castles and cities in the kingdom were taken; that all the Catholics in Ireland should else have been compelled to go to Church or they should have been all hanged before their own doors on Tuesday then next, and asked this deponent if he were not privy to such a plot among the English.
  This deponent further saith, that upon the Tuesday night after the beginning of the rebellion, being the 26th of October, 1641, Colonel Richard Plunkett and Captain Nugent, both rebels, came to Virginia, and the said Colonel would needs make this deponent believe that all the cities and castles in Ireland were taken by the Catholics, the city and castle of Dublin only excepted, and that there was assuredly great wars raised in England.
  The said Colonel Plunkett also said he had a contract under the hands of all the Earls and Lords in Ireland that were Catholics, to stand firm in this insurrection. ' *What !* ' said this deponent, ' *you have a covenant among you as the Scots have.*' ' *Yea,*' said he, ' *the Scots have taught us our A B C ;* ' in the meantime he so trembled that he could scarce carry a cup of drink to his head. This deponent further saith, that upon Wednesday, October 17th, 1641, there came to Virginia four hundred and forty stripped English Protestants, many of them sore wounded, and this deponent desiring the said Colonel Plunkett to come to the door and to look on the first fruits of this war, the said Colonel at the sight wept and said Rory Maguire

had undone them all: their plot was not to kill or to rob any man, but to seize on the persons and estates of all the British, and when they had all in their hands then to present their petition to the House of Commons in England, and if their petitions were granted then to restore every man as he was; if it were not granted, then to do as seemed good unto them. After this came a great number of stripped Protestants from about Ballyhayes in the county of Cavan, and afterwards about 1,400 from Belturbet in the same county, and after many more from about Cavan, and the parish of Dun (*illegible*). All whom this deponent, by God's especial providence and through the favour of his parishioners and the O'Reillys (being left among them as yet not robbed being a Scottish man), to his power having store of provisions relieved: who in all likelihood, had not the Almighty so prevented the rebels that they spared him (this deponent), had perished all or the most part of them by famine, starving with cold, or the rebels' malice ere they could have reached Dublin.

And further saith, that the English who came from northward told him, this deponent, and the company that was with him at Virginia aforesaid that the Irish that pillaged them told them that they should be of good comfort because they were sent away with their lives, but that they had a sorer matter to put in execution against the Scots. And further saith, that he had heard some of the rebels say that their purpose at first was to spare the Scots and to make them all prisoners, and then if their countrymen would relinquish the quarrel of the English and be content that their friends in Ireland should be despoiled of their goods and lands, then they would spare the prisoners' lives, otherwise they would put all the Scots to death. But the blessed providence of God setting limits to their proceedings and saving the castle of Dublin all their purposes and resolutions were altered, and what they did but feignedly pretend in sparing the Scots before they heard of the castle of Dublin being safe, now they did desire that the Scots should believe to be intended with all reality; for having before they were aware so much provoked the English, it was very likely they would have willingly made the Scots their friends, being wonderfully dismayed when they heard they had failed in their main design of taking the castle of Dublin; for some of them came to this deponent desiring advice what they should do with some Englishmen's goods that they had gotten into their hands. And the Irish would tell this deponent that the Scots were their kindred and had not oppressed them in their government, and if the Scots would be honest men and ttake heir parts they would share the kingdoms among them; they (the Irish) believed that the Scots would not forget the great trouble (as they said) the English procured lately in Scotland; now (they said) it was their case with the English, and they resolved never to have any Englishman to be Chief Governor of Ireland but either an Irishman, a Scotsman, or an ould Brittayne (*sic*).

This deponent further saith, that upon Thursday, October the 28th, 1641, Captain Owen MacShane MacPhillip O'Reilly and one Maolmore O'Reilly coming from Dublin to Virginia, being saluted by this deponent, he observed that their hands trembled exceedingly; those two among others were appointed to assist in taking the castle of Dublin and were once, as they said, taken themselves, but made an escape. All of them looked with heavy countenances, and Captain Nugent before named said to this deponent that he believed if they who began this business had it yet to begin they would never go in hand with it. And this deponent further saith, that when the O'Reillys of the county Cavan assembled in great companies to go to the belengueering, or as they called it the taking of Drogheda, and Philip MacHugh MacShane, Colonel and chief of the rebels of that county, seemed slow in bringing in his men so that some stayed (waited) for him a while at Virginia, their general rendezvous, so that the rebels there seemed suspicious that he would forsake them, the mother of the said Philip being their prisoner gave her counsel that if he failed them they should send their soldiers and pillage his tenants.

This deponent further saith, that Mr. Daniel Crean, an Irishman and some time a priest of the Romish Church, then minister of the next adjoining parish, did at Virginia, before one Thomas MacKernan, guardian of Dundalk, with great confidence affirm that the friars had preached in his parish that the Irish should not leave with any English Protestant twopence worth of goods, of which the said Mr. Crean did likewise complain before divers of the Irish, and (said) that the priests and friars had formerly undone O'Neil and O'Donnell and had now raised up a mischief that would go near to undo the whole kingdom, which words of his (Mr. Crean's) had almost cost him his life, one seeking to save him, another to betray him.

And this deponent observed that it pleased God so to divide the Irish amongst themselves thereby the lives of many have been saved, as was not only this Mr. Crean but also this deponent and many in his company several times at Virginia, where one great rebel or the meaner rout would seek to destroy them and another would for that time save them. Albeit the main thing that delivered him and his company from the malice of the priests and friars his

greatest enemies, who once persuaded and sent men to destroy
them, from whom they were hardly by others delivered was a message
sent from Sir Paul Davis, clerk of the county, and Captain
William Cadogan, who enjoined one Friar Nugent, who had license
to pass for exchange of prisoners, to tell the priests and friars of
that county, that if this deponent miscarried, his death should be
revenged on all the priests and friars that should be found about
Dublin. By which means he had from the rebels greater respect
and his enemies were his guards against their will. This deponent
further saith, that after the overthrow of the six hundred English
at Gillianstown going to Drogheda, it is incredible how the Irish
were lifted up, how all that were something friendly before to this
deponent and his company had now changed their countenances,
and that this deponent was informed by the rebels that at the overthrow
Colonel Byrne was a principal actor, the first man that discharged
his pistol exhorted to spare none, but kill all, now was the
ime of their deliverance. And further saith, that he heard credibly
that friars were dispersed among the rebel soldiers, who with tears
exhorted and set them on to kill the English, whom God had so
wonderfully given into their hands, and the rebel soldiers assured
him and others at Virginia that they had killed divers whom they
would have spared but that their captains would have otherwise
killed them.

This deponent further saith, that some of the Irish rebels told
him that they admired (*i.e.* wondered) at the behaviour of the
English, being so many and well armed, why they did not at once
at least discharge their muskets, and that if they had made but ten
shots the Irish would have fled, they concluded that God had taken
away the heart of the English, and now they would destroy them
all out of the kingdom (their words being ' *now we will devour the
seed of the English out of the land* '), and they said when they had
rid them out of Ireland, they would go over into England and not
leave the memorial of the English name under heaven, and some
said they would have England as long in possession as the English
had possessed Ireland.

The O'Reillys did much extol themselves for being the destroyers
of those 600 English, for that by their valour, as they said, all the
pale before that morning and all Ireland was brought together to
be joined in that war. This deponent further deposeth, that he and
others in his company heard from divers persons bitter words cast
out about Dublin, viz. that they would burn and ruin it, destroy all
records and manuscripts of the English Government, they spake of
laws to be made that the English tongue should not be spoken, but

this deponent remembereth not whether that law should take place through Ireland or Ulster only, and that all the names given to lands or places by the English should be abolished and the ancient names restored. And that the Earl of Fingal demanded of this deponent what was the ancient name of Virginia, who replied, as this deponent could remember, Aghanure, whereupon the said Earl said that must be the name thereof again.

This deponent further saith, that he had conference with divers of the pale gentlemen, concerning the bitterness of the Irish against the English, and they acknowledged that it was common for them to hear the same and a great deal more than this deponent had observed, saying withal that they were surely all bewitched to join with such bitter cursed people, from whom they were sure to find as bitter persecution as from the English, and that Sir Phelim Roe O'Neil had told them that they (meaning the old Irish) hoped they had now requited them (meaning those of the pale) for helping the English in former times against the Irish; 'you,' said they (the Irish), 'broke our heads heretofore, now we hope we have broken yours, you brought plantations into our land, now we hope to have the plantations in the counties of Meath and Dublin.' This deponent further saith, that it was declared to this deponent and others of his company by divers of the Irish, that upon the overthrow of the aforesaid six hundred (English) the O'Reillys had concluded to kill all the Protestants that were in the county of Cavan, however it pleased God to divert that their cruel resolution, though while they spared this deponent and his company they were as dead men every hour, seeing their lives not so much regarded as the life of a dog.

This deponent further saith, that about the 19th of February, 1641, about ten or twelve of the rebels assaulted the house wherein this deponent and his company was, and had not a neighbour and parishioner to this deponent by persuasions diverted them would have put them all to the sword, alleging to that neighbour of his that they had directions from the priests and friars to kill them. This deponent further saith, that the rebels after they failed in their hopes of taking Drogheda, as they came home were more mild in their behaviour than before and began to pray for peace and at last to curse them that began the war.

This deponent further saith, that the Popish pretended Bishop of Kilmore, returning from a great meeting of the Popish clergy held at Kells about the 23rd of March, then next told this deponent that the council of their (the Irish) commonwealth had made a law that all that went not to mass should be sent out of the country, and afterwards put it to this deponent's choice whether he would go to mass or be sent to the gaol of Cavan, at which words one Phelim MacShemen sitting near this deponent whispered him in the ear, '*Mr. Crichton, they speak of carrying you to gaol, but you are to be killed before you come there.*'

The same bishop going out of town a dog ran fiercely at his horse, and the bishop having drunk very much, was almost cast to the ground. Whereat, '*do you see,*' said he (the bishop), '*the very dogs here are not yet converted.*'

This deponent further saith, after the O'Reillys were returned from Drogheda the Earl of Fingal went for them to come into this country of Meath; that one of the O'Reillys read the letter to this deponent, and that this deponent perceived that the O'Reillys were suspicious the pale had some purpose to bring the people of Ulster into a snare and revenge their cruel oppression and pillaging wherewith they had wasted the county of Meath. And further saith, that the Earl of Fingal was his bitter enemy, and that the Countess of Fingal told him (the Earl) that this deponent had made a catalogue of all the English driven out of the country and had sent it to the justices.

This deponent further saith, that being in distress in his own parish and having requested the Popish priest of the parish to put his neighbours in mind to supply him with some victuals, some of them told this deponent that the parish priest said to the people that the Protestants there (all in distress) were no better than dogs, that they were altogether unworthy that they should give them anything, but they might give it if they would, but strictly forbade them to visit or converse with this deponent.

This deponent further saith, that he never saw such base covetousness as did show itself in these Irish rebels, such bitter inveighings and emulations, such oppositions and divisions behind the backs of one another; sometimes the chief of the Irish would make heavy moan for the great evils they perceived were coming on their country and kindred, and said they saw utter destruction at hand, for they had carried so great bitterness for so long time in their hearts and had now so suddenly broken out against them that had brought them up, kept them in their houses like their own children and made no difference between them and their English friends and kindred, by all which the English had so well deserved of them and they had requited them so evil, that the English would never trust them hereafter, so that now it remained that either they must destroy the English or the English must destroy them.

This deponent further saith, that one time Colonel Plunkett the

Earl of Fingal's brother, and one Mr. Strake of Ballhurne (*sic*) told this deponent that it was their priests and friars that had undone them, they had no want of wealth and good land and liberty of conscience they said, and yet they must not they know not what for their clergy to make them great. They cursed themselves if ever they would believe either priest or friar, whom they had found to be such cheating knaves, and such as to save a priest or friar would not care if their best gentlemen were hanged.

This deponent further saith, that the Lord of Gormanstown was pleased one day to fall into discourse with this deponent and made great complaint of the misfortune of these times, that he had adhered to the English in the beginning and received arms out of the king's store, that when he saw there was danger to lose them he had sent them to Drogheda, but in the end he spake many bitter words against the Lords Justices and of all the Privy Counsellors by name that did then, as he said, frequent the council board. And this was most manifest in almost all the gentlemen of the pale, and greater eagerness did show itself in the gentlewomen than in the men, that they were irreconcilable enemies to the English nation, for such were their words that they were sorry that they suffered any English to pass safe to Dublin; and in their discourses among themselves, speaking of what number of English were killed in the several counties of the kingdom, the men of Fingal and the pale did maintain they had killed far more than other counties; and at other times those people of the pale driven from their own homes by our forces and being at Virginia and thereabouts among the Irish, charged the northern Irish to be the men that had undone the whole kingdom, saying it was that covetousness that hath wronged us all, for '*if* (said they) *you had destroyed the English in their several dwellings and maintained them on their own goods then had we had pledges in our hands that might have stood us in good stead.*' '*You,*' said the O'Reillys, '*might have then killed them, for we sent them to you.*' And those two enemies were thus every day in one jar or another, and as this deponent believeth, hate one another, as much as any two nations in the world.

After they had had these controversies amongst themselves they would many times apart make their complaints to this deponent; the people of the pale saying, how unfortunate they were to be joined to such people (as the Irish), who had ever been their enemies, or to have need of such, in whom there was neither honesty nor worth; 'a people' (they said) '*proud without anything that was honourable, covetous without industry, and bragging without valour,*' calling them '*a company of thieves,*' which this deponent knoweth they had reason to call them, for that the northern Irish stole their English muttons as being such as were taken from the English, and every day some of their horses would be missing and the O'Reillys got many a crown to find them for their owners and within a while they were stolen again.

The O'Reillys would have drink from the pale people had they money to pay for it or not. And the northern Irish would call the pale men cowards, saying they had no heart, nor durst fight with the English; they would (*illegible*) where there was a good sword or piece, and by night, sometimes by day, would enter the houses of the men of the pale and take what they would; they raised continual taxes and levies and cessed soldiers upon the pale so that if the Turks had been their lords they could not, as this deponent conceiveth, have done worse.

This deponent further saith, that the priest of the parish of Lurgan did so hate the pale people that he would not that any of their priests or friars should say mass in his parish, and the people of the pale did so hate him that they would not come to hear him. Neither party believed each other, the Irish would usually abuse those of the pale with news of foreign aids landed at Wexford and Kinsale, and while they were thus telling lies one to another and seemed to give themselves comfort in telling them, some would sometimes come in from Dublin and tell them some news that would change all their cheer and then how earnestly would they pray for peace and many a bitter curse would they give to them that began the war. They would affirm that the parliament of England was the cause of all their harms, and being by this deponent demanded what laws they had made to their prejudice he was answered that they (the English) were about to make (them). This deponent further saith, that in the parish of Kells, in the county of Meath, the year before this rebellion a hundred and forty women bare so many children unlawfully begotten, three score whereof lived in the town of Kells, this was often acknowledged to this deponent to be true by the Papists themselves. This deponent further saith, that he observed that the Irish after the overthrow of our men at Gellingstown grew more proud and cruel, and that one Turlogh O'Reilly that had a sore hand, going to the siege of Drogheda, being after his return demanded by one of this deponent's family how his hand did, replied '*very well now since I have been killing English people!*' and divers the like expressions of their affection to the English they heard from the rebels. This deponent further saith, that the O'Reillys who had been at the slaughter of the English at Gellingstown aforesaid acknowledged that the English did yield themselves and called to their old acquaintances and friends amongst the rebels for mercy, but they spared not any. And further this deponent saith, that during his abode among the rebels, about the time that so many stripped English passed through Virginia divers women constantly witnessed and affirmed to this deponent that in their company and fights a young woman then present with them being almost naked was near this deponent's house set upon by a rebel, who demanding money of her and she answering that she had none, the rebel told her that if she would not deliver her money he would kill her with his sword, and therewith drew it, to whom the young woman replied ' you cannot kill me unless God gives you leave and His will be done,' and instantly the rebel struck three times at her naked body with his drawn sword and yet never cut her skin, albeit those that know the Irish know that they carry no swords unless they be very sharp and therewithal the rebels seemed confounded and left her.

Jurat. 15th die April, 1643,
  Coram, JOHN STERNE.
    WM. ALDRICH.

COUNCIL BOOKS OF COMMONWEALTH.

(*Dublin P.R.O.*)

To the Rt. Hon. the Lord Deputy and Council in Ireland.

MY LORDS,—Edward Plunkett, one of the sons of Luke Earl of Fingal in Ireland, having by petition to his Highness set forth there being a small estate in lands called Drumbarah and Caslaughton in the county of Meath of about the yearly value of 100*l*. settled on him by his said father in his lifetime, he was shortly after his father's death, which he allegeth to be in the year 1635, the petitioner being then in his minority, sent by his friends to travel in foreign parts for his education, where he continued about nine or ten years, and on his return towards England was taken by the Turks and was carried to Sallee, where he remained in captivity five years, and about January last arrived in England, having not been in Ireland since his travels and captivity. And therefore expresses his hopes that his estate so settled on him shall not be adjudged liable to forfeiture or sale, his Highness and the Council in consideration thereof have thought fit to refer it to your Lordships to examine the petitioner's title to the said estate, and if you shall find the same to be as is before set forth then you are desired and hereby authorised to cause possession thereof to be forthwith delivered to him.

Signed, &c.,

Whitehall,   HEN. LAWRENCE,
21 *October,* 1656.   *Pres.*

CROMWELL TO SAME.

GENTLEMEN,—Having received the two enclosed petitions and paper of John Prendergast and the Widow Brooke, whose cases have been so represented to me which if true may deserve some tender regard. Wherefore I thought fit to recommend to your consideration that they may be permitted to reside on and enjoy their present estates and habitations unless there be some instant cause to the contrary. However, I would have their transplantation to be suspended until I receive from you an accompt of their particular cases and conditions and that you receive further order therein.

Your loving friend,

Whitehall,   OLIVER P.
22nd *March,* 1653.

FOR THE LORD HENRY CROMWELL.

Upon the addresses of James Coppinger, Esq., finding that his case if truly stated by the enclosed to be different from many others, and in respect his father was faithful to the parliament in assisting against the rebellion and lending at the first 500*l.* towards the maintenance of the army, and supplying it with victuals and other necessaries, upon which account the rebels burned his house and his castles, and that he himself never acted against the parliament, and hath lately married a gentlewoman who is a Protestant, and of good repute, we desire that all favour may be shown him, both as to his estate and also in exempting him from transplantation and rest.

Your loving father,

Whitehall,   OLIVER P.
14*th August,* 1655.

ORDER.

It is desired that Dudley Colley of Carberry, in the county of Kildare, who is called Captain Colley, and was lately governor of Carberry Castler, on the enemy's behalf may be forthwith sent for as criminal for the murder of one John Brown.

2nd Jan. 1652,

  Rob. MEREDITH.
  RALPH HUNT.
  P. W. PIERS.

For the Registrar of the High Court of Justice.

The Examination of NICHOLAS SIMPSON, *of the town of Glaslogh, in the county of Monaghan, Esquire, Knt. of the Shire in Parliament for the same county.*

This examt., duly sworn, deposeth (*inter alia*) that on Saturday, the 23rd of October, 1641, divers of the Sept of the MacWades (*sic*), fosterers to Tirlogh Oge O'Neil, came to the town of Glaslogh aforesaid, being market day, pretending that the said Tirlogh had lost thirty English sheep, whose track they brought to the end of the town, for the following of which track they borrowed all the weapons they could get in the town. Then came the whole Sept of the MacWades (*sic*) into the town and brake into every man's house on the sudden, and possessed themselves of their weapons and wished every man to yield and that no hurt should be to any man; for it was not their doing, but they had good warrant for what they did, and it was only to secure themselves against an order made at the Council Table of Ireland to hang all them that should refuse to go to church on the All Saints' Day after; which order divers friars affirmed in this deponent's hearing that they had seen, and that they had asked Sir Edward Trevor, a privy councillor, and then in their hands at the Newry, whether there was not such an order made at the Council Board, and that he had confessed there was such an order and that his hand was to it. And the said friars further confidently affirmed that the warrants were out in every county under the hands of the justices of the peace, whose hands they said were to every warrant; and although all the justices of the peace present protested to the contrary, yet the multitude believed their holy friars, and this was the greatest cause, as they pretended, of their cruel murders committed on the British.

And this deponent further saith, that when those MacWades (*sic*) came in such multitudes upon the British in the town, which were but few, for the greater part there were Irish and ran to them, they the British were not able to resist them, for besides the suddenness they had no powder amongst them; the late proclamation against any having powder being so strict that none could be gotten but by license from the Newry, but yet they refused to yield to those rebels until some gentlemen of quality in the county came to them. And further saith, that presently after night falling, Tirlogh Oge came and went directly into the castle and took possession thereof, and sent for all the British in the town unto him, and wished them to fear nothing, for there was no hurt intended against them, it was but to secure the Catholics, and he kept this deponent and divers others with him that night, when he affirmed to this deponent that all the noblemen of Ireland had their heads and hands in this insurrection, and many of the noblemen of England, but that he, the said Tirlogh, knew not of it above a fortnight before. And this deponent asked him (Tirlogh), knowing he married the Earl of Antrim's bastard sister, whether the E/il had any knowledge of it, he told this deponent he could not tell, but he was sure his Duchess had divers letters from many of the noblemen of England about it. He told this deponent further when he first heard of it, which was from his brother Sir Phelimy, that he utterly disliked it, and persuaded Sir Phelimy from it and thought he had prevailed with him, until he heard he, Sir Phelimy, had taken Charlemont, and he assured this deponent that Monaghan, Newry, and Dublin and all the forts and castles of Ireland were taken before that time, for that was the day of taking them; and that my Lord Maguire and Hugh MacMahon were gone out of the north to take Dublin, and every messenger that came to him he said had brought him letters that Dublin and the castle were taken.

But at last came Ever MacMahon, the Vicar-General of Clogher, or titulary Bishop of Down, (who this deponent thinketh was one of the principal plotters of this treason) and he, knowing that my Lord Maguire and Hugh MacMahon were apprehended, desired to draw certain remonstrances of their grievances, with the reasons of this their insurrection, and seizing on the king's forts, and in every county thereabouts made choice of some gentlemen to send them up to the State, thence to be sent into England to his Majesty; and told this deponent that the gentlemen of the county of Monaghan had chosen him (*illegible*) to be their messenger to present them, and left a copy of the said remonstrance and a copy of the protestations of their loyalty with him, (both which this deponent delivered to Sir Robert Meredith) and so departed, going as he, the Vicar-General, said, to get the hands of the gentlemen of the county to these instruments and to provide the deponent money and a pass for his journey; and presently after his departure was the overthrow of the 600 near Drogheda, of which he sent notice to Tirlogh Oge by his letters, which caused great triumphing amongst them, leaping and dancing and crying '*Victoria!* God Almighty had put us all into their hands,' from which time the deponent never saw the Vicar-General, but is sure that he was a continual bloody persecutor of the British, and chief inciter to all the barbarous murders in the north.

And the deponent further saith, that Tirlogh Oge O'Neil having gotten all the money, plate and goods, and cattle about Glaslogh into his possession, and conveyed them to his own castle and lands, he left Glaslogh and went to Armagh, and by the way protested very much against those courses of his brother Sir Phelimy, and that he, being sheriff of that county, would keep the British from all oppression and wrong, and that he would carry the king's money he had received to Dublin and pass his accompts. And when this deponent with other of the British came to Armagh, they found Sir Phelimy O'Neil, Rory O'More, and divers other principal rebels there; to whom the town had then yielded upon promise, under Sir Phelimy's hand and seal which this deponent saw, which he (Sir Phelimy) offered to sign with his blood, and to deliver his son in pledge that they (the Armagh Protestants) should not be molested, or troubled either in their lives or estates, but should enjoy all they had as quietly and peaceably as they did before (*illegible*), and in a great bravado offered fifty townlands for fifty barrels of powder, and fifty muskets, and bragged that he had got one barrel of powder out of the store in Dublin, in his own name, his brother's, and Sir William Brownlow's; and that my Lord Maguire had brought down many muskets and corslets in trunks and chests from Dublin, and that Philip O'Reilly had made 5,000 pikes out of the woods of Loughrea. Sir Phelimy stayed in the town two or three days after it was yielded up, and then departed, leaving one Hugh Buie Mac Gonnell (*sic*), a man before that time of base condition, governor, who presently pillaged all the houses and shops at his pleasure, took up the best house in town, commanded every man to send him in provisions, and domineered upon the spoil like an Emperor; Tirlogh Oge living then in town (and seeing the port and state of this base fellow) and his wife being a woman of a haughty and high spirit and basely covetous, thinking anything too much that passed by her, persuaded her husband to take upon him the government of the town, and at Sir Phelim's next coming he was made governor of the county of Armagh, and what Hugh Buie had left he took into his possession; he made the shopkeepers both in Armagh and Loghgall to be accountable to his wife for all the wares they sold out of their shops. In this his government he forgot his promise to the British to protect them, and by the setting on of his wife and mother, a most cruel woman to the English, he turned a bloody persecutor of them, and was the cause, as this deponent and other British conceived, of the death of about 2,000 persons by drowning, hanging, pistolling, stabbing, and starving.

These that the deponent knew to be murdered thereabouts and saw most of them carried to their ends were as followeth, viz. at Corbridge sixty-eight drowned; at Portadown one hundred and fifty drowned in one week or thereabouts led out by one Manus O'Cahane; at Armagh a hundred and twenty-six drowned; at Loughgall eighteen at one time drowned; besides this deponent observed that out of that parish and Kilmore, where they reported there were three or four thousand communicants, there came not above two or three alive from them; at Glaslogh thirteen drowned; at Kinard that night, and the night before my Lord Caulfield was shot by them, fifty at least killed in the town besides many in the county. Mr. James Maxwell, Mr. Henry Cowell, Hugh Echlin and his son and his servants hanged, and James Maxwell's wife, being in strong labour, drawn down to the river by the hair of her head and she and her infant drowned; at least three hundred killed and burned when Armagh was burned. This deponent speaketh not of Clones and thereabouts, where the first day they killed all they lighted on, besides afterwards many hanged and drowned; nor of Monaghan, Carrick, Castleblancy, and Drumbo, where multitudes were hanged and drowned; nor of small numbers, as Carsnett Clinton, (who) being blind and led by his grandchild they cast them both into the river and drowned them; nor of Ambrose Blancy, Ensign Pierce, and many others. They hanged Ensign Pugh twice or thrice till he was half dead and then let him down and afterwards killed him and his wife, and, as this deponent heard, set a Scottishwoman upon a hot gridiron and bored another through the hands to make them confess their money.

To strip men and women stark naked as they were born, was their ordinary sport. Nor did the malice of those friars and priests end with the death of the poor British, but when they had murdered them or that they died they denied them burial in the churchyard, but made them be buried in gardens, and flung them they killed into ditches, or left them to the dogs to devour their carcases, and excommunicated all them that relieved them alive, or buried them being dead. And the friars preached in their sermons that it was as lawful to kill an Englishman as a dog.

And this deponent further saith, that while he and other of the British were in Armagh, Sir Phelimy was created O'Neil and Earl of Tyrone at Tullaghoge, and proclamations were often made in the market-place in the name of O'Neil. He took petitions directed to him as Earl of Tyrone, and so he subscribed them and his letters. And he, this deponent, and others heard Tirlogh Oge's son, a youth of twelve or thirteen years of age, say that his uncle Sir Phelimy should be king of Ireland, and Sir Phelimy himself said that he would have that statute repealed that men born in this kingdom should not be governors thereof, and they would give his Majesty the double revenue he now received out of Ireland by way of tribute. And at a meeting at Carrick there were various statutes made for the government of the county in Sir Phelimy's name, wherein he gave every gentleman power to try treasons and felonies, and all other actions and to keep courts on his own lands. This authority this deponent saw and read in his (Sir Phelim's) own name, and under his own hand and seal, wherein he wrote WE, after the manner of kings, and according to OUR royal intentions, *etc.* In this, his commission, the gentlemen had power to cess all the lands in the county towards the maintenance of the Catholic army, except Church lands, which were exempted at a former meeting at Cavan. It seems the rebellion was not so sudden as they pretended, for in the former assizes before in the county of Monaghan, there was one Shane O'Neil of Tyrone indicted before Sir Samuel (*illegible*) for stealing of cows, whereof he was apparently guilty, yet by the cunning of one William Kelly of Carrick, now a great rebel, he was acquitted. And Neale McKenna told this deponent, that if Shane O'Neil had been hanged, there were five hundred horsemen well weaponed that would have hanged both the judge and the sheriff, before they came to Armagh.

And this deponent further saith, that when he was relieved and came to the army who quartered near Armagh, he and his company went into the town, but there was not a roof on church or house to cover them, all was burnt; and looking into some houses they found divers dead bodies burnt in the chimneys and the stones in the streets were all bloody, and like the floor of a butcher's slaughter-house, since the day of the murdering of the inhabitants, which was three weeks before.

And further saith, that the men and women rebels did not only commit those cruel murders, but by their example, and no doubt by their encouragement, the fry of young children of 12 or 13 years of age, with skeans, would stab and kill poor women and children they met in the fields; nay, the very spawn of six or seven years of age that could not use a skean had daggers, made of laths, with which they would follow the English in the streets, pushing at them with those laths and crying ' *Boddagh Sassanagh !* ' (*i.e.* English churls) and none durst speak a word or reprove them for fear of murdering.

And further saith, that Sir Phelimy O'Neil scoffing, as it now appears, at our laws whose execution upon his prodigal riotousness had brought his great estate to nothing, which was more likely the cause of his entering into rebellion than religion, would oftentimes ask him, this deponent, where were now our laws, statutes, staples, or executions, and our *dedimus potestationes ?* (*sic*), he cared not now (he said) a farthing for them all, nor for our pursuivants and serjeants-at-arms.

And they (the Irish) had a proverb among them in every man's mouth, that ' *the horse had been a long time atop of the rider, but that now, God be thanked, the rider had gotten atop of the horse again.*'

And further saith, that the rebels of that county hanged Mr. Richard Blaney in the orchard of the castle of Monaghan, and refused him to have a minister come to him, but scornfully offered him a priest, and being dead they cast him into a bag scarce covering his corpse, and the Lady Blaney procuring him to be coffined, could not obtain so much favour of the friars and priests as to bury him in the churchyard, but was suffered to have him buried in the said orchard, and they that coffined him were threatened to be hanged. And when this deponent next met with Sir Phelimy O'Neil he asked him, this deponent, ' *what was become of the fallen knight of the shire of the county Monaghan ?* ' to which this deponent making no answer, Sir Phelimy told him, he had sent a warrant to hang him and said it was done by very good advice.

And Tirlogh Oge told this deponent that his name was in that warrant also to be hanged, but that he, the said Tirlogh, procured him to be struck out. The rebels also at that time hanged another gentleman, one Luke Ward, at Monaghan, and flung his body into a ditch, and would not suffer his wife to take him out and bury him.

And further saith, that Tirlogh Oge oftentimes persuaded this deponent to stay with him at mass in his own house; this deponent answered him that he, the said Tirlogh, pretended that religion was the cause of this general insurrection, because they (the Catholics) would not be enforced to church, and desired him not to enforce him (this deponent) to mass, for he was resolved to die in the religion he had been bred. The said Tirlogh said he would not enforce him (to go to mass) but because he loved him (this deponent) and for his soul's sake persuaded him ; but when he (Tirlogh) saw he could not prevail with him, he wished him before Sir William Brownlow, then a captive with him, to shift for himself, saying that he (the said Tirlogh) could no longer protect him. And this deponent demanding the reason of this sudden alteration the said Tirlogh Oge answered him, that he was persuaded it was a mortal and unpardonable sin to protect heretics. And this deponent heard by one that was near him that it was his mother's and the friars' persuasion. And afterwards this deponent was always in fear of murdering.

And this deponent further saith, that they, meaning the British, had every Sunday sermons in Armagh, and every month at the farthest communions, and that the rebels led out the curate, one Mr. Griffin, to be drowned, and that he, this deponent, and Sir William Brownlow entreated for him, and Sir Phelimy told them that the said Mr. Griffin was their chaplain, and at that time they prevailed for him, but when Armagh was burned he and his family were murdered, with two or three other ministers.

And further saith, that his, this deponent's, son being a minister, and then lately come out of an extreme fit of the gout, was carried to the gaol and sent with many others to be drowned ; and not being able to go, one Manus O'Cahane, that Arch Devil and executioner of all the British thereabouts, beat him with a cudgel, till he was like to murder him ; but by the means of Mr. Henry O'Neil the deponent got him recalled, but he was stript of his clothes and all the rest were drowned.

And further saith, that the said Mr. Henry O'Neil entertained a gentleman, one Brownlow Taylor,[1] to follow him, and going with him towards Charlemont on May Eve, 1642, being unwilling that Sir Phelimy should see him in his company, turned him back to Armagh, who going to a farm his father had, was apprehended by some of Tirlogh Oge's company, and carried to him to Loghgall, who sent him to Charlemont to Sir Phelimy and Mr. Henry O'Neil, returning that night without him, his mother made a great moan for her son. At last they heard that he was with Tirlogh Oge and sent unto him for him. The said Tirlogh told the messenger that he was sent to Charlemont, but that he would send for him, and so it seems he did, for the next morning being Sunday by four of the clock he was hanged at Charlemont.

[1] *v. ante*, p. 158.

And this deponent further saith, that the rebels pistolled many men as they walked in the streets of Armagh, for every rogue would kill any man upon any grudge between them, and one of them pistolled a smith in the town in the sight of his wife and son, and divers other English, whereof when he, this deponent, complained unto Tirlogh Oge, and told him it was contrary to his promise of protecting the British, and contrary to his own proclamation which he had publicly made in the town, he called a council, but neither wife, nor son, nor any other that saw the murder committed and knew the murderer, durst come in and give any evidence against him. If they had they had been sure to be murdered themselves, and so not only he, but many other murderers in that town escaped unpunished.

N. SIMPSON.

Jurat. 6*th April,* 1643,
Coram, JOHN STERNE.
RANDALL ADAMS.

THE CASE OF PHELIM McFEAGH O'BYRNE.

I FIND it necessary to qualify very slightly the statement I made at p. 40, vol. i. respecting the documents in Trinity College library, Dublin, relating to the O'Byrnes of Wicklow. My reference to them was incidental, and was made chiefly for the sake of contrasting the ready acceptance those copies of depositions in favour of Phelim MacFeagh had met with from some modern historians, who contemptuously rejected all official copies of depositions made by the plundered colonists in 1641. I had not made a very close examination of the O'Byrne MSS., but writing of them from memory I said that they were unsigned and unofficial. I judged them to be mere copies by a private collector of historical MSS. of the lost official copies of lost originals. They are written in a small, weak hand, very unlike that of an official copyist. While the foregoing pages were passing through the press, Mr. S. R. Gardiner wrote to ask me if I was certain that the O'Byrne depositions were not duly certified official copies with signatures and the words '*copia vera*' at foot of each. He added that such copies were always considered in the Public Record Office to be only second in value to original documents. I was quite aware of this, and had I found the O'Byrne documents in the Public Record Office, I would have set more value upon them, notwithstanding their very unofficial appearance, and the absence of signatures and the words '*copia vera*' to many, if not all of them. Determined, however, not to trust to my memory of them, seeing that I had not examined them very closely as I had examined the 1641-52 depositions, I wrote to the learned and courteous librarian of Trinity College, Dr. Ingram, F.T.C.D., to ask his opinion of them, and in a few days received the following reply :—

'Dear Miss Hickson—I looked carefully into the depositions in the O'Byrne case which are given in our volumes F. 3. 15, and F. 3. 17. There is nothing to show that they are certified official copies. The words "*copia vera*" are at the foot of *some* of them, but there is no signature to attest their being true copies. I think it probable that they are copies of certified official copies as you suggest. The signatures (at the end of all) of Loftus, the Archbishop of Armagh, etc., are not in the handwriting of those persons, but in that of the person who wrote the documents to which they are appended. In other words, these signatures also are copies, most probably at second hand. "*Copia vera*" occurs but twice, once in each volume, and perhaps is meant to apply to all the entries about the case collectively. The signatures of Loftus, the Archbishop, etc., occur only in one of the volumes.

'Yours truly,
'JOHN K. INGRAM.'

Thus while I may have misled my readers into thinking that all the O'Byrne depositions were unsigned and without the words '*copia vera*,' in the main my judgment of them was right. They are mere copies of official copies, many of them unsigned, and the words '*copia vera*' do not appear at the foot of each document. They are not absolutely worthless, nor do I think of asserting that they are forgeries, or even inaccurate copies of the lost official copies, but they can by no means be classed with regular official copies preserved in a State Paper Office, and to compare them in value with the duly certified official copies of the depositions of witnesses in 1641-2, having the words '*Examined and entered*,' or '*copia vera*' written at foot over the original signatures of well known officials, much more to reject the latter because they are copies and accept the second hand unofficial copies in the O'Byrne case, is most inconsistent and absurd. It is an instance of that unreal and fanciful way of dealing with the materials of Irish history to which I have before referred. Moreover, if every one of these documents could be proved an original, or a certified official copy of an original, with all of them before us we should still have only half the case whereon to pronounce judgment, all the depositions, originals, and copies taken against Phelim O'Byrne having been lost or destroyed.

ADDENDA. 407

N.B. In copying the depositions relating to the massacres for print, I have followed the plan adopted by the official copyist of 1645-8, who made those duplicates present in the Harleian MSS. and in the MS. volume which Warner prized so highly (v. vol. i. p. 126), that is to say, I have omitted all the superfluous words, repetitions, and the long inventories of stolen or destroyed goods and chattels, over which Mr. Waring drew lines of abbreviation (v. ante, p. 199). I have carefully preserved the total money value of those as it is inserted by the said copyist. A comparison of the facsimile of John Dartnell's deposition (v. vol. i. p. 129) with the printed abbreviated copy of the same at page 141 of this volume will make this explanation clearer and will show how mistaken Dr. Warner and Mr. Gilbert have been in supposing that the abbreviating lines (called by them cancellings) can in the slightest degree invalidate the original, or that the omission of the portions of it over which those lines were drawn can invalidate any copy of it, printed or written. As Dartnell's deposition is one of those in the Waterford book which Mr. Gilbert says contains so many crossed-out passages, I have selected it for reproduction by photography and lithography. The former process being too expensive for these volumes, I had a limited number of excellent photographs (autotypes) taken from the original MS. in the Waterford book by Mr. Chancellor, 55 Lower Sackville Street, Dublin. These can now be seen in the library of Trinity College, Dublin, the libraries of the Royal Dublin Society and Royal Irish Academy, the British Museum Library, the London Library, and the Free Library at Hastings, founded, I believe, by the munificence of Sir Thomas Brassey. Although my researches chiefly lay in the MS. departments of the first-mentioned libraries, I cannot refrain from expressing my obligations to the London and Hastings libraries, for the many valuable rare old books of reference I was able to obtain from both. It is impossible to exaggerate the value of those libraries to authors and readers, and the admirable way in which they are managed by their generous and courteous patrons and librarians. In copying all the foregoing seventeenth century documents I have modernised the spelling, because it seems to me that the preservation of the old-fashioned contractions ' y^e ' for ' the ' ' w^{ch} ' for ' which ' and the doubling of the final consonants in such words as ' faithfull ' only puzzle and tire the majority of readers. Those who want the old spelling *literatim* will go to the original MSS.

THE END.

Spottiswoode & Co., Printers, New-street Square London.

This book is a preservation photocopy.
It was produced on Hammermill Laser Print natural white,
a 60# book weight acid-free archival paper
which meets the requirements of
ANSI/NISO Z39.48-1992 (permanence of paper)

Preservation photocopying and binding
by
Acme Bookbinding
Charlestown, Massachusetts
1997

www.ingramcontent.com/pod-product-compliance
Lightning Source LLC
Chambersburg PA
CBHW050844300426
44111CB00010B/1126